Open Source
E-mail Security

RICHARD BLUM

201 West 103rd Street, Indianapolis, Indiana 46290

Open Source E-mail Security

Copyright © 2002 by Sams Publishing

International Standard Book Number: 0-672-32237-4

Library of Congress Catalog Card Number: 2001089510

Printed in the United States of America

First Printing: October 2001

04   03   02   01   4   3   2   1

Trademarks

Warning and Disclaimer

Associate Publisher
Jeff Koch

Acquisitions Editor
Katie Purdum

Managing Editor
Matt Purcell

Project Editor
Christina Smith
Emily Morgan

Copy Editor
Lisa M. Lord

Indexer
Eric Schroeder

Proofreader
Jody Larsen
Kelly Thompson

Technical Editor
David Taylor

Team Coordinator
Chris Feather

Interior Designer
Gary Adair

Cover Designer
Bill Thomas

Page Layout
Rebecca Harmon
Michelle Mitchell

Contents at a Glance

Contents

Part II   Server Security

About the Author

Rich Blum has worked for the past 13 years as a network and systems administrator for the U.S. Department of Defense at the Defense Finance and Accounting Service. There he has been using Unix operating systems as an FTP server, TFTP server, e-mail server, mail list server, and network monitoring device in a large networking environment. Rich currently serves on the board of directors for Traders Point Christian Schools and is active on the computer support team at the school, helping to support a Microsoft network in the classrooms and computer lab of a small K–8 school. Rich has a bachelors of science degree in electrical engineering, and a masters of science degree in management, specializing in Management Information Systems, both from Purdue University. When Rich is not being a computer nerd, he is either playing electric bass for the church worship band or spending time with his wife, Barbara, and two daughters, Katie Jane and Jessica.

Dedications

This book is dedicated to my dad and stepmom, Mike and Jean Blum. "Moreover, we have all had human fathers who disciplined us and we respected them for it. How much more should we submit to the Father of our spirits and live!" Hebrews 12:9 (NIV)

Acknowledgments

First, all honor, glory, and praise goes to God, who through His Son all things are possible, and who gave us the gift of eternal life.

I would like to thank all the great people at Sams for their help, guidance, and professionalism. Thanks to Katie Purdum, the Acquisitions Editor, for offering me the opportunity to write this book, and for helping things out along the way. Also thanks to Christina Smith, the Project Editor, for guiding this book along the publishing process and making things go smoothly.

Many thanks to Lisa Lord, the Copy Editor, for making this book readable by correcting my terrible grammar, and to Dave Taylor, the Technical Editor, for doing an excellent job of pointing out my technical goofs and making suggestions to help make this book more useful. As always, thanks also to the interior design group at Sams for turning my scribbles into great-looking figures.

Finally, I would like to thank my family. My parents, Mike and Joyce Blum, for their dedication and support, and my wife, Barbara, and daughters Katie Jane and Jessica for their love, faith, and understanding, especially while I was writing this book.

Tell Us What You Think!

As the reader of this book, *you* are our most important critic and commentator. We value your opinion and want to know what we're doing right, what we could do better, what areas you'd like to see us publish in, and any other words of wisdom you're willing to pass our way.

As an Associate Publisher for Sams Publishing, I welcome your comments. You can fax, e-mail, or write me directly to let me know what you did or didn't like about this book—as well as what we can do to make our books stronger.

Please note that I cannot help you with technical problems related to the topic of this book, and that due to the high volume of mail I receive, I might not be able to reply to every message.

When you write, please be sure to include this book's title and author's name as well as your name and phone or fax number. I will carefully review your comments and share them with the author and editors who worked on the book.

Fax: 317-581-4770
E-mail: feedback@samspublishing.com
Mail: Jeff Koch
         Associate Publisher
         Sams Publishing
         201 West 103rd Street
         Indianapolis, IN 46290 USA

INTRODUCTION

It is said that every computer platform has a "killer application" that makes it marketable. Many consider e-mail the killer application for the Internet.

Internet e-mail has become a vital resource for businesses and home users alike. Many corporations use e-mail for official communications internally as well as with external customers. E-mail server downtime can severely affect communications in many corporations.

Unfortunately, not everyone using e-mail plays by the same rules. The increasing popularity of the Internet has sparked growing abuse of e-mail systems. The same people who have deluged the postal mail system with massive mailings trying to sell every type of item imaginable have found Internet e-mail. The prospect of mass-marketing items to millions of people with a single computer program has attracted many unsavory businesses to the Internet. The influx of unsolicited commercial e-mail (UCE, or spam) clogs both network bandwidth and mailboxes of users to the point of overloading the mail system.

Another misuse of Internet e-mail systems is the attack by hackers sending malicious virus programs. Before the popularity of e-mail, a virus creator had to rely on people sharing files with floppy disks or downloading files from bulletin boards to spread their destructive programs. With the popularity of e-mail (and "user friendly" e-mail client programs), it became all too easy to infect thousands of computers with a single virus sent to a handful of people.

As a mail administrator, it has most likely become your job to protect your users from unnecessary junk e-mail and malicious viruses. In today's e-mail environment, however, this task has become a difficult one.

For mail administrators in the Unix environment, many choices of open source e-mail server software are available to use, thus giving you several different ways to protect your network from spam and viruses. Naturally, each Unix e-mail server product has its pros and cons in various e-mail environments.

Over the short history of Unix e-mail, three separate open source products have proved to be more popular than the rest. By far the most popular Unix e-mail package used today is the sendmail package, developed by the Sendmail Consortium. After sendmail, two other packages have attracted a large following of users: qmail, developed by Dan Bernstein, and Postfix, developed by Weitse Venema. All three packages are complete e-mail server packages that can be configured to block both spam and viruses. The purpose of this book is to help the mail administrator understand and use the spam- and virus-blocking features of these packages.

Knowledge is the best security tool any administrator can have. Understanding the protocols used for e-mail systems on the Internet is crucial in helping you improve e-mail security. The first part of this book is dedicated to helping novice mail administrators understand e-mail protocols and thus understanding how e-mail viruses and attacks work. If you already have a good understanding of how Internet e-mail works, feel free to skip the first section of the book and use it for reference while reading the other sections.

The second part of this book focuses on how to achieve a more secure e-mail server, from the point of view of both a Unix system and an e-mail server. Before you can achieve a secure e-mail environment, however, you must have a secure Unix system that prevents and detects intruder access, as well as a secure e-mail server configuration that blocks spam and viruses. By understanding how the different Unix e-mail server software packages work, you can decide which one is best for your particular e-mail environment.

Finally, the last section of the book shows some examples of using security in real-life e-mail server situations. One of the best tools available for e-mail security is an e-mail firewall, preventing prying eyes on the Internet from gathering information from your e-mail server. Next, secure POP3 and IMAP servers and secure Webmail servers are discussed, offering ways for your users to securely read their mail messages from remote locations.

How This Book is Organized

The three separate parts of the book are broken down into the following chapters:

Chapter 1, "E-mail Basics," describes the history of e-mail and how e-mail on the Unix platform works.

Chapter 2, "SMTP," describes the Simple Mail Transfer Protocol, the core protocol used for sending messages to hosts across the Internet.

Chapters 3, "POP3," and 4, "IMAP," describe the Post Office Protocol and Internet Mail Access Protocol, two protocols used to allow remote users to retrieve mail messages from a mail server.

Chapter 5, "MIME," describes the standard format used for e-mail messages and attachments, including the S/MIME and PGP methods of incorporating security in e-mail messages.

Chapter 6, "Reading E-mail Headers," helps the novice mail administrator decode the message headers used on Internet mail to help track down senders of spam and malicious viruses.

Chapter 7, "Securing the Unix Server," helps the novice mail administrator understand the basics of Unix server security, along with some examples of open source products that can help secure the server and identify tampering attempts.

Chapters 8, "The sendmail E-mail Package," 9, "The qmail E-mail Package," and 10, "The Postfix E-mail Package," describe the sendmail, qmail, and Postfix open source e-mail server packages. Each chapter shows how the individual packages are installed and how they can be configured for a more secure e-mail environment.

Chapter 11, "Preventing Open Relays," shows how to prevent spammers from using your mail server to forward spam mail to others and how to avoid receiving spam mail from known open relays on the Internet.

Chapter 12, "Blocking Spam," shows how to incorporate spam-filtering features in standard open source e-mail server packages.

Chapter 13, "Filtering Viruses," shows two techniques used to help stop viruses from entering your e-mail system: virus filtering and virus scanning using a commercial anti-virus package.

Chapter 14, "Using E-mail Firewalls," describes techniques that can be used to create a separate e-mail firewall server to protect your users' addresses and mailboxes from external hackers.

Chapter 15, "Using SASL," demonstrates a common method used to require remote servers to authenticate to your server before allowing them to forward mail messages.

Chapter 16, "Secure POP3 and IMAP Servers," shows how to incorporate the SSL protocol with the OpenSSL open source package with POP3 and IMAP servers to give your users a secure way to read their mail messages remotely.

Chapter 17, "Secure Webmail Servers," ends the book by showing how to provide a full-featured, secure Webmail interface to your mail server for remote users.

A Few Disclaimers

This book uses many e-mail addresses and domain names in the examples. When possible, all examples use fictional domain names and addresses that at the time of writing were not registered with the Internet Corporation for Assigned Names and Numbers (ICANN). Should any of the sample addresses be registered by the time you read this book, there's no association with this book and the owner(s) of the address(es).

Also, all IP addresses used in this book are for examples only. When possible, public IP addresses are used and should be replaced with the IP addresses that have been assigned to your particular organization. When that is not possible, fictitious IP addresses have been selected and are not associated with any existing IP networks. Please consult your Internet service provider before assigning any IP addresses to your network if it is connected to the Internet.

Conventions Used in This Book

Features in this book include the following:

NOTE

Notes give you comments and asides about the topic at hand, as well as full explanations of certain concepts.

CAUTION

Cautions warn you against making your life miserable and show you how to avoid the pitfalls in networking.

At the end of each chapter you'll find a handy summary that recaps the main themes explored in the chapter.

In addition, you'll find various typographic conventions throughout this book:

- *Italics* are used to set apart new terms and are occasionally used for emphasis.
- Commands, variables, and code elements appear in text in a special `monospaced` font.
- Throughout the code listings and code examples, I use a **`boldface monospace type`** to emphasize command lines entered by the reader.
- Placeholders in syntax descriptions appear in `monospace italic typeface`. This indicates that you should replace the placeholder with the actual filename, parameter, or other element it represents.

PART I

E-mail Principles

CHAPTER 1

E-mail Basics

This chapter starts the journey into e-mail security by describing the basics of an e-mail server and how e-mail messages are transferred across the Internet. Understanding the fundamentals of how open source e-mail software and protocols work is the first step to understanding e-mail security.

Unix E-mail Systems

Since its inception in the late 1970s, the Unix operating system has become a popular platform for multiuser applications. E-mail is no different. The majority of Internet e-mail servers use some type of Unix system, and Unix and its variations—Linux, FreeBSD, and NetBSD—have become the operating systems of choice for open source software developers.

The Unix operating system changed the way e-mail software was approached. One of the main innovations of the Unix operating system was to make software modular. Instead of having one gigantic program that handled all the required pieces of a function, smaller programs were created that could work together. Each program handled a smaller piece of the system's total functionality. This philosophy was used to implement Unix e-mail systems. E-mail functions were broken into separate pieces and assigned to separate programs. Figure 1.1 shows how most open source e-mail software modularizes e-mail functions in the Unix environment.

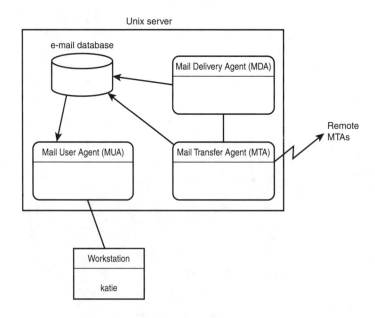

FIGURE 1.1

Unix modular e-mail environment.

As you can see in Figure 1.1, the e-mail server is normally divided into three separate functions:

- The Mail Delivery Agent (MDA)
- The Mail Transfer Agent (MTA)
- The Mail User Agent (MUA)

The lines between these three functions are often fuzzy. Some e-mail packages combine functionality for the MDA and MTA functions, while others combine the MDA and MUA functions. The following sections describe these basic e-mail agents and explain in more detail how they are implemented in Unix systems.

Unix Mail Delivery Agent

Often Unix e-mail implementations rely on separate standalone MDA programs to deliver messages to local users. Because these MDA programs concentrate only on delivering mail to local users, they can add bells and whistles that aren't available on MTA programs that include MDA functionality. This focus enables the mail administrator to offer additional mail features to mail users.

The MDA program concentrates only on the message destined for a user on the local mail server. It receives messages from the MTA program and then determines how those messages are to be delivered. Figure 1.2 demonstrates how the MDA program interacts with the MTA program.

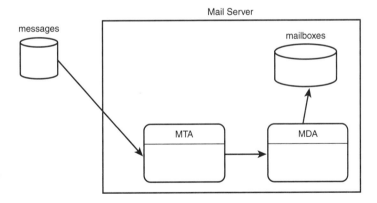

FIGURE 1.2

Using an MDA program on a mail server.

When the MTA program determines that a message is destined for a local user, it passes the message to the MDA program. At this point, the MDA program ensures that the message gets delivered to the proper location, either to the local user's mailbox or to an alternative location defined by the local user.

MDA Functions

As mentioned, the MDA program's main function is to deliver mail to users on the local mail server. To do this, the MDA program must know the location and type of mailboxes used by the e-mail system. There are currently three different types of user mailboxes commonly used on Unix systems:

- /var/spool/mail files
- $HOME/mail files
- Maildir-style mailbox directories

Each mailbox type has its own features that make it attractive to use. Maildir-style mailbox directories offer increased performance, security, and fault-tolerance, but many popular MDA and MUA programs are not able to use them. However, just about all MDA and MUA programs can use the /var/spool/mail mailbox files.

Several other features can be added to the basic MDA program. Different MDA programs combine various features that make them useful to the mail administrator. These features are some of the more popular ones:

- Automatic mail filtering
- Automatic mail replying
- Automatic program initialization by mail

The following sections describe these features and how they are implemented.

Automatic Mail Filtering

Possibly the most helpful and most used feature of MDA programs is the ability to filter incoming mail messages. For users who get lots of e-mail, this feature can be a lifesaver. Messages can be automatically sorted into separate folders based on a subject header value or even just one word in a subject header. Figure 1.3 illustrates this process.

The MDA program uses a configuration file that allows the user to specify standard text expressions (including wildcard characters) to search fields in the incoming message header. As expressions are matched, the message is saved in a predetermined folder in the user's mail area or dealt with in another way the user has set up.

This feature can also be used to filter and throw away undesirable messages, which is helpful for reducing unwanted unsolicited commercial e-mail (UCE).

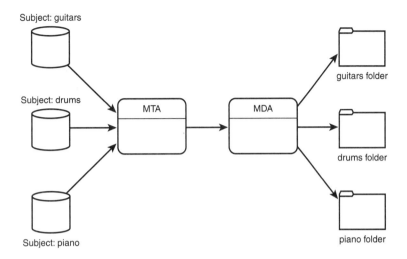

FIGURE 1.3

Sorting incoming mail messages into separate folders.

Automatic Mail Replying

Another feature used in MDA programs is the ability to configure an auto-reply for e-mail messages. Much like message filtering, many MDA programs also allow the mail user to send reply messages based on values defined in the subject header field. Mail users can customize the auto-reply function to support many different types of responses to received messages. Figure 1.4 illustrates the use of the auto-reply feature.

The mail user can configure the MDA program to send mail responses to the original message sender based on predetermined values in the configuration file. Different values can solicit different text messages in the reply message. The user can also determine whether the original message should be stored in a mail folder or discarded after responding to it.

Automatic Program Initialization by Mail

Still another common feature in MDA programs is the ability for the mail user to run a program initiated by receiving a message, as shown in Figure 1.5. The MDA program can also start different processes based on different text in messages.

With many MDA programs, the mail user can create a configuration so that programs are started based on values in the mail message, such as subject header values. This feature offers such functions as producing different workstation sounds based on a new message with a particular subject heading or starting a monitoring process on your workstation if you receive a particular message. (Some people monitor their networks while they are gone using this method.)

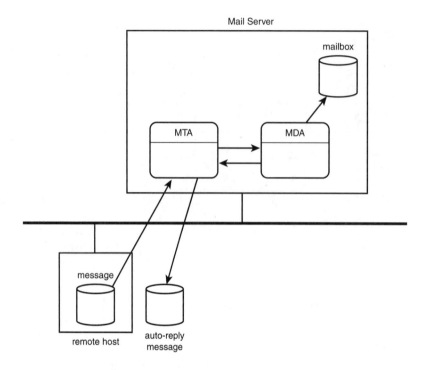

FIGURE 1.4

Using an auto-reply MDA feature to respond to e-mail messages.

Open Source MDA Programs

There are several open source MDA programs available for the mail administrator to incorporate with the e-mail system. Two of the most popular programs are binmail and procmail, described in the following sections.

The Binmail Program

The binmail program is the most popular MDA program used on Unix systems. You might not recognize it by its official name, but you most likely have used it by its system name: mail.

The name *binmail* comes from its normal location on the system, /bin/mail. The binmail program actually has two separate versions: one for SRV4 versions of Unix and one for V7 versions. You must be careful to use the version that is applicable to your version of Unix. Most Linux distributions use the V7 version of binmail.

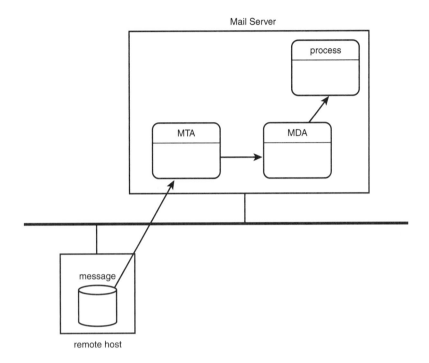

FIGURE 1.5

Starting a process from a mail message.

The binmail program has become popular because of its simplicity. No configuration is required for binmail to do its job. Unfortunately, its simplicity means it is limited in its functions. Because of that, some mail administrators have sought alternative MDA programs.

The Procmail Program

Another popular MDA program is the procmail program written by Stephen R. van den Berg. It has become so popular that many Unix implementations now install it by default, and many MTA programs use it in default configurations.

The popularity of the procmail program comes from its versatility in creating user-configured "recipes" that can allow a user to direct how received mail is processed. The user can create his own .procmailrc file to direct messages based on regular expressions to separate mailbox files, alternative e-mail addresses, or even to the /dev/null file to automatically trash unwanted mail.

Unix Mail Transfer Agent

The MTA software is responsible for handling both incoming and outgoing mail messages. For each outgoing mail message, the MTA determines the destination of the recipient addresses. If the destination host is the local machine, the MTA can deliver it to the local mailbox directly or pass the message off to the local MDA for delivery.

However, if the destination host is a remote mail server, the MTA must establish a communication link with the remote host to transfer the message. For incoming messages, the MTA must be able to accept connection requests from remote mail servers and receive messages for local users. Many different protocols can be used to transfer messages between two remote hosts, but the most common protocol used for Internet mail transfer is the Simple Mail Transfer Protocol (SMTP).

The Unix environment has many different types of open source MTA programs, and each offers different features for the mail administrator. You should choose the MTA program that meets the most requirements of your particular e-mail environment. These are some of the most common features MTA programs offer:

- Security
- Ease of configuration
- Processing speed

The following sections describe these features in more detail.

MTA Security

In these days of increasing security awareness, any software that interacts with remote hosts is scrutinized for weaknesses that can be exploited by hackers. MTA software is no different.

Various safeguards are used to protect the MTA software from attacks from remote hosts. Many MTA programs run as separate usernames rather than as the root user to help protect the mail server; these special user accounts on the server prevent a hacker from taking over the server if the software is compromised. Even tighter security is available in some packages by creating a chroot environment. The chroot environment limits the MTA package to a specific area on the filesystem by restricting access to the regular filesystems. Instead, the MTA is restricted to a single directory on the filesystem. Of course, all files and directories needed by the MTA program must be present in that directory for it to function properly. Extensive logging of each connection attempt is another valuable security feature found in most MTA packages.

Ease of Configuration

Although the advent of security features has made MTA software more complex, it's a relief to see software that can be fine-tuned for a particular e-mail environment without having to study a 1,000-page scripting language manual. Most MTA software packages allow the administrator to make configuration changes to control the behavior of the MTA software and how it reacts to particular e-mail situations.

Different MTA software packages handle configuration options differently. Some software packages create one or two monolithic configuration files that contain all the parameters used by the MTA software. Others divide configuration parameters into separate configuration files.

Processing Speed

With many companies and ISPs having large e-mail systems, performance is crucial. Most customers expect their e-mail recipients to receive the messages instantly. Using servers that hold messages in message queues for a few hours usually isn't tolerated in today's e-mail environment.

Most MTA packages implement some form of queuing strategy to handle e-mail traffic as efficiently as possible. Some newer features include creating separate message queues to handle different classes of messages (such as new messages, bounced messages, and mail list messages). By prioritizing messages, the MTA program can efficiently transfer messages even in high-volume situations. It's extremely frustrating to have your e-mail held up while the mail server is processing a message sent to the company's 10,000 member mailing list.

Unix MTA Programs

Many open source MTA programs are available for the Unix environment. Again, it is the job of mail administrators to determine which MTA program meets most of the e-mail requirements of their particular environments. This book specifically covers three popular MTA packages that are in wide use on the Internet:

- sendmail
- qmail
- Postfix

The following sections describe these three MTA programs in more depth.

The sendmail Program

The sendmail MTA program is one of the most popular Unix MTA programs available, originally written by Eric Allman while at the University of California, Berkeley. The Sendmail Consortium (http://www.sendmail.org) currently maintains the source code for it. Eric has moved on to Sendmail, Inc., which provides commercial versions of the sendmail program and support to the Sendmail Consortium.

The sendmail program has gained popularity mainly from its ability to be extremely versatile. Many of sendmail's standard features have become synonymous with e-mail systems—virtual domains, message forwarding, user aliases, mail lists, and masquerading.

You can use sendmail for many types of e-mail configurations—large corporate Internet e-mail servers, small corporate servers that dial into ISPs, and even standalone workstations that forward mail through a mail hub. Simply changing a few lines in sendmail's configuration file can change its characteristics and behavior.

In addition to changing its server characteristics, sendmail can also parse and handle mail messages according to predefined rule sets. Mail administrators often need to filter messages depending on particular mail requirements. To do that, they can simply add new rules to the sendmail configuration file.

Unfortunately, with versatility comes complexity. The sendmail program's large configuration file often becomes overwhelming for novice mail administrators to handle. Many books have been written to help the mail administrator determine the proper configuration file settings for a particular e-mail server application.

The qmail Program

The qmail program is a complete MTA program written and maintained by Dan Bernstein (http://www.qmail.org). It supports all the core MTA functionality of the sendmail program.

However, qmail takes the idea of modular e-mail software one step further. It was written as a set of modular programs to break down the MTA functions into several modules and use separate programs to carry out each function.

With qmail, you need to add several different user IDs on the mail server. Each program module runs under a different user ID. If an intruder compromises one module, most likely it won't affect the other modules. The security features of qmail are often touted as its best advantage.

Still another feature of qmail is its reliability. As each message enters the qmail system, it is placed in a mail queue. Qmail uses a system of mail subdirectories and message states to ensure that no message stored in the message queue is lost. As an added feature, qmail can also use Maildir-style mailboxes that further safeguard against messages getting corrupted or lost in the message mailbox.

The qmail program uses multiple configuration files, one for each feature. This setup avoids the problem of one large configuration file, but novice administrators often get confused as to which feature is configured in which file.

The Postfix Program

Wietse Venema wrote the Postfix program to be a complete MTA package. Similar to qmail, Postfix is written as a modular program; it uses several different programs to implement the MTA functionality.

Postfix requires a separate user ID to be added to the mail server. Unlike qmail, which uses a separate user ID for each module, Postfix runs each module under one user ID.

However, even if intruders compromise a Postfix module, they probably won't be able to control the mail server.

One of Postfix's best features is its simplicity. Instead of one large complex configuration file, or multiple small configuration files, Postfix uses two files with plain-text parameter and value names to define functionality. Most of the parameters default to common values so that mail administrators can configure a complete mail server with minimum effort.

Unix Mail User Agent

The Unix e-mail model uses a local mailbox for each user to hold messages for that user. MUA programs became available as an interface for users to read messages stored in their mailboxes. MUAs do not receive messages; they only display messages that are already in the user's mailbox. Many MUA programs also offer the ability to create separate mail folders for the user to store mail.

Many different open source MUA programs have been available for the Unix platform. These programs use different features to distinguish themselves from other MUA programs, in particular the location where the MUA program stores mail, and the method used to display the messages.

Mail Location

Over the brief history of Internet mail, two different philosophies have developed on where user mail messages should be stored. Both philosophies have proponents and opponents, but in reality, each one can be beneficial given a particular e-mail environment.

One philosophy is to download messages directly to the user's workstation, thus freeing up disk space on the mail server. This method makes the mail administrator's job easier, but it often leads to confusion for users who check their mail from multiple workstations. For example, often a user checks mail messages from home (thus downloading them to his home workstation), and then goes into work. Unfortunately, the messages are located on the home workstation and have been deleted from the mailbox account. When the user gets to work, he finds the messages can't be retrieved from his workstation, which could be a bad (if not confusing) situation.

The second philosophy solves the problem of multiple workstations by keeping all the messages on the mail server. As each user reads her mail, only a copy of the message is sent to the workstation for display purposes. The actual message is still stored in a file or directory on the mail server. No matter which workstation the user checks her mail from, the same messages are available for viewing. Although this method makes life easier for the user, the mail administrator's life is more complicated because disk space has become a crucial factor with all messages being stored on the mail server.

Displaying Messages

With the advent of fancy graphical user interface (GUI) devices, MUA programs have become more sophisticated in how they can display messages. Many Unix MUA Programs still use text mode graphics to display text messages. However, many Mac, X Window System, and Windows-based programs now have the ability to display rich text and HTML-formatted documents.

To accommodate this feature, many e-mail MUAs support the multipurpose Internet mail extensions (MIME) format. MIME allows messages to contain multiple versions of the same message, each formatted using a different display method. The MUA's job is to determine which display method to use for the message. Therefore, text-based terminals display the message in text mode, and GUI terminals display the message in a more visually complex and sophisticated mode.

Although users often like the look of HTML-formatted messages, they quickly become troublesome for mail administrators. A simple three-sentence message can turn into a large mail message because of added HTML formatting, complete with fancy background graphics and signature blocks that include pictures. It doesn't take long for these messages to clog up the mail system.

MUA Programs

Again, several excellent open source MUA programs are available for the mail administrator to choose from. When choosing an MUA program, the administrator must find one that works on the operating system the client workstations will be using.

The open source movement has created several very good MUA programs for Unix operating systems:

- binmail for text terminals
- pine for graphical text terminals
- kmail for X Window System terminals

The Binmail MUA Program

The binmail program was discussed as an MDA program, but it does double duty as an MUA program. The mail program allows users to access their mailboxes to read stored messages and to send messages to other mail users. Listing 1.1 shows a sample mail session.

LISTING 1.1 Sample Mail Program Session

```
$ mail
Mail version 8.1 6/6/93.  Type ? for help.
"/var/spool/mail/rich": 4 messages 4 new
```

LISTING 1.1 Continued

```
>N  1 barbara@shadrach.isp   Tue Apr 10 18:47 12/417 "This is the first tes"
 N  2 katie@shadrach.isp1.   Tue Apr 10 18:57 12/415 "Second test message"
 N  3 jessica@shadrach.isp   Tue Apr 10 19:23 12/413 "Third test message"
 N  4 mike@shadrach.ispnet   Tue Apr 10 19:42 12/423 "Fourth and final test"
& 1
Message 1:
From barbara@shadrach.isp1.net Tue Apr 10 18:47:05 2001
Date: 10 Apr 2001 23:47:05 -0000
From: barbara@shadrach.isp1.net
To: rich@shadrach.isp1.net
Subject: This is the first test message

Hi, This is a test message

& d
& 2
Message 2:
From katie@shadrach.isp1.net Tue Apr 10 18:57:32 2001
Date: 10 Apr 2001 23:57:32 -0000
From: katie@shadrach.isp1.net
To: rich@shadrach.isp1.net
Subject: Second test message

Hi, this is the second test message

& q
Saved 3 messages in mbox
$
```

The first line shows the mail program being executed with no command-line options. By default, this line allows users to check the messages in their mailboxes. After entering the `mail` command, a summary of all the messages in the user's mailbox is displayed. By default, the mail program reads messages only from `/var/spool/mail` style mailboxes or `$HOME/mail` style mailboxes. The default location of the users' mailboxes depends on the particular flavor of Unix the mail server is using. On FreeBSD servers, the default mailbox directory location is `/var/mail`; on Linux they are located at `/var/spool/mail`.

Each user has a separate file that contains all his messages. The filename is usually the system username of the user and located in the system mailbox directory. Thus, all messages for username *rich* are stored in the file `/var/spool/mail/rich` on a Linux system. As the user receives new messages, they are added to the end of the file.

The Pine Program

As advancements were made to the Unix environment, MUA programs became fancier. One of the first attempts at graphics on Unix systems was the ncurses graphics library. Using ncurses, a program could manipulate the location of a cursor on the terminal screen and place characters almost anywhere on the screen.

One MUA program that takes advantage of the ncurses library is the pine program. When you start pine, you see a user-friendly menu on the terminal screen, as shown in Figure 1.6.

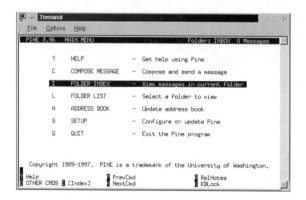

FIGURE 1.6

The pine program's main menu screen.

The pine program assigns any messages in the user's mailbox to a special folder labeled INBOX (which is actually the standard /var/spool/mail mailbox). All new messages appear in the INBOX. The user can create separate folders to hold mail that has already been read, thus making message storage and retrieval easier. As you can see in Figure 1.6, pine also includes an address book feature, allowing the user to save important e-mail addresses in a single location.

The Kmail Program

Almost all Unix systems support the graphical X Window System environment. Linux uses the Xfree86 software to run X Window System programs on the system console or a remote X terminal on the network. Many e-mail MUA programs utilize the X Window System to display message information. For example, the kmail MUA program can be used to read and send messages from an X Window System using the KDE desktop manager. Figure 1.7 shows a sample kmail session screen.

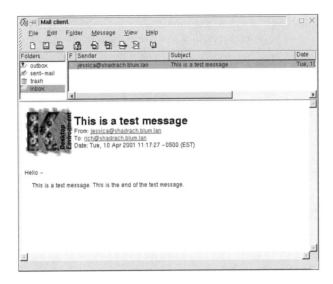

FIGURE 1.7

The kmail MUA program's main screen.

E-mail Protocols

Using open source e-mail packages means you must also use open source protocols to communicate messages between packages. Several protocols have been developed to allow messages to be transferred between mail servers and to allow network clients to read their messages from the mail server. This section gives you an overview of the protocols that are explained in more depth in subsequent chapters.

Mail Transfer Agent Protocols

MTA programs must be able to communicate messages between packages. Several transfer messages to users on remote mail servers. To do this, one MTA package must be able to communicate with another MTA package to move not only the mail message, but also the information needed for the remote server to identify the mail message. MTA programs use the protocols covered in the following sections to transfer messages and information between remote hosts.

Simple Mail Transfer Protocol

The Simple Mail Transfer Protocol (SMTP) was developed as the primary method for transferring messages across the Internet between MTA servers. Any host connected to the Internet could use the SMTP protocol to send a mail message to any other host.

The SMTP protocol uses simple commands to establish a connection and to transfer information and data between hosts, thus the word *simple* in the title. Commands consist of a single word with additional information following the command, such as the SMTP command:

```
MAIL FROM: <rich@shacrach.ispnet1.net>
```

This command tells the remote mail server who the message originated from. Each command line is transmitted across the Internet in plain ASCII text. After each command, the remote host sends a reply code to the originating host to indicate whether the command was successful. Figure 1.8 illustrates a sample SMTP connection between two hosts.

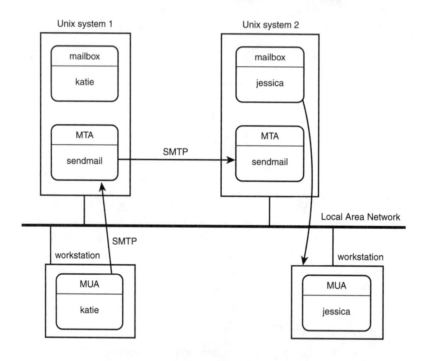

FIGURE 1.8

Sample SMTP connection between two hosts.

No login is required on the remote host, as no functions are performed on the host. It is the remote host's responsibility to interpret the received message and decide whether to accept it and forward it to the appropriate local mailbox. The full SMTP protocol is described in Chapter 2, "SMTP."

To identify remote hosts, the SMTP protocol uses the Domain Name System (DNS). DNS is a distributed database on the Internet that allows hosts to be uniquely identified by a name as well as an IP address. Each area within the Internet has a DNS server responsible for maintaining the DNS database for the area, or zone. Any Internet hosts in that zone that use a registered DNS name have an entry in the database on the DNS server. The entry maps the host's IP address to its official DNS name.

Extended Simple Mail Transfer Protocol

As SMTP became more popular, some shortcomings were identified in the original protocol. Rather than create a new protocol, developers decided to extend the basic SMTP commands with new commands. The new protocol was named the Extended Simple Mail Transfer Protocol (ESMTP). For the past several years, its new functionality has proved to be more robust than SMTP and more than capable of supporting the mail transfer environment between MTA hosts.

One important security feature that ESMTP has implemented is the ability for MTA hosts to log in to the receiving ESMTP host. As mentioned in the SMTP section, the original SMTP protocol did not have a method to authenticate the client host's identity, which led to some "interesting" situations. To compensate for this limitation, the ESMTP protocol implements the AUTH command. The client host can use the AUTH command to send a username/password pair to the server host to authenticate itself. This authentication method helps ensure that the remote client is who it says it is. The ESMTP commands are also discussed in more detail in Chapter 2.

Mail User Agent Protocols

The purpose of the MUA protocols is to allow users to read messages from their mailboxes. On a single-user Unix system this is not usually a problem—the user is logged in to the system from the console. However, in a multiuser environment, multiple users need to access their mailboxes to read their messages, which is practically impossible to do from a single console screen.

To accommodate this scenario, protocols have been developed to allow remote network users to log in and read messages in their mailboxes on the network mail server. Each user can connect to her mailbox on the mail server through an MUA program that resides on her workstation. The MUA program uses special protocols to connect to the mail server and manipulate messages in the mailbox. The following sections describe the two most popular MUA protocols in use.

The Post Office Protocol

The simplest MUA protocol is the Post Office Protocol (POP). The current version of POP is version 3, thus the term *POP3*. MUA programs on the workstation use the POP3 protocol to access and read messages in the user's mailbox. Figure 1.9 shows an example of a workstation using the POP3 protocol to read mail messages.

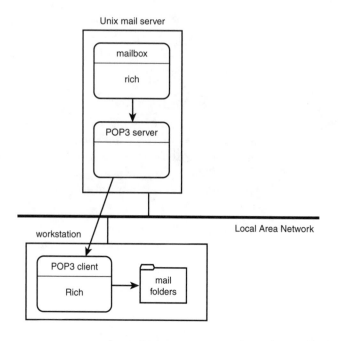

FIGURE 1.9

A sample POP3 connection.

When using the POP3 protocol, all messages for the user are read from the user's mailbox and stored on the local workstation. Usually, when using the POP3 protocol, the workstation MUA program deletes messages from the server mailbox as they are read, thus freeing up space on the mail server.

The Interactive Mail Access Protocol

Another commonly used MUA protocol is the Interactive Mail Access Protocol (IMAP). The IMAP protocol is currently at version 4, revision 1, thus the term *IMAP4rev1* is often used. MUA programs on workstations can use the IMAP program to manipulate mail messages in folders that reside on the mail server. Figure 1.10 shows an example of a workstation using the IMAP protocol.

In an IMAP connection, all of the user's mail messages reside on the mail server. Messages are downloaded only for the purpose of displaying the message on the workstation screen. This protocol is useful if the user must access his mailbox from several different computers. Each time the user accesses his mailbox when using the POP3 protocol, the current messages would be downloaded to the workstation that was used for access. This method could easily distribute messages to several different computers. IMAP prevents this situation by keeping all the messages on the mail server, no matter which workstation is used to display the messages. Although this method is more convenient for the user, it makes the mail administrator's job much more difficult. Disk space on the mail server must be carefully watched, as it can quickly fill up with undeleted messages.

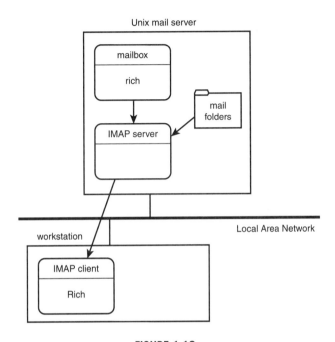

FIGURE 1.10

A sample IMAP connection.

E-mail Security

There are many parts to e-mail security. This section describes the three most important elements that the average mail administrator must monitor to help ensure a safe e-mail environment:

- Avoiding open relays
- Preventing spam
- Preventing viruses

Avoiding Open Relays

In the early days of the Internet, it was considered a common courtesy to accept all mail messages that were sent to your mail server. If a message was not destined for a local user, the mail server assumed the task of attempting to pass the message off to the proper destination. This simple act made life much easier for many mail administrators. Instead of constantly worrying about connecting to every possible remote mail server to deliver a message, they could count on some other remote server to do that for them.

When a mail server automatically passes a mail message from a remote client to the proper destination mail server (other than itself), it is called *relaying*. When a mail server relays any message from any remote client to any remote host, that mail server is called an *open relay*.

Open relays were useful in the early days of the Internet, but they too were abused just as other components of the Internet. It didn't take long before people found out that by relaying messages through an open relay, you could easily mask the origin of the message from the recipient. Using this feature, many commercial mass marketers send out thousands of unsolicited commercial e-mails (UCE). When victims receive them, it is often difficult to track the messages back to a source e-mail address.

Because of this, most open source e-mail packages have implemented *limited relaying*. Instead of relaying messages from all clients, only a preconfigured subset of clients are allowed to relay messages. Any other client attempting to relay a message is blocked.

Preventing Spam

As mentioned in the preceding section, UCE mail is the less controversial term for unwanted e-mail advertisements. The term *UCE* is often found in technical literature addressing the issue, but the more common name for UCE is *spam*.

NOTE

The Hormel Corporation has agreed that the use of the term *spam* in relation to UCE does not violate the trademark for its canned luncheon meat product, as long as the term is not printed in all capital letters. Please do not misuse the Hormel trademark when referring to UCE (see `http://www.spam.com/ci/ci_in.htm`).

Although most people are glad to avoid receiving spam messages, mail administrators must walk a fine line when trying to reduce spam on their mail server. An overzealous mail administrator can block out legitimate messages as well as spam messages. There are a few different techniques used to block spam:

- Block messages from known spam hosts.
- Block messages with known commercial subject headers.
- Block messages from hosts listed in a worldwide spam database.
- Accept messages only from known hosts.

Some spam solutions may be less controversial than others, depending on your e-mail environment. An internal corporate e-mail server might decide to block all messages from hosts known to send spam messages; however an ISP could get complaints from customers who receive messages from other users on the same spam host. For example, if you receive spam from a Yahoo account, blocking all Yahoo addresses will most likely result in complaints from your users. The option of accepting messages only from known hosts is a harsh solution to the spam problem, but can be easily implemented in a private e-mail network environment.

Preventing Viruses

The greatest fear of the Internet community is the plague of destructive viruses. A single virus can delete any or all files on the computer, often without the user knowing what is happening.

Although the mail server itself is not normally susceptible to viruses, it can be used as a tool to help block viruses from being transmitted via e-mail to unsuspecting users. As with controlling spam, there are many methods commonly used to help block virus-laden e-mails:

- Block all messages with a known virus subject header.
- Perform a virus scan on all mail attachments.
- Block all messages that contain an attachment.
- Block all messages with a particular type of attachment.

Often just the simple act of scanning messages' subject header lines is enough to block known viruses from entering the e-mail site. Unfortunately, you must know ahead of time which mass virus messages contain which headers. Scanning every mail attachment on the mail server can have serious performance consequences, especially on lower-end hardware servers. Much like spam control, the extent of virus control your e-mail site uses will most likely be a political decision more than a technical one.

Summary

To understand e-mail security, it is best to start by understanding how e-mail works. Most open source e-mail packages use three parts to deliver messages in the Unix environment: the Mail Delivery Agent (MDA), the Mail Transfer Agent (MTA), and the Mail User Agent (MUA). Each part performs a separate function in the e-mail process.

The MDA package is responsible for delivering messages to local users on the mail server. Often the messages are passed from the MTA program to the MDA program for delivery. Common Unix MDA programs are binmail and procmail.

The MTA package is responsible for delivering messages to users on remote mail servers. It usually uses the Internet with the SMTP protocol to communicate with remote hosts. Common Unix MTA programs are sendmail, qmail, and Postfix.

The MUA package is responsible for allowing remote users to read messages in their mailboxes on the local mail server. Often remote users connect to the mail server using the Post Office Protocol (POP) or the Interactive Mail Access Protocol (IMAP). Local users can also use MUA packages to access messages in their mailboxes. The binmail, pine, and kmail packages are popular open source MUA programs used on the Unix platform.

Internet e-mail security starts at the mail server. There are several things you can do as the mail administrator to help protect your users from e-mail problems. Open mail relays allow unsolicited commercial e-mail (UCE, or spam) to be passed through the mail server to remote users, which gives spammers a way to hide their identity in their mail messages.

You can help prevent spam from getting to your users' mailboxes by using simple filtering methods on the mail server. By blocking known spam hosts and messages with known spam headers, you can decrease the amount of spam mail on your server.

Computer viruses are also a security threat on the Internet. Mail messages containing attachments with viruses are the cause of many Internet virus problems. You can help block virus-laden mail by blocking known virus e-mails or scanning all messages with attachments that enter your mail system.

CHAPTER 2

SMTP

The Simple Mail Transfer Protocol (SMTP) has been used since 1982 to relay e-mail messages and attachments to many different types of computer systems. Its ease of use and portability made it the standard protocol used to transfer messages between computer systems on the Internet. To have an understanding of how e-mail works, you should get to know SMTP.

This chapter describes SMTP and shows how Unix e-mail servers use it to send mail messages.

SMTP Description

SMTP was designed to work on many different types of transport media. The most common transport medium is the Internet, using a Transmission Control Protocol/Internet Protocol (TCP/IP) connection on port 25, the SMTP service port. A common troubleshooting technique to check whether a remote server is running an SMTP server package is to use telnet on TCP port 25 and see if you get a response. You can test this out on your own Unix server by using telnet with the hostname localhost on port 25. Listing 2.1 shows a sample Telnet session to a Unix server running the Postfix Mail Transfer Agent (MTA) package.

LISTING 2.1 Sample Telnet Session to Port 25

```
[rich@shadrach]$ telnet localhost 25
Trying 127.0.0.1...
Connected to localhost.
Escape character is '^]'.
220 shadrach.ispnet1.net ESMTP Postfix
QUIT
221 Bye
Connection closed by foreign host.
[rich@shadrach]$
```

The first line shows the telnet command format using host localhost and TCP port 25. If the server is running an SMTP package, you should see a response similar to the one shown. The first number is a three-digit response code. This code can be used for troubleshooting purposes if mail is not being transferred properly. Next, the hostname of the SMTP server and a description of the SMTP software package the server is using are displayed. This server is using the Postfix SMTP software package with the smtpd program to accept incoming SMTP connections. You can close the Telnet connection by typing QUIT followed by pressing the Enter key. The SMTP server should send you a closing message and close down the TCP connection.

As you can tell from this example, SMTP uses simple ASCII text commands and returns three-digit reply codes with optional ASCII text messages. SMTP is defined in Internet

Request for Comment (RFC) document 821, maintained by the Internet Engineering Task Force (IETF), and was first published on August 21, 1982. Several modifications have been made to SMTP over the years, but the basic protocol commands still remain in use.

Basic SMTP Client Commands

When a TCP session has been established and the SMTP server acknowledges the client by sending a welcome message (as shown in Listing 2.1), it is then the client's responsibility to control the connection between the two computers. The client accomplishes this by sending special commands to the server. The server should respond accordingly to each command sent.

RFC 821 defines the basic client commands an SMTP server should recognize and respond to. Since then, there have been several extensions to SMTP that not all servers have implemented. This section documents the basic SMTP keywords defined in RFC 821. The section "Extended SMTP" later in this chapter covers some of the new extensions that have been implemented by several SMTP software packages.

This is the basic format of an SMTP command:

```
command [parameter]
```

In this syntax, *command* is a four-character SMTP command and *parameter* is optional qualifying data for the command. Table 2.1 shows the basic SMTP commands that are available.

TABLE 2.1 SMTP Basic Commands

Command	Description
HELO	Opening greeting from client
MAIL	Identifies sender of message
RCPT	Identifies recipients
DATA	Identifies start of message
SEND	Sends message to terminal
SOML	Carries out SEND *or* MAIL commands
SAML	Carries out SEND *and* MAIL commands
RSET	Resets SMTP connection
VRFY	Verifies username on system
EXPN	Queries for lists and aliases
HELP	Requests list of commands
NOOP	No operation; does nothing

TABLE 2.1 Continued

Command	Description
QUIT	Stops the SMTP session
TURN	Reverses the SMTP roles

The following sections describe these commands in more detail.

HELO Command

This command name is not a typo. By definition, SMTP commands are four characters long; therefore, the client's opening greeting to the server is the HELO command. The format for this command is as follows:

HELO *hostname*

The purpose of the HELO command is for the client to identify itself to the SMTP server. Unfortunately, this method was devised in the early days of the Internet before mass hacker break-in attempts. As you can see, the client can be identified as whatever it wants to use in the text string. That being the case, most SMTP servers use this command just as a formality. If they really need to know the client's identity, they try to use a reverse Domain Name System (DNS) lookup of the client's IP address to determine the client's DNS name.

For security reasons, many MTA packages can be configured to refuse to talk to hosts whose IP address does not resolve to a proper DNS hostname or whose reverse-DNS hostname doesn't match the hostname specified in the opening HELO message. By sending the HELO command, the client indicates that it wants to initialize a new SMTP session with the server. By responding to this command, the server acknowledges the new connection and should be ready to receive further commands from the client.

MAIL Command

The MAIL command is used to initiate a mail session with the server after the initial HELO command is sent. It identifies the message sender, and uses the following format:

MAIL *reverse-path*

The *reverse-path* argument not only identifies the sender, but also identifies how to reach the sender with a return message. If the sender is a user on the client computer that initiated the SMTP session, the format for the MAIL command would look something like this:

MAIL FROM:rich@shadrach.ispnet1.net

Notice how the MAIL FROM section denotes the proper e-mail address for the sender of the message, including the full hostname of the client computer. This information should appear in the text of the e-mail message in the From: section (but more on that later).

Often, mail from clients on private networks has to traverse several mail relay points before getting to the Internet. The *reverse-path* information is often useful in troubleshooting e-mail problems or in tracking down e-mailers who are purposely trying to hide their identity by bouncing their e-mail messages off several unknowing SMTP servers.

RCPT Command

The RCPT command defines the recipients of the message. The same message can have multiple recipients. Each recipient is normally listed in a separate RCPT command line. This is the format of the RCPT command:

RCPT *forward-path*

The *forward-path* argument defines the e-mail's ultimate destination. It's usually a fully qualified e-mail address, but could be just a username that is local to the SMTP server. For example, the following RCPT command would send the message to user haley on the SMTP server processing the message:

RCPT TO:haley

Messages can also be sent to users on other computer systems that are remote from the SMTP server the message is sent to.

For example, sending the following RCPT command to the SMTP server on computer shadrach.ispnet1.net would force the SMTP server on shadrach.ispnet1.net to make a decision:

RCPT TO:riley@meshach.ispnet1.net

Because the user is not local to shadrach, it must decide what to do with the message. There are three possible actions shadrach could take with the message:

- shadrach could forward the message to the destination computer and return an OK response to the client. In this scenario, shadrach would add its hostname to the Received: header fields to indicate that it is part of the return path routing a message back to the original sender.
- shadrach could refuse to forward the message, but would send a reply to the client specifying that it was not able to deliver the message. The response could also verify that the address of meshach.ispnet1.net was a correct address for another server. The client could then try to re-send the message directly to meshach.ispnet1.net.

- Finally, shadrach might not forward the message, and would send a reply to the client specifying that this operation (relaying) is not permitted from this server. It would be up to the system administrator at shadrach to figure out what happened and why.

In the early days of the Internet, it was common to run across computers that used the first tactic and blindly forwarded e-mail messages across the world. Unfortunately, that technique became popular with e-mail spammers who could protect their identity through these "open relay" servers. Nowadays, most ISPs allow their customers to relay e-mail from their mail server, but restrict outside computers from that privilege.

In the case of multiple recipients, it is up to the client how to handle situations in which some of the recipients are not acknowledged. Some clients abort the entire message and return an error to the sending user. Some continue sending the message to the recipients that are acknowledged and list the recipients that aren't acknowledged in a return message.

DATA Command

The DATA command is the meat-and-potatoes of the SMTP operation. After the MAIL and RCPT commands are hashed out, the DATA command is used to transfer the actual message. The format of the DATA command is

```
DATA
```

Anything after that command is treated as the message to transfer. Usually the SMTP server adds a timestamp and the return-path information to the head of the message as the data is received (you can see this in your own e-mail messages with the Received: headers). The client indicates the end of the message by sending a line with just a single period, as shown here:

```
<CR><LF>.<CR><LF>
```

The carriage return (<CR>) and line feed (<LF>) characters ensure that the period is on a line by itself. When the SMTP server receives this sequence, it knows that the message transmission is done, and should return a response code to the client indicating whether the message is accepted.

Much work has been done on the format of the actual DATA messages. Technically, there is no wrong way to send a message, although efforts have been made to standardize a method. However, any combination of valid ASCII characters will be transferred to recipients. Listing 2.2 shows a sample session sending a short mail message to a local user on an SMTP server.

LISTING 2.2 Sample SMTP Session

```
$ telnet localhost 25
Trying 127.0.0.1...
Connected to localhost.ispnet1.net.
Escape character is '^]'.
220 shadrach.ispnet1.net ESMTP
HELO localhost
250 shadrach.ispnet1.net
MAIL FROM: rich@localhost
250 ok
RCPT TO:rich
250 ok
DATA
354 go ahead
This is a short test of the SMTP e-mail system.
.
250 ok 959876575 qp 40419
QUIT
221 shadrach.ispnet1.net
Connection closed by foreign host.
you have mail
$ mail
Mail version 8.1 6/6/93.  Type ? for help.
"/var/mail/rich": 1 message 1 new
>N  1 rich@localhost        Thu Jun  1 11:22     8/339
& 1
Message 1:
From rich@localhost Thu Jun  1 11:22:55 2000

This is a short test of the SMTP e-mail system.

& x
$
```

Listing 2.2 shows a typical SMTP exchange between two hosts performing the transmission of a one-line e-mail message. After entering the message header information, the client enters the DATA command, and the server responds. Next the client sends the text message. Following the completed message is the terminating period, indicating the end of the message to the server. As you can see, the SMTP server transferred the message to the local user's mailbox account exactly as the server received it. Also note how the SMTP server included a timestamp and the return-path information in the text of the e-mail message (as part of the From line).

Much work has been done toward standardizing the format of Internet mail messages. RFC 822 specifies a standard format for sending text mail messages between hosts. The section "Message Formats" later in this chapter covers some of these features.

SEND Command

The SEND command is used to send a mail message directly to the terminal of a logged in user. This command works only when the user is logged in and usually pops up as a message much like the Unix write command works. This command does have a serious drawback. It is an easy way for an external user to determine who was logged into a computer system at any given time without having to log in to the system. Hackers have taken advantage of this "feature" by searching the Internet for unsuspecting victims' user IDs and when they are logged in. Because it is such a security threat, most SMTP software packages do not enable this command anymore.

SOML Command

The SOML command stands for "send or mail." If the recipients are logged on to the computer system, it behaves like the preceding SEND command. If not, it behaves like the MAIL command and sends the message to the recipients' mailbox. The "exploit-ability" of this command has made it another victim of the Internet world, so it is usually disabled on newer SMTP server packages.

SAML Command

The SAML command stands for "send and mail." This command tries to cover both bases by both sending a message to the terminal of a logged in user and placing the message in the users' mailbox. Again, the "exploit-ability" of this command has rendered it unsafe to use.

RSET Command

The RSET command is short for "reset." If the client somehow gets confused by responses from the server and thinks the SMTP connection has gotten out of sync, it can issue the RSET command to return the connection back to the HELO command state. Therefore, any MAIL, RCPT, or DATA information entered will be lost. Often this command is used as a "last-ditch effort" when the client has lost track of where it was in the command series or did not expect a particular response from the server.

VRFY Command

The VRFY command is short for "verify." You can use it to determine whether an SMTP server can deliver mail to a particular recipient before entering the RCPT command mode. The command's format looks like this:

```
VRFY username
```

When received, the SMTP server determines whether the user is on the local server. If the user is local to the server, the SMTP server returns the user's full e-mail address. If the user is not local, the SMTP server can return a negative response to the client or indicate that it is willing to forward any mail messages to the remote user—depending on whether the SMTP server will forward messages for the particular client.

The VRFY command can be a valuable troubleshooting tool. Often users incorrectly type a username or hostname in an e-mail message and don't know why their mail message did not get where they wanted it to go. Of course, the first thing they do is complain about the lousy mail system, and then contact you—the mail administrator.

As the mail administrator, you can attempt to verify the e-mail address in two ways. First, use the DNS host command or the nslookup utility to determine whether the domain name is correct and has a mail server associated with it. Then you can issue the telnet command on port 25 of the mail server and use the VRFY command to see whether the user name is correct. Listing 2.3 shows an example of using the VRFY command to check the validity of usernames.

LISTING 2.3 Example of the VRFY Command

```
$ telnet localhost 25
Trying 127.0.0.1...
Connected to localhost.
Escape character is '^]'.
220 shadrach.ispnet1.net ESMTP Sendmail 8.9.3/8.9.3;
➥ Thu, 26 Aug 1999 19:20:16 -050
HELO localhost
250 shadrach.ispnet1.net Hello localhost [127.0.0.1], pleased to meet you
VRFY rich
250 <rich@shadrach.ispnet1.net>
VRFY prez@mechach.ispnet1.net
252 <prez@mechach.ispnet1.net>
VRFY jessica
550 jessica... User unknown
QUIT
221 shadrach.ispnet1.net closing connection
Connection closed by foreign host.
$
```

Note the difference between the return codes for the username rich and prez. The VRFY command for rich returns a 250 code, which indicates the server will accept messages for rich, who is a local user. The result from the VRFY command for prez is 252, which indicates the user is not local, but the mail server is willing to forward the message for him.

The result codes are explained in more detail later in the "Server Responses" section.

Much like some of the other useful commands, the VRFY command has the capability of being exploited by hackers and spammers. Because of this potential problem, many sites disable the VRFY command.

EXPN Command

The EXPN command is short for "expand." This command queries the SMTP server for mailing lists and aliases. Mailing lists are handy ways of sending mass mailings to groups of people with just one address. This is the format of the EXPN command:

EXPN *address*

In this format, *address* is the name of the mailing list or alias. The SMTP server returns an error code if the client does not have privileges to see the list or returns the complete mailing list, one e-mail address per line. Again, most servers disable EXPN *address* to hide the membership addresses of mailing lists.

HELP Command

The HELP command is used to return a list of SMTP commands that the SMTP server understands. Most all SMTP software packages understand and process the basic RFC 821 commands listed here (except, of course, ones that could cause security issues). Where differences occur are with the extended SMTP options. Listing 2.4 shows the output from a HELP command issued to a Linux server running the sendmail SMTP package version 8.11.3.

LISTING 2.4 SMTP HELP Command Output

```
$ telnet localhost 25
Trying 127.0.0.1...
Connected to localhost.
Escape character is '^]'.
220 test.ispnet.net ESMTP Sendmail 8.11.3/8.11.3; Fri, 6 Apr 2001 07:25:37
HELO localhost
250 test.ispnet.net Hello IDENT:rich@localhost [127.0.0.1], pleased to
➥ meet you
HELP
214-2.0.0 This is sendmail version 8.11.3
214-2.0.0 Topics:
214-2.0.0        HELO    EHLO    MAIL    RCPT    DATA
214-2.0.0        RSET    NOOP    QUIT    HELP    VRFY
214-2.0.0        EXPN    VERB    ETRN    DSN     AUTH
```

LISTING 2.4 Continued

```
214-2.0.0      STARTTLS
214-2.0.0 For more info use "HELP <topic>".
214-2.0.0 To report bugs in the implementation send email to
214-2.0.0      sendmail-bugs@sendmail.org.
214-2.0.0 For local information send email to Postmaster at your site.
214 2.0.0 End of HELP info
HELP RCPT
214-2.0.0 RCPT TO: <recipient> [ <parameters> ]
214-2.0.0    Specifies the recipient.  Can be used any number of times.
214-2.0.0    Parameters are ESMTP extensions.  See "HELP DSN" for details.
214 2.0.0 End of HELP info
QUIT
221 2.0.0 test.ispnet.net closing connection
Connection closed by foreign host.
$
```

Two levels of help are available. If you send the HELP command alone, the SMTP server gives a brief overview of all of the available commands. If you send the HELP command with an argument that is another SMTP command, the server returns a more detailed description of the command, including any parameters that are required.

NOOP Command

The NOOP command is short for "no operation." This command has no effect on the SMTP server other than having it return a positive response code. This command is often useful for testing connectivity without actually starting the message transfer process.

QUIT Command

The QUIT command does what it says. It indicates that the client computer is finished with the current SMTP session and wants to close the connection. It is the responsibility of the SMTP server to respond to this command and to initiate the closing of the TCP connection. If the server receives a QUIT command in the middle of an e-mail transaction, any data previously transferred should be deleted and not sent to any recipients.

TURN Command

The TURN command is not used on SMTP servers today for security reasons. It is part of the RFC 821 standard because it was a great idea that, unfortunately, was exploited by hackers. The TURN command idea was modified in the extended SMTP RFCs, and it is discussed in the section "Extended SMTP" later in this chapter. It is described here as a background reference for the extended SMTP version ETRN.

The purpose of the TURN command is to allow two-way mail transfer between two computers during one TCP connection. Normally, the SMTP protocol sends mail in only one direction for each connection. The client host is in control of the transmission medium and directs the actions of the server by the SMTP commands that are sent. Mail can be sent only from the client to the server. Usually when a host connects with a remote host via SMTP, it not only needs to send messages, but also needs to receive messages.

As discussed previously, the server uses the domain name indicated by the HELO command text string to identify the client it is talking to. The idea of the TURN command is to allow the SMTP server to switch roles with the client and send any mail destined for the client's domain name to the client. The problem with this idea is the SMTP server relying on the client actually being who it says it is. If a hacker connects to the SMTP server and identifies himself as another computer domain name, the server would unknowingly send all the mail messages destined for that domain name to the hacker. Ouch!

Server Responses

For each command the client sends to the SMTP server, the server must reply with a response message. As you can see from Listings 2.2 and 2.3, response messages are made up of two parts. The first part is a three-digit code used by the SMTP software to identify whether the command was successful, and if not, why. The second part is a text string that helps humans understand the reply. Often the SMTP software displays the text string to the user as part of a response message.

Usually a space separates the code from the text string. In the case of multiline responses (such as the HELP and EXPN commands in Listing 2.4), a dash (-) separates the code from the text on all but the last line, which conforms to the normal pattern of using a space. This helps the client host know when to expect more lines from the server. There are four different groups, or categories, of reply codes, explained in the following sections.

Error SMTP Response Codes

Table 2.2 shows the response codes for error conditions that could occur from various problems in the SMTP transaction.

TABLE 2.2 SMTP Error Response Codes

Code	Description
500	Syntax error, command not recognized
501	Syntax error in parameters
502	Command not implemented
503	Bad sequence of commands
504	Command parameter not implemented

SMTP error responses are not overly descriptive. They just give a general idea of what might have gone wrong in the SMTP process. When troubleshooting mail problems, it is helpful to be able to watch the actual SMTP transactions for command errors if you are communicating with an unfamiliar SMTP server. Often 500, 502, and 504 errors occur when trying to use extended SMTP commands with older SMTP software servers.

Informational SMTP Response Codes

The next category of response codes is informational codes, which are used to display additional information about a command. Table 2.3 shows these codes.

TABLE 2.3 SMTP Informational Response Codes

Code	Description
211	System status, or system help
214	Help message

As shown in Listing 2.4, the 214 response code is used when displaying output from the HELP command. When there are multiple lines of output, a dash after the response code signifies that more lines are coming. The last line uses a space to separate the response code from the text.

Service SMTP Response Codes

Another response code category is service codes, which are used to mark the status of the SMTP service in the connection. Table 2.4 lists these codes.

TABLE 2.4 SMTP Service Response Codes

Code	Description
220	Service ready
221	Service closing transmission channel
421	Service not available

Each of these response codes includes the hostname of the SMTP server in the text string portion, as well as the text description. The 421 response code is a little misleading. Many mail administrators think this response code is returned when there is no SMTP software available on the remote server. Although that can happen, this response code usually means there is an SMTP server, but it's not accepting mail messages at the time. Sometimes this is the case if a server locks its file system to perform nightly data backups. The SMTP server would be unable to store mail messages on the locked file system, so the SMTP server shuts down temporarily while the backup is running. Trying to connect to the same server a little later in the evening would result in a successful transaction.

Action SMTP Response Codes

The last response code category relates to replying to SMTP client actions. Table 2.5 shows the action codes used in an SMTP transaction.

TABLE 2.5 SMTP Action Response Codes

Code	Description
250	Requested mail action okay, completed
251	User not local, will forward to `<forward-path>`
354	Start mail input: End with `<CR><LF>.<CR><LF>`
450	Requested mail action not taken: Mailbox unavailable
451	Requested action aborted: Error in processing
452	Requested action not taken: Insufficient system storage
550	Requested action not taken: Mailbox unavailable
551	User not local: Please try `<forward-path>`
552	Requested mail action aborted: Exceeded storage allocation
553	Requested action not taken: Mailbox name not allowed
554	Transaction failed

Action codes are a result of the SMTP server trying to perform a function requested by the client, such as MAIL, RCPT, and DATA commands. They return the status of the requested action so that the client knows what actions to take next in the SMTP process.

SMTP server response codes are often "behind-the-scenes" players in the SMTP world. Some e-mail client packages forward any error response codes they receive back to the e-mail sender. When that happens, it is easy to check the response codes against the code lists to determine what went wrong. Sometimes it is difficult to determine what went wrong with an e-mail message that does not get processed properly. A returned e-mail message does not get routed back properly to the client, so no error text is sent to the user. Often the mail administrator has to resort to using network analyzers to watch the actual TCP packets on the local area network (LAN) to see the response codes coming from the SMTP server. Remember that the SMTP data packets are ASCII text, so they are easy to read and decode.

Extended SMTP

Since its invention in 1982, SMTP has performed well in transporting messages between computers across the Internet. As mail systems advanced and the demand for faster processing increased, however, system administrators began to recognize its limitations. Instead of trying to replace a standard protocol that was in use all over the world, work was done to improve basic SMTP by keeping the original specifications and adding new features.

RFC 1869, published in 1995, defined a method of extending the capabilities of SMTP, calling it "SMTP Service Extensions." Extended SMTP is implemented by replacing the original SMTP greeting (HELO) with a new greeting command—EHLO. When an SMTP server receives this command, it should realize that the client is capable of sending extended SMTP commands. Listing 2.5 shows a sample EHLO session and the commands that are available.

LISTING 2.5 Extended SMTP Commands

```
$ telnet localhost 25
Trying 127.0.0.1...
Connected to localhost.
Escape character is '^]'.
220 test.ispnet.net ESMTP Sendmail 8.11.3/8.11.3; Fri, 6 Apr 2001 07:30:10
EHLO localhost
250-test.ispnet.net Hello IDENT:rich@localhost [127.0.0.1], pleased to meet you
250-ENHANCEDSTATUSCODES
250-EXPN
250-VERB
250-8BITMIME
250-SIZE
250-DSN
250-ONEX
250-ETRN
250-XUSR
250-AUTH LOGIN
250 HELP
HELP AUTH
214-2.0.0 AUTH mechanism [initial-response]
214-2.0.0     Start authentication.
214 2.0.0 End of HELP info
HELP ETRN
214-2.0.0 ETRN [ <hostname> | @<domain> |
214-2.0.0     Run the queue for the specified <hostname>, or
214-2.0.0     all hosts within a given <domain>, or a specially-named
214-2.0.0     <queuename> (implementation-specific).
214 2.0.0 End of HELP info
QUIT
221 2.0.0 test.ispnet.net closing connection
Connection closed by foreign host.
$
```

Notice the server indicates that more commands are available now that it is in "extended" mode. One of the new groups of commands is the Delivery Status Notification (DSN) options. These options can be used on the MAIL and RCPT commands to indicate the delivery status of a particular e-mail message for the client. Two additional ESMTP commands that are extremely useful are ETRN and AUTH.

ETRN Command

The TURN SMTP command was briefly mentioned in the previous descriptions of the basic SMTP client commands. This command is extremely useful, but not very secure. To compensate for that, RFC 1985 defines a new, more secure method of implementing the TURN command.

The ETRN command allows an SMTP client to issue a request for the SMTP server to initiate another SMTP connection with the client to transfer messages back to it. This method differs from the original TURN command in that the ETRN command is just a request to start another SMTP session, not to transfer data on the existing session. This way, the SMTP server can then contact the client computer using the normal DNS hostname resolution methods. ETRN does not rely on the client computer being who it says it is. If a hacker establishes an unauthorized SMTP connection and issues an ETRN command, the SMTP server just starts an SMTP connection with the real client and sends any waiting mail—no harm done.

The format for the ETRN command is as follows:

ETRN *name*

In this command, *name* can be an individual hostname or a domain name if you are requesting mail for an entire domain. The ETRN command is a valuable tool for the mail administrator. If you elect to have an ISP spool mail for your e-mail server, you might use this method to notify the ISP when you are ready to receive your spooled mail.

AUTH Command

Another extended SMTP command gaining in popularity is the AUTH command, which allows the SMTP client to properly identify itself with the SMTP server using a user ID and password or other type of authentication technique. Here is the format of the AUTH command:

AUTH *mechanism*

The *mechanism* parameter identifies the authentication method the ESMTP client can use. Several different authentication mechanisms are currently supported by ESMTP. Table 2.6 lists the commonly used authentication mechanisms.

TABLE 2.6 ESMTP Authentication Mechanisms

Mechanism	Description
PLAIN	Uses a plain text username, authentication ID, and password.
LOGIN	Uses a base-64 encrypted username and password.
CRAM-MD5	Uses an MD5 encrypted username and password.
DIGEST-MD5	Uses an MD5 encrypted digest value of the username and password.
KERBEROS_V4	Uses a Kerberos authentication key.
GSSAPI	Uses a Generic Security Service (GSS) authentication key.

Although some administrators equate ESMTP AUTH with security, this is not necessarily the case. As you can see in Table 2.6, the PLAIN and LOGIN authentication methods can be easily captured by network snoopers and used to steal the identity of the ESMTP client. Listing 2.6 shows a sample ESMTP AUTH session.

LISTING 2.6 Sample ESMTP AUTH Session

```
[rich@test rich]$ telnet localhost 25
Trying 127.0.0.1...
Connected to localhost.
Escape character is '^]'.
220 test.ispnet.net ESMTP Sendmail 8.11.3/8.11.3; Fri, 6 Apr 2001 08:36:45
EHLO localhost
250-test.ispnet.net Hello IDENT:rich@localhost [127.0.0.1], pleased to meet you
250-ENHANCEDSTATUSCODES
250-EXPN
250-VERB
250-8BITMIME
250-SIZE
250-DSN
250-ONEX
250-ETRN
250-XUSR
250-AUTH LOGIN
250 HELP
AUTH LOGIN
334 VXNlcm5hbWU6
cmljaA==
334 UGFzc3dvcmQ6
dGVzdA==
235 2.0.0 OK Authenticated
```

LISTING 2.6 Continued

```
MAIL FROM: <rich@ispnet.net>
250 2.1.0 <rich@ispnet.net>... Sender ok
RCPT TO: <richard.blum@otherplace.net>
250 2.1.5 <richard.blum@otherplace.net>... Recipient ok
DATA
354 Enter mail, end with "." on a line by itself
This is a test message, using the AUTH command.
.
250 2.0.0 f36DbVn12406 Message accepted for delivery
QUIT
221 2.0.0 test.ispnet.net closing connection
Connection closed by foreign host.
[rich@test rich]$
```

As seen in Listing 2.6, after entering the AUTH LOGIN command, the ESMTP client is sent an encoded challenge. The client responds with the base-64 encrypted version of the username. Next, another encoded challenge for the password is sent, and the encoded password is returned.

After the client is positively identified with the server, it may be allowed to perform special functions, such as using the server as a mail relay, something non-authenticated clients would not be allowed to do. Note that although the LOGIN authentication method uses encrypted usernames and passwords, it would not be too difficult for a network snoop to capture the pair and work on decoding them at his leisure.

The Message Digest 5 (MD5) authentication methods utilize a secret word for encrypting the username and password pair based on a seed value provided by the server. Each time the client logs into the server, a different seed value is used, thus producing a different encoding. This method is much more secure than the LOGIN method.

Message Formats

Listing 2.2 showed a simple example of an SMTP session. The format of the message was extremely basic, just one line of text. As shown in the example, the resulting e-mail message was functional, but not too exciting. Today's e-mail messages are much more complex, and users are beginning to expect that level of sophistication from their e-mail service. Niceties such as Subject, Cc:, and Bcc: lines are now the norm in e-mail text. RFC 822 describes a standard e-mail message format that most SMTP systems implement to "standardize" the look and feel of e-mail. Simple one-line text messages are now unacceptable in the business world.

Standard RFC 822 Header Fields

RFC 822 specifies splitting the message into two separate parts. The first part is called the header. Its job is to identify the message. The second part is the body of the message. The header consists of data fields that can be used whenever additional information is needed in the message. The header fields should appear before the text body of the message and should be separated by one blank line. Header fields do not need to appear in any particular order, and the message can have multiple occurrences of any header field. Figure 2.1 shows what a basic RFC 822–compliant message would look like.

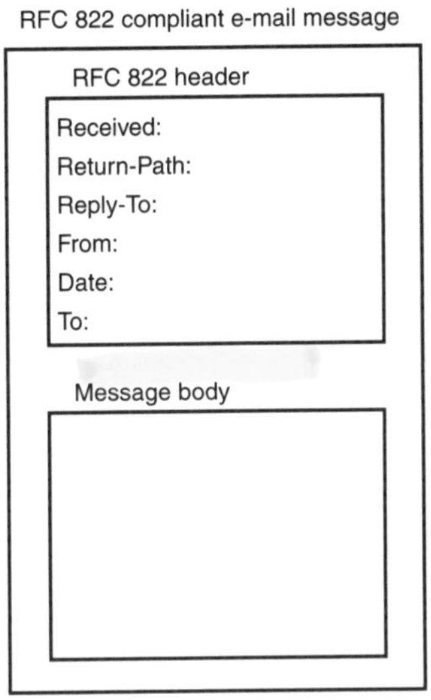

RFC 822 compliant e-mail message

RFC 822 header

Received:
Return-Path:
Reply-To:
From:
Date:
To:

Message body

FIGURE 2.1

The RFC 822 message format.

Received: Header Field

The format for the Received: header field is as follows:

```
Received:
    from host name
    by host name
    via physical-path
    with protocol
    id message-id
    for final e-mail destination
```

The `Received:` header field is used to identify the SMTP servers that relayed the e-mail message from the originating sender to the destination. Each server adds a new `Received:` field to the e-mail message supplying specific details about itself. The subfields in the `Received:` header field further identify the path, protocol, and computers used in transferring the e-mail message. It is the responsibility of the receiving MTA as to which subfields in the `Received:` field are used, so you might see many variations between the separate `Received:` fields in a single message.

Return-path: Header Field

The `Return-path:` header field format is as follows:

`Return-path: route`

The last SMTP server in the relay chain adds the `Return-path:` field to the message. The purpose of the `Return-path:` field is to identify the route that was taken to pass the message to the destination server. If the message was sent directly to the destination server, there will be only one address in this field. Otherwise, the field will list the path that was taken to transfer the message.

Originator Header Fields

The originator field shows the address the message originated from. This information is extremely useful on messages that have been bounced around several times on private networks before making it to the Internet. The format of this field looks like this:

`Reply-To: address`

The originator field does not have to be an e-mail address. If the message is sent in the context of an SMTP session, the originator field is a small subset of the full-blown authentic header field. It serves as an easier way for smaller SMTP packages to implement this feature without having to use a full-blown authentic header field.

Authentic Header Fields

The authentic header fields identify the sender of the e-mail message. This is the format of the authentic field:

`From:    user-name`
`Sender:  user-name`

The `From:` field identifies the author of the original message. Usually the `From:` and `Sender:` fields are the same user, so only one is needed. If the sender of the e-mail is not the original author (for example, a secretary might send e-mail on behalf of someone else), both fields can be identified for return mail purposes.

Date: Header Field

The Date: header fields are used to timestamp the message as the client sends it to the server. The format for the Date: field is as follows:

```
Date:   date-time
```

The Date: header field passes the data information in the message header exactly as it is entered in the original message. This field is useful for tracking message times in responses, especially multiple responses.

Destination Header Fields

The destination header fields identify e-mail addresses that are the intended recipients of the mail message. These fields are purely informational. The SMTP server does not send a message to a user mailbox unless a RCPT command has been issued for that user (see the "Basic SMTP Client Commands" section earlier in this chapter). These fields use the following format:

```
To: address
Cc: address
Bcc: address
```

The To:, Cc:, and Bcc: fields have set a standard in the way e-mail is processed. Most e-mail packages now use this terminology to classify the recipients of a message. The To: field is intended for the main recipient of the message. The Cc: fields, much like "carbon copies" in a printed business memo, are recipients that should receive a "copy" of the message but are not the primary recipients. A blind carbon copy (Bcc:) goes to a recipient whose address isn't listed on the message for other people to see (sneaky but useful!). There has been some debate in computer ethics circles over the appropriate use of bccs, but practically every e-mail package in use today offers this feature.

Optional Header Fields

Optional header fields further identify the message to the SMTP server, but are not required for a message to be RFC 822 compatible. These fields are some of the niceties mentioned earlier that many e-mail customers now expect to see. The format for some of the optional header fields is as follows:

```
Message-ID:  message-id
Resent-Message-ID:  message-id
In-Reply-To: message-id
References: message-id
Keywords: text-list
Subject: text
Comments: text
Encrypted: word
```

The most useful and typically used optional header field is the Subject: field. E-mail packages allow the sender to include a one-line subject that identifies the e-mail message's topic for the recipient. This text string is then used in the e-mail client package when listing multiple e-mail messages.

Other optional header fields help identify the e-mail message. The Message-ID: fields supply a unique message ID that can be included in log files in transit and referred to in return messages. The Encrypted: field indicates whether the e-mail message has been encrypted for security purposes, and the Keyword: field offers keywords that can be used when searching for specific content in multiple messages.

Resent Header Fields

The resent header fields identify an e-mail message that for some reason had to be re-sent from the client. The format for this field is to add the tag Resent to the original header field:

```
Resent-Reply-To: address
Resent-From: user-name
Resent-Sender: user-name
Resent-Cc: address
Resent-To: address
Resent-Bcc: address
Resent-Date: date-time
```

The resent fields behave just like the original fields. They just signify that the e-mail message was re-sent from the client for some unknown reason.

Using the RFC 822 Format in an SMTP Mail Transaction

A sample SMTP mail transaction using full RFC 822 message formats is shown in Listing 2.7. Line numbers have been added to aid in the following discussion.

LISTING 2.7 Sample SMTP RFC 822 Message Transaction

```
1  [rich@shadrach rich]$ telnet localhost 25
2  Trying 127.0.0.1...
3  Connected to localhost.
4  Escape character is '^]'.
5  250 shadrach.ispnet1.net Hello localhost [127.0.0.1], pleased to meet you
6  MAIL FROM:rich@localhost
7  250 rich@localhost... Sender ok
8  RCPT TO:rich
9  250 rich... Recipient ok
10 DATA
```

LISTING 2.7 Continued

```
11 354 Enter mail, end with "." on a line by itself
12 Return-Path:rich@localhost
13 Received: from localhost by localhost with TCP/IP id 1 for Richard Blum
14 Reply-to:rich@localhost
15 From:rich
16 Date:8/27/99
17 To:rich
18 Cc:jessica
19 Cc:katie
20 Bcc:barbara
21 Bcc:haley
22 Message-ID:1
23 Subject:Test RFC 822 message
24
25 This is a test message sent from the local host to rich.
26 This message is a little larger, but in the right format.
27 .
28 250 PAA02866 Message accepted for delivery
29 QUIT
30 221 shadrach.ispnet1.net closing connection
31 Connection closed by foreign host.
32 You have new mail in /var/spool/mail/rich
33 [rich@shadrach rich]$ mail
34 Mail version 8.1 6/6/93.  Type ? for help.
35 "/var/spool/mail/rich": 1 message 1 new
36 >N  1 rich@shadrach.smallo  Fri Aug 27 18:50  18/622   "Test RFC 822 message"
37 &1
38 Message 1:
39 From rich@ispnet1.net  Fri Aug 27 18:50:21 1999
40 From: rich@shadrach.ispnet1.net
41 Reply-to: rich@shadrach.ispnet1.net
42 Date: 8/27/99
43 To: rich@shadrach.ispnet1.net
44 Cc: jessica@shadrach.ispnet1.net
45 Cc: katie@shadrach.ispnet1.net
46 Subject: Test RFC 822 message
47
48 This is a test message sent from the local host to rich.
49 This message is a little larger, but in the right format.
50
51 &x
52 [rich@shadrach rich]$
```

This example is similar to the example in Listing 2.2, but notice the differences. Lines 12 through 23 show the RFC 822 header fields used for the message. Line 36 shows how the e-mail reader package has used the RFC 822 Subject: field as a short description of the e-mail message. Lines 39 through 46 show how the header fields were displayed by the e-mail reader package in the message. One thing that stands out is the missing Bcc: fields. The Bcc: fields are for identifying blind carbon copies to the MTA. Because the message recipients shouldn't know those bcc recipients got copies, it makes sense that those fields do not show up in the e-mail reader.

Another obvious difference is the Date: line. Line 28 in Listing 2.2 shows a complete date that was automatically added by the MTA. Line 42 in Listing 2.7 shows the date as it was set by the RFC 822 message. This e-mail reader package allowed the RFC 822 field to override its automatic field insertion.

Summary

The Simple Mail Transfer Protocol (SMTP) allows computers to transfer messages from a user on one computer to a user (or multiple users) on another computer using a standard method. This protocol, outlined in RFC 821, defines a standard set of commands used to identify the mail sender and recipients as well as transfer the message.

SMTP has been extended with additional features in Extended SMTP (ESMTP). One of the additional features is the AUTH command, which allows a client to authenticate itself to the ESMTP host. After being authenticated, the client can be granted special privileges on the host, such as relaying messages to other hosts.

The actual SMTP message can be in any form, but a standard format has been set forth in RFC 822. This format provides for two different sections—the message header and the message body. The message header contains fields that identify important parts of the message, such as the sender, recipients, subject, and comments.

CHAPTER 3

POP3

The previous chapter described how to send mail to a user at a remote mail server using the SMTP protocol. After the message is received by the mail server and placed in a user's mailbox, the user must have a method to retrieve and read that message.

Back in the old days (the '80s), that user would have to sit at a dumb terminal, log in to the host computer, and read his or her mail message via a character-based text e-mail processor. Now things are different. Computer users want to have the freedom of reading their mail from anywhere at any time, as well as having fancy GUI interfaces to do that. If the user cannot be at the mail server using X Window System to view the e-mail, the next best thing is to let him connect to the mail server via a network to read his mail using a client software package on the local computer. One popular protocol that allows a client to retrieve e-mail messages that are on a remote server is defined in Request for Comment (RFC) 1939 and called the Post Office Protocol (POP). Currently, this protocol is at version three, thus the common name POP3.

Description of the Post Office Protocol

Much like Simple Mail Transfer Protocol (described in Chapter 2, "SMTP"), POP3 is a command-based protocol. The POP3 server listens for connection requests on Transmission Control Protocol (TCP) port 110 and responds by issuing a welcome message indicating it is ready for commands. One method of determining whether a host is running a POP3 server is to use `telnet` on port 110 and see if you get a POP3 greeting. Listing 3.1 shows an example of this method.

LISTING 3.1 Sample POP3 Client Session

```
$ telnet localhost 110
Trying 127.0.0.1...
Connected to localhost.
Escape character is '^]'.
+OK POP3 localhost v7.59 server ready
QUIT
+OK Sayonara
Connection closed by foreign host.
$
```

When the connection to TCP port 110 is made, the POP3 server produces a welcome message to identify itself. After receiving the response, the client sends a QUIT command to log off the server.

In a POP3 session, the first step for the client is to log in to the server. There are several different methods to do this. After logging in to the POP3 server, the client can query the server to see if there are any mail messages in the mailbox assigned to the username the client logged in with. It is not the intent of POP3 to allow the client to do extensive manipulation of messages in its mailbox. POP3 can simply send a list of messages to the client and transfer each message individually for the client to manipulate locally.

POP3 Authentication Methods

After the POP3 client has established a TCP connection to the server, it must be able to identify itself to the server so that the server knows it is sending the right e-mail messages to the right user. The original POP3 authentication method uses a username/password command set. Unfortunately, this method uses a clear text transmission of the username and password to log in to the server. This method is not preferred, especially if you are connecting to a remote server where your packets will traverse unknown networks. To provide a solution for this problem, RFCs 1734 and 1939 describe two different secure methods of logging in to a POP3 server. All three methods are described in the following sections.

USER/PASS Commands

The USER/PASS command combination is the easiest to implement, but again, the most dangerous to use. Each time a client wants to log in to the POP3 server to check mail, his or her complete username and password are transmitted across the network in plain ASCII text format—risky, to say the least. This is the format for these commands:

USER *username*
PASS *password*

The *username* parameter must be a valid username for the host POP3 server. The *password* parameter must also be the server password associated with that username. Listing 3.2 shows a sample POP3 session with a client using the USER/PASS combination.

LISTING 3.2 Sample USER/PASS POP3 Client Login

```
$ telnet localhost 110
Trying 127.0.0.1...
Connected to localhost.
Escape character is '^]'.
+OK POP3 localhost v7.59 server ready
USER melanie
+OK User name accepted, password please
PASS toybox
+OK Mailbox open, 0 messages
QUIT
+OK Sayonara
Connection closed by foreign host.
$
```

In this example, the client is using the USER command with her username in plain text. The POP3 server responded, asking for the matching password for the username. After the password is received, the username/password combination is compared for validity. One security feature of POP3 is that it won't immediately tell the client if a username is invalid until after the password is entered, so a hacker can't easily use a POP3 server to find valid usernames on the host system. Listing 3.3 shows the difference between a valid user with a bad password and an invalid user.

LISTING 3.3 Example of POP3 Login Attempts

```
$ telnet localhost 110
Trying 127.0.0.1...
Connected to localhost.
Escape character is '^]'.
+OK POP3 localhost v7.59 server ready
USER rich
+OK User name accepted, password please
PASS hello
-ERR Bad login
USER baduser
+OK User name accepted, password please
PASS hello
-ERR Bad login
QUIT
+OK Sayonara
Connection closed by foreign host.
$
```

This example shows how the POP3 server handles two different situations: a valid user login with an invalid password and an invalid user login. In both situations the POP3 server's response is purposely generic. In this case, the use of generic error messages helps prevent a hacker from using the POP3 server to find valid usernames on the system. Of course, the downside is that it is not very helpful for mail administrators trying to troubleshoot connection problems with the host.

Using clear text usernames and passwords in the POP3 connection is even more dangerous if the client logs in to the POP3 server several times a day (or hour) to check for new mail messages. Many e-mail client packages can be configured to check for new mail at regular intervals, which gives a hacker with a network analyzer the opportunity to capture usernames and passwords. To compensate for this situation, RFC 1939 offers some relief with the APOP command.

Another feature to point out is the return codes generated by the server in response to client requests. Two different request codes can be returned: +OK and -ERR. Even though the meaning of the return codes is obvious, most server commands also return a text response to clarify the situation.

APOP Command

The client can use the APOP command in place of the USER/PASS combination to log in to the POP3 server. The APOP command allows the client to log in to the server without sending a plain text version of the password. Instead, the APOP command uses a Message Digest 5 (MD-5)–encrypted version of the password. Its format looks like this:

APOP *name digest*

The *name* parameter is the normal username the client wants to log in as. The *digest* parameter allows the client to send an MD-5–encoded digest value to the server to authenticate who it is.

The MD-5 encryption algorithm, invented by Ron Rivest, is described in RFC 1321. It uses a hashing algorithm to combine a known message with a shared secret word that only both entities should know. The result of the hashing algorithm is the *digest* parameter supplied by the client.

Obviously, for this encryption method to work, both the client and server must have a predetermined secret word to use for the algorithm. The known message is supplied by the POP3 server on the greeting issued when the TCP connection is established. The known message is usually a message ID followed by the hostname of the POP3 server. A sample APOP session is shown in Listing 3.4.

LISTING 3.4 Sample APOP Session

```
$telnet meshach 110
Trying 198.162.0.5...
Connected to meshach.smallorg.org.
Escape character is '^]'.
+OK POP3 server ready <1896.698370952@meshach.smallorg.org>
APOP chris c4c9334bac560ecc928e58001b3e22fb
+OK maildrop has 1 message (369 octets)
QUIT
+OK Sayonara
Connection closed by foreign host.
$
```

This example shows the different greeting displayed by the POP3 server using APOP authentication. The known message used for the MD-5 encryption is supplied by the greeting. It is the timestamp and the hostname within angle brackets. The entire value is used for the known message. The APOP authentication command uses the username and the MD-5 hash value of the known message along with the shared secret to create the digest value. The actual text password is never transmitted across the network. Without the knowledge of the shared secret word, it would be difficult to break the MD-5–encoded password for this client.

The APOP command is not a required command for a POP3 server to support. The easiest way to determine whether a POP3 server supports the APOP command is to observe the greeting when you connect to the server. The POP3 server on the sample mail server shown in Listing 3.1 did not supply the necessary message for the MD-5 algorithm; therefore a client would not be able to use the APOP method to log in to this server. In fact, trying to use the APOP command produces a negative response error message from the server.

AUTH Command

Another method of secure user identification is the AUTH command described in RFC 1734. It has been adapted from the newer Interactive Message Access Protocol (IMAP) (see Chapter 4, "IMAP") that has more functionality than POP3 for handling mailbox messages . The format of the AUTH command is as follows:

AUTH *mechanism*

In this command, *mechanism* is a method of authenticating the user that the client can negotiate with the server. After an authentication method is agreed on, the actual user-name authentication takes place. Table 3.1 shows the valid authentication methods that can be used in increasing order of security.

TABLE 3.1 POP Authentication Methods

Method	Description
PLAIN	Client sends a plain text username/password combination.
LOGIN	Client sends a base64 encoded username/password combination.
SKEY	Client sends a base64 encoded username and a one-time password combination.
GSSAPI	Client sends a Generic Security Service Application Interface (GSSAPI) encoded username and password.
KERBEROS	Host sends a ready response with a random 32-byte number, and the client responds with a Kerberos ticket and authenticator for the username.

The client initiates the negotiation method, first issuing an AUTH command with the highest level of authentication encryption it can support. If the server does not support that encryption technique, a negative response is sent to the client. The client can then issue another AUTH command with a different mechanism specified. This negotiation can go back and forth until the client and server find a common authentication encryption technique, or they resort to using the USER/PASS technique. Listing 3.5 shows a sample AUTH negotiation session with a POP3 server.

LISTING 3.5 Sample AUTH Negotiation Session

```
$ telnet localhost 110
Trying 127.0.0.1...
Connected to localhost.
Escape character is '^]'.
+OK POP3 localhost v2000.69 server ready
AUTH GSSAPI
-Err Bad authentication
AUTH LOGIN
+ VXN1ciBOYW1lAA==
cmljaA==
+ UGFzc3dvcmQA
dGVzdA==
+OK Mailbox open, 0 messages
QUIT
+OK Sayonara
Connection closed by foreign host.
$
```

Listing 3.5 shows the client using the LOGIN method of authentication with the POP server. As you can see in the listing, the encrypted username and password are sent to the server. Unfortunately, this information can also be easily captured by a network sniffer and used to log in to the server from a different client.

The MD-5 and Kerberos authentication methods rely on encrypting the password with a secret word that only the client and POP server know. This technique prevents network sniffers from being able to duplicate the login credentials.

POP3 Client Commands

After the POP3 client has successfully logged in to the server, it enters the transaction mode. It must issue commands to control the transfer of messages from the server to the client. Each command elicits a specific POP3 action from the server.

STAT Command

The STAT command has no parameters. It is used to obtain a *drop listing* from the POP3 server, which is a formatted line of text that indicates the mailbox's current status. The line is formatted in the following way:

+OK *nn mm*

The format of the STAT response is standard so that e-mail clients can parse the response for the information. The *nn* value represents the total number of messages in the user's mailbox. Messages that have been marked as deleted are not counted in this value; however, messages that have already been read are counted. The *mm* value represents the total byte count of the messages represented by the count number. The STAT command is often used by the e-mail client program to quickly check on the status of the mailbox. By logging in and issuing a STAT command, the e-mail package can compare the message count number to the value obtained at the last mail check. If the number is different, the e-mail package can then proceed further in retrieving the messages. The only problem with this method is that the e-mail client has no idea how many of the messages have been downloaded previously and not deleted, or if an equal number of messages have been deleted and added.

LIST Command

The LIST command is used to get a *scan listing* of the mailbox, which is a brief synopsis of the mailbox contents that includes the message number and its size in bytes. The LIST command issued with no parameters displays the scan listing of all the messages in the mailbox. If you include a message number as a parameter, the LIST command displays the scan listing for that individual message. A sample LIST command session is shown in Listing 3.6.

LISTING 3.6 Sample LIST Command

```
$ telnet localhost 110
Trying 127.0.0.1...
Connected to localhost.
Escape character is '^]'.
+OK POP3 localhost v6.50 server ready
USER alex
+OK User name accepted, password please
PASS tarzan
+OK Mailbox open, 2 messages
LIST
+OK Mailbox scan listing follows
1 355
```

LISTING 3.6 Continued

```
2 465
.
LIST 1
+OK 1 355
LIST 2
+OK 2 465
LIST 3
-ERR No such message
QUIT
+OK Sayonara
Connection closed by foreign host.
$
```

In this example, the client issues the LIST command with no parameters to the server. The server responds with a positive acknowledgment and then the individual message scan listings. In some POP3 server implementations, the positive acknowledgment response includes the STAT output to summarize the messages, but the client software cannot count on that being the case (as shown by this example). Next, the client issues a LIST command for individual messages, with the server's responses shown. Finally, the client issues a LIST command for a nonexistent message number. The server returns a negative response.

RETR Command

The RETR command is used to retrieve the text of individual messages from the mailbox. The parameter used with this command is a message number as returned by the LIST command described previously. If the message number is valid, the server responds with a positive acknowledgment line and the complete text of the message followed by a terminating character (a single period on a line by itself). The message sent to the client should be the full RFC 822–formatted message that is contained in the mailbox on the server as received by the host software (typically an SMTP-based MTA). The POP3 server does not format or manipulate the message in any way. The job of the POP3 server is to transfer the message in its entirety to the client. A sample RETR command session is shown in Listing 3.7.

LISTING 3.7 Sample RETR Command

```
$ telnet localhost 110
Trying 127.0.0.1...
Connected to localhost.
Escape character is '^]'.
+OK POP3 localhost v6.50 server ready
```

LISTING 3.7 Continued

```
USER rich
+OK User name accepted, password please
PASS guitar
+OK Mailbox open, 2 messages
LIST
+OK Mailbox scan listing follows
1 355
2 465
.
RETR 1
+OK 355 octets
Return-Path: <rich>
Received: (from rich@localhost)
        by indy-mon.dfas.mil (8.8.7/8.8.7) id KAA00648
        for rich; Thu, 2 Sep 1999 10:15:25 -0500
Date: Thu, 2 Sep 1999 10:15:25 -0500
From: rich@shadrach.smallorg.org
Message-Id: <199909021515.KAA00648@shadrach.smallorg.org>
To: rich@shadrach.smallorg.org
Subject: Message 1
Status:  O

This is test message 1
.
QUIT
+OK Sayonara
Connection closed by foreign host.
$
```

In this example the client issues the RETR command for message number 1. The POP3 server sends the message text in its entirety to the client. It is the client's responsibility to have a storage buffer large enough to store the message after it's received (that's why the LIST command returns the size of the message).

DELE Command

The DELE command is used for deleting messages from the mailbox on the server. Its single parameter is the message number identified from the LIST command. Actually, the DELE command does not delete the message; it just marks it for deletion. The actual deletion does not take place until the session is properly terminated with the QUIT command (described after the following listing). Be careful when using the DELE command because the message numbering system must be closely watched. Listing 3.8 shows the results of deleting a message from the scan listing.

LISTING 3.8 Results of Using the DELE Command

```
$ telnet localhost 110
Trying 127.0.0.1...
Connected to localhost.
Escape character is '^]'.
+OK POP3 localhost v7.59 server ready
USER rich
+OK User name accepted, password please
PASS guitar
+OK Mailbox open, 3 messages
LIST
+OK Mailbox scan listing follows
1 377
2 387
3 396
.
DELE 1
+OK Message deleted
LIST
+OK Mailbox scan listing follows
2 387
3 396
.
QUIT
+OK Sayonara
Connection closed by foreign host.
$ telnet localhost 110
Trying 127.0.0.1...
Connected to localhost.
Escape character is '^]'.
+OK POP3 localhost v7.59 server ready
USER rich
+OK User name accepted, password please
PASS guitar
+OK Mailbox open, 2 messages
LIST
+OK Mailbox scan listing follows
1 387
2 396
```

LISTING 3.8 Continued

```
.
QUIT
+OK Sayonara
Connection closed by foreign host.
$
```

In this example the client issues a LIST command to check whether there are any messages in his mailbox, and then issues the DELE command to delete the first message. The POP3 server confirms the action with an OK response. The new scan listing from the server now shows only messages 2 and 3 available for downloading. The client decides to terminate the POP3 session at that point. Upon receiving the QUIT command, the POP3 server actually deletes message 1 (recall that DELE only queues messages for deletion).

Next, the client initiates a second POP3 session. In this session, a new LIST command is issued. As before, the POP3 server indicates that there are two messages available in the mailbox. However, notice that in this new POP3 session, the server renumbered the messages. The message that used to be message 2 is now message 1, and the message that used to be message 3 is now message 2.

This example shows that message numbers using the LIST commands are not static entities. The message numbers are valid only for the current POP3 session. Any attempt by the client to use the message numbers between POP3 session almost always ends up with unexpected results. The UIDL command mentioned in the following section is an optional command that some POP3 servers support in an attempt to uniquely identify messages between sessions.

UIDL Command

The UIDL command is another optional POP3 server command. Its purpose is to uniquely identify messages in the mailbox between POP3 sessions. As shown for the LIST command, messages are normally numbered sequentially during the POP3 session. When a client terminates one session and begins another, the messages are renumbered sequentially. Therefore, if the client had 10 messages in her mailbox and deleted message 6 during a POP3 session, the next POP3 session would have nine messages renumbered 1 through 9. This is not an easy way for the e-mail client software to keep track of messages, however.

To solve this problem, some POP3 servers implement the UIDL, or unique-ID listing, command. Each message is assigned a unique character string ID consisting of 1 to 70 printable ASCII characters. That ID remains with the message for as long as it is in the mailbox. Often the message's UIDL is obtained by performing a hash algorithm on } the message header. Using this technique, it is possible for two identical copies of the same message to have the same UIDL. The client e-mail software should be capable of recognizing this situation and handling it accordingly. Listing 3.9 shows an example of listing and deleting messages identified by a UIDL.

LISTING 3.9 Sample of the `UIDL` Command

```
$ telnet localhost 110
Trying 127.0.0.1...
Connected to localhost.
Escape character is '^]'.
+OK POP3 localhost v7.59 server ready
USER rich
+OK User name accepted, password please
PASS guitar
+OK Mailbox open, 3 messages
UIDL
+OK Unique-ID listing follows
1 37cabbcb00000009
2 37cabbcb0000000a
3 37cabbcb0000000b
.
DELE 1
+OK Message deleted
UIDL
+OK Unique-ID listing follows
2 37cabbcb0000000a
3 37cabbcb0000000b
.
QUIT
+OK Sayonara
Connection closed by foreign host.
[rich@shadrach rich]$ telnet localhost 110
Trying 127.0.0.1...
Connected to localhost.
Escape character is '^]'.
+OK POP3 localhost v7.59 server ready
USER rich
+OK User name accepted, password please
PASS guitar
+OK Mailbox open, 2 messages
UIDL
+OK Unique-ID listing follows
1 37cabbcb0000000a
2 37cabbcb0000000b
```

LISTING 3.9 Continued

```
.
QUIT
+OK Sayonara
Connection closed by foreign host.
$
```

In this example, the client issues the UIDL command to display the unique IDs of the messages in the mailbox. After displaying the unique IDs, the client issues the DELE command to delete message number 1. Next, another UIDL command is issued to show that the remaining message UIDLs have not changed. In the next POP3 session, the messages have been renumbered for the new session, but the UIDL numbers for the remaining messages have stayed the same between POP3 sessions. This information enables the client to identify individual messages between POP3 sessions.

TOP Command

The TOP command, an optional POP3 command that servers can choose to implement, is a handy way for the client to get a brief synopsis of messages available in the mailbox. It returns the RFC 822 header fields for a message, along with a designated number of lines from the body of the message. The TOP command has two parameters that are both required and uses the following format:

TOP *msg n*

The *msg* parameter is the message number from a LIST scan listing, and *n* is an integer representing the number of lines from the message body that will be displayed. E-mail clients often use this command to display messages' subject header fields in a list of messages without having to download the entire text of the messages. Listing 3.10 shows an example of the TOP command being used.

LISTING 3.10 Sample of the TOP Command

```
$ telnet localhost 110
Trying 127.0.0.1...
Connected to localhost.
Escape character is '^]'.
+OK POP3 localhost v7.59 server ready
USER rich
+OK User name accepted, password please
PASS guitar
+OK Mailbox open, 5 messages
LIST
```

LISTING 3.10 Continued

```
+OK Mailbox scan listing follows
1 387
2 396
3 374
4 375
5 383
.
TOP 1 0
+OK Top of message follows
Return-Path: <rich>
Received: (from rich@localhost)
        by shadrach.smallorg.org (8.9.3/8.9.3) id MAA00496
          for rich; Thu, 2 Sep 1999 12:35:51 -0500
Date: Thu, 2 Sep 1999 12:35:51 -0500
From: rich@shadrach.smallorg.org
Message-Id: <199909021735.MAA00496@shadrach.smallorg.org>
To: rich@shadrach.smallorg.org
Subject: Test message 1
Status:   O


.
TOP 4 10
+OK Top of message follows
Return-Path: <rich>
Received: (from rich@localhost)
          by shadrach.smallorg.org (8.9.3/8.9.3) id NAA00588
          for rich; Thu, 2 Sep 1999 13:32:35 -0500
Date: Thu, 2 Sep 1999 13:32:35 -0500
From: rich@shadrach.smallorg.org
Message-Id: <199909021832.NAA00588@shadrach.smallorg.org>
To: rich@shadrach.smallorg.org
Subject: Sample message #4
Status:

This is the fourth sample message.
.
QUIT
+OK Sayonara
Connection closed by foreign host.
$
```

This example shows the client issuing the TOP command to display the RFC 822 header field information from each message. By using the TOP command with the value of 0, no lines from the message body are displayed. In the next TOP command, the client uses the value of 10, asking to see the message header and the first 10 lines of the message body. As the message body has only one line, the server responds by displaying the entire header and message body.

NOOP Command

The NOOP command does what is says—nothing. After receiving a NOOP command, the POP3 server returns a positive response. This command can be used to determine the POP3 server's state and responsiveness. It can be issued only after establishing a session by logging in to the server.

RSET Command

The RSET command resets the session back to its start after the authentication of the client with the server (the client does not have to log back in). The important thing to know about the RSET command is that it causes the server to unmark any messages marked for deletion. The unmarked messages are returned to the scan listing with their original message numbers.

QUIT Command

The QUIT command is used to terminate the POP3 session. When the server receives a QUIT command, it deletes any messages that had been marked for deletion from the user's mailbox and terminates the TCP session. If the POP3 session should terminate before the client issues a QUIT command, any messages marked for deletion are restored and not deleted.

Open Source POP3 Implementations

Several open source software packages are available that allow Unix servers to offer POP3 clients and servers. This section discusses three of the more popular packages used on many Unix mail servers.

Open Source POP3 Client

By far the most popular open source POP3 client package is the fetchmail program written by Eric Raymond. Calling it a POP3 program is actually a misnomer, as it does much more than just POP3 client functions. It can retrieve messages from a mailbox on a remote host using the POP3, IMAP4, or SMTP ETRN (the Extended SMTP version of the TURN command) protocols. However, with the popularity of POP3 mail services being offered by ISPs, fetchmail has become the standard software package for many Unix users wanting to retrieve their Internet mail using POP3. Fetchmail automatically determines which protocols the remote server supports and attempts to choose the best method to transfer messages. After it downloads the message, it attempts to pass it to the local Mail Delivery Agent (MDA) on the mail server for delivery to the local user.

One use of fetchmail that is becoming popular is downloading mail for an entire domain using a single ISP mailbox. The ISP configures its Mail Transfer Agent (MTA) to forward any message sent to any user at a domain to a single username. For example, any messages sent to prez@smallorg.org, viceprez@smallorg.org, or janitor@smallorg.org are forwarded by the ISP to the account smallorg@ispnet.net. The mail server for smallorg.org then uses fetchmail and POP3 to download the messages for smallorg@ispnet.net. Although each message is sent to the same mailbox, they all have different values in the RFC 822 To: header field (see Chapter 2). The fetchmail program can be configured to forward each of the received messages to the appropriate local mailbox on the mail server based on the To: header field values.

Installing fetchmail

Because of fetchmail's popularity, many Unix distributions come with a binary package. If your distribution did not include the fetchmail package, or you want to use the most current version (currently 5.8.0), you can download the fetchmail source code from the fetchmail home page at http://tuxedo.org/~esr/fetchmail/.

You should have a C compiler, as well as a current copy of the flex and yacc programs installed on your Unix system. After the source code is downloaded, you can unpack it into a working directory by typing

```
tar -zxvf fetchmail-5.8.0.tar.gz -C /usr/local/src
```

This command creates a subdirectory named /usr/local/src/fetchmail-5.8.0 with the source code and related files needed for compiling. These are the steps necessary to create the fetchmail executable:

1. Run the configure program, which checks for compiler-specific options available on your Unix distribution that you need to properly create the makefile. The configure program performs tests of libraries, include files, and compiler options and displays the results as it goes along. If you want to customize your fetchmail implementation, you can use the configure parameters to change parts of the program, such as leaving out IMAP or SMTP support if they are not needed to produce a smaller binary footprint.

2. Run the make utility to process the makefile created in the previous step. This step compiles the source code pieces and produces two binary files: fetchmail and fetchmailconf.

3. As the `root` user, run `make install` to place the executables in the proper location so that any user on the Unix system can use them without permissions problems (unless, of course, you do not want any user to be able to use them).

After the executables are created and installed, you must create a configuration file for each fetchmail user so that fetchmail can properly connect to the remote server and retrieve your mail.

Configuring Fetchmail

Each fetchmail user requires a configuration file, which is located in $HOME/.fetchmailrc. When fetchmail runs, it checks for the existence of this file, and complains if it is not found with the following message:

```
fetchmail: no mailservers have been specified.
```

The .fetchmailrc file is a standard ASCII text file defining what server fetchmail should connect to, what protocol(s) to use, and what user ID and password method it should use to retrieve mail messages. The format of the configuration file takes an odd form—half configuration and half narrative. A sample .fetchmailrc file is shown in Listing 3.11.

LISTING 3.11 Sample .fetchmailrc File

```
# Configuration created Wed Apr 11 19:16:53 2001 by fetchmailconf
set postmaster "rich"
set bouncemail
set properties ""
poll 192.168.1.1 with proto POP3
        user "rich" there with password "guitar" is rich here
```

In the sample .fetchmailrc file, the last two lines set the `fetchmail` configuration parameters for the username `rich`. The remote host address, protocol, username, and password are all configured in this file. This configuration file instructs fetchmail to connect to the POP3 server 192.168.1.1 using POP3 as the protocol. It checks messages for the remote user `rich` and passes them to the local Unix username `rich`. You do not have to match up the usernames, but be careful of using too many unrelated usernames as it could get extremely confusing.

By default, fetchmail attempts to detect whether the POP3 server supports APOP and AUTH authentication. If it does, fetchmail sends the username/password combination using the highest level of security supported by the POP3 server.

CAUTION

You might have noticed that the .fetchmailrc configuration file includes the username and password of the main POP3 account in plain text form. This can be a serious security problem. Please make sure this file can't be read by other system users.

Using Fetchmail

After the .fetchmailrc configuration file is completed, you can use the fetchmail program to retrieve mail from the POP3 server. In interactive mode, all that is needed is to type the command `fetchmail`. This command causes fetchmail to read the configuration file, log in to the configured servers, and transfer the mail messages to the appropriate user-names on the local Unix computer. Fetchmail can also be used with command-line parameters that alter its behavior. Table 3.2 shows some of the options available for using fetchmail in POP3 mode.

TABLE 3.2 Fetchmail Command-Line Options

Option	Description
-V	Displays version of fetchmail
-c	Checks for mail without downloading any messages
-s	Silent mode; suppresses output
-v	Verbose mode; extra output
-a	Retrieve all messages from server
-k	Keep messages on the remote server after they have been downloaded
-K	Delete messages on the remote server after they have been downloaded (default)
-F	Flush—delete old messages before retrieving new messages
-p	Specify a transfer protocol
-U	Use the UIDL to identify messages
-P	Use a different TCP port
-t	Set a different timeout value

Fetchmail can also be used as a background program by specifying the poll frequency in the configuration file. This method allows fetchmail to run in the background and check for new mail messages on a regular basis.

Open Source POP3 Server

There are also several open source POP3 server implementations that give remote users the ability to check and retrieve mail messages on the local host. Each e-mail user must have his or her own username on the mail server, and each username should have access to a single mailbox. The server can then run POP3 server software as a background process to watch the network for POP3 connections.

The qpopper package is an open source POP3 server package originally released by the University of California at Berkeley, but now maintained by the Qualcomm Corporation. Qpopper was written to provide POP3 server software for most types of Unix servers.

Qpopper supports both the normal user/password POP3 logins and the APOP POP3 encrypted authentication. The user/password login feature supports using the standard Unix system password files. The APOP feature supports encrypted passwords using a separate password database file that must be maintained separately by the mail administrator.

Information about qpopper can be found on its Web site:

```
http://www.eudora.com/qpopper/
```

The current release version of qpopper at the time of this writing is version 4.0.2.

CAUTION

If you happen to come across a version of qpopper earlier than version 3.0, don't use it. There were some serious security problems with the earlier versions that could allow a hacker to gain root access to your mail server.

Downloading Qpopper

The Qualcomm FTP site hosts the most current version of qpopper. The FTP server is at `ftp://ftp.qualcomm.com`, and this is the directory where qpopper is located:

```
/eudora/servers/unix/popper
```

At the time of this writing, the most current version is 4.0.2. Make sure you are using the FTP BINARY mode and download the version you want to use. For this example, the file qpopper4.0.2.tar.gz is used:

```
ftp://ftp.qualcomm.com/eudora/servers/unix/popper/qpopper4.0.2.tar.gz
```

After the file is downloaded (the 4.0.2 version is a little over 2.3MB), you can extract the source code files into a working directory:

```
tar -zxvf qpopper4.0.2.tar.gz -C /usr/local/src
```

The Unix tar utility creates a subdirectory, /usr/local/src/qpopper4.0.2, and places the source code files in subdirectories beneath it.

Compiling Qpopper

The qpopper program utilizes the configure program to examine the operating environment and create a makefile that references the specific locations of the C compiler, libraries, and include files. The configure program also uses command-line parameters to change specific features you might want to include in your implementation of the qpopper server.

The default qpopper configure environment uses no extra command-line parameters, and can be built by using these commands:

```
./configure
make
```

These commands create a default POP3 server that does not recognize the APOP authentication method or the shadow password database used on many Unix systems. To include different authentication methods, you must run the configure program with the appropriate parameters (more on this in the "Shadow Password Support" section).

The qpopper executable program, called popper, is located in the popper subdirectory beneath the qpopper 4.0.2 directory. You need to copy this program to a common location as the root user. The qpopper documentation recommends using the /usr/local/lib directory.

The popper program can use command-line parameters to modify the behavior of the POP3 server. Table 3.3 shows the available command-line parameters.

TABLE 3.3 Popper Command-Line Parameters

Parameter	Description
-b	Changes the default directory for bulletins (systemwide messages)
-c	Changes all usernames to lowercase
-d	Enables debugging
-e	Sets POP3 extensions
-k	Enables Kerberos support
-s	Enables statistics logging
-t	Defines an alternative debug and log file
-T	Changes the default timeout waiting for reads
-R	Disables reverse client address lookups

Popper uses the inetd program to start when a POP3 session is received. This program listens for network connections and passes those connections to the appropriate program, depending on the TCP or User Datagram Protocol (UDP) port number the connection is established on.

The first part of the inetd configuration is to make sure it recognizes the POP3 TCP port (number 110). This information is in the /etc/services file. The pertinent line should look like the following:

```
pop-3        110/tcp            # POP version 3
```

After ensuring that the /etc/services file supports POP3, the next step is to configure the inetd configuration file—/etc/inetd.conf—to support POP3. A line should be added to the configuration file that corresponds to the tag in the /etc/services line (pop-3) and tells the program to start when a connection is established. The new line should look like the following:

```
pop-3  stream  tcp nowait  root    /usr/local/lib/popper    popper -s
```

This inetd.conf entry assumes that the popper program is located in the /usr/local/lib directory and that statistics logging is enabled (the -s option). By default, statistics are logged in the Unix default syslog file (usually /var/log/messages) or in a separate mail log file defined on some Unix systems.

To activate the new inetd.conf settings, the currently running inetd daemon must be restarted. You can do that by sending a SIGHUP signal to it with the following commands:

```
[root@shadrach rich]# ps ax | grep inetd
  327 ?         S       0:00 inetd
12600 pts/2     S       0:00 grep inetd
[root@shadrach rich]# kill -HUP 327
[root@shadrach rich]#
```

The kill command is used to send a SIGHUP signal to the inetd process ID. This command uses the signal's abbreviated name (HUP). You can test the qpopper installation by using the Telnet program and connecting to port 110 on the mail server, as shown in Listing 3.12.

LISTING 3.12 Sample POP3 Session

```
$ telnet localhost 110
Trying 127.0.0.1...
Connected to localhost.
Escape character is '^]'.
+OK QPOP (version 4.0) at shadrach.smallorg.org starting.
QUIT
+OK Pop server at shadrach.smallorg.org signing off.
Connection closed by foreign host.
$
```

Listing 3.12 shows the greeting message produced by the installed qpopper program.

The default qpopper configuration works fine in some simple POP3 implementations running on basic Unix mail servers. However, you can use other features to make qpopper more versatile.

Shadow Password Support

A common Unix feature is to make use of *shadow passwords*, which help prevent unauthorized users from accessing the encrypted password file to try brute-force attacks. FreeBSD supports shadow passwords by using the /etc/master.passwd file. By default, qpopper recognizes the FreeBSD shadow password file without any modifications.

However, many Unix distributions have incorporated the use of a different shadow password file system. The normal /etc/passwd file still contains usernames, but the encrypted passwords are stored in a separate file that can be made inaccessible to users. When a shadow password file is used, programs that verify user IDs must be aware of its existence.

For qpopper to work with Unix shadow password files, you must include additional parameters in the configure command line.

If you have previously compiled a version of qpopper, you must clean the object and executable files from the build directory. You can accomplish this by using the following command from the qpopper4.0 directory:

```
make clean
```

This command removes files that have been added or modified by the install script. The next step is to run the configure script with the parameter that includes shadow password support, using the following format:

```
./configure —enable-specialauth
```

This command re-creates the makefile using parameters necessary for the GNU gcc compiler to add support for shadow password files. After the configure program finishes building the makefile, you can then run the GNU's Not Unix (GNU) command `make` against it to create a new popper executable program in the popper subdirectory. Again, you must copy this file to the location specified in the inetd.conf file as the `root` user. There is no need to restart the inetd daemon because the configuration file /etc/inetd.conf was not modified.

After copying the new executable popper file to the appropriate directory, you can test the configuration by using `telnet` on port 110 and attempting to log in as a user. An example of this method is demonstrated in Listing 3.13.

LISTING 3.13 Sample POP3 Login Session

```
$ telnet localhost 110
Trying 127.0.0.1...
Connected to localhost.
Escape character is '^]'.
+OK QPOP (version 4.0) at shadrach.smallorg.org starting.
USER riley
+OK Password required for riley.
PASS firetruck
+OK riley has 3 messages (1162 octets).
QUIT
+OK Pop server at shadrach.smallorg.org signing off.
Connection closed by foreign host.
$
```

APOP Authentication Support

As shown in Listing 3.13, our poor e-mail client had to send the username and password in clear text to the qpopper server. Had Riley been checking his mail from across the Internet, it's possible this information could have been captured by a hacker and used for illegal purposes. However, POP3 has a solution for this problem.

POP3 can use alternative methods to authenticate a user. The qpopper program supports the APOP method of authenticating a user. This method uses encrypted passwords, which greatly reduce the risk of being compromised. To accommodate the different passwords, the APOP method requires that the mail administrator create a separate user password database.

It is often best to create a new system user (often called pop) to control the qpopper access database. This method reduces the risk of logging in as root to add new users.

To add this capability to the popper executable program, you must recompile the program. First, you must remove the object and executable files created from any previous builds, using the following command:

```
make clean
```

Next, you must run the configure script again, including parameters to define the location of the APOP password database and the user ID of the APOP administrator:

```
./configure —enable—apop=/etc/pop.auth —with-popuid=pop
```

This line creates a new makefile using the value /etc/pop.auth for the authentication database location, with the user pop being the database administrator. You can then create the new executables by using the GNU make command. With the APOP option, two executable files are created: popper and popauth.

As before, copy the popper executable file to the location specified in the inetd.conf file (such as /usr/local/lib). The popauth program created allows the APOP administrator to add users to the APOP authentication database specified in the configure command line.

To test the new qpopper configuration, you can use telnet on port 110 and observe the new greeting. Listing 3.14 shows an example of a qpopper server using APOP authentication.

LISTING 3.14 Sample Qpopper Greeting Using APOP

```
$ telnet localhost 110
Trying 127.0.0.1...
Connected to localhost.
Escape character is '^]'.
+OK QPOP (version 4.0) at shadrach.smallorg.org starting.
[ic:ccc] <17166.940368317@shadrach.smallorg.org>
QUIT
+OK Pop server at shadrach.smallorg.org signing off.
Connection closed by foreign host.
$
```

The new greeting generated by qpopper differs from the greeting shown in Listing 3.13 in that it includes the APOP seed information. The POP3 server supplies this seed value on the greeting for the client to use in encrypting the password. Both sides of the POP3 connection must know the secret word so that the hashed value can be matched. The qpopper server stores the secret words in the authentication database.

To create the APOP authentication database, as the root user enter the command:

popauth -init

This command creates a new authentication database in the location specified when the configure program was run (/etc/pop.auth in the example). The username specified in the -with-popuid parameter is now the APOP administrator and can add users to the authentication database. One strange characteristic about qpopper is that after a username is added to the authentication database, that user *must* use APOP authentication to connect to the POP3 server.

To add a new user to the authentication database, the APOP administrator can type the command:

popauth -user *user*

The *user* parameter is the Unix system username of the user. The popauth program queries the administrator for a user password to be used for APOP authentication. This password can be different from the normal Unix system login password. To remove a user from the authentication database, the administrator can type the following:

```
popauth -delete user
```

In this line, *user* is the Unix system username of the user to be removed. Individual users can change their APOP passwords by using the popauth command without any parameters.

Summary

After mail has been transferred to the mail server, users must be able to connect to the server to retrieve their mail. The Post Office Protocol version 3 (POP3) is used to download messages to the user's local PC so they can be read using graphical e-mail packages.

POP3 is not as robust as newer protocols used, but its simplicity in configuration and use make it a common tool for mail transfers. There is open source software available for Unix to implement POP3 both as a server and as a client.

The open source fetchmail package can be used to provide POP3 client services for a Unix mail server. The fetchmail program can connect to a remote mail server using POP3 and retrieve mail messages from a single mailbox.

The open source qpopper package is used to provide POP3 server functionality to a Unix server so that users can retrieve their mail messages remotely from the server.

POP3 has its limitations, and over the past few years a trend has developed toward more advanced mail retrieval protocols, such as IMAP, which is covered in the next chapter.

CHAPTER 4

IMAP

The previous chapter discussed the Post Office Protocol version 3 (POP3)—a popular way of retrieving e-mail messages from a remote server. Although POP3 is easy to implement and widely supported in e-mail client programs, it does have its drawbacks. Mainly, it lacks any serious message-handling capabilities. Messages are usually downloaded en masse from the mail server, and then deleted from the server. This technique is good for the ISP hosting the mail server because it saves on required disk space, but for the mail user it can quickly get confusing. By downloading the messages, they become "tied down" to the PC where the download was performed. If your users retrieve mail from only a single workstation on the network, that might not be a problem, but if they need to access their mailbox from home as well as work, it can be a big problem. That means their mailbox messages get split between two workstations located in different areas.

To compensate for this situation, a new protocol was devised. The Interactive Message Access Protocol (IMAP), developed at the University of Washington, allows e-mail users to access their mailboxes from multiple locations without splitting their mail between computers. This is accomplished by maintaining the mailbox on the mail server and allowing the client PC to manipulate the messages on the server. Of course, the downside to this scenario is that the mail server must maintain *all* the mail on its own disk, which can lead to some scary disk space situations for the mail administrator. Care must be taken when administering an IMAP server so that the system does not max out on disk space and crash (with all the mailboxes and messages on it).

This chapter outlines the IMAP protocol and shows how it is implemented using open source software. The current version of IMAP is version 4 revision 1, or IMAP4rev1 for short. It is described in RFC 2060.

Description of the Interactive Message Access Protocol

Just like its cousin POP3, IMAP uses a client/server command method of transferring messages from the server to the client. The client establishes a TCP connection to port 143 of the server to initiate the connection. The server should respond with a greeting. Listing 4.1 shows a sample IMAP session.

LISTING 4.1 Sample IMAP Session

```
$ telnet localhost 143
Trying 127.0.0.1...
Connected to localhost.
Escape character is '^]'.
* OK shadrach.smallorg.org IMAP4rev1 v12.250 server ready
a001 LOGOUT
* BYE shadrach.smallorg.org IMAP4rev1 server terminating connection
```

LISTING 4.1 Continued

```
a001 OK LOGOUT completed
Connection closed by foreign host.
$
```

This example shows a `telnet` session to TCP port 143 (the default IMAP port). After the connection is established, the IMAP server presents the greeting message. The client sends the `LOGOUT` command to the server to close the IMAP session.

Each command from the client must start with a unique identifier. The server uses this identifier when responding to the command so that the client knows which command the server is responding to if multiple commands are being processed. The identifier is usually a short alphanumeric string generated by the client. The sixth line in Listing 4.1 shows that the client chose the tag `a001` to represent the first command-line identifier. Often client command identifiers increment sequentially throughout the IMAP session to simplify things.

When the client establishes a connection, it starts out in an un-authenticated state. For the client to be allowed to perform any operations with the mailbox, it must first authenticate itself with the server. After the client has authenticated itself to the server, it can issue IMAP commands to manipulate mail messages.

IMAP supports each user having multiple mailboxes on a server. The client can read, transfer, and delete messages to and from any mailbox he or she has access to on the server. This feature is a vast improvement over POP3.

IMAP Authentication Methods

Also like its cousin POP3, IMAP allows several methods to authenticate a client, some more secure than others. Unlike POP3 clients, however, IMAP clients often keep established sessions open for extended periods of time while they process their messages. Therefore, the username and password pair are not transferred across the network several times each hour as with POP3. Nonetheless, it is still beneficial to transmit username and password information using an encrypted method if possible.

LOGIN Command

The `LOGIN` command allows the client to use plain text usernames and passwords to log in to the IMAP server. Although this is not necessarily the best method to use, sometimes it's the only method a client and server can agree on. Listing 4.2 shows a sample IMAP login session using the `LOGIN` command.

LISTING 4.2 Sample *LOGIN* Command Session

```
$ telnet localhost 143
Trying 127.0.0.1...
Connected to localhost.
Escape character is '^]'.
* OK localhost IMAP4rev1 v12.250 server ready
a001 LOGIN katie boxcar
a001 OK LOGIN completed
a002 LOGOUT
* BYE shadrach.smallorg.org IMAP4rev1 server terminating connection
a002 OK LOGOUT completed
Connection closed by foreign host.
$
```

This example shows the IMAP user katie logging in to the server with the LOGIN command. Note how the server includes the command identifier code (a001) from the client's command to tag the response. The user password is included on the same line as the username, separated by a space. The server returns a positive response if the login was successful.

AUTHENTICATE Command

The AUTHENTICATE command allows a client to use alternative methods to log in to the IMAP server without having to send a plain text username/password pair. The implementation of individual authentication methods is optional, and not all IMAP servers support the same set of methods. Table 4.1 lists the different authentication methods available in IMAP.

TABLE 4.1 IMAP Authentication Methods

Method	Description
PLAIN	Client sends a plain text username/password combination.
LOGIN	Client sends a base-64–encoded username/password combination.
SKEY	Client sends a base-64–encoded username and one-time password combination.
GSSAPI	Client sends a Generic Security Service Application Interface (GSSAPI) encoded username and password.
KERBEROS	Host sends a ready response with a random 32-byte number, and the client responds with a Kerberos ticket and authenticator for the username.

When the client issues a valid AUTHENTICATE command, the server responds with a challenge string. It is the responsibility of the client to respond to the challenge with the appropriate response. If the IMAP server does not support the authentication method proposed by the client, it responds with a NO message. The client must attempt to negotiate a common authentication method, falling back to the LOGIN method as a last resort. Listing 4.3 shows a sample AUTHENTICATE session.

LISTING 4.3 Sample AUTHENTICATE Session

```
$ telnet localhost 143
Trying 127.0.0.1...
Connected to localhost.
Escape character is '^]'.
* OK localhost IMAP4rev1 v12.264 server ready
a001 AUTHENTICATE
a001 BAD Missing required argument to AUTHENTICATE
a002 AUTHENTICATE KERBEROS
a002 NO AUTHENTICATE KERBEROS failed
a003 AUTHENTICATE LOGIN
+ VXN1ciBOYW11AA==
cmljaA==
+ UGFzc3dvcmQA
dGVzdA==
a003 OK AUTHENTICATE completed
a004 LOGOUT
* BYE test.ispnet.net IMAP4rev1 server terminating connection
a004 OK LOGOUT completed
Connection closed by foreign host.
$
```

This example shows a failed attempt by the client to negotiate the KERBEROS IMAP authentication method. Next, the client attempts to use the LOGIN authentication method. The server responds by issuing a base-64–encoded challenge. The client responds with the appropriate encoded username and password.

IMAP Client Protocol

After the client is authenticated with the IMAP server, it can begin manipulating messages. IMAP provides a number of different commands to read, move, and delete mail messages from within different mailboxes on the server. Remember, IMAP specifies that all messages reside on the server. Downloading messages is purely for display purposes; no messages should be stored on the client in lieu of server-side storage.

The default mailbox for a client is called the INBOX. All new messages appear in the INBOX. The client has the ability to create new mailboxes (sometimes called *folders* by e-mail client software) to move messages from the INBOX to other areas, thus reducing clutter.

Each message is assigned a unique identifier (UID) to identify it in the mailbox. The UID should persist between sessions so that the IMAP client software can properly identify messages. Each mailbox has a unique identifier validity tag (UIDVALIDITY). The UIDVALIDITY tag should persist between sessions only if the UIDs of the messages in the mailbox remain the same. If there are any different UIDs in the mailbox, then the UIDVA-LIDITY value for the mailbox should become larger for the next IMAP session. Clients can then quickly determine whether anything has changed since the last time a mailbox was opened.

Each message is also tagged with flags that indicate the message's status. A flag can be valid for the single session only or permanently across all sessions. Permanent flags can be changed by the client and persist between sessions. Session-only flags apply only for the current IMAP session. Table 4.2 shows different flags available for mail messages.

Table 4.2 IMAP Mail Message Flags

Flag	Description
\Seen	Message has been read
\Answered	Message has been answered
\Flagged	Message is marked as urgent
\Deleted	Message has been deleted
\Draft	Message is not in final form
\Recent	New mail in mailbox

A mail message can have zero or more flags associated with it. The flag information is transferred with the message to the client. It is the client's responsibility to handle the flag accordingly.

The following sections define the IMAP commands a client can issue to the IMAP server. The server should respond to every command with either the requested information or a negative response if the command is not formatted properly or not supported.

SELECT Command

The SELECT command is used to select an active mailbox. By default, no mailboxes are selected for use when the client first authenticates to the server. The client must select a mailbox to work in. Usually, the first mailbox selected is the special mailbox called INBOX, where new messages are placed. The format of the SELECT command is as follows:

```
SELECT mailbox
```

The *mailbox* parameter is the text name of the desired mailbox. Only one mailbox can be active at a time per IMAP connection. If the mailbox exists and the client has proper access to it, the server returns a multiline response describing the mailbox's status. A sample SELECT session is shown in Listing 4.4.

LISTING 4.4 Sample *SELECT* Session

```
$ telnet localhost 143
Trying 127.0.0.1...
Connected to localhost.
Escape character is '^]'.
* OK localhost IMAP4rev1 v12.250 server ready
a1 LOGIN alex drums
a1 OK LOGIN completed
a2 SELECT INBOX
* 2 EXISTS
* 1 RECENT
* OK [UIDVALIDITY 936033227] UID validity status
* OK [UIDNEXT 3] Predicted next UID
* FLAGS (\Answered \Flagged \Deleted \Draft \Seen)
* OK [PERMANENTFLAGS (\* \Answered \Flagged \Deleted \Draft \Seen)]
* OK [UNSEEN 2] first unseen message in /var/spool/mail/alex
a2 OK [READ-WRITE] SELECT completed
a3 LOGOUT
* BYE test.ispnet.net IMAP4rev1 server terminating connection
a3 OK LOGOUT completed
Connection closed by foreign host.
$
```

Here, user alex issues the SELECT command for the INBOX mailbox. The server responds by indicating that two messages exist in the mailbox, with one new message for alex. The current FLAG status for the mailbox is reported to the client, as well as additional information for the messages and mailbox.

NOTE

The UIDVALIDITY value for the mailbox and the next available UID to be used in the mailbox are both used to track messages in the mailbox, and are discussed later in the "UID Command" section.

The FLAGS settings supported by the mailbox for both session-only and permanent use are displayed to the client. The client is allowed to change the status of these flags for each message in the mailbox. The IMAP command used to change flags for individual messages is the STORE command, discussed later in this chapter.

EXAMINE Command

The EXAMINE command is used to open the mailbox in read-only mode. The server response to the EXAMINE command is the same as for the SELECT command. The command-line parameter for EXAMINE is the mailbox to be opened. When a mailbox is opened using the EXAMINE command, no manipulation of the messages is allowed, so you cannot add or remove flags from messages.

CREATE Command

The CREATE command is used to create a new mailbox on the IMAP server for the client. The pathname of the new mailbox follows normal Unix pathname specifications. A mailbox name with no path is created in the client's $HOME directory. For example, if the client's home directory is /home/haley, and she issues a CREATE command to create a mailbox called stuff/junk, the new mailbox created on the mail server will have the pathname /home/haley/stuff/junk. This example assumes a mail server that uses the slash (/) character as the hierarchy separator, but this is not always the case with other IMAP servers.

Some IMAP clients use the term *folder* to refer to new mailboxes. Some IMAP clients also allow users to create folders several layers deep, so use caution when creating new folders (mailboxes). It's easy to get lost in a chain of pathnames.

Listing 4.5 shows a sample IMAP session that creates a new mailbox and makes it the active mailbox for a user.

LISTING 4.5 Sample CREATE IMAP Session

```
$ ls -l
total 0
[alex@shadrach alex]$ telnet localhost 143
Trying 127.0.0.1...
Connected to localhost.
Escape character is '^]'.
* OK localhost IMAP4rev1 v12.250 server ready
a1 LOGIN alex drums
a1 OK LOGIN completed
a2 CREATE stuff/junk
a2 OK CREATE completed
a3 SELECT stuff/junk
* 0 EXISTS
* 0 RECENT
* OK [UIDVALIDITY 936998958] UID validity status
* OK [UIDNEXT 1] Predicted next UID
```

LISTING 4.5 Continued

```
* FLAGS (\Answered \Flagged \Deleted \Draft \Seen)
* OK [PERMANENTFLAGS (\* \Answered \Flagged \Deleted \Draft \Seen)]
a3 OK [READ-WRITE] SELECT completed
a4 LOGOUT
* BYE test.ispnet.net IMAP4rev1 server terminating connection
a4 OK LOGOUT completed
Connection closed by foreign host.
[alex@shadrach alex]$ ls -lR
.:
total 1
drwx------   2 alex      alex          1024 Apr 10 16:29 stuff

stuff:
total 1
-rw-------   1 alex      alex           516 Apr 10 16:29 junk
$
```

This example shows the test user alex listing the contents of his empty home directory. Next, he establishes a telnet connection to the local IMAP server. After logging in, Alex issues a CREATE command to create a new mailbox in his system. The mailbox stuff/junk represents a mailbox file named junk in a new directory called stuff. The server responds positively by indicating that the new directory and new mailbox have been created.

Alex then tries to use the new mailbox by issuing a SELECT command for the new mailbox name (stuff/junk). The IMAP server responds, showing the relevant information for the new mailbox (there are no new or old messages in the new mailbox). After being satisfied that the new mailbox actually does exist, Alex then proceeds to log out of the IMAP server.

To complete this example, our hero performs another listing of his home directory. This time a new directory named stuff and a new file under the directory named junk exist. Notice that the new mailbox is a file, not a directory. Messages placed in this mailbox will be appended to this file, just as with the standard /var/spool/mail/alex file.

DELETE Command

The DELETE command deletes mailboxes, not messages. The IMAP server attempts to delete the mailbox name specified as the argument to the DELETE command. Again, standard Unix pathnames apply to the argument, in relation to the $HOME directory location unless preceded with a leading slash (/). Messages in deleted mailboxes are lost and gone forever.

RENAME Command

The RENAME command allows the client to change the name of a mailbox. It uses two parameters: the name of the mailbox you want to change and the new mailbox name. The standard rules for pathnames applies for both parameters. Remember that pathnames without a leading slash (/) are relative to the $HOME directory of the logged in user. Listing 4.6 shows an example of renaming a mailbox.

LISTING 4.6 Sample RENAME Command Session

```
$ ls -1R
.:
total 1
drwx------   2 alex     alex          1024 Sep 10 16:48 stuff

stuff:
total 1
-rw-------   1 alex     alex           918 Sep 10 16:44 junk
$ telnet localhost 143
Trying 127.0.0.1...
Connected to localhost.
Escape character is '^]'.
* OK localhost IMAP4rev1 v12.250 server ready
a1 LOGIN alex drums
a1 OK LOGIN completed
a2 RENAME stuff/junk newbox
a2 OK RENAME completed
a3 SELECT newbox
* 1 EXISTS
* 0 RECENT
* OK [UIDVALIDITY 936998958] UID validity status
* OK [UIDNEXT 2] Predicted next UID
* FLAGS (\Answered \Flagged \Deleted \Draft \Seen)
* OK [PERMANENTFLAGS (\* \Answered \Flagged \Deleted \Draft \Seen)]
OK [READ-WRITE] SELECT completed
a4 LOGOUT
* BYE test.ispnet.net IMAP4rev1 server terminating connection
a4 OK LOGOUT completed
Connection closed by foreign host.
$ ls -1R
.:
total 2
```

LISTING 4.6 Continued

```
-rw-------   1 alex      alex           918 Sep 10 16:44 newbox
drwx------   2 alex      alex          1024 Sep 12 13:59 stuff

stuff:
total 0
$
```

This listing shows our user alex first displaying the contents of his home directory. As in the last example, he has a mailbox called stuff/junk that created a directory named stuff and a file named junk. Next Alex establishes an IMAP session with the local host, and after the usual logon formalities, Alex issues the RENAME command, renaming his old stuff/junk mailbox to a new name, newbox. The IMAP server returns a positive response to the command. Alex then makes the new mailbox active by issuing the SELECT command. The server responds with the current information for the new mailbox.

If Alex had previously stored a message in the stuff/junk mailbox, the new mailbox, newbox, would have one message in it. This shows that renaming a mailbox does not change its contents, just the name. After disconnecting from the IMAP session, Alex performs another listing of his home directory. Much to his surprise, the stuff directory is still there, but the junk file has vanished. The IMAP server properly deleted the junk file from the stuff/junk mailbox, but left behind the stuff subdirectory, which is now empty. The new mailbox was created as a new file named newbox.

SUBSCRIBE Command

The SUBSCRIBE command is used to add a mailbox to the list of active mailboxes for the client. The SUBSCRIBE command uses a single parameter: the mailbox you want to add. The current active mailboxes can be listed by using the LSUB command, described later in this chapter. The mailbox does not necessarily have to exist for it to be added to the active mailbox list. This feature can be used to add active mailboxes that don't yet exist or mailboxes that get deleted when they are empty.

UNSUBSCRIBE Command

The UNSUBSCRIBE command is used to remove a mailbox from the list of active mailboxes for the client. It uses a single parameter: the mailbox you want to remove from the list. The mailbox itself is not deleted, just removed from the client's active list. The current active mailboxes can be listed by using the LSUB command.

LIST Command

The LIST command is used to display a list of mailboxes available to the client. The LIST command uses two parameters with the following format:

LIST *reference mailbox*

The *reference* parameter is the directory that the mailbox names are relative to. If you use an empty string ("") for this parameter, the mailboxes listed are relative to your $HOME directory. The second parameter, *mailbox*, is the mailbox name you want to list. This value can include wildcard characters much like a normal directory listing. If the mailbox name is an empty string (""), the server returns the hierarchy delimiter (/ for Unix) and the root name of the *reference* parameter. Listing 4.7 shows a sample LIST session.

LISTING 4.7 Sample LIST Session

```
$ telnet localhost 143
Trying 127.0.0.1...
Connected to localhost.
Escape character is '^]'.
* OK localhost IMAP4rev1 v12.250 server ready
a1 LOGIN alex drums
a1 OK LOGIN completed
a2 CREATE new/anotherbox
a2 OK CREATE completed
a3 LIST "" *
* LIST (\NoInferiors) "/" .Xdefaults
* LIST (\NoInferiors \UnMarked) "/" .bash_logout
* LIST (\NoInferiors \UnMarked) "/" .bash_profile
* LIST (\NoInferiors \UnMarked) "/" .bashrc
* LIST (\NoSelect) "/" stuff
* LIST (\NoInferiors \UnMarked) "/" .mailboxlist
* LIST (\NoInferiors \UnMarked) "/" .bash_history
* LIST (\NoInferiors) "/" newbox
* LIST (\NoSelect) "/" new
* LIST (\NoInferiors) "/" new/anotherbox
* LIST (\NoInferiors) NIL INBOX
a3 OK LIST completed
a4 LOGOUT
* BYE test.ispnet.net IMAP4rev1 server terminating connection
a4 OK LOGOUT completed
Connection closed by foreign host.
$
```

In this example, the test user `alex` issues a `CREATE` command to create a new mailbox. Next, he issues a `LIST` command with the parameters `""` and `*`. The first parameter indicates that the mailbox names specified will be relative to his $HOME directory. The second parameter is the `*` wildcard character, indicating that he wants a listing of all mailboxes in his $HOME directory. The IMAP server sends a listing that shows a lot more than just mailboxes. It assumes that every file in Alex's $HOME directory is related to the mail system. While this is somewhat true, there is a potential security problem with hidden configuration files, and certainly this can cause confusion for the user when non-mailbox files are listed in an IMAP client program.

The username `alex` was created as a normal Unix user on this system. Therefore, his $HOME directory was created using a standard home directory template. This template created a few configuration files used for things such as the bash shell and X Window System. Unfortunately, these files come across the IMAP server as mailboxes. This suggests that if you are creating new users on a Unix system for purely e-mail purposes, you should try to avoid the normal user creation techniques, or at least remember to remove the standard configuration files that are often created by default.

Another point this example illustrates is how the `LIST` command displays the mailboxes it lists. It shows the mailboxes that the IMAP server thinks are on the server. Notice how the files listed show the mailbox flag `\NoInferior`, which indicates there are no mailboxes under this name. Also, notice how the subdirectories stuff and new have the `\NoSelect` flag, indicating they cannot be activated by using the `SELECT` command. Finally, notice how the `LIST` command automatically lists the `INBOX` mailbox, even though no file actually exists in the $HOME directory for this mailbox.

LSUB Command

The `LSUB` command is used to correct the problem described with the `LIST` command. The `LIST` command returns everything in a client's $HOME directory, but the `LSUB` command lists only the mailboxes that have been tagged as being active for the client, using the `SUBSCRIBE` command. The parameters for the `LSUB` command are a reference name and a mailbox name. Like the `LIST` command, the reference parameter points to the directory where the mailbox names are relative to ($HOME if `""`), and the mailbox parameter is the mailbox you want to list (including wildcard characters).

Mailboxes can be added to the active mailbox list by using the `SUBSCRIBE` command and removed from the active list by using the `UNSUBSCRIBE` command.

Listing 4.8 shows a sample `LSUB` session.

LISTING 4.8 Sample LSUB Command Session

```
$ telnet localhost 143
Trying 127.0.0.1...
Connected to localhost.
Escape character is '^]'.
* OK localhost IMAP4rev1 v12.250 server ready
a1 LOGIN alex drums
a1 OK LOGIN completed
a2 SUBSCRIBE new/anotherbox
a2 OK SUBSCRIBE completed
a3 LSUB "" *
* LSUB () "/" stuff/junk
* LSUB () "/" newbox
* LSUB () "/" new/anotherbox
a3 OK LSUB completed
a4 LOGOUT
* BYE test.ispnet.net IMAP4rev1 server terminating connection
a4 OK LOGOUT completed
Connection closed by foreign host.
$
```

This example shows Alex adding the new mailbox created in Listing 4.7 to his list of subscribed mailboxes. He issues the LSUB command to see what mailboxes he has subscribed to. Notice that the LSUB parameters point to his $HOME directory and use the * wildcard character (to list all the mailboxes under his $HOME directory that appear in his subscription list). The IMAP server's response differs greatly from the LIST response shown in Listing 4.7.

You might have noticed one oddity in Listing 4.8. The stuff/junk mailbox had been successfully renamed back in Listing 4.6, but it shows up as a subscribed mailbox here. What happened? Remember that subscribing to a mailbox does not necessarily mean the mailbox is still available. The LSUB command keeps any previously subscribed mailboxes in its active list, regardless of the actual mailbox status. This allows mailboxes to be temporarily deleted when they are empty and re-created when they get messages, without clients having to resubscribe to them.

STATUS Command

The STATUS command is used to request the current status of a mailbox. The first parameter for this command is the name of the mailbox. The second parameter is a list of items the client wants information on enclosed in parentheses. The STATUS command can be used to get mailbox information without having to issue the SELECT (open) or EXAMINE (open, read-only) commands to actually open the mailbox.

The items that the STATUS command can retrieve information on are shown in Table 4.3.

TABLE 4.3 STATUS Command Data Items

Item	Description
MESSAGES	Total number of messages in mailbox
RECENT	Number of messages in mailbox flagged with the \RECENT flag
UIDNEXT	Next available UID to assign to a new message
UIDVALIDITY	The UID validity identifier for the mailbox
UNSEEN	Number of messages in mailbox not flagged with the \SEEN flag

A sample IMAP session using the STATUS command is shown in Listing 4.9.

LISTING 4.9 Sample STATUS Command

```
$ telnet localhost 143
Trying 127.0.0.1...
Connected to localhost.
Escape character is '^]'.
* OK localhost IMAP4rev1 v12.250 server ready
a1 LOGIN alex drums
a1 OK LOGIN completed
a2 STATUS inbox (messages recent unseen)
* STATUS inbox (MESSAGES 1 RECENT 0 UNSEEN 0)
a2 OK STATUS completed
a3 STATUS newbox (messages uidnext unseen)
* STATUS newbox (MESSAGES 1 UNSEEN 0 UIDNEXT 2)
a3 OK STATUS completed
a4 LOGOUT
* BYE test.ispnet.net IMAP4rev1 server terminating connection
a4 OK LOGOUT completed
Connection closed by foreign host.
$
```

This example shows Alex issuing the STATUS command asking for information about the total number of messages, the number of recent messages, and the number of unseen messages from the special INBOX mailbox. The server responds with the requested information. Next, Alex issues another STATUS command for another mailbox. Notice the IMAP server response. The server responds with the information requested for the mailbox, but not in the order it was requested. The IMAP server always uses a consistent

order in returning the information: MESSAGES, RECENT, UNSEEN, UIDNEXT, and
UIDVALIDITY.

APPEND Command

The APPEND command is an interesting addition to the IMAP command family. Normally,
IMAP is used exclusively for reading mail from mailboxes, but the APPEND command gives
IMAP the ability to send messages to a mailbox by adding the message to the end of the
mailbox file. This is an extremely tricky and dangerous practice, and is not recommended
as a normal replacement for using SMTP software to deliver messages. It's more of a
"nice to have" feature of IMAP just in case the need arises. This is the basic format of the
APPEND command:

```
APPEND mailbox [(flags)] [date/time string] {message size} message
```

This is an awkward command to carry out (and even more awkward to try to simulate).
Listing 4.10 shows an attempt to push a message into a mailbox. Of course, the client
needs read/write capabilities for the mailbox.

LISTING 4.10 Sample APPEND Command Session

```
$ telnet localhost 143
Trying 127.0.0.1...
Connected to localhost.
Escape character is '^]'.
* OK localhost IMAP4rev1 v12.250 server ready
a1 LOGIN alex drums
a1 OK LOGIN completed
a2 CREATE testbox
a2 OK CREATE completed
a3 APPEND testbox (\SEEN) {23}
+ Ready for argument
This is a test message.
a3 OK APPEND completed
a4 SELECT testbox
* 1 EXISTS
* 1 RECENT
* OK [UIDVALIDITY 937242636] UID validity status
* OK [UIDNEXT 2] Predicted next UID
* FLAGS (\Answered \Flagged \Deleted \Draft \Seen)
* OK [PERMANENTFLAGS (\* \Answered \Flagged \Deleted \Draft \Seen)]
a4 OK [READ-WRITE] SELECT completed
a5 LOGOUT
```

LISTING 4.10 Continued

```
* BYE test.ispnet.net IMAP4rev1 server terminating connection
a5 OK LOGOUT completed
Connection closed by foreign host.
$ mail -f testbox
Mail version 8.1 6/6/93.  Type ? for help.
"testbox": 2 messages
>   1 MAILER-DAEMON@test.i Mon Apr 16 19:11  12/516 "DON'T DELETE THIS MES"
    2 alex@test.ispnet.ne  Mon Apr 16 19:11   8/128
& 2
Message 2:
From alex@test.ispnet.net Mon Sep 12 19:11:18 1999 -0500

This is a test message.
Status: RO
X-Status:
X-Keywords:
X-UID: 1

&
```

Here Alex creates a brand-new empty mailbox for testing. Next, he uses the APPEND command to insert a message into the new mailbox. The appended message is flagged as \SEEN and is 23 bytes long. The message size includes all CR–LF combinations in the message, with the exception of the terminating CR–LF at the end of the last line entered. For this example, Alex uses a very simple message. After he presses Enter, the IMAP server returns a positive response and prompts Alex to enter the "argument" for the APPEND command. Alex responds by typing the message, which is successfully added to the client's mailbox.

Next Alex issues the mail -f testbox command to read the mail in the testbox mailbox. By displaying the message, you can see that this is the message that was added with the APPEND command, although the IMAP server tried to make a normal message out of the test text. Had this been a real message, Alex (or his e-mail package) would have sent a properly formatted RFC 822 message, and the IMAP server would have handled it properly.

CHECK Command

The CHECK command is used to initiate a checkpoint for the mailbox. Any pending operations, such as writing data from server memory to disk, are performed to place the mailbox in a consistent state. The CHECK command does not use any parameters.

Unix experts will recognize CHECK as the IMAP equivalent of the sync command, which ensures that the in-memory disk buffers are all written out to the disk.

CLOSE Command

The CLOSE command does what it says—it closes the mailbox. When a mailbox is closed, any messages tagged with the \DELETED flag are physically removed from the mailbox. The CLOSE command is also implicitly performed on an open mailbox when a new mailbox is opened. Also, an open mailbox is implicitly closed when a LOGOUT command (described later in this chapter) is issued or the connection is unexpectedly terminated. The CLOSE command does not have any parameters.

EXPUNGE Command

The EXPUNGE command is used to remove all messages in a mailbox tagged with the \DELETED flag without closing the mailbox. The EXPUNGE server response is a list of the mailbox's new status. Listing 4.11 is a sample EXPUNGE session.

LISTING 4.11 Sample EXPUNGE Session

```
$ telnet localhost 143
Trying 127.0.0.1...
Connected to localhost.
Escape character is '^]'.
* OK localhost IMAP4rev1 v12.250 server ready
a1 LOGIN alex drums
a1 OK LOGIN completed
a2 SELECT newbox
* 6 EXISTS
* 0 RECENT
* OK [UIDVALIDITY 937243866] UID validity status
* OK [UIDNEXT 8] Predicted next UID
* FLAGS (\Answered \Flagged \Deleted \Draft \Seen)
* OK [PERMANENTFLAGS (\* \Answered \Flagged \Deleted \Draft \Seen)]
* OK [UNSEEN 1] first unseen message in /home/alex/newbox
a2 OK [READ-WRITE] SELECT completed
a3 STORE 1 +flags \DELETED
* 1 FETCH (FLAGS (\Deleted))
a3 OK STORE completed
a4 STORE 2 +flags \DELETED
* 2 FETCH (FLAGS (\Deleted))
a4 OK STORE completed
a5 STATUS newbox (messages unseen)
* STATUS newbox (MESSAGES 6 UNSEEN 6)
a5 OK STATUS completed
a6 EXPUNGE
```

LISTING 4.11 Continued

```
* 1 EXPUNGE
* 1 EXPUNGE
* 4 EXISTS
* 0 RECENT
a6 OK Expunged 2 messages
a7 STATUS newbox (messages unseen)
* STATUS newbox (MESSAGES 4 UNSEEN 4)
a7 OK STATUS completed
a8 LOGOUT
* BYE test.ispnet.net IMAP4rev1 server terminating connection
a8 OK LOGOUT completed
Connection closed by foreign host.
$
```

In this example Alex selects the mailbox named newbox. The server response shows that there are six messages in the mailbox. Next Alex uses the STORE command (discussed later in this chapter) to flag the first two messages as \DELETED. After flagging the two messages, Alex issues a STATUS command for the mailbox. The server response shows that the IMAP server still sees six messages in the mailbox, even though two of them are now marked for deletion.

Next Alex issues the EXPUNGE command to remove the messages marked for deletion. The server responds by indicating that two messages were expunged (deleted), and four messages still exist in the current mailbox. This information is verified by issuing a STATUS command on the mailbox. The server then responds by showing only four messages remaining in the mailbox.

SEARCH Command

The SEARCH command, a powerful tool in the IMAP command arsenal, searches messages in an active mailbox based on search criteria and displays the matching message numbers. The format for the SEARCH command looks like this:

```
SEARCH [CHARSET specification] (search criteria)
```

In this command, CHARSET specification consists of the word CHARSET followed by a registered CHARSET symbol set. The default CHARSET is US-ASCII, so this parameter is usually omitted. The search criteria parameter specifies keys and values to search for in the messages. Table 4.4 lists the search keys that can be used.

TABLE 4.4 SEARCH Command Defined Search Keys

KEY	Description
message set	Messages with message numbers corresponding to the specified message sequence number set
ALL	All messages in the mailbox
ANSWERED	Messages with the \ANSWERED flag set
BCC string	Messages that contain the string specified in *string* in the Bcc: header field
BEFORE date	Messages whose internal date is before *date*
BODY string	Messages that contain the *string* specified in string in the body of the message
CC string	Messages that contain the *string* specified in string in the Cc: header field
DELETED	Messages with the \DELETED flag set
DRAFT	Messages with the \DRAFT flag set
FLAGGED	Messages with the \FLAGGED flag set
FROM string	Messages that contain the *string* specified in string in the From: header field
HEADER field name STRING	Messages that contain the specified header *field name* and the string *string* in that field (for example, HEADER Keyword email)
KEYWORD flag	Messages with the specified keyword set
LARGER n	Messages with a size larger than *n*
NEW	Messages with the \RECENT flag set but not the \SEEN flag
NOT search key	Messages that don't contain the *search* key specified in search key (such as NOT NEW)
OLD	Messages that do not have the \RECENT flag set
ON date	Messages whose internal date is *date*
OR searchkey1 searchkey2	Messages that contain either searchkey1 or searchkey2
RECENT	Messages that have the \RECENT flag set
SEEN	Messages that have the \SEEN flag set
SENTBEFORE date	Messages whose Date: header field is before *date*
SENTON date	Messages whose Date: header field is *date*
SENTSINCE date	Messages whose Date: header field is on or after *date*
SINCE date	Messages whose internal date is on or after *date*
SMALLER n	Messages whose message size is smaller than *n*
TEXT string	Messages that contain the string specified in *string* in either the header or body
UID message set	Messages whose UID corresponds to *message set*
UNANSWERED	Messages that do not have the \ANSWERED flag set

TABLE 4.4 Continued

KEY	Description
UNDELETED	Messages that do not have the \DELETED flag set
UNDRAFT	Messages that do not have the \DRAFT flag set
UNFLAGGED	Messages that do not have the \FLAGGED flag set
UNKEYWORD flag	Messages that do not have the keyword *flag* set
UNSEEN	Messages that do not have the \SEEN flag set

As you can see in Table 4.4, there are many things you can search for in messages. This command is extremely handy when trying to find specific messages in mailboxes that have become cluttered. Listing 4.12 shows a short example of using the SEARCH command.

LISTING 4.12 Sample SEARCH Command Session

```
$ telnet localhost 143
Trying 127.0.0.1...
Connected to localhost.
Escape character is '^]'.
* OK localhost IMAP4rev1 v12.250 server ready
a1 LOGIN alex drums
a1 OK LOGIN completed
a2 SELECT inbox
* 2 EXISTS
* 0 RECENT
* OK [UIDVALIDITY 936999597] UID validity status
* OK [UIDNEXT 5] Predicted next UID
* FLAGS (\Answered \Flagged \Deleted \Draft \Seen)
* OK [PERMANENTFLAGS (\* \Answered \Flagged \Deleted \Draft \Seen)]
* OK [UNSEEN 1] first unseen message in /var/spool/mail/alex
a2 OK [READ-WRITE] SELECT completed
a3 SEARCH header subject test
* SEARCH 1 2
a3 OK SEARCH completed
a4 SEARCH header subject another
* SEARCH 2
a4 OK SEARCH completed
a5 SEARCH unseen
* SEARCH 1 2
a5 OK SEARCH completed
a6 LOGOUT
```

LISTING 4.12 Continued

```
* BYE test.ispnet.net IMAP4rev1 server terminating connection
a6 OK LOGOUT completed
Connection closed by foreign host.
$
```

This listing shows three examples of using the SEARCH command. In each example a different word is searched for in the Subject: header field. The server response is a list of message numbers that match the search criteria. If no matches are found, the server returns the word SEARCH with no UIDs.

FETCH Command

The FETCH command is used for retrieving the text of the mail message. It is used for display purposes only. Unlike POP3, the IMAP client should not retain a copy of the message on the client workstation. It is the server's responsibility to maintain the messages in mailboxes. The format of the FETCH command is as follows:

```
FETCH messageset datanames
```

The *messageset* parameter is a list of message numbers you want to retrieve, and *datanames* is a list of data items from each message you want to retrieve.

The *messageset* can be a single message number, a list of specific numbers separated by commas, or a range of numbers separated by a colon. The IMAP server returns the specified data items for all the messages in the message set.

The *datanames* item is a complex specification of pieces of the message that can be returned individually. Three special macros return specific message information: ALL, BODY, and BODY[section].

The ALL macro does not return the entire message as you might expect, but a formatted synopsis of the message that includes the flags set, the internal date, and the message envelope. The IMAP client can parse this standard message into the relevant parts to display information about the message.

The BODY macro does not return the actual text of the body, but a synopsis of the type of text and the size of the body. Again, the IMAP client can parse this information to give the user more detailed information about the message.

The BODY[section] macro can be used to return individual pieces of the message. RFC 2060 lists each of the specific RFC 822 message parts that can be used in this section. Two of the most common are HEADER and TEXT. The BODY[HEADER] macro returns the complete header of the message. You can get even more specific by specifying only certain header fields, such as BODY[HEADER.FIELDS (SUBJECT)] to return the Subject:

header field of a message. Multiple fields can be displayed by separating them with spaces within the parentheses.

The BODY[*section*] macro can also be modified by using the *partial* field, which consists of two numbers separated by a period. The first number is a starting position octet in the data output you want to display. The second number is the number of octets from the data output you want to display. This feature can be used to further format the output. For example, if you want to display only the first 10 characters in the message body of message 1, you would use the following command:

```
FETCH 1 BODY[TEXT]<0.10>
```

This command fetches the first 10 characters of the body section defined as *text*. If there were less than 10 characters in the message body, the whole message body would be displayed.

Listing 4.13 shows some more examples of using the FETCH command.

LISTING 4.13 Sample FETCH Command Session

```
$ telnet localhost 143
Trying 127.0.0.1...
Connected to localhost.
Escape character is '^]'.
* OK localhost IMAP4rev1 v12.250 server ready
a1 LOGIN alex drums
a1 OK LOGIN completed
a2 SELECT inbox
* 6 EXISTS
* 0 RECENT
* OK [UIDVALIDITY 937321060] UID validity status
* OK [UIDNEXT 7] Predicted next UID
* FLAGS (\Answered \Flagged \Deleted \Draft \Seen)
* OK [PERMANENTFLAGS (\* \Answered \Flagged \Deleted \Draft \Seen)]
a2 OK [READ-WRITE] SELECT completed
a3 FETCH 3:5 body[header.fields (date from subject)]
* 3 FETCH (BODY[HEADER.FIELDS ("DATE" "FROM" "SUBJECT")] {112}
Date: Tue, 14 Sep 1999 10:09:50 -0500
From: alex@shadrach.smallorg.org
Subject: This is the first test message

)
* 4 FETCH (BODY[HEADER.FIELDS ("DATE" "FROM" "SUBJECT")] {113}
Date: Tue, 14 Sep 1999 10:10:04 -0500
```

LISTING 4.13 Continued

```
From: alex@shadrach.smallorg.org
Subject: This is the second test message

)
* 5 FETCH (BODY[HEADER.FIELDS ("DATE" "FROM" "SUBJECT")] {112}
Date: Tue, 14 Sep 1999 10:10:26 -0500
From: alex@shadrach.smallorg.org
Subject: This is the third test message

)
a3 OK FETCH completed
a4 FETCH 4 body[text]
* 4 FETCH (BODY[TEXT] {42}
This is the fourth test message for IMAP
)
a4 OK FETCH completed
a5 LOGOUT
* BYE test.ispnet.net IMAP4rev1 server terminating connection
a5 OK LOGOUT completed
Connection closed by foreign host.
$
```

This listing shows samples of using the FETCH command to retrieve message data. The first FETCH command requests the Date:, From:, and Subject: header fields from messages 3 through 5 (note the use of a colon as the range delimiter in 3:5, not a dash as is more common in Unix commands). The server responds by listing the data for each message requested. The second FETCH command requests the text of the body from message 4. The IMAP server responds by displaying the text of the message body.

By default, the BODY[section] macro alters the message by setting the \SEEN flag. If you want to look at a part of the message without flagging it as being seen, you can substitute the BODY[section] macro with BODY.PEEK[SECTION]. This performs the same function as the BODY[section] macro without setting the \SEEN flag for the message.

STORE Command

The STORE command is used to alter information associated with the message and uses the following format:

STORE *messageset dataname datavalue*

The *messageset* parameter is a list of message numbers to perform the STORE operation on. There are currently only two data item types available for the STORE command. FLAGS identifies a list of flags set for the message. FLAGS.SILENT identifies a list of flags that are set for the message, but with this option the IMAP server does not return the new value as part of the response.

The behavior of the two data items can be further modified by preceding them with a plus sign or a minus sign. The plus sign signifies that the data item value will be added to the message, and the minus sign signifies that the data item value will be removed from the message.

Listing 4.11 showed a good example of using the STORE command to set flags for messages. Line 17 showed setting the \DELETED flag for message 1 in the active mailbox (STORE 1 +flags \DELETED). Notice how the flags parameter was preceded by a plus sign. You could use a minus sign to remove the \DELETED flag from the message (a way to undelete a message before the next checkpoint takes effect). Remember, when a message is flagged as \DELETED, it's not actually removed from the mailbox until a checkpoint is performed on the mailbox using the CHECK, EXPUNGE, SELECT, or LOGOUT commands.

COPY Command

The COPY command is used to copy messages from one mailbox to another. The format for the COPY command is as follows:

COPY *messageset mailboxname*

In this command, *messageset* is a list of messages you want to copy from the active mailbox, and *mailboxname* is the mailbox you want the messages to go to.

There is no "move" command defined in IMAP, but it should be fairly obvious that a move is nothing more than copying messages to a new mailbox and setting the \DELETED flag on the original messages. After the next mailbox checkpoint occurs, the original messages are deleted and the new messages are present.

UID Command

The UID command is used with the FETCH, COPY, STORE, or SEARCH commands. It allows these commands to use actual UID numbers instead of sequence numbers in their message sets. The UID number is a 32-bit integer that uniquely identifies the mailbox messages within the mail system. Normally, these functions use the sequence number to identify the messages in the mailbox. Using the UID number allows the IMAP client to remember messages between IMAP sessions.

CAPABILITY Command

The CAPABILITY command requests a list of capabilities that the IMAP server supports. Listing 4.14 shows a sample CAPABILIY command session.

LISTING 4.14 Sample CAPABILITY Command Session

```
$ telnet localhost 143
Trying 127.0.0.1...
Connected to localhost.
Escape character is '^]'.
* OK localhost IMAP4rev1 v12.250 server ready
a1 LOGIN riley firetruck
a1 OK LOGIN completed
a2 CAPABILITY
* CAPABILITY IMAP4 IMAP4REV1 NAMESPACE IDLE SCAN SORT MAILBOX-REFERRALS
[ic:ccc] LOGIN-REFERRALS AUTH=LOGIN THREAD=ORDEREDSUBJECT
a2 OK CAPABILITY completed
a3 LOGOUT
* BYE test.ispnet.net IMAP4rev1 server terminating connection
a3 OK LOGOUT completed
Connection closed by foreign host.
$
```

When the client issues the CAPABILITY command, the server responds by listing the capabilities this particular IMAP server software supports. The server supports all the commands in the IMAP4 and IMAP4rev1 protocols listed in this chapter. Note that the server also lists other nonstandard commands as well as the authentication methods it is capable of supporting.

NOOP Command

The NOOP command does what it says—nothing. It can be used to send automatic commands to the server to prevent an inactivity logout timer from expiring. The server response to the NOOP command should always be positive. Because the server is allowed to return status update information from any command, the NOOP command can often trigger a status report from the server. If something happened to the mailbox during the period of inactivity with the client, such as if the server deleted messages because of a mailbox rule set by the mail administrator, the new status can be returned as a response to the NOOP command.

LOGOUT Command

The LOGOUT command is used to log the current username out of the mail server and close any open mailboxes. If any messages were flagged \DELETED, they are removed from the mailbox at this time.

Open Source IMAP Implementations

There have been a few open source IMAP software packages written for the Unix platform, both for IMAP clients and IMAP servers. With the growing popularity of IMAP4, you should expect to see more activity in this area of software development. This section looks at the most popular Unix packages for IMAP server software and IMAP client software.

Open Source IMAP Server

The imapd software package is a popular IMAP4 server implementation developed at the University of Washington. It is included in many Unix distributions as a binary package. If you do not have a binary distribution, or want to install the latest version, you can get the source code from the University of Washington's FTP site at ftp.cac.washinton.edu in the /mail directory. The most recent version is always named imap.tar.Z. At the time of this writing, the current version is imap-2001.BETA.

The imapd program is invoked by the inetd program, and by default listens for connection requests on the standard IMAP TCP port 143. This is the configuration line in the /etc/inetd.conf file necessary for inetd to run imapd:

```
imap    stream  tcp     nowait  root    /usr/sbin/imapd  imapd
```

The default mail directory for an IMAP client is the Unix $HOME directory specified in the /etc/passwd file for the username.

Open Source IMAP Client

The fetchmail program discussed in Chapter 3, "POP3," can be configured to use IMAP to retrieve mail from one or more mailboxes on an IMAP server. You can use the fetchmailconf program to configure the basic settings for the IMAP server, specifying IMAP as the mail transport protocol. The fetchmailconf program creates a .fetchmailrc configuration file for the default mailbox for the user, usually the special INBOX mailbox. If you want to check other mailboxes that have been configured on the IMAP server, you can use the -r option in fetchmail:

```
fetchmail -r mailbox
```

The *mailbox* parameter is the name of the mailbox (or folder) that is checked instead of the default INBOX mailbox. Be careful when using this option, though, as fetchmail forwards any messages it retrieves to your normal local mailbox on your workstation. Messages that were once separated into different mailboxes are now combined into a single place.

Summary

The Interactive Message Access Protocol (IMAP) was developed to retrieve mail that remains on remote mail servers. This method of mail retrieval has the advantage of a user's mail always staying in one place; it can't get scattered among different client PCs.

IMAP provides for multiple mailboxes, or folders, that reside on the server. The client can move messages around to different folders on the server. This type of client mail retrieval requires close administration because all mail messages and mailboxes reside on the server. If the server crashes or loses connectivity, or the disk space fills up, all users lose their ability to retrieve mail. The mail administrator responsible for an IMAP server must pay close attention to details on the mail server.

Several open source software packages are available for Unix systems that use IMAP. The imapd software program developed at the University of Washington implements IMAP server functions. Also, the standard fetchmail mail client program can be configured to use IMAP to retrieve mail from a remote IMAP server.

CHAPTER 5

MIME

Chapter 2, "SMTP," discussed how mail servers send messages across the Internet using Simple Mail Transfer Protocol (SMTP). You may have noticed that the only SMTP command used to transmit information was the DATA command. You have probably also noticed that the DATA command is limited to transmitting ASCII text to the remote mail server.

At this point, you might be wondering how you are able to send non-ASCII things, such as foreign character set documents, fancy pictures, and programs, to your friends and relatives if the mail servers can send only ASCII data. The answer is simple. Somewhere along the e-mail process binary data must be converted into ASCII text. The ASCII text is then sent via SMTP to the remote mail server, where it must be converted back to the original binary data, whether it was a Chinese character document, a picture of the new baby, or the monthly sales figures in Microsoft Excel format.

This chapter describes the methods used to transmit binary data to remote mail servers on the Internet. It covers the two most popular methods used to encode binary data: uuencode and the multipurpose Internet mail extensions (MIME) format.

The Uuencode Program

Several years before SMTP was invented, Unix system administrators were sending binary data across modem lines by converting it to ASCII text and embedding it in mail messages. The method they used to convert binary data into ASCII text was called *uuencode*. The *uu* stands for "Unix-to-Unix," part of the Unix-to-Unix Copy Protocol (UUCP) suite that was developed to help transfer data between Unix computers, using both dial-up and dedicated modems.

When SMTP became popular, it was natural for Unix system administrators to use existing utilities for transferring binary data within an SMTP message across the Internet. Therefore, many original SMTP e-mail packages used the uuencode method of sending binary data. Many e-mail packages still use this method for encoding binary data to send via SMTP. Unfortunately, some newer e-mail packages don't include uuencode, thus creating incompatibilities in the e-mail world.

If you receive a message that has been uuencoded but your e-mail package does not support it, all you will see is a jumbled mess of text characters. You can, however, still manually decode the message. Similarly, if you know you are sending a message to another person whose e-mail package supports only uudecoding, you can manually uuencode your binary files. The following sections describe how to manually encode and decode binary files using the uuencode programs.

Encoding Binary Data

The uuencode program has become almost standard software on most Unix systems. All Linux distributions install it by default, as well as the FreeBSD setup. If your Unix distribution does not include the uuencode program, you can download the source code from a Unix utility Web site, such as sunsite.unc.edu, and install it yourself.

After the uuencode program is installed on your system, you can manually encode any binary or text file. Uuencode uses a *3-to-4 encoding scheme*, in which 3 bytes of binary data are converted to 4 bytes of ASCII text. This scheme significantly increases the size of the file you want to transmit. Remember not to compress the encoded file, as it would then cease to be an ASCII text file. Instead, compress the binary file before encoding it.

To demonstrate encoding a binary file, first you must have a sample binary file. You can create a simple binary file by creating a simple "Hello World" C program and compiling it. Listing 5.1 shows a simple C program that you can use.

LISTING 5.1 Sample Hello World Program

```
#include <stdio.h>

main()
{
printf("Hello, World\n");
}
```

This program can be saved as a text file called hello.c. After creating the text file, you can compile it to create the binary executable file using this command:

```
cc -o hello hello.c
```

This command creates a binary file named hello. You can then run the binary file from the command line to test it:

```
[rich@test rich]$ ./hello
Hello, World
[rich@test rich]$
```

You are now ready to encode the binary file by using the uuencode command, which follows this format:

```
uuencode [file] name
```

The *file* parameter allows the user to specify the file to be encoded (by default, the uuencode program takes its input from standard input), and the *name* parameter defines the filename used to identify the binary file in the encoded file (more on this later).

CAUTION

Some uuencode versions include an -m option to force it to use base-64 encoding instead of the standard uuencode encoding. This option can be dangerous, as most uuencode programs expect an uuencoded file to be in the original uuencode format.

To encode the sample binary file, you should use the following command:

```
uuencode hello hello > hello.uue
```

This command encodes the binary file hello, identifying it as the filename hello in the encoded file, and directing the encoded file output to the file hello.uue. By default, the uuencode program sends its output to standard output. Listing 5.2 shows a partial listing of the resulting file.

LISTING 5.2 Partial hello.uue Listing

```
begin 755 hello
M?T5,1@$!`0`````````(`'P`!````4(,"4'$``#H&``
M`"`'0`:8`````T````-(`$$(!!C!`!````!@(`0$!`0`
M`#0`0]`0$(`$$('`#0````A`T````$```((````"#0
M>G`%````@`<(!$`````"#[BC9@`!````!@(`0$!`0`
M`(_```,`````W`P`)@!@0`%#$`````"````%````!
M````$@`````L`H`````A`4H``$(!!@$`#0````A`T`
M````````("````H````!(`#0````A`T`````````
M`````%````$````@`@`(H`````!`````8`@!!@$`$`
.
.
.
M7S(N``````@`*@`!(`4@`H;`I`"@````$``,`````#
M;`!`1($!!@$`#0````A`T``````````````%`HB0`H
M;P.`8`!`I`P`B07!B!.`P````A`T```!!!@$`#0````
M@@C``Q3@`!`(!!@$`#0````A`T`P`P`Y*]@`A`$``>
&87)T7U
```

```
end
```

Notice that the encoded file contains a header line that identifies the start of the encoded file, along with a Unix permissions number and a name. The name is the filename you specified in the uuencode command. The permissions are the Unix permissions that the original binary file had. In this example, the binary file had rwxr-xr-x permissions, which translates into the number 755.

Also notice that the end of the encoded file is identified with a separate footer line, end, along with a trailing blank line. By explicitly specifying the beginning and end of the encoded file, the uudecode program can strip out any extraneous text that might be before or after the encoded file. This often happens when the file is included in an e-mail message.

You can compare the sizes of the original and encoded files by using the Unix ls command:

```
[rich@test tmp]$ ls -l
total 32
-rwxr-xr-x   1 rich      rich           11295 Apr 19 10:43 hello
-rw-r--r--   1 rich      rich              57 Apr 19 10:43 hello.c
-rw-r--r--   1 rich      rich           15584 Apr 19 10:43 hello.uue
[rich@test tmp]$
```

Notice that the encoded file is 15584 bytes, while the original binary file was only 11295 bytes. Using uuencode on large binary files can produce extremely large text files.

After the file is encoded and sent to the remote user, it must be decoded back into the binary file. The next section describes this process.

Decoding the Data

The companion to the uuencode program is the uudecode program, which takes an encoded ASCII text file and extracts the original binary data file. The format of the uudecode command looks like this:

```
uudecode [-o outfile] [ file ]
```

By default, the uudecode program decodes the data from standard input. Alternatively, you can specify the ASCII text file to decode by using the file parameter. Also by default, uudecode creates the filename specified in the encoded file header. If you want to decode it to a different filename, you can use the -o option and the outfile parameter. Using the sample hello.uue file created in the previous section, you would use this command:

```
uudecode hello.uue
```

This command would decode the encoded binary file and place it in the filename specified in the encoded header text, in this case the program name hello. If you do not want to overwrite the original hello program, you can specify an alternative output name:

```
uudecode -o hello2 hello.uue
```

This command overrides the internal filename specified in the encoded file header, and instead creates the file hello2 with the decoded data. To see if the decoded file is the same, you can try running it from the command prompt:

```
[rich@test mime]$ ./hello2
Hello, World
[rich@test mime]$
```

Indeed, the new file runs with the same results.

NOTE

When sending binary files to others, remember that not all binary files are compatible on all Unix systems. Often it is easier to send the source code of programs and allow the recipients to compile the program on their Unix system.

MIME and Binary Data

The reason many newer e-mail packages don't use uuencode to encode files is because an Internet standard for encoding binary data has been created: MIME. RFCs 2045 and 2046 describe the MIME message format. MIME is more versatile than uuencode in that it passes additional information about the file to the decoder, allowing the decoder to automatically detect and decode different types of binary files.

MIME enables binary data to be directly incorporated into a standard RFC 822 message. Five new header fields were defined to identify binary data types embedded in the RFC 822 message. E-mail packages that can handle MIME messages must be able to process these five new header fields. Figure 5.1 demonstrates how the new header fields fit together with the original RFC 822 header fields in a standard e-mail message.

MIME Header Fields

The five additional header fields that MIME uses help identify how the data is encoded in the MIME sections. Table 5.1 describes these new header fields.

TABLE 5.1 MIME Message Header Fields

Field	Description
MIME-Version	Specifies the version of MIME used
Content-Transfer-Encoding	Specifies the encoding scheme used to encode the binary data into ASCII
Content-ID	Specifies a unique identifier for the message section
Content-Description	A short description identifying the message section
Content-Type	Specifies the type of content contained in the encoded data

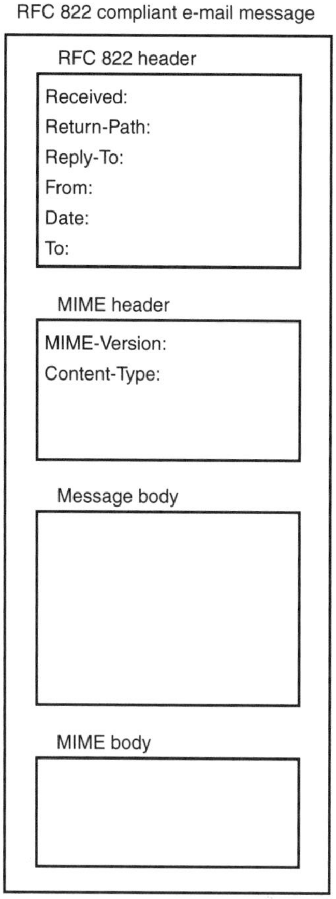

RFC 822 compliant e-mail message

```
┌────────────────────────────────────┐
│         RFC 822 header             │
│  ┌──────────────────────────────┐  │
│  │ Received:                    │  │
│  │ Return-Path:                 │  │
│  │ Reply-To:                    │  │
│  │ From:                        │  │
│  │ Date:                        │  │
│  │ To:                          │  │
│  └──────────────────────────────┘  │
│                                    │
│          MIME header               │
│  ┌──────────────────────────────┐  │
│  │ MIME-Version:                │  │
│  │ Content-Type:                │  │
│  │                              │  │
│  │                              │  │
│  └──────────────────────────────┘  │
│                                    │
│         Message body               │
│  ┌──────────────────────────────┐  │
│  │                              │  │
│  │                              │  │
│  │                              │  │
│  │                              │  │
│  │                              │  │
│  └──────────────────────────────┘  │
│                                    │
│           MIME body                │
│  ┌──────────────────────────────┐  │
│  │                              │  │
│  │                              │  │
│  │                              │  │
│  └──────────────────────────────┘  │
└────────────────────────────────────┘
```

FIGURE 5.1

The MIME message header fields.

Not all five fields have to be present in the MIME message header. Only the Content-Type field is required. The receiving e-mail server must be able to identify the message data from the MIME header fields, so the more information provided, the more accurate the decoder can be.

The following sections describe the MIME header fields in more detail.

MIME-Version Header Field

The first additional header type identifies the version of MIME that the sender used to encode the message. Currently this value is always 1.0:

MIME-Version: 1.0

Alternatively, e-mail packages can add additional text to the `MIME-Version` header, such as a vendor implementation version number:

```
MIME-Version: 1.0 (software test 2.3a)
```

The MIME translation software of the receiving mail server ignores the additional text.

Content-Transfer-Encoding **Header Field**

The `Content-Transfer-Encoding` header field identifies how the binary data embedded in the message is encoded. There are currently seven different methods, listed in Table 5.2, used to encode binary data in a MIME message.

TABLE 5.2 MIME Encoding Methods

Method	Description
7-bit	Standard 7-bit ASCII text
8-bit	Standard 8-bit ASCII text
binary	Raw binary data
quoted-printable	Encodes data to printable characters in the US-ASCII character set
base64	Encodes 6 bits of binary data into an 8-bit printable character
ietf-token	Extension token encoding defined by an RFC
x-token	Two characters, x- or x-, followed, with no intervening space, by any token

Note that the first three methods define no encoding of the data. The `7-bit` encoding method assumes that the encoded data is standard 7-bit ASCII text characters, and is the default method used if the `Content-Transfer-Encoding` field is not present. Of course, this method assumes a standard ASCII text message in the message body.

The `binary` encoding method assumes that the transport protocol being used supports sending raw binary data within the e-mail message. This is not the case in SMTP, so this encoding is not used.

The most common method used to encode binary data is the `base64` method, which encodes the binary data by mapping 6-bit blocks of binary data to 8-bit bytes of ASCII text. Table 5.3 shows the standard base-64 character set used to encode the 6-bit data.

TABLE 5.3 The base64 Encoding Method

Value Encoding	Value Encoding	Value Encoding	Value Encoding
0 A	17 R	34 i	51 z
1 B	18 S	35 j	52 0
2 C	19 T	36 k	53 1

TABLE 5.3 Continued

Value Encoding	Value Encoding	Value Encoding	Value Encoding
3 D	20 U	37 l	54 2
4 E	21 V	38 m	55 3
5 F	22 W	39 n	56 4
6 G	23 X	40 o	57 5
7 H	24 Y	41 p	58 6
8 I	25 Z	42 q	59 7
9 J	26 a	43 r	60 8
10 K	27 b	44 s	61 9
11 L	28 c	45 t	62 +
12 M	29 d	46 u	63 /
13 N	30 e	47 v	(pad) =
14 O	31 f	48 w	
15 P	32 g	49 x	
16 Q	33 h	50 y	

Each line of the encoded text contains 76 characters, with a line break at the end of each line. The last line uses pad characters to complete the line. This format is similar to the uuencode method shown earlier.

Content-ID Header Field

The Content-ID header field is used to identify MIME sections with a unique identification code. A MIME content section can refer to another MIME message by using the unique Content-ID.

Content-Description Header Field

The Content-Description header field is an ASCII text description of the data to help identify it in the e-mail message. The format of this field is as follows:

```
Content-Description: message
```

The message parameter can be any ASCII text of any length. This header field comes in handy when sending binary data such as word processing documents or graphic images that would otherwise be unidentifiable by their base-64 encoding. The Content-Description helps the recipient identify the type of data in the message.

Content-Type Header Field

The Content-Type header field is where the action is. This field identifies the data enclosed in the MIME message.

Two separate values, a type and a subtype, identify the data contained in the MIME section. The format of the Content-Type header field looks like this:

Content-Type: *type/subtype*

In this line, *type* is the general content format, and *subtype* is the specific content format that further defines the data type. There are currently seven basic types of Content-Type identified by MIME:

- text
- message
- image
- video
- audio
- application
- multipart

The following sections describe these types in more detail.

The text Content Type

The text content type identifies data that is in ASCII format and can be read by almost all e-mail packages. There are three subtypes:

- plain, which signifies unformatted ASCII text.
- html, which signifies using standard HTML tags to format the text.
- enriched, which signifies formatting features similar to the rich text format (RTF) used by many word processing packages.

The text content type should also specify the character set used to encode the data by using the charset parameter, as shown in this example:

Content-Type: text/plain; charset=us-ascii

This example shows that the enclosed MIME data is plain ASCII text using the ASCII character set. The html and enriched subtypes identify text that uses special formatting tags to produce features such as underlining, bold, different font sizes, and colors. Most newer e-mail client packages can display html and enriched text e-mail messages.

The message Content Type

The message content type allows the e-mail package to send multiple RFC 822 messages within a single e-mail message. These are the subtypes for this content type:

- `rfc822` specifies a normal embedded RFC 822–formatted message.
- `partial` specifies one section of a long e-mail messages that was broken up into separate sections.
- `external-body` specifies a pointer to an object that is not within the e-mail message.

The `image` Content Type

The `image` content type defines embedded binary data streams that represent graphic images. Currently, two subtypes are defined: the `jpeg` format and the `gif` format.

These types identify the standard JPEG and GIF image types. Of course, the actual image files must be encoded using a standard MIME encoding type, identified by the `Content-Type-Encoding` field.

The `video` Content Type

The `video` content type defines embedded binary data streams that represent video data. The only subtype defined at this time is the `mpeg` format.

Similar to the `image` type, the MPEG video file must be encoded using a standard MIME encoding type and identified in a `Content-Type-Encoding` field.

The `audio` Content Type

The `audio` content type defines embedded binary data streams that represent audio data. Currently, it has only one subtype: `basic`, which defines a single-channel Integrated Services Digital Network (ISDN) mu-law encoding at an 8KHz sample rate.

Yet again, the audio data file must be encoded using a standard MIME encoding method and identified using the `Content-Type-Encoding` field.

The `application` Content Type

The `application` content type is used to identify embedded binary data that represents application data, such as spreadsheets, word processing documents, and other applications. Currently, there are two formal subtypes defined:

- `postscript`, which defines a Postscript-formatted print document.
- `octet-stream`, which defines a message containing arbitrary binary data.

Often, the `octet-stream` subtype is used when embedding application-specific data, such as Microsoft Word documents and Microsoft Excel spreadsheets.

The `multipart` Content Type

The `multipart` content type is a special type. It identifies messages that contain different data content types combined in one message. This format is common in e-mail packages that can present a message in a variety of ways, such as ASCII text, HTML, and audio formats, as well as messages that include binary file attachments.

A boundary identifier separates each content type, and each content type is identified with its own separate `Content-Type` header field. The boundary identifier must be specified at the start of the `multipart` content type definition:

```
Content-Type: multipart/alternative; boundary=bounds1
```

The boundary identifier recognizes the start and end of each section of the `multipart` message. Two leading dashes are added to the boundary identifier to denote the separation of the sections. At the end of the last section, two additional trailing dashes are added to denote the end of the multipart message:

```
Content-Type: multipart/mixed; boundary=bounds2


--bounds2
    Content-Type: text/plain; charset=us-ascii
      First section


--bounds2
      Content-Type: text/plain; charset=us-ascii
        Second section


--bounds2
      Content-Type: text/plain; charset=us-ascii
        Last section


--bounds2--
```

Each section in the `multipart` content type is identified with a `Content-Type` header field to identify the type of data within the section.

The `multipart` Content type has four subtypes:

- `mixed` subtype means that each of the separate parts are independent of one another. Each part should be presented to the recipient in the order they were embedded in the message.
- `parallel` subtype specifies that each of the separate parts are independent of one another, and can be presented to the recipient in any order.
- `alternative` subtype indicates that each of the separate parts represent different ways of presenting the same data. Only one part should be presented to the recipient, and the best method available should be used.
- `digest` subtype identifies the same method as the `mixed` subtype, but specifies that the body of the message is always in RFC 822 format.

Listing 5.3 demonstrates the use of Content-Type definitions in a multipart e-mail message. Line numbers have been added to aid in the following discussion.

LISTING 5.3 Sample SMTP Multipart MIME Message Session

```
1   $ telnet localhost 25
2   Trying 127.0.0.1...
3   Connected to localhost.
4   Escape character is '^]'.
5   220 shadrach.ispnet1.net ESMTP
6   HELO localhost
7   250 shadrach.ispnet1.net
8   MAIL FROM:rich@localhost
9   250 ok
10  RCPT TO:rich
11  250 ok
12  DATA
13  354 go ahead
14  From:"Rich Blum" <rich@localhost>
15  To:"rich"<rich@localhost>
16  Subject:Formatted text message test
17  MIME-Version: 1.0
18  Content-Type: multipart/alternative; boundary=bounds1
19
20  --bounds1
21  Content-Type: text/plain; charset=us-ascii
22
23  This is the plain text part of the message that can be read by simple
24  e-mail readers.
25
26  --bounds1
27  Context-Type: text/enriched
28
29  This is the <bold>rich text</bold> version of the <bigger>SAME</bigger>
➥message.
30
31  --bounds1--
32  .
33  250 ok 959882500 qp 84053
34  QUIT
35  221 shadrach.ispnet1.net
36  Connection closed by foreign host.
38  $
```

The sample message shows a two-part MIME message. Line 18 shows the content type definition for the entire message. The `multipart/alternative` type/subtype indicates that there are multiple content types included in this message, separated by the boundary identifier `bounds1`, and that only one of the parts should be presented to the recipient. The first part starts at line 21, and is a simple ASCII plain text message that can be read by virtually any e-mail reader.

The second section starts at line 27 and uses the `text/enriched` type definition. This is an RTF-formatted version of the message. Because the MIME content type specified for the message was `multipart/alternative`, it is up to the discretion of the e-mail reader which content type version of the message to present.

Figure 5.2 shows an example of how a Eudora reader would display the message. Notice how the plain ASCII text part of the message was discarded, and the enriched text part was presented to the reader. In a real e-mail message, both parts would contain the same text message. I purposely made them different to demonstrate which version the e-mail reader would use.

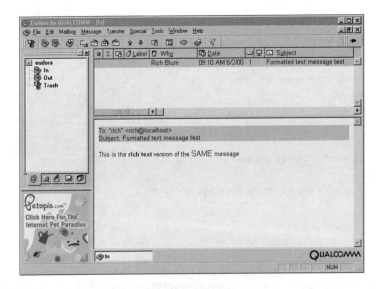

FIGURE 5.2

Using Eudora to read a MIME multipart message.

S/MIME

The MIME extensions have been augmented over the years to add additional functionality. Many RFCs have been proposed, creating new types and subtypes to add features that were not present in the core set of features described in the previous section. One of the new features added to MIME is security.

Secure MIME (S/MIME) was created as a way to allow secure e-mail messages to be sent across the Internet. The standard MIME types only allow for encoding binary data information into ASCII characters before sending the data. The information itself can easily be intercepted and decoded. This does not make for a secure method of communication.

S/MIME attempts to solve this problem by not only encoding the raw data, but also using a security algorithm to encrypt the data. Any plain text message can be encrypted first, and then encoded using a standard MIME encoding technique to convert it to ASCII text. After it is ASCII text, it can be sent via SMTP to a remote recipient. Although the ASCII text can still be decoded back to the binary data, it is much more difficult to decrypt the encrypted information it contains. Remember that encrypted data is not totally secure. Given enough time, someone can decrypt the message.

The following sections describe different methods that have been added to MIME types to incorporate security features.

S/MIME MultiPart Subtype

This method involves adding a subtype to the multipart type. The signed subtype identifies a clear-signed message that contains two parts: the standard message and a digital signature. The digital signature is a method for a person to "sign" a message with a unique digital code. Other people can verify that code with a public key. This method does not encrypt the original message, so e-mail readers without S/MIME capabilities can still read the message.

Of course, the digital signature in the subtype's second section must be encoded to convert it to ASCII text before sending via SMTP. This encoding is usually done with base-64. The receiving e-mail reader must decode the signature section before validating it. An example of a multipart/signed message is shown in Listing 5.4.

LISTING 5.4 Sample Multipart/Signed Message

```
Content-Type: multipart/signed;
        protocol="application/pkcs7-signature";
        micalg=sha1; boundary=boundary42

--boundary42
Content-Type: text/plain

This is a clear-signed message.

--boundary42
```

LISTING 5.4 Continued

```
Content-Type: application/pkcs7-signature; name=smime.p7s
Content-Transfer-Encoding: base64
Content-Disposition: attachment; filename=smime.p7s
```

```
ghyHhHUujhJhjH77n8HHGTrfvbnj756tbB9HG4VQpfyF467GhIGfHfYT6
4VQpfyF467GhIGfHfYT6jH77n8HHGghyHhHUujhJh756tbB9HGTrfvbnj
n8HHGTrfvhJhjH776tbB9HG4VQbnj7567GhIGfHfYT6ghyHhHUujpfyF4
7GhIGfHfYT64VQbnj756
```

```
--boundary42--
```

The main Content-Type header field identifies the message as being multipart/signed. Besides the normal boundary parameter used with multipart messages, two additional parameters are defined. The protocol and micalg parameters define the protocol method used to produce the digital signature. The receiving e-mail reader must use the same protocol to authenticate the digital signature.

CAUTION

Remember that the message in the first section is sent in ASCII text with no encryption. This format allows standard e-mail readers to process the message, but does not protect the original message from a security standpoint. For message protection, you must use an alternative S/MIME function, described in the "S/MIME application Subtypes" section.

S/MIME application Subtypes

The pkcs7-mime application subtype has been created to offer several different security features for e-mail messages. Each feature is identified using a separate parameter within the pkcs7-mime subtype, specified with the tag smime-type. The format for these header fields is as follows:

```
Content-Type: application/pkcs7-mime; smime-type=feature; name=filename
```

The *feature* parameter defines the security feature that the message contains. The *filename* parameter is the name of the file the data should be saved to; for pkcs7-mime files, it should always end in .p7m. Table 5.4 shows the list of security features you can use with the pkcs7-mime subtype.

TABLE 5.4 *pkcs7-mime* Features

Feature	Description
data	Unencrypted message text
encrypted-data	Encrypted message text
signed-data	Unencrypted message text plus a digital signature
enveloped-data	Encrypted message text
signed-and-enveloped-data	Encrypted message text plus an encrypted digital signature
digest-data	Hashed message text used to authenticate the original message

Not all e-mail packages that support S/MIME are required to support all of these features. Only the data, signed-data, and enveloped-data features must claim S/MIME functionality. Packages can add the other features, but that could create some compatibility issues between mailers. The following sections describe these subtypes in more detail.

The data Feature

The data feature is used in other Content-Type sections to indicate that the message content has had security services applied to it. The data contained in the pk7cs-mime section defined with the data feature is not encrypted.

The encrypted-data Feature

The encrypted-data feature is used in other Content-Type sections to indicate that the message content has been encrypted. Data is encrypted by using a public key encryption method. The encrypted data is then encoded using a standard MIME encoding method, such as base-64, to convert it to ASCII text.

The signed-data Feature

The signed-data feature, which is similar to the multipart/signed method, allows the sender to send a digital signature with a plain text message. Unlike the multipart/signed method, however, the application/signed-data method uses public key encryption to both encrypt and sign the original message. The result is then encoded with base-64 to produce ASCII characters that can be sent via SMTP. The receiving e-mail reader must be able to decrypt the message for the recipient to read the message text.

The enveloped-data Feature

The enveloped-data feature is used to provide public key encryption services to messages, but it does not provide authentication services.

The signed-and-enveloped-data Feature

The signed-and-enveloped-data feature combines public key encryption and digital signature services in a message. Again, the receiving e-mail must be able to decrypt the message as well as the digital signature for the recipient to be able to read the text and determine who actually sent the message.

The digest-data Feature

The digest-data feature is used to authenticate the message content sent in the message. When the original message is sent, the sender performs a hash function on the text message along with his digital signature. The hash function determines a value based on a predetermined algorithm run on the data. The result is placed in the digest-data section, which is added to the normal message section. The recipient can then hash the original message with the digital signature and compare the result to the digest-data information. If they match, the recipient can assume that the message is authentic.

NOTE

To encrypt messages and create digital signatures in S/MIME, you must have a valid, unique digital identification key. There are several companies that can provide this key (usually for a fee). For more information about obtaining digital identification keys, you can visit the Verisign Web site at http://www.verisign.com/products/class1/index.html.

Open Source MIME Packages

Most MUA packages can automatically handle MIME messages with no external help. Users who use packages such as Eudora, Netscape Messenger, and Microsoft Outlook can view MIME messages and click on attachments to save them to their hard drives.

In case of problems, the mail administrator has a choice of several open source utilities to manually manipulate MIME messages on the mail server. This section describes two of the more popular Unix MIME-handling utilities: metamail and reformime.

The Metamail Utility

One of the most popular MIME decoder packages in use is the metamail package. Developed by Nathaniel Borenstein while working at BellCore, it has not been updated for a few years, and as such has not kept up with some of the newer MIME types. Still, it often comes standard as a binary distribution on many Unix systems and can be used by the mail administrator when in trouble. The following sections describe metamail in more detail.

Installing Metamail

As mentioned, the metamail package is often found on most Unix distributions. The Red Hat 7.0 Linux system includes a Red Hat package management (RPM) formatted package named metamail-2.7-25.i386.rpm. You can install it using the standard RPM installation utility:

```
rpm -Uvh metamail-2.7-3mdk.i586.rpm
```

Metamail uses a file named mailcap to define how it should handle different MIME content types. Red Hat has also developed a standard mailcap distribution file named mailcap-2.0.9-2.noarch.rpm. It should also be installed, using this command:

```
rpm -Uvh mailcap-2.0.9-2.noarch.rpm
```

If your Unix distribution does not include metamail, at the time of this writing you can still download the source at ftp://thumper.bellcore.com in the directory /pub/nsb. The latest version developed was mm2.7.tar.Z, dated February 18, 1994.

After metamail is installed you can use it to view messages and extract MIME attachments.

Using Metamail

To test metamail, you need a mail message with a binary attachment. You can use the hello program created in Listing 5.1 and any MUA program to send it as an attachment to a user on the local system. When the message is received, you should save it as a text file so that you can use the metamail program. To do that, use the standard Unix mail program. Listing 5.5 shows an example of performing these steps.

LISTING 5.5 Saving a MIME Message to a File

```
$ echo "This is a test message" | mutt -s "Test message"
➥ -a hello rich
[rich@test rich]$mail
Mail version 8.1 6/6/93.  Type ? for help.
"/var/spool/mail/rich": 1 message 1 new
>N  1 rich@test.ispnet.net  Tue Apr 24 15:19 239/16089 "Test message"
& s 1 test.txt
"test.txt" [New file]
& d
& q
$
```

This example uses the common mutt Unix program to send a message that contains the hello program as a binary attachment. The mail program is then used to save the sample message to a file named test.txt. The contents of test.txt include the full RFC 822 message headers and the encoded attachment. Listing 5.6 shows a partial listing of the message.

LISTING 5.6 Partial Listing of the Sample Message

```
From rich@test.ispnet.net  Tue Apr 24 17:19:01 2001
Return-Path: <rich@test.ispnet.net>
Delivered-To: rich@test.ispnet.net
Received: by test.ispnet.net (Postfix, from userid 500)
    id 3430AC352; Tue, 24 Apr 2001 17:18:59 -0500 (EST)
Date: Tue, 24 Apr 2001 17:18:59 -0500
From: Rich Blum <rich@test.ispnet.net>
To: Rich Blum <rich@test.ispnet.net>
Subject: Test message
Message-ID: <20010424151859.A4998@test.ispnet.net>
Mime-Version: 1.0
Content-Type: multipart/mixed; boundary="J2SCkAp4GZ/dPZZf"


--J2SCkAp4GZ/dPZZf
Content-Type: text/plain; charset=us-ascii

This is a test message

--J2SCkAp4GZ/dPZZf
Content-Type: application/octet-stream
Content-Disposition: attachment; filename=hello
Content-Transfer-Encoding: base64

f0VMRgEBAQAAAAAAAAAAAAIAAwABAAAAIIMECDQAAAC4IAAAAAAAADQAIAAGACgAHQAaAAYA
AAAQAAAANIAECDSABAjAAAAwAAAAAUAAAAEAAAAwAAAPQAAAD0gAQI9IAECBMAAAATAAAA
BAAAAAEAAAABAAAAAAAAACABAgAgAQISgQAAEoEAAAFAAAAABAAAAEAAABMBAAATJQECEyU
BAjgAAAA+AAAAAYAAAAEAAAAgAAAIwEAACM1AQIjJQECKAAAACgAAAABgAAAAQAAAAEAAAA
CAEAAAiBBAgIgQQIIAAAACAAAAAEAAAABAAAAC9saWIvGQtbGludXguc28uMgAABAAAABAA
AAABAAAAR05VAAAAAAACAAAAAAAAAAAAAADAAAABwAAAAYAAAADAAAABQAAAAAAAAAAAAAAA
.
.
.
XzIuMABkYXRhX3N0YXJJ0AHByaW50ZkBAR0xJQkNfMi4wwAF9maW5ppAF9lZGF0QBfR0xPQkFM
X09GRlNFVF9UQUUUJMRV8AX2VuZABfSU9fc3RkaW5fdXNlZABfX2RhdGFfc3RhcnQAX19nbW9u
X3N0YXJ0X18A

--J2SCkAp4GZ/dPZZf--
```

The MIME Content-Type header field indicates the multipart MIME type and the mixed subtype, along with the boundary identifier. The first section uses the text/plain content type and contains the text entered in the message body. The second section uses the application/octet-stream content type and contains the base-64–encoded hello program.

To use the metamail program to extract the binary attachment, you'll need to use some command-line options, and the metamail program has lots of them. Table 5.5 lists the options that can be used.

TABLE 5.5 Metamail Command-Line Options

Option	Description
-b	Used when only the body of the message is present
-B	Displays message in the background
-c content-type	Uses the content type specified in content-type rather than the one listed in the header to interpret the data
-d	Does not ask any questions during processing
-e	Disregards leading newline characters in the message body
-E content-encoding	Uses the encoding method specified in content-encoding rather than the one listed in the header to decode the data
-f from-name	Specifies the sender of the address, rather than the one used in the RFC 822 header
-h	Indicates that the output will be printed, and any attachments will not be executed
-m mailer-name	Specifies the name of the mail program that called metamail
-p	Shows output one page at a time
-P	Shows output one page at a time, and waits for a RETURN character from the user at the end of the display
-q	Specifies that no output should be displayed
-r	Allows metamail to be run as root
-R	Resets the terminal before starting to display text
-s subject	Specifies the subject of the mail message instead of using the one in the RFC 822 header
-w	Writes attachments directly to files using raw binary mode
-x	Specifies that metamail is not running on a terminal
-y	Attempts to "yank" a MIME message from a misformatted message
-z	Deletes the input file when finished

In its simplest form, you can use metamail with no command-line options. If you do, metamail automatically detects any attachments that must be extracted and queries you for how to handle them one by one. Listing 5.7 demonstrates using the metamail program with the sample saved message.

LISTING 5.7 Using Metamail

```
$ metamail test.txt
Date: Tue, 24 Apr 2001 17:18:59 -0500
From: Rich Blum <rich@test.ispnet.net>
To: Rich Blum <rich@test.ispnet.net>
Subject: Test message

This is a test message


This message contains raw digital data, which can either be viewed as text
or written to a file.

What do you want to do with the raw data?
1 -- See it as text
2 -- Write it to a file
3 -- Just skip it

2
Please enter the name of a file to which the data should be written
(Default: /tmp/mm.UuEKQ7) > hello
Wrote file hello
$ chmod 700 hello
$ ./hello
Hello, World
$
```

When metamail was run, it displayed the text portion of the message. Next, it determined that there was an attachment of raw binary data and queried the user as to how to handle it. In this example, the binary data was written to a separate file. The file was then converted to an executable file using the standard Unix chmod program and adding the executable permissions, and the hello program was successfully run.

The Reformime Utility

The Courier MTA package, developed by the Inter7 Corporation, contains several utility packages that are also distributed separately (http://www.courier-mta.org). One of those packages is the Maildrop package. The maildrop program is used as an MDA to parse messages for local users and deliver them as directed by a user-configurable file.

One component of the Maildrop package is the reformime program, which is used by maildrop to extract MIME attachments to e-mail messages. The reformime program can also be used by itself to decode MIME messages and extract attachments.

Installing Reformime

As mentioned, reformime is included in the Maildrop package, which can be downloaded from the Courier download Web site (`http://www.courier-mta.org/download.php`). At the time of this writing, this is the link for downloading the current maildrop package:

```
http://download.sourceforge.net/courier/maildrop-1.3.1.tar.gz
```

After it's downloaded, extract the Maildrop package into a working directory and compile it using the following commands:

```
tar -zxvf maildrop-1.3.1.tar.gz -C /usr/local/src
cd /usr/local/src/maildrop-1.3.1
./configure
make
```

CAUTION

The Maildrop package uses both C and C++ code for its modules. You should ensure that you have the proper C++ executables and libraries installed for your compiler. On my Mandrake Linux system I had to install RPM packages `gcc-c++-2.95.2-4mdk`, `libstdc++-2.95.2-4mdk`, and `libstdc++-compat-2.95.2-4mdk`.

If you do not want to install the complete Maildrop package, you can copy just the reformime executable to a location that will make it accessible to whoever needs to use it:

```
cp /usr/local/src/maildrop-1.3.1/rfc2045/reformime /usr/local/bin
```

Using Reformime

The reformime program reads a standard MIME message as standard input, and manipulates the message based on command-line options. Table 5.6 lists the available options that can be used.

TABLE 5.6 Reformime Command-Line Options

Option	Description
-d	Parse a Delivery Status Notification (DSN) message.
-D	Same as -d, but lists the original recipient address.
-e	Displays the contents of a particular MIME section. It must be used with the -s option.
-x	Extracts the contents of the indicated MIME section to a file.
-X	Pipes the contents of the indicated MIME section to a program
-i	Displays the MIME information for each section.
-s section	Displays the MIME information for the section specified in section.
-r	Rewrites the message using standard MIME headers.
-r7	Converts MIME sections with 8-bit encoding to quoted printable encoding.
-r8	Converts MIME sections with quoted printable encoding to 8-bit encoding.
-m file1 file2	Creates a MIME message digest from file1 and file2.

To test reformime, you must have a MIME–formatted message handy. If you have been following along in the chapter, you can use the one created in Listing 5.5 and saved as file test.txt. If not, refer back to that listing and create the test.txt file.

In its most basic form, reformime lists the separate sections it finds in a MIME message:

```
$ cat test.txt | reformime
1
1.1
1.2
$
```

Remember that reformime reads the message from standard input, so you must use the Unix cat command and pipe the output to the reformime package.

The output generated by reformime lists the MIME sections it found. The output from the preceding example shows that one MIME message was found with two separate sections though this information is not too helpful. To get more information, use the -i option, as shown in Listing 5.8.

LISTING 5.8 Sample Reformime Output

```
$ cat test.txt | reformime -i
section: 1
content-type: multipart/mixed
```

LISTING 5.8 Continued

```
content-name:
content-transfer-encoding: 8bit
charset: us-ascii
starting-pos: 0
starting-pos-body: 577
ending-pos: 16099
line-count: 240
body-line-count: 224

section: 1.1
content-type: text/plain
content-name:
content-transfer-encoding: 8bit
charset: us-ascii
starting-pos: 597
starting-pos-body: 641
ending-pos: 664
line-count: 3
body-line-count: 1

section: 1.2
content-type: application/octet-stream
content-name:
content-transfer-encoding: base64
charset: us-ascii
content-disposition: attachment
content-disposition-filename: hello
starting-pos: 684
starting-pos-body: 806
ending-pos: 16076
line-count: 214
body-line-count: 210

$
```

This information is more useful. It shows that there is indeed one MIME message of type multipart/mixed. The first section is of type text/plain, and the second section is of type application/octet-stream. If you want to extract the attachment, you can use the -x option:

```
$ cat test.txt | reformime -x
Extract text/plain? y
```

```
Filename [988218546.11645-0.test.ispnet.net]: test
Extract application/octet-stream? y
Filename [hello]:
$ chmod 700 hello
$ ./hello
Hello, World
$
```

When the -x option is used, reformime queries you for each MIME section. If you want to save the section to a file, you must either accept the default value supplied by reformime, or enter the one you want to use. As you can see in the example, reformime properly extracted the hello program from the MIME e-mail message.

MIME with PGP

Besides the standard defined S/MIME types, many e-mail packages include external security features with standard RFC 822–formatted messages. One commonly used security package for e-mail messages is the Pretty Good Privacy (PGP) package created by Phil Zimmermann.

The PGP package was created to provide both signing and encrypting of files using a variety of standard security algorithms. The PGP package uses a standard public/private key combination to allow a user to sign a file with a private key, and enable a remote user to authenticate the file with the public key. When users encrypt files, it is done with the recipients' public keys so that only the intended recipients can decrypt the file with their private keys.

The PGP package has been released as freeware for noncommercial users, but commercial users must pay a license fee. Because of this fee, many MUA packages do not include PGP support. To use PGP support, the user must encrypt the message separately before sending it in the e-mail message. After the message has been encrypted, the PGP software can also encode it to a base-64–encoded ASCII file so that it can be sent directly in an e-mail message.

The following sections describe the PGP package in more detail.

Installing PGP

There are many different distributions of the PGP software. The PGP Corporation (http://www.pgp.com/) offers free versions of the PGP software for noncommercial users on both Microsoft Windows and Apple Macintosh platforms. This might not be too much of an inconvenience, though, as most messages are composed on the user's workstation, which is usually either Windows or Macintosh.

Alternatively, you can download the PGP files from several different sites, and either compile them on your Unix system or install the binary distribution on your Windows or Macintosh computer. Here's one site that offers the PGP binary executable software for Microsoft Windows:

```
ftp://ftp.csua.berkeley.edu/pub/cypherpunks/pgp/pgp262/pgp262.zip
```

After it's downloaded, you must extract the files into a working directory using the pkunzip program.

Using PGP to Encrypt Messages

Before a message can be encrypted or signed, you must first create your own unique digital signature (called a *key pair*). There are two parts of the digital signature: the private key and the public key.

The *private key* is what PGP uses to digitally encrypt your messages and decrypt messages sent to you from other PGP users. You must never release your private key to another individual, or your digital signature could become forged. The *public key* is what is released to other people so they can authenticate your digital signature and send you encrypted messages.

Each person must maintain a *keyring* that contains the public key of each individual they might send encrypted messages to or receive signed messages from. This is where the PGP method becomes complicated.

You must possess a public key for each person you want to securely interact with. In large organizations, however, this can become quite complicated, especially in companies with high employee turnover. You can easily see why the S/MIME method of authentication uses centralized commercial digital signature authenticators to simplify the process.

To create your own private/public key pair, you can use the pgp command with the -kg option:

```
pgp -kg
```

The PGP program queries you for a user ID and a secret pass phrase to create your digital keys. The user ID identifies who you are to other individuals. Usually e-mail addresses are used to create a unique identification. You must remember your secret pass phrase to be able to sign and encrypt future messages.

To extract your public key to send to others, you use the -kx option. To extract it in ASCII mode for mailing, you must also use the -a option:

```
pgp -kxa username
```

The *username* parameter is the user ID you selected for yourself when you created your key. The resulting text can be sent to any other user who might need to authenticate messages sent from you or needs to send you an encrypted message. Listing 5.9 shows a sample public key file.

LISTING 5.9 Sample Public Key File

```
-----BEGIN PGP PUBLIC KEY BLOCK-----
Version: 2.6.2

mQBtAzrlrpgAAAEDAL324EGxQeAnR/qxqSgW3xojmYjM7ak17oEy7vdZRoRFJ/IC
zeMM+ZS43QeNVGdP5NJAmmKBtAK6/VoEKlF8BNMYsze8q0183KneILH15QMut81M
nuu+2GnYQ9LrPNZD5QAFEbQEcmljaA==
=gePp
-----END PGP PUBLIC KEY BLOCK-----
```

After a public/private key combination is created, you can begin signing messages with your digital signature. The -s option is used to sign a text file containing the message. Again, to make the resulting message ASCII text for mailing, include the -a option:

```
pgp -sa message.txt
```

The PGP program queries you for your secret pass phrase to verify that it is really you who's signing the message. After you are authenticated, it produces a separate file containing both the original message and digital signature.

When encrypting messages to send to others, you must use the recipient's public key, not your private key, to encrypt the message. This method enables only the recipients to decrypt the message using their private key. You can specify multiple recipients when encrypting the message. To encrypt a message with another user's public key, use this format:

```
pgp -ea file user1 [, user2, ...]
```

The *file* parameter is the file to encrypt, and *user1* is the recipient's PGP user ID. You can also sign an encrypted file, using your key to sign it and the recipients' keys to encrypt it:

```
pgp -esa file user1 [, user2, ...]
```

After the signed and encrypted file is created, it can be e-mailed to recipients using a standard mail package.

Using PGP to Decrypt Messages

To authenticate signed messages you must possess the sender's public key. Usually senders identify their public keys as an ASCII text string, as shown in Listing 5.9. After you have that information, add it to your keyring so that PGP can recognize it.

To add new public keys to your keyring, use the `-ka` option as shown here:

```
pgp -ka katie.asc
```

This command adds Katie's public key stored in the text file katie.asc to your keyring. After her key is added, you can properly decrypt and authenticate messages sent from her.

The format for decrypting and/or authenticating messages is simple:

```
pgp filename
```

The `filename` is the name of the file the message has been saved to. If the message was signed, the PGP program determines the source of the message and uses the appropriate key in the keyring. After authenticating the sender's key, PGP informs you who it came from. If the sender encrypted the message using your public key, PGP decrypts the message using your private key. Before decrypting the file, PGP queries you for your secret pass phrase to make sure it is really you who's requesting to decrypt the file.

Summary

Sending binary data via SMTP can be a complicated process. There are currently two popular methods for doing this. The oldest method is the uuencode program. It converts binary data into an ASCII text file, which can be sent via SMTP to a remote mail server. The message recipient can use the uudecode program to convert the message back into a binary file.

Alternatively, the MIME protocol can be used to convert and tag binary data before sending it to a remote mail server. MIME-formatted messages contain separate sections that encapsulate the different types of data sent. Plain text data can be enclosed with no encoding. Binary data, such as pictures and executable files, can be encoded with base-64 encoding and attached as separate sections. A MIME header field identifies each section so that the receiving mail server can decode the sections.

The S/MIME format adds security functions to the standard MIME message format. Additional MIME header types are used to identify signed messages as well as encrypted messages. Message encryption is done using commercial digital keys. The receiving mail server must be able to identify the digital key used to encrypt the message.

An alternative to using S/MIME is the use of external encryption software. The Pretty Good Privacy (PGP) program offers a way for users to encrypt and sign messages before mailing them. The recipient must have the sender's digital key to be able to properly authenticate and/or decrypt the message.

CHAPTER 6

Reading E-mail Headers

Possibly one of the most important jobs you have as a mail administrator is to be able to track e-mail messages received by your users. Often users receive messages that they have questions about, either because a message was delivered with a delay ("I should have received this message yesterday"), or because it came from a sender the user doesn't know ("I've been spammed"). It is your job as the mail administrator to be able to track down the origin of the message, how it was transported to your e-mail server, and what servers handled the message as it made its way across the Internet to your mail server.

These days it is not always easy to track down e-mail messages. Spammers use sophisticated methods of hiding their true identities in the e-mail message header. This chapter describes a few techniques the mail administrator can use to read e-mail headers and track down the origin and path of e-mail messages.

Decoding Forged E-mail Headers

One of the biggest problems in tracking e-mail messages is dealing with forged e-mail headers. There are many commercial spam packages that help marketing professionals send thousands of forged e-mail messages to unsuspecting customers (victims).

The first step in tracking down e-mail messages is to decode the standard e-mail headers that are part of the message and attempt to separate the true information from the forged information. Although the message headers might contain forged data, the mail administrator can still extract and use some valuable information. The following sections describe how to extract this information.

The To: Header Field

One of the most confusing parts of a spam message for users is the RFC 822 To: header field. By strict RFC 822 rules, the   : and From: headers should represent the e-mail address of the message recipient and sender, as shown here:

```
To: rich@ispnet.net
From: barbara@schoolnet.net
```

However, this is often not the case with spam mail. Both the To: and the From: headers can be forged.

You might be wondering how this could be possible. It's easy to see that the From: header field could be forged, but if the To: header field is wrong, the message would not get delivered to the intended recipient. However, this is not true.

Chapter 2, "SMTP," described in detail the SMTP commands used to send mail via the Internet. These commands control how the message is sent from the client e-mail server to a remote host e-mail server. The RCPT command is used to inform the remote e-mail server to whom the message should be delivered. The e-mail server uses this information, not the To: header field, to deliver the message.

In a normal e-mail situation, the sender creates a message with the proper To: field(s) for the intended recipient(s). The local Mail Transfer Agent (MTA) program then uses this information to create the proper SMTP RCPT command(s) to identify the recipient(s) to the remote mail server. In a normal mail message, these values are the same.

However, for spam messages, the spammer uses software that forges the To: header field in the message and uses the proper recipient addresses in either Bcc: fields or the SMTP RCPT commands. By forging the To: header field, the spammer can mass-mail the same message to thousands of customers.

The trick is not that the To: header field is forged, but that the message is not sent using a standard MTA program. Instead, the spammer uses a special MTA program that reads a list of the intended customer addresses and uses them in the Bcc: fields or the SMTP RCPT command instead of the normal To: header field values. This technique delivers the forged mail message to the proper e-mail addresses, even though the message header fields are incorrect.

You can test this method yourself by using telnet on TCP port 25 on your local mail server and creating a forged e-mail session. Listing 6.1 shows an example of how to do this.

LISTING 6.1 Sample Forged To: Header Field

```
[rich@test rich]$ telnet localhost 25
Trying 127.0.0.1...
Connected to localhost.
Escape character is '^]'.
220 test.ispnet.net ESMTP Postfix
EHLO dude
250-test.ispnet.net
250-PIPELINING
250-SIZE 10240000
250-ETRN
250 8BITMIME
MAIL FROM: <badguy@nowhere.net>
250 Ok
RCPT TO: <rich@ispnet.net>
250 Ok
DATA
```

LISTING 6.1 Continued

```
354 End data with <CR><LF>.<CR><LF>
From: badguy@nowhere.net
To: phonyuser@yourplace.com
Subject: This is a forged message

This is a test of a forged To: header message.
This is the end of the message test.

.
250 Ok: queued as 03792C36A
QUIT
221 Bye
Connection closed by foreign host.
[rich@test rich]$ mail
Mail version 8.1 6/6/93.  Type ? for help.
"/var/spool/mail/rich": 1 message 1 new
>N  1 badguy@nowhere.net  Tue May  1 11:19  16/599 "This is a forged mess"
&
Message 1:
From badguy@nowhere.net  Tue May  1 11:19:29 2001
Delivered-To: rich@test.ispnet.net
From: badguy@nowhere.net
To: phonyuser@yourplace.com
Subject: This is a forged message
Date: Tue,  1 May 2001 19:18:46 -0500 (EST)

This is a test of a forged To: header message.
This is the end of the message test.

&
```

This sample SMTP session uses the correct recipient address in the RCPT command. When the DATA command is entered, the message text is sent to the remote e-mail server as a single block of data, containing both the RFC 822 header fields and the message body. Because the header fields are considered part of the message, the MTA program on the receiving e-mail server does not attempt to verify the addresses in the To: header field. Anything can be placed in that field by the sending MTA program. As shown in this example, the receiving MTA program delivered the message to the user as addressed in the RCPT command and ignored the value used in the To: message header field.

This explains why most spam messages contain forged To: header fields, but are delivered by the MTA program anyway. Remember that almost all spam messages also forge the From: header field, hiding where the message originated. The next section describes how you can still use information in the message header to help track down the origin of a message.

The Received: Header Field

Spammers seldom send messages directly to their victims. Instead, they usually use intermediate e-mail servers, often unsuspecting, as go-betweens in the e-mail process. This tactic helps make the e-mail headers more complex so that normal recipients can't figure out how to track them down. Figure 6.1 shows how forwarding e-mail messages off another e-mail server works.

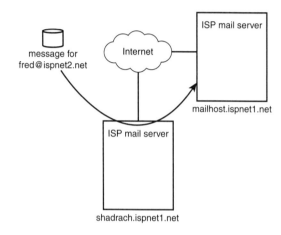

FIGURE 6.1

Bouncing e-mail messages off an intermediate server.

The spammer's mail server relies on remote mail servers that support *open relaying*. This feature allows a mail server to forward a message that it receives for a recipient on another mail server.

NOTE

Chapter 11, "Preventing Open Relays," describes how to prevent your mail server from being abused as an open mail relay server.

As each e-mail server in the e-mail path receives messages via SMTP, it adds an RFC 822 Received: header field to the message before passing it along. This allows you to track the path the e-mail message took by examining the Received: header fields contained in the received message.

This is the format of the `Received:` header field:

```
Received:
    from host name
    by host name
    via physical-path
    with protocol
    id message-id
    for final e-mail destination
```

Table 6.1 describes the various parameters in the `Received:` header field.

TABLE 6.1 `Received:` Header Field Parameters

Parameter	Description
from host_name	The host that sent the message
by host_name	The host that received the message
via physical_path	How the message was sent
with protocol	What protocol the message was sent using
id message-id	A unique message ID from the receiver
for final_e-mail_destination	The recipient's e-mail address

Each e-mail server that passes the message along the path to the destination server adds a `Received:` header field. This process creates multiple `Received:` header fields for a single message. Each receiving e-mail server adds its `Received:` field to the top of the message. Therefore, to track the path of the message, you must read the `Received:` fields from the bottom up.

First, take a look at a normal e-mail message. Listing 6.2 shows an example of a message header from a normal message I recently sent to an Internet e-mail account. You should be able to follow the `Received:` header fields to see where the message originated.

LISTING 6.2 Sample Message Showing `Received:` Fields

```
Return-Path: <xxxxx@juno.com>
Received: from m8.boston.juno.com (sourcenat1.bigmailbox.com
➥ [209.132.220.250])
    by mailrecv5.bigmailbox.com (8.10.0/8.10.0) with ESMTP id f3TKmZl06274
    for <xxxxx@my-deja.com> ; Sun, 29 Apr 2001 13:48:35 -0700
Received: from cookie.juno.com by cookie.juno.com for
<"u3y6yWLwCx8wc9ilpwKBmA+Cfy20HkUFCY/b+AyjpzoE730TvIoqlA==">
Received: (from xxxxx@juno.com)
  by m8.boston.juno.com (queuemail) id F38KV5; Sun, 29 Apr 2001 16:47:59 EDT
```

LISTING 6.2 Continued

```
To: xxxx@my-deja.com
Date: Sun, 29 Apr 2001 15:51:57 -0500
Subject: Test message
Message-ID: <20010429.155159.-462747.0.xxxxx@juno.com>
X-Mailer: Juno 4.0.11
MIME-Version: 1.0
Content-Type: text/plain
Content-Transfer-Encoding: 7bit
X-Juno-Att: 0
X-Juno-RefParts: 0
From: Richard Blum <xxxxx@juno.com>
```

This simple example generated three separate `Received:` header fields. To track the path of the e-mail message, you must read them from the bottom up, starting with the first one:

```
Received: (from xxxxx@juno.com)
 by m8.boston.juno.com (queuemail) id F38KV5; Sun, 29 Apr 2001 16:47:59 EDT
```

The first `Received:` field was generated by my ISP as it received the message from my home workstation. It identified the user address it received the message from using the `from` parameter (the actual username has been replaced with `xxxxx` to help minimize getting any more spam than I already get). It also identified itself by using the `by` parameter and a unique message ID by using the `id` parameter. Note that the time the ISP received the message was also placed in the `Received:` field.

The following `Received:` header field identifies the next stop on the message path:

```
Received: from cookie.juno.com by cookie.juno.com for
 <"u3y6yWLwCx8wc9ilpwKBmA+Cfy20HkUFCY/b+AyjpzoE730TvIoqlA==">
```

This example probably doesn't look too exciting because the `from` and `by` hostnames are identical (`cookie.juno.com`). This information documents that the message was passed from one interface on a mail server to another interface on the same server. You often see this configuration in messages that have passed through firewalls or internal e-mail relay servers (the latter being the situation here).

The last `Received:` header field identifies the final destination mail host:

```
Received: from m8.boston.juno.com (sourcenat1.bigmailbox.com
➥ [209.132.220.250])
    by mailrecv5.bigmailbox.com (8.10.0/8.10.0) with ESMTP id f3TKmZl06274
    for <xxxxx@my-deja.com> ; Sun, 29 Apr 2001 13:48:35 -0700
```

Notice that it not only documents the hostname of the original e-mail server it received the message from (`m8.boston.juno.com`), but it also supplies the hostname and IP address (sourcenat1.bigmailbox.com and 209.132.220.250) of an internal firewall that received the incoming message. This information can help if the sending host is not using its correct hostname in the SMTP session commands. Again, note the timestamp on the Received: header field. It indicates the time the e-mail server received the message from the sending e-mail server. Also notice that extended SMTP (ESMTP) was the agreed on delivery protocol used for the message at this final step.

When a customer complains about receiving an e-mail message late, you can determine which server was at fault by observing the timestamps on the Received: header fields. Each Received: header field contains a timestamp placed by the mail server when it receives the message. Often, as in this example, you must first convert the times from the different Received: field time zones into a standard format to properly compare them. There is no standard method used by all e-mail servers to identify the time the message was received.

With all this information, you can see the whole picture. The e-mail message originated from a user on a juno.com mail server (m8.boston.juno.com), was passed through an internal mail server at Juno (cookie.juno.com), and then was delivered to a mail server that accepts messages for the my-deja.com domain (mailrecv5.bigmailbox.com).

Now that you have seen an example of a normal e-mail message, it is time to look at an example of a spam message. Listing 6.3 shows a sample spam message received on one of my Internet e-mail accounts.

LISTING 6.3 Sample Spam Message Header Fields

```
Return-Path: <alfki@miesto.sk>
Received: from moon1.kimo.com.tw (sourcenat1.bigmailbox.com
➥ [209.132.220.250])
   by mailrecv22.bigmailbox.com (8.10.0/8.10.0) with ESMTP id f3L9Eex32005;
   Sat, 21 Apr 2001 02:14:41 -0700
Received: from netposta.net ([208.187.10.89]) by
        moon1.kimo.com.tw (Netscape Messaging Server 4.15) with SMTP id
        GC3CG500.F3W; Fri, 20 Apr 2001 20:38:29 +0800
Message-ID: <00000ad359dd$00003352$000076da@netposta.net>
To: <173@artic.net>
From: alfki@miesto.sk
Subject: FW:
Date: Thu, 19 Apr 2001 18:52:52 -0800
MIME-Version: 1.0
Content-Type: text/html;
    charset="iso-8859-1"
Content-Transfer-Encoding: quoted-printable
X-Priority: 3
X-MSMail-Priority: Normal
Attachments: msg1.html
```

As discussed in the previous section, the first thing you should notice is the forged To: in this message. The e-mail account this message was received on was not on artic.net, nor was the username 173. This is the first indication that you are looking at a spam message. You can trace the path this message took by examining the Received: header fields.

The top Received: field, shown in the following line, indicates that the message was passed by moon1.kimo.com.tw (again received through the firewall sourcenat1.bigmailbox.com, which has the IP address 209.132.220.250) to mailrecv22.big-mailbox.com, the destination mail server:

```
Received: from moon1.kimo.com.tw (sourcenat1.bigmailbox.com
➡ [209.132.220.250])
    by mailrecv22.bigmailbox.com (8.10.0/8.10.0) with ESMTP id f3L9Eex32005;
    Sat, 21 Apr 2001 02:14:41 -0700
```

Next you need to determine where moon1.kimo.com.tw received the message from. The next Received: field indicates that the message was sent to the moon1.kimo.com.tw mail server from the netposta.net (IP address 208.187.10.89) mail server, as shown here:

```
Received: from netposta.net ([208.187.10.89]) by
        moon1.kimo.com.tw (Netscape Messaging Server 4.15) with SMTP id
        GC3CG500.F3W; Fri, 20 Apr 2001 20:38:29 +0800
```

This line indicates that the moon1.kimo.com.tw server was used (possibly without its knowledge) as a relay mail server for the spam message.

The true culprit in this spam message was the netposta.net mail server. Armed with this information, you can begin hunting for information about this domain.

The Message-ID: Header Field

Sometimes you do not need to trace the Received: header fields back to find the source of the e-mail. Often you can identify the origin of a message by examining the RFC 822 Message-ID: header field. This field, generated by the originating e-mail host, usually contains the server's hostname. You can see that the Message-ID: field used in the e-mail message header in Listing 6.2 contains the sender's proper domain name:

```
Message-ID: <20010429.155159.-462747.0.xxxxx@juno.com>
```

In this case, the Message-ID: field shows not only the hostname, but also the sender's username (replaced with xxxxx). This is an ideal situation, as you can track the message down to a specific username on a specific mail server. You will find that most spam you receive doesn't contain this much information (otherwise your job would be too easy, wouldn't it?).

It is still possible to use some of the information in the Message-ID: field. In the spam message example in Listing 6.3, this field might not show the originating username, but at least it gives a clue as to the originating mail server:

```
Message-ID: <00000ad359dd$00003352$000076da@netposta.net>
```

The mail domain listed in the Message-ID: field indicates that the message originated in the netposta.net domain. After you have the mail domain, you can try to find the responsible mail server for that domain. Most likely the message originated from a user on that mail server.

The next section describes some Unix open source programs that are available to help you find DNS information for domains and hosts.

Using DNS Programs to Track E-mail Hosts

When you know the domain that the offending spam message came from, you can use several different open source programs to find information about the spammer, or at least his Internet service provider (ISP). Often, if enough people complain to an ISP about a spammer, the ISP will remove the spammer from its site.

The following sections describe three open source tools normally found on Unix systems that can be used to help the mail administrator gain information about a spammer.

The Whois Program

The whois program can be used to find information about registered Internet networks. It contacts various Network Information Centers (NICs) to retrieve registered information about the requested network address. The format of the whois command looks like this:

```
whois [-adgimpQrR6] [-h host] name ...
```

Table 6.2 lists the command-line parameters available for the whois command.

TABLE 6.2 Whois Command-Line Parameters

Parameter	Description
-a	Uses the American Registry for Internet Numbers (ARIN) database for .com, .net, and .org networks
-d	Uses the U.S. Department of Defense database for .mil networks
-g	Uses the U.S. nonmilitary government database for .gov networks
-i	Uses the Network Solutions Registry for Internet Numbers database
-m	Uses the Route Arbitrator Database (RAD)
-p	Uses the Asia/Pacific Network Information Center (APNIC) database
-Q	Does a quick lookup
-r	Uses the Réseaux IP Européens (RIPE) database for European information

TABLE 6.2 Continued

Parameter	Description
-R	Uses the Russia Network Information Center (RNIC) database for .ru networks
-6	Uses the IPv6 Resource Center (6bone) database for IPv6 networks
-h host	Uses the host database specified by *host* to find the information

You can use the spammer netposta.net as an example for the whois command, shown in Listing 6.4.

LISTING 6.4 Sample whois Session

```
$ whois netposta.net

Whois Server Version 1.3

Domain names in the .com, .net, and .org domains can now be registered
with many different competing registrars. Go to http://www.internic.net
for detailed information.

   Domain Name: NETPOSTA.NET
   Registrar: NETWORK SOLUTIONS, INC.
   Whois Server: whois.networksolutions.com
   Referral URL: http://www.networksolutions.com
   Name Server: NS.TELNET.HU
   Name Server: NS.TOLNA.NET
   Updated Date: 01-mar-2001


>>> Last update of whois database: Thu, 3 May 2001 09:08:52 EDT <<<

The Registry database contains ONLY .COM, .NET, .ORG, .EDU domains and
Registrars.

$
```

The whois query returned some information on the netposta.net domain. It shows that it was registered on the Internet by Network Solutions, Inc., and lists the two name servers that service this domain. You can continue using the whois command on these servers to determine where the domain is located and possibly who operates it.

The Nslookup Program

The nslookup program is an extremely versatile tool that can also be used to get network information from a spam message. You can run nslookup under two modes. In non-interactive mode, it behaves much like the whois command discussed previously, supplying network information for a specific hostname. The interactive mode is where you find all the fun. This mode can give you more detailed information about remote computers and domains because you can change options as you traverse the DNS database. The basic format of the nslookup command is as follows:

```
nslookup [-option ...] [host-to-find | -[server]]
```

If you enter the *host-to-find* parameter on the command line, nslookup operates in non-interactive mode and returns the result of the query. If no arguments are given, or the first argument is a hyphen (·), nslookup enters interactive mode. If you want to use a different DNS server, you can specify that by using the -server argument; server is the IP address of the DNS server to use. Otherwise, nslookup uses the default DNS server. Unix systems define the default DNS server in the resolv.conf text file, which is normally located in the /etc directory.

There are three ways to change option settings in the nslookup program. One way is to list them as options in the nslookup command line. Another way is to specify them by using the set command on the interactive command line when nslookup starts. The third way is to create a file in your $HOME directory named .nslookuprc, with the options entered one option per line. A list of available options is shown in Table 6.3.

TABLE 6.3 Nslookup Options

Option	Description
all	Prints current values of options
class	Sets the DNS class value (default = IN)
debug/nodebug	Turns debugging mode on (or off) (default = nodebug)
d2/nod2	Turns exhaustive debugging mode on (or off) (default = nod2)
domain=name	Sets the default domain name to name
srchlist=name1/name2...	Changes the default domain name to name1 and the search list to name1, name2, and so on
defname/nodefname	Appends the default domain name to a single component lookup request (default = defname)
search/nosearch	Appends the domain names in the search list to the hostname (default = search)
port=value	Changes the TCP/UDP port to the port specified by *value* (default = 53)
querytype=value	Changes the type of information requested to the type specified by *value* (default = A)
type=value	Same as querytype

TABLE 6.3 Continued

Option	Description
recurse/norecurse	Tells the name server to query other servers to find an answer (default = recurse)
retry=number	Sets the number of retries to what's specified by *number* (default = 4)
root=host	Changes the name of root server to what's specified by *host* (default = ns.internic.net)
timeout=number	Changes the initial timeout interval to wait for a reply to the time specified by *number* (default = 5 seconds)
vc/novc	Always uses a virtual circuit (default = novc)
ignoretc/noignoretc	Ignores packet truncation errors (default = noignoretc)

Listing 6.5 shows a sample nslookup session used to get information for the netposta.net domain. By using the interactive mode and setting the query's querytype option to any, all the available network information for the domain name is returned.

LISTING 6.5 Sample Nslookup Session

```
$ nslookup
Default Server:  dns.ispnet.net
Address:  10.0.0.1

> set querytype=any
> netposta.net
Server:  dns.ispnet.net
Address:  10.0.0.1

Non-authoritative answer:
netposta.net    nameserver = ns.telnet.hu
netposta.net    nameserver = dns.telnet.hu
netposta.net    preference = 20, mail exchanger = booster.telnet.hu
netposta.net    preference = 10, mail exchanger = mx1.netposta.net
netposta.net    internet address = 212.75.128.65

Authoritative answers can be found from:
netposta.net    nameserver = ns.telnet.hu
netposta.net    nameserver = dns.telnet.hu
ns.telnet.hu    internet address = 212.75.128.43
dns.telnet.hu   internet address = 195.70.46.3
booster.telnet.hu       internet address = 212.75.128.38
mx1.netposta.net        internet address = 212.75.128.65
>
```

This example shows the results of using the nslookup program's any query type for the netposta.net domain. The information returned lists the mail servers, name servers, and IP addresses for the domain. One thing that appears obvious from this listing is that many of the hosts are in the .hu domain, indicating that the netposta.net domain most likely originates in Hungary.

If you want to extend this example, you could change the default DNS server to one of the authoritative DNS servers listed (by using the server command) and retry the query to see whether any additional information appears from the authoritative DNS server for the domain.

The Dig Program

The dig program uses a simple command-line format to query DNS servers for domain information. The format for the dig command is as follows:

```
dig [@server] domain [query-type] [query-class] [+query-option]
➥ [-dig-option] [%comment]
```

The *server* parameter is an optional DNS server you can specify. By default, dig uses the DNS server defined in the /etc/resolv.conf file. You can specify the *server* option by using an IP address in numeric dot notation or as a hostname. If you use a hostname for the *server* option, dig uses the default DNS server to resolve the hostname, and then uses that DNS server to find the information on the domain.

The *query-type* parameter is the DNS resource record (RR) type information you are requesting:

- A—Internet address
- SOA—Start of authority
- NS—Name server
- MX—Mail server

You can use a *query-type* of any to return all information available about a domain.

The *query-class* parameter is the network class of information you are requesting. The default value is Internet (IN), which is the type of information you are looking for in these examples.

The *+query-option* parameter is used to change an option value in the DNS packet or to change the format of the dig output. Many of these options mirror options available in the nslookup program. Table 6.4 shows the available query options.

TABLE 6.4 Dig Query Options

Option	Description
debug/nodebug	Turns debugging on or off (default = debug)
d2/nod2	Turns extra debugging on or off (default = nod2)
recurse/norecurse	Specifies whether recursive lookups are used (default = recurse)
retry=#	Sets number of retries
time=#	Sets timeout length
ko/noko	Keeps option list open (implies virtual circuit) (default = noko)
vc/novc	Specifies whether virtual circuits are used (default = novc)
defname/nodefname	Indicates whether default domain names are used (default = defname)
search/nosearch	Determines whether domain search lists are used (default = search)
domain=NAME	Sets the default domain name to what's specified in NAME
ignore/noignore	Determines whether truncation errors are ignored (default = noignore)
primary/noprimary	Specifies whether primary servers are used (default = noprimary)
aaonly/noaaonly	Sets an authoritative query only flag (default = noaaonly)
cmd/nocmd	Echoes parsed arguments (default = cmd)
stats/nostats	Prints query statistics (default = stats)
Header/noHeader	Prints basic header (default = Header)
header/noheader	Prints header flags (default = header)
ttlid/nottlid	Prints time-to-lives (TTLs) (default = ttlid)
cl/nocl	Prints class info (default = nocl)
qr/noqr	Prints outgoing query (default = noqr)
reply/noreply	Prints reply (default = reply)
ques/noques	Prints question section (default = ques)
answer/noanswer	Prints answer section (default = answer)
author/noauthor	Prints authoritative section (default = author)
addit/noaddit	Prints additional section (default = addit)
pfdef	Sets to default print flags
pfmin	Sets to minimal print flags
pfset=#	Sets print flags to the number specified by #
pfand=#	Bitwise combine # AND print flags
pfor=#	Bitwise combine # OR print flags

The *-dig-option* parameter is used to specify other options that affect the operation of dig. Table 6.5 shows some of the other options available to fine-tune the dig command and its output.

TABLE 6.5 Options for the -dig-option Parameter

Option	Description
-x	Specifies inverse address mapping in normal dot notation
-f	Reads a file for batch mode processing
-T	Time in seconds between batch mode command processing
-p	Port number to use
-P	After a response, issues a ping command
-t	Specifies type of query
-c	Specifies class of query
-envsav	Specifies that the dig options should be saved to become the default dig environment

A sample dig session output is shown in Listing 6.6. As you can see, the dig command produces the same information as nslookup, but shows more detail on where the answers came from and how you get them.

LISTING 6.6 Sample Dig Output

```
$ dig netposta.net any

; <<>> DiG 8.2 <<>> netposta.net any
;; res options: init recurs defnam dnsrch
;; got answer:
;; ->>HEADER<<- opcode: QUERY, status: NOERROR, id: 4
;; flags: qr rd ra; QUERY: 1, ANSWER: 5, AUTHORITY: 2, ADDITIONAL: 4
;; QUERY SECTION:
;;      netposta.net, type = ANY, class = IN

;; ANSWER SECTION:
netposta.net.          11h1m56s IN NS  ns.telnet.hu.
netposta.net.          11h1m56s IN NS  dns.telnet.hu.
netposta.net.          11h1m56s IN MX  20 booster.telnet.hu.
netposta.net.          11h1m56s IN MX  10 mx1.netposta.net.
netposta.net.          11h2m50s IN A   212.75.128.65

;; AUTHORITY SECTION:
netposta.net.          11h1m56s IN NS  ns.telnet.hu.
netposta.net.          11h1m56s IN NS  dns.telnet.hu.
```

LISTING 6.6 Continued

```
;; ADDITIONAL SECTION:
ns.telnet.hu.           23h1m56s IN A   212.75.128.43
dns.telnet.hu.          23h1m56s IN A   195.70.46.3
booster.telnet.hu.      23h2m7s IN A    212.75.128.38
mx1.netposta.net.       11h1m56s IN A   212.75.128.65

;; Total query time: 15 msec
;; FROM: shadrach.ispnet1.net to SERVER: default -- 207.133.66.126
;; WHEN: Thu May  3 17:13:08 2001
;; MSG SIZE  sent: 30  rcvd: 226

$
```

The output from the `dig` command shows the DNS records used in the `netposta.net` domain. This example shows the name server (`NS`), mail server (`MX`), and Internet address (`A`) DNS records that are registered for the `netposta.net` domain.

Using External Spam Services

With the rising use of spam mail, many Web sites are now devoted to helping mail administrators deal with spam. These Web sites offer tools to help the mail administrator in different ways. This section describes two popular Internet Web sites that demonstrate the different types of assistance available to mail administrators.

SpamCop

The SpamCop Web site at `http://www.spamcop.net` offers two different services for mail administrators. The free statistical information service lists hostnames of current spam hosts that you can use to help block spam messages from your mail server. A second service that SpamCop offers is enabling individual users to filter all their incoming e-mail messages for spam. By forwarding all your incoming e-mail messages to SpamCop, you can significantly reduce the amount of spam you get. SpamCop charges a fee for this service.

Chapter 12, "Blocking Spam," describes in detail how you can configure your open source MTA program to block incoming messages from known spam hosts. The trick is finding a current list of known spam hosts to use. The SpamCop Web site helps you collect addresses of known spam offenders.

The SpamCop Web site has four different lists of spam addresses:

- Network addresses of sites known to produce spam messages
- Network addresses of sites known to relay spam messages

- Network addresses of Web sites found in spam messages
- E-mail addresses mentioned in spam messages

Most MTA programs allow you to filter incoming messages based on any of these values. To keep the lists current, they are updated every hour when the SpamCop system is not under a heavy load. Table 6.6 shows a sample list of network addresses known to produce spam messages.

TABLE 6.6 Sample SpamCop Offenders List

Network	Age	IP Address
postmaster@edbasa.no	6 min.	212.18.128.133
abuse-noverbose@uu.net	6 min.	63.39.114.85
postmaster@attglobal.net	8 min.	12.64.72.186
aol_proxy@admin.spamcop.net	8 min.	172.158.193.25
abuse@psi.com	9 min.	38.29.64.22
abuse@bigmailbox.com	9 min.	209.132.220.203
postmaster@bigmailbox.com	9 min.	209.132.220.203
abuse@pacific.net.sg	11 min.	203.120.47.7
abuse@kornet.net	11 min.	210.217.27.75
abuse@wcom.net	12 min.	216.192.206.146
abuse@jtibs.net	12 min.	212.9.24.140
abuse@thegrid.net	13 min.	216.224.158.112
abuse@singnet.com.sg	15 min.	203.126.130.116

The list shown in Table 6.6 is only a small sample of the hosts identified by SpamCop. The original network usernames are replaced with generic names, such as abuse and postmaster, in the SpamCop statistics to protect individual privacy. The Age field shows how recently a spam message has been received from the host. After you have this information, you can use it to configure your MTA package to stop known spam sources from sending messages to your e-mail users.

CAUTION

Remember that not all users on a particular host are spammers. Blocking messages from an entire ISP because of a single spammer can result in some valid e-mail messages also getting blocked. Depending on your e-mail environment, this can be irritating to your customers, and possibly disastrous for your corporation. See Chapter 12 for more details on how to block spam messages.

Sam Spade

Another popular spam Web site tool is Sam Spade (http://www.samspade.org). This site supplies standard network lookup tools, such as whois, traceroute, and nslookup, via a Web interface. With these tools, mail administrators who do not have access to standard Unix tools can find information about spam sites. Figure 6.2 shows the standard tools Web page.

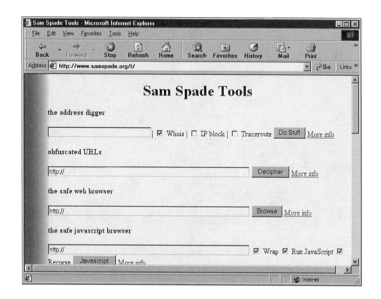

FIGURE 6.2

Sam Spade tools Web page.

The Sam Spade site offers many different tools the mail administrator can use. These are some of the more useful ones:

- **The address digger**   Uses the standard Unix tools whois and traceroute to find information on a domain.
- **Obfuscated URLs**   Decodes cryptic Web site addresses found in spam mail to produce the source Web site address.
- **The safe Web browser**   Connects to a remote Web site without passing your IP address, accepting any cookies, or running any scripts or applets. The raw HTML response from the server is returned.
- **The safe JavaScript browser**   Connects to a remote Web site and runs a JavaScript program without passing your IP address or accepting any cookies or applets. The raw HTML response from the server is returned.

To test out Sam Spade, you can enter the `netposta.net` domain you have been investigating into the address digger tool. Figure 6.3 shows part of the results.

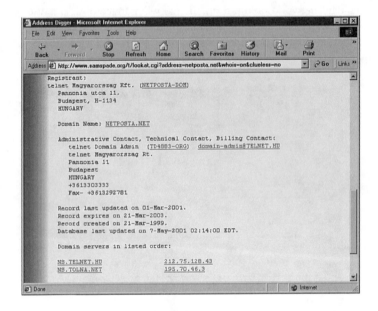

FIGURE 6.3

Results of the address digger tool.

As you can see, the address digger tool has found the registrant for the `netposta.net` domain. It appears to be registered in Budapest, Hungary.

Summary

The ability to decode e-mail headers and track messages is a vital skill for mail administrators. Spammers can create e-mail messages with forged header information, so you must be able to dig through the information to determine where and when the message originated.

You can track forged e-mail messages by examining the RFC 822 `Received:` header field. As each MTA server handles an e-mail message, it places its information in a separate `Received:` header field added to the original message. By following the path of the `Received:` header fields, you can often determine the origin of e-mail messages or determine which MTA server delayed the transmission of the message.

If you are trying to track down a spammer, there are some open source DNS programs that can help you. The whois program can be used to find registration information for IP addresses and domain names. The nslookup and dig programs can provide information about registered mail and name servers.

As a final line of defense, you can use external spam resources. Two popular spam resources are SpamCop and Sam Spade. SpamCop supplies real-time addresses of known spam hosts that can be used in e-mail filters to block spam before it gets to your customers' mailboxes. Sam Spade offers a simple Web interface for the standard whois and nslookup programs.

PART II

Server Security

CHAPTER 7

Securing the Unix Server

Before discussing e-mail security, it is a good idea to first look at server security. Having the most secure e-mail software in the world won't compensate for having a server that can be easily broken into through an open "backdoor."

This chapter describes some methods you can use to help ensure that the Unix server platform your e-mail software is running on is as secure as possible. To do that, you can use both internal security methods and external server security packages.

Monitoring Log Files

Unix has the capability to track events that occur on the system and log messages for each event in system log files. The program that handles this function is syslogd. With this program, you can locate the log files and track any problems or security events that may appear in them. You should get in the habit of scanning through the log files at least once a day to watch for possible system or security problems.

This section describes the syslogd program and how to configure it to log events in log files.

The Syslogd Program

The command syntax of syslogd varies for different Unix systems. For Linux systems, this is the command syntax:

```
syslogd [ -a socket ] [ -d ] [ -f config ] [ -h ] [ -l hostlist ]
➥ [ -m interval ] [ -n ] [ -p socket ] [ -r ] [ -s domainlist ]
➥ [ -v ]
```

Table 7.1 describes the options available for the Linux version of syslogd.

TABLE 7.1 Syslogd Options

Option	Description
-a socket	Specifies additional sockets to listen to for remote connections.
-d	Turns on debugging mode.
-f config	Uses the configuration file specified by config.
-h	Forwards any remote messages to forwarding hosts.
-l hostlist	Specifies a list of hosts that are logged only by hostname.
-m interval	Sets the MARK timestamp interval in the log file. Setting it to 0 disables the timestamp.
-n	Avoids running in background mode.
-p socket	Specifies an alternative socket to listen for remote syslogd connections on.

TABLE 7.1 Continued

Option	Description
-r	Enables receiving remote syslogd connections from other servers.
-s *domainlist*	Specifies a list of domain names that will be stripped off before logging.
-v	Prints syslogd version.

The syslogd program is normally started at boot time by an init script and quietly runs in background mode. Most Unix distributions start syslogd by default. You can check to see whether syslogd is running on your Unix system by using the command:

```
ps ax | grep syslogd
```

The syslogd program should appear in the list of processes running on your system. When syslogd starts, it reads a configuration file to determine what types of messages to log and how to log them. The next section describes the format of this configuration file.

The Syslogd Configuration File

The syslogd configuration file is located by default at /etc/syslog.conf. It contains directives that instruct the syslogd program what type of events to log and how to log them. Table 7.2 shows the different event types that syslogd can log.

TABLE 7.2 Syslogd Event Types

Event	Description
auth	Security/authorization events
authpriv	Private security/authorization events
cron	Cron program daemon events
daemon	System daemon events
kern	System kernel events
lpr	Line printer events
mail	Mail program events
mark	Internal check
news	Network News program events
syslog	Internal syslogd events
user	User-level events
uucp	Unix-to-Unix Copy Protocol (UUCP) program events
local*n*	Locally defined events ($n = 0$–7)

Each event type has a hierarchy of message priorities. Lower priorities mean smaller problems; higher priorities mean bigger problems. Table 7.3 shows the available event priorities in ascending order of importance, with debug having the lowest priority and emerg having the highest.

TABLE 7.3 Syslogd Message Priorities

Priority	Description
debug	Debugging events
info	Informational events
notice	Normal notices
warning	Warning messages
err	Error condition events
crit	Critical system conditions
alert	System alerts
emerg	Fatal system conditions

The format of an entry in the /etc/syslog.conf file looks like this:

```
event.priority          action
```

Each entry in the /etc/syslog.conf file represents different actions. There are four actions that can be taken for events:

- Displaying the event message to the system console
- Logging the event message to a log file
- Sending the event message to the users' console screen if they are logged in
- Sending the event message to a remote log host

The syslogd configuration file consists of combinations of events and actions that define the characteristics of the syslogd program. This is best explained by an example. Listing 7.1 shows a sample /etc/syslog.conf file. Line numbers have been added to the normal file for explanation purposes.

LISTING 7.1 Sample /etc/syslog.conf File

```
1   # Log all kernel messages to the console.
2   # Logging much else clutters up the screen.
3   kern.*                      /dev/console
4
5   # Log anything (except mail) of level info or higher.
6   # Don't log private authentication messages!
```

LISTING 7.1 Continued

```
7   *.info;mail.none;authpriv.none                    /var/log/messages
8
9   # The authpriv file has restricted access.
10  authpriv.*                      /var/log/secure
11
12  # Log all the mail messages in one place.
13  mail.*                          /var/log/maillog
14
15  # Everybody gets emergency messages, plus log them on another
16  # machine.
17  *.emerg                              *
18  *.emerg                     @meshach.ispnet.net
19
20  # Save mail and news errors of level err and higher in a
21  # special file.
22  uucp,news.crit                  /var/log/spooler
```

Lines 1 and 2 start off by showing how to use comments in the configuration file. These lines are not processed by syslogd. Line 3 is an example of using wildcard characters in the configuration file (in this example, * is used). It indicates that all kernel event messages of any priority will be sent to the system console.

Line 7 is a good example of a complex configuration that lists multiple events on a single action line. A semicolon is used to separate event and priority pairs. The first pair on line 7 is *.info, which defines all events of informational priority and higher. It is important to remember that by specifying a particular priority, you are also including the priorities higher in the list (refer back to Table 7.3).

The second pair—mail.none—may look confusing. You might be thinking there is no "none" priority. What this event pair is defining is that all mail events of any priority should be excluded from the previous definition. The next pair—authpriv.none—does the same thing. This statement, in effect, is logging all events, except mail and authpriv events, of informational priority and higher to the log file /var/log/messages.

Lines 10 and 13 define what is happening to the authpriv and mail events. Line 10 defines that all authpriv events of any priority get logged to a separate file called /var/log/secure. Similarly, line 13 defines that all mail events of any priority get logged to a separate file named /var/log/maillog. This is an extremely handy way of parsing event messages by separating them into their own log files. As the mail administrator, it is a good idea to define a separate place to put all mail-related event messages, making it easier to spot mail problems on the system.

Line 18 shows an example of using a remote syslogd server to log messages. Any emergency priority messages are sent to the remote host meshach.ispnet.net. If there is a serious error on the host, you might not get a chance to see the log fil, so it is often a good idea to send these messages elsewhere (assuming that the serious error does not prevent the system from sending the messages).

Using a remote host to log server messages is also wise from a security standpoint. If a server is compromised, you must also assume that the log files have been tampered with. A good hacker always deletes pertinent log file entries to cover his tracks. If the server is also logging messages to a remote host that the hacker can't access, you have a copy of the original messages that the hacker can't tamper with (you hope).

TIP

If a remote syslogd host is not available, another logging trick is to create secondary log files on the server in nonstandard locations. Most hackers know to look for logs in the /var/log directory, but few think to scan the /etc/syslogd.conf file to see where else they could be logged. Sending log messages to the standard files as well as secondary files located in an odd directory (such as /.log) is a clever way to trick some hackers.

Watching for Attacks

Often the mail administrator can get clues about illegal activity from the log files. Listing 7.2 shows part of a sample /var/log/maillog file from a Linux mail server.

LISTING 7.2 Sample Log File with SMTP Session

```
May  2 19:09:12 shadrach sendmail[5365]: NOQUEUE: "wiz" command from
➡ [192.168.1.15] (192.168.1.15)
May  2 19:09:14 shadrach sendmail[5365]: NOQUEUE: "debug" command from
➡ [192.168.1.15] (192.168.1.15)
```

This listing shows two attempts to access the sendmail program via the network. Both times the hacker attempted to use the archaic sendmail hacker commands wiz and debug that have long since been disabled. By reading the log file, you can determine the source address the commands were sent from. It is proper Internet protocol to inform your ISP of this illegal attempt on your mail server. With any luck, they can track down the source of the hacking attempts.

Besides MTA event messages, you might also find other types of mail messages in the /var/log/maillog log file. Listing 7.3 shows an example of a client trying to log in to the POP3 server.

Listing 7.3 Sample Log File with POP3 Session

```
May  2 16:24:49 shadrach ipop3d[5373]: port 110 service init
➡ from 192.168.1.15
May  2 16:24:49 shadrach ipop3d[5373]: Login failure user=rich
➡ host=[192.168.1.15]
May  2 16:24:52 shadrach ipop3d[5373]: AUTHENTICATE LOGIN failure
[ic:ccc host=[192.168.1.15]
May  2 16:24:52 shadrach ipop3d[5373]: Command stream end of file while
➡ readingline user=??? host=[192.168.1.15]
May  2 16:24:55 shadrach ipop3d[5374]: port 110 service init from
➡ 192.168.1.15
May  2 16:24:55 shadrach ipop3d[5374]: Login failure user=rich
➡ host=[192.168.1.15]
May  2 16:24:58 shadrach ipop3d[5374]: AUTHENTICATE LOGIN failure
➡ host=[192.168.1.15]
```

This listing shows the log file for the mail events generated by a mail user that did not know his password. Notice how the POP3 server program generated a warning message about the failed login attempts; the message includes the source IP address of the site attempting to log in, as well as the user ID that tried to log in. Had this been a real hacker, you could attempt to trace the IP address back to determine where the hacker was trying to log in from.

Preventing Network Attacks

One common rule of thumb in the network world is that if your server is connected to a network, someone will try to break into it. Even with servers connected to local area networks (LANs) protected by firewalls, you must always be on guard against intruders originating in your own organization.

The first step in protecting the mail server is to disable any network services that are not being used. Many network services can be exploited by hackers, but by disabling unused network services, you can decrease the chance of a network break-in.

The inetd program is a single network program that listens for any network connection requests from remote clients. If a connection request is identified, a specific application is called by inetd and the connection is passed off to the application. Figure 7.1 illustrates how the inetd program is used.

By using a single program to listen for all network connections, system resources are not needlessly used running multiple applications. Not only does this save on system resources, but it also creates a single place for performing all network configurations.

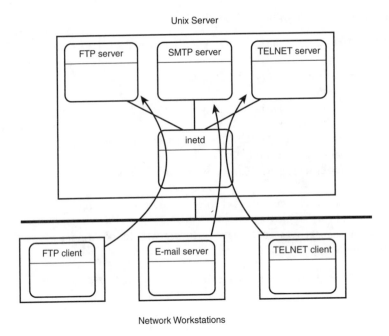

Unix Server

FIGURE 7.1

The Unix inetd program.

The inetd program has been a source of network attacks for several years. There are some simple things you can do to help defend yourself against these attacks, however. The following sections describe the inetd program and how to help make it more secure.

Using the Inetd Program

Two different versions of the inetd program are used in different Unix distributions. Both versions of the inetd program utilize two configuration files as well as command-line parameters to control the program's operation.

Unfortunately, the two inetd programs have different command-line formats. The BSD version of inetd uses this format:

```
inetd [-d] [-l] [-w] [-W] [-c maximum] [-C rate] [-a address] [-p filename]
➡ [-R rate] [configuration file]
```

FreeBSD and other variations of BSD Unix use this format. The command-line parameters used for this version of inetd are described in Table 7.4.

TABLE 7.4 Command-Line Parameters for the BSD Inetd Program

Parameter	Description
-d	Turns on debugging
-l	Turns on logging
-w	Turns on TCP wrapping for external services
-W	Turns on TCP wrapping for internal services
-c *maximum*	Specifies the maximum number of services that can be started
-C *rate*	Specifies the maximum times a service can be started from a single IP address per minute
-a *address*	Specifies a specific IP address to bind to
-p *filename*	Specifies an alternative file for storing the process ID
-R *rate*	Specifies the maximum number of times a service can be invoked in one minute (default = 256)
configuration file	Specifies an alternative configuration file

In contrast, the Unix System V version of inetd uses this format:

```
inetd [-d] [-q queuelength] [configuration file]
```

Linux and other System V–based versions of Unix use this format. The command-line parameters used for this version of inetd are described in Table 7.5.

TABLE 7.5 Command-Line Parameters for the Unix System V Inetd Program

Parameter	Description
-d	Turns on debug mode
-q *queuelength*	Sets size of socket listen queue to *queuelength* (default = 128)
configuration file	Defines an alternative configuration file

In both instances, the system boot scripts start the inetd program. For Linux systems, the inetd program startup script is located in the /etc/init.d/inet file and is started by the /etc/rc.d/rc3.d/S50inet and /etc/rc.d/rc5.d/S50inet files (which are linked to the /etc/init.d/inet script).

For FreeBSD systems, the inetd program is started directly from the /etc/rc startup script. These are the pertinent inetd lines in the /etc/rc script:

```
echo -n starting standard daemons:
if [ "X${inetd_enable}" != X"NO" ]; then
        echo -n ' inetd';        inetd ${inetd_flags}
fi
```

Two environment variables are used for the FreeBSD inetd startup script: ${inetd enable} and ${inetd flags}. These variables are set in the /etc/defaults/rc.conf file as follows:

```
inetd_enable="YES"          # Run the network daemon dispatcher (or NO).
inetd_flags="-wW"           # Optional flags to inetd.
```

The Inetd Configuration Files

When the inetd program runs, it reads two separate configuration files to determine how it operates. The /etc/services configuration file defines which TCP and UDP network ports the Unix server will communicate on. Listing 7.4 shows a partial listing of an /etc/services file from a FreeBSD server.

LISTING 7.4 Partial /etc/services File

```
ftp-data        20/tcp    #File Transfer [Default Data]
ftp-data        20/udp    #File Transfer [Default Data]
ftp             21/tcp    #File Transfer [Control]
ftp             21/udp    #File Transfer [Control]
ssh             22/tcp    #Secure Shell Login
ssh             22/udp    #Secure Shell Login
telnet          23/tcp
telnet          23/udp
#               24/tcp    any private mail system
#               24/udp    any private mail system
smtp            25/tcp    mail        #Simple Mail Transfer
smtp            25/udp    mail        #Simple Mail Transfer
nsw-fe          27/tcp    #NSW User System FE
nsw-fe          27/udp    #NSW User System FE
msg-icp         29/tcp    #MSG ICP
msg-icp         29/udp    #MSG ICP
msg-auth        31/tcp    #MSG Authentication
msg-auth        31/udp    #MSG Authentication
dsp             33/tcp    #Display Support Protocol
dsp             33/udp    #Display Support Protocol
#               35/tcp    any private printer server
#               35/udp    any private printer server
time            37/tcp    timserver
time            37/udp    timserver
rap             38/tcp    #Route Access Protocol
rap             38/udp    #Route Access Protocol
rlp             39/tcp    resource    #Resource Location Protocol
```

LISTING 7.4 Continued

```
rlp             39/udp      resource    #Resource Location Protocol
graphics        41/tcp
graphics        41/udp
nameserver      42/tcp      name        #Host Name Server
nameserver      42/udp      name        #Host Name Server
```

Notice that most protocols reserve a port for both the TCP and UDP protocols. Although the SMTP port is reserved for both protocols, modern SMTP programs use only TCP to communicate with remote servers.

The core of the inetd program is the inetd.conf configuration file. This file defines what network ports inetd will listen for connections on and what programs it should pass accepted connections to. The inetd.conf file is located in the /etc directory. Listing 7.5 shows a simplified listing of a /etc/inetd.conf file for a FreeBSD server.

LISTING 7.5 Partial /etc/inetd.conf File

```
#ftp     stream  tcp     nowait  root    /usr/libexec/ftpd        ftpd -l
telnet   stream  tcp     nowait  root    /usr/libexec/telnetd     telnetd
#shell   stream  tcp     nowait  root    /usr/libexec/rshd        rshd
#login   stream  tcp     nowait  root    /usr/libexec/rlogind     rlogind
#finger  stream  tcp     nowait/3/10 nobody /usr/libexec/fingerd  fingerd -s
#exec    stream  tcp     nowait  root    /usr/libexec/rexecd      rexecd
#uucpd   stream  tcp     nowait  root    /usr/libexec/uucpd       uucpd
#nntp    stream  tcp     nowait  usenet  /usr/libexec/nntpd       nntpd
#comsat  dgram   udp     wait    tty:tty /usr/libexec/comsat      comsat
#ntalk   dgram   udp     wait    tty:tty /usr/libexec/ntalkd      ntalkd
#tftp    dgram   udp     wait    nobody  /usr/libexec/tftpd       tftpd /tftpboot
#bootps  dgram   udp     wait    root    /usr/libexec/bootpd      bootpd
pop3     stream  tcp     nowait  root    /usr/local/libexec/popper   popper -s
imap4    stream  tcp     nowait  root    /usr/local/libexec/imapd    imapd
```

Each line in the inetd.conf file represents a protocol that inetd must monitor for connections. Lines that begin with a pound sign (#) are commented out from the configuration and are not active. Most inetd.conf files are largely comment lines. The format of an inetd.conf file line looks like this:

```
[serv name] [socket type] [protocol] [wait/nowait] [user] [program] [arguments]
```

The *serv name* should match an entry in the /etc/services file. It defines the TCP or UDP port that inetd should monitor. The next three parameters describe the type of network connection required for the application; each application should specify the *socket type*, *protocol*, and wait parameters required to communicate with the application. The *user* parameter specifies the username for running the application when a connection is established on the port. The *program* parameter is used to map a particular application to the network port.

Removing Unnecessary Services

By default, the inetd program supports many different types of network services, many of which are not necessarily needed on a mail server. It is a good idea to disable any services you are not using to decreases the chance that a hacker can use them to break into your server.

Disabling services is easy. Simply place a comment character (#) in front of the service definition in the /etc/inetd.conf file. After you restart the inetd program, the service will be disabled.

If the server is being used only for e-mail, you can disable almost all the other network services. The example shown in Listing 7.5 has only the telnet, pop3, and imap4 services enabled. Even the ftp service has been disabled as it is not needed for this server. If you normally log in to the server using the console port, it is advisable to disable the telnet and login services to help prevent any unauthorized network connections to the server.

Blocking Network Access to the Server

If you do not want to completely disable network services on your server, you can at least block access to the server from networks other than your own. Linux allows you to filter packets received on any network interface—Ethernet cards, dial-up Serial Line Internet Protocol (SLIP) lines, and dial-up Point-to-Point Protocol (PPP) lines. By filtering packets you can also block specific IP address ranges for specific TCP and UDP ports.

There are two parts to filtering the network packets that come into the Linux server. The first part resides in the actual Linux kernel. Packet filtering support has been added to the Linux kernel since version 2.1.

Because all packets received by the server are passed through the kernel, this method is a quick way to check and block unwanted packets (much as a firewall does). The kernel maintains a Network Address Translation (NAT) table that indicates how individual packets should be handled. The NAT table contains sets of rules that dictate when and how packets are forwarded on the various network interfaces on the server. By creating rules that block specific types of packets, such as from specific network addresses or for certain ports, you can effectively create a firewall-type environment for your server.

An external program is used to configure rules in the NAT table, the second part required for packet filtering. Unfortunately, three different programs have been used to support the packet filtering feature, depending on which version of the Linux kernel you are using:

- Kernel 2.0 uses the ipfwadm program.
- Kernels 2.1 and 2.2 can use either the ipfwadm or ipchains programs.
- Kernel 2.4 can use either the ipchains or iptables programs.

By manipulating rules in the NAT table, you can control how your server reacts to various types of network packets it receives. By blocking access to common services, such as telnet, from unauthorized sites, you can still use the services yourself without worrying about hackers abusing them.

At the time of this writing, the majority of current Linux distributions use the 2.2 kernel. Because the newer 2.4 kernel also supports ipchains, this section describes the ipchains method of filtering packets. This method works for both 2.2 and 2.4 kernel–based Linux systems.

Installing Ipchains

The ipchains program was written and is maintained by Rusty Russell. The main ipchains Web site is located at:

```
http://www.rustcorp.com/linux/ipchains
```

Most Linux distributions that use the version 2.2 or higher kernel include a binary distribution of ipchains. The most current version of ipchains at the time of this writing is version 1.3.10. It can be downloaded from this FTP site:

```
ftp://ftp.rustcorp.com/ipchains/ipchains-1.3.10.tar.gz
```

After you download it, you can unpack and compile it to create the binary executable file ipchains. Besides the ipchains program, you get three scripts that can be used to simplify ipchains administration: ipchains-save, ipchains-restore, and ipchains-wrapper. The ipchains-wrapper script can be used if you are currently using ipfwadm and want to convert to ipchains after upgrading your Linux kernel. The additional scripts can also be downloaded from this FTP site:

```
ftp://ftp.rustcorp.com/ipchains/ipchains-scripts-1.1.2.tar.gz
```

The ipchains-save and ipchains-restore scripts are discussed later in this chapter in the "Saving Ipchains Filters" section.

NOTE

At the time of this writing, the `rustcorp.com` Web and FTP sites were experiencing difficulties. To compensate for this, an alternative Web site had been created, `http://netfilter.file-watcher.org/ipchains`, which contains links to all the download files. It is not known at this time when the original `rustcorp.com` Web site will be back.

Using Ipchains

The ipchains program manipulates rules in the kernel's NAT table. When the kernel processes a packet and checks it against the NAT table, it performs certain actions if the packet address is found in the NAT table. Actions configured in the table include blocking the packet, forwarding the packet, and changing the packet's address.

The ipchains program inserts addresses and actions into the NAT table using four different categories:

- IP input chain
- IP output chain
- IP forwarding chain
- User-defined chains

The ipchains program uses the concept of chaining rules together to filter packets as they pass through the Linux server. Figure 7.2 shows a diagram of how the chains are configured.

The processes shown in Figure 7.2 control how packets are processed in the Linux server. Table 7.6 describes these processes.

TABLE 7.6 Ipchains Packet Filtering Processes

Process	Description
checksum	Checks for corrupted packets
sanity1	Checks for malformed packets
input chain	Firewall input chain check
demasquerade	If reply to a masqueraded packet, must be converted back to original packet address
routing	Destination checked to see whether it is local or needs to be forwarded
sanity2	Checks for malformed packets
forward chain	Firewall forward chain check
sanity3	Checks for malformed packets
output chain	Firewall output chain check

The packet must successfully pass each of the appropriate processes listed in Table 7.6 before it is accepted to be processed on the local host or forwarded to a remote host.

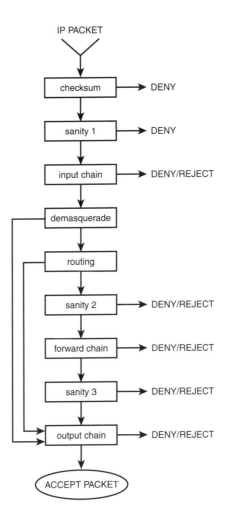

FIGURE 7.2

Ipchains rule processing.

The input, forward, and output chains use rules that are set in the NAT table by the ipchains program. The format of the ipchains command varies, as shown in the following lines, depending on the category that is used:

```
ipchains -[ADC] chain rule-specification [options]
ipchains -[RI] chain rulenum rule-specification [options]
ipchains -D chain rulenum [options]
ipchains -[LFZNX] [chain] [options]
ipchains -P chain target [options]
ipchains -M [ -L | -S ] [options]
```

The first parameter is the command that controls the function ipchains performs. Table 7.7 lists the commands available to use.

TABLE 7.7 Ipchains Command Types

Command	Description
-A	Appends one or more rules
-D	Deletes one or more rules
-C	Checks the packet against selected chain
-R	Replaces a rule in the selected chain
-I	Inserts one or more rules as the given rule number
-L	Lists all rules in the selected chain
-F	Flushes the selected chain
-Z	Zeros the counters for all chains
-N	Creates a new user-defined chain
-X	Deletes selected user-defined chain
-P	Sets the policy for the chain
-S	Sets the TCP timeout values in packets
-M	Views the current masqueraded connections

The next parameter in the ipchains command, *chain*, is the chain name. It can be one of the system chains—input, output, or forward—or a user-defined chain name created by using the -N command. User-defined chains are often used to help simplify complex rules. The *rulenum* parameter is used to specify a certain rule number to alter. As each rule is added to the NAT table, it is assigned a number. You can reference the rules by their rule numbers.

The *rule-specification* parameter specifies the actions taken in the rule. Table 7.8 lists the available parameters.

TABLE 7.8 Ipchains Parameter Types

Parameter	Description
-p protocol	Protocol to check
-s address[/mask]	Source address to check
--source-port *port*	Source port to check
-d address[/mask]	Destination address to check
--destination-port *port*	Destination port to check
--icmp-type	Internet Control Message Protocol (ICMP) type to check

TABLE 7.8 Continued

Target	Description
-j *target*	Target to jump to if packet matches
-i *name*	Interface name
-f	Rule refers to fragment packets

There are six special targets the -j option can jump to when a packet matches the rule. The *targets* are tags that point to routines that handle the packet. Table 7.9 lists the available targets.

TABLE 7.9 Ipchains Target Types

Target	Description
ACCEPT	Allows packet to pass
DENY	Prevents packet from passing
REJECT	Prevents packet from passing and returns ICMP error to sender
MASQ	Masquerades forward packets
REDIRECT	Sends packet to local port instead of destination
RETURN	Drops out of chain immediately

Besides parameters, there are additional options, listed in Table 7.10, used to further define the rule.

TABLE 7.10 Ipchains Option Types

Option	Description
-b	Bidirectional mode
-v	Verbose output
-n	Numeric output
-l	Turn on logging
-o [*maxsize*]	Copy matching packets to userspace device
-m *markvalue*	Mark matching packets
-t *andmask xormask*	Masks used to modify the TOS field
-x	Expand numbers
-y	Match only TCP packets with SYN set and ACK and FIN cleared

The option types further instruct ipchains on what to do with matching packets. Note that varying things can be accomplished. The -b option, for example, allows the rule to be used for both incoming and outgoing packets. The -l option instructs ipchains to create a log file entry for the matching packet. The -o option instructs ipchains to copy the packet to a storage area.

The -y option is used to filter out packets that have the SYN TCP bit set. The SYN bit is used to identify the start of a new TCP session. By blocking only this packet, you can effectively prevent a remote host from starting a TCP session with your server.

Saving Ipchains Filters

As each ipchains command is entered, the NAT table is modified accordingly. When the server is rebooted, the NAT table resets and any changes made previously are lost. To solve this problem, ipchains uses two script files to save the NAT table in a file that can be read back into the NAT table at boot time.

The ipchains-save script is used to save the existing NAT table configuration into a specified file. This is the format of the ipchains-save command:

```
ipchains-save > filename
```

The filename parameter is the name of the file where you want to save the NAT table configuration. You must be logged in as the root user to execute this command. To restore the NAT table, you can create an initialization script that uses the ipchains-restore script. The format of the ipchains-restore command looks like this:

```
ipchains-restore < filename
```

The filename parameter is the full pathname of the location where the original NAT table configuration was stored. Again, this command should be run as the root user, preferably during the server initialization scripts.

An Ipchains Example

Listing 7.6 shows an example of ipchains commands that can be used to block all network access except incoming SMTP sessions on a Linux server.

LISTING 7.6 Sample Ipchains Commands

```
/sbin/ipchains -P forward DENY/sbin/ipchains -A forward -i ppp0 -j MASQ
/sbin/ipchains -A input -I ppp0 --destination-port smtp -y -j ACCEPT
/sbin/ipchains -A input -i ppp0 -l -y -j DENY
```

The first entry sets a default policy of DENY for the forward chain. This command ensures that any packet not specifically allowed will be blocked. The second entry appends a rule to the forward chain. Any packets forwarded to the ppp0 interface will be passed to the MASQ target first. The ppp0 interface is most often a Point-to-Point Protocol (PPP) link to the ISP for Internet connectivity. As shown in Table 7.9, the MASQ target specifies sending the packet through the masquerading table in the NAT table. By masquerading packets, you can change the outgoing IP address of packets. This procedure is most often used when your internal network uses a common network address, but you want to communicate with the Internet using a single Internet IP address supplied by your ISP.

The third and fourth entries add the packet filtering features. The third entry allows connection requests on the SMTP port for external hosts. This connection enables hosts to send mail messages to the mail server via SMTP, which listens on port 25.

The last entry denies any remaining TCP SYN packet coming into the input chain on the ppp0 interface. Assuming the ppp0 interface is the server's connection to the ISP, this entry prevents Internet hosts from establishing connections with hosts on the office network. The use of the -1 option allows any connection attempt to be logged in the kernel log file. By carefully monitoring the log files, the system administrator can detect hackers' unauthorized attempts to connect to internal workstations and hosts.

NOTE

Chapter 14, "Using E-mail Firewalls," describes in more detail how to configure an e-mail server for use in a firewalled network.

The Bastille Project

The idea of disabling services and blocking network connections has been taken even one step further. The Bastille Project is a group of people dedicated to creating secure Linux servers. They provide the Bastille package, which can completely lock down a Linux server.

The Bastille Project created a package that automates creating ipchains or iptables rules based on a script that asks the server administrator simple questions. After defining the specific network applications and IP networks that you want to allow access for, Bastille creates the appropriate rules and enters them into the NAT table for you. This feature greatly simplifies the process for the server administrator.

Besides creating the NAT table rules, Bastille also locks down system commands and resources to prevent wayward internal server users from causing damage on the system. This added security helps create a completely locked-down server that minimizes the risk of tampering from both internal and external hackers.

The Bastille package is available from the Bastille Project's Web site http://www.bastille.org as either an RPM package or a compressed tar file of the source code. At the time of this writing, the most current beta version of the Bastille package is version 1.2.0.

Detecting Break-ins

Disabling network services and checking log files often are not enough to keep hackers from managing to work their way into your server. When a hacker breaks into your server, he will most likely tamper with the system files in one way or another, whether it's leaving Trojan horses for you to run as root or altering the system log files to hide his activity. Even after you realize that a hacker has been in your system, it might not always be obvious what files he has tampered with.

One way to help solve this problem is to use the tripwire program, which maintains an encrypted database of files and directories you want to monitor and checks them on a regular basis. If tripwire determines that monitored files or directories have been tampered with, it automatically reports the discrepancy with a log report or an e-mail warning. The following section describes how you can install and configure tripwire on your server.

Downloading and Installing Tripwire

Two different versions of the tripwire package are available. The commercial version, called Tripwire Manager, can be used on Solaris, HP-UX, IBM AIX, and Windows NT servers. There is a fee for installing and using this package. The second package is an open source version available only for Linux servers. This section describes how to download and install the open source tripwire package on a Linux server.

The open source tripwire package is available on the Tripwire Web site (`http://www.trip-wire.org`). Binary distributions can be downloaded as a RPM installation file or as a compressed tar file. The URL for downloading the tar file distribution is currently:

```
http://www.tripwire.org/files/tripwire-2.3-47.bin.tar.gz
```

After the file has been downloaded, you then uncompress and untar it with the following command:

```
tar -zxvf tripwire-2.3-47.tar.gz -C /usr/local/
```

This command creates the directory /usr/local/tripwire-2.3 and places the binary executables for tripwire there. After extracting the executables, you must check the install.cfg file to determine how you want tripwire installed on your system.

There are many parameters used that specify the default installation directories tripwire has for its various pieces, such as executables, man pages, and log files. For most systems, you can use the default values. One parameter to be careful of, however, is the default `sendmail` command, used to mail reports to an e-mail address. If you are using an alternative MTA package, such as qmail or Postfix, you must replace the default value with the location of the installed sendmail wrapper program used on your system:

```
TWMAILPROGRAM=/usr/sbin/sendmail -oi -t"
```

After modifying the install.cfg file, you can run the install.sh script to install tripwire. You are asked several questions during the installation. One of the queries is for a passphrase to use for the tripwire databases. You must select a phrase for encrypting the tripwire files used on your system. By encrypting the tripwire files, you can deter any intruders from tampering with the tripwire database.

CAUTION

Please remember the passphrase, as you'll need it when trying to modify any tripwire features in the future. If you forget the passphrase, you have to completely remove and reinstall tripwire.

After the installation is finished, both an encrypted and a plain text configuration file are created. You can check the text file to ensure that tripwire was installed as you expected; the file is located at /etc/tripwire/twcfg.txt. If you need to change any of the configuration parameters from the original installation, you can use the twadmin command:

```
twadmin --create-config filename
```

The *filename* is the name of the text configuration file you created. This command re-creates the encrypted configuration file that tripwire uses. After you are satisfied with the configuration, it is a good idea to delete the text version of the file so hackers can't figure out what is and isn't protected by the tripwire facility.

After you delete the text configuration file, you can view the current tripwire configuration by using the twadmin command:

```
twadmin --print-cfgfile
```

This command prints the configuration parameters and their current values. To change any of the parameter values, you must create a new configuration text file, and use the twadmin command to replace the existing configuration parameters. As with the original configuration, it is best to delete the text version of the configuration file after updating the configuration.

Before you can run tripwire, you must first set policies for it to follow. The next section describes how to do that.

Configuring Tripwire

The core of the tripwire configuration is the policy file, which defines the files and directories tripwire will monitor for tampering. Similar to the configuration file, to prevent tampering with the policy file, tripwire uses the passphrase entered at installation time to encrypt the file.

A plain text version of the policy file is used to create the encrypted file. The default location of this file is /etc/tripwire/twpol.txt. The default values in the policy file configure tripwire to monitor the standard files and directories found on a Red Hat 7.0 Linux distribution. If you are not running Red Hat 7.0, you need to modify the files listed in the policy file.

The policy file consists of a series of rules that define what file and directory features tripwire should monitor and how to report any discrepancies. Each rule has this format:

```
(
rulename="rulename",
severity = level,
emailto = remoteuser
)
{
    filename      -> security;
}
```

Here's what the parameters in these rules mean:

- *rulename* defines a name for the rule.
- *level* defines a severity level that is logged if an inconsistency occurs.
- *remoteuser* defines one or more e-mail addresses to mail inconsistencies to.
- *filename* defines the file or directory to monitor.
- *security* defines a set of file or directory properties to monitor.

The file and directory properties that tripwire can monitor consist of different standard Unix file attributes. Table 7.11 defines these properties.

TABLE 7.11 Tripwire File Properties

Property	Description
a	Access timestamp
b	Number of blocks
c	Inode timestamp
d	Inode storage disk device number
g	File owner's group ID
i	Inode number
m	Modification timestamp
n	Inode reference count
p	Permissions and file mode bits
r	Device number
s	File size

TABLE 7.11 Continued

Property	Description
t	File type
u	File owner's user ID
l	File is increasing in size
c	CRC-32 hash value
M	MD5 hash value
s	SHA hash value
H	Haval signature value

The CRC-32, MD5, SHA, and Haval values are common algorithms that can be used to determine whether a file has been modified. If the file has been modified in any way, the result of the algorithm will change. By comparing before and after values, tripwire can determine when a file has been tampered with.

These *security* parameters can be combined using standard Unix variables to make definitions simpler. If you constantly use a set of parameters, such as the p, i, n, g, u, and s parameters, you can assign them together to a Unix variable:

```
SEC_CRIT = +pingus
```

This entry assigns the variable SEC_CRIT to monitor the permissions (p), inode number (i), inode reference count (n), file owner group ID (g), file owner user ID (u), and file size (s). If any of these properties change in the file, tripwire detects the change and alerts the administrator. For each file or directory listed in the rules, you can use the created variable to identify the security level:

```
/sbin/ping     -> $(SEC_CRIT)
```

To help the configuration process, tripwire defines nine different security-level variables, described in Table 7.12, in the sample policy file.

TABLE 7.12 Tripwire Security Levels

Level	Description
SEC_CRIT	Critical files that cannot change
SEC_SUID	Binary files with the SUID or SGID bit set
SEC_BIN	Binary files that should not change
SEC_CONFIG	Configuration files that are changed infrequently, but are read often by applications
SEC_LOG	Log files that grow, but never change ownership
SEC_INVARIANT	Directories that should never change ownership or permissions
SIG_LOW	Noncritical files that have minimal security impact

TABLE 7.12 Continued

Level	Description
SIG_MED	Noncritical files that have a significant security impact
SIG_HI	Critical files that have a high security impact if compromised

You can add and delete file and directory entries in the policy file as necessary to match your Linux and security environment. Remember that each rule should define related entries, and each entry must be matched with a corresponding security level. Listing 7.7 shows a few sample policy file entries.

LISTING 7.7 Sample Policy File Entries

```
(
  rulename = "Login Scripts",
  severity = $(SIG_HI)
  emailto = "rich@ispnet.net rich@alt.ispnet.net"
)
{
  /etc/csh.cshrc                  -> $(SEC_CONFIG) ;
  /etc/csh.login                  -> $(SEC_CONFIG) ;
  /etc/tsh_profile                -> $(SEC_CONFIG) ;
  /etc/profile                    -> $(SEC_CONFIG) ;
}

# Libraries
(
  rulename = "Libraries",
  severity = $(SIG_MED)
  emailto = rich@mechach.ispnet.net
)
{
  /usr/lib                        -> $(SEC_BIN) ;
  /usr/local/lib                  -> $(SEC_BIN) ;
}
```

This example shows two separate rules for the policy file. The first rule identifies the login scripts used on the Linux system and associates them with a high security level (SIG_HI). The individual files in the login script group are marked as configuration files that are read often but change infrequently (SEC_CONFIG). The rule defines an action of e-mailing a notice to two separate e-mail accounts should there be a discrepancy with the files.

The second example shows marking directories in the policy file. The libraries rule identifies two directories that contain system libraries. The individual directories are marked as containing binary files that should not change (SEC_BIN). If any new libraries are added, or if a hacker modifies any existing library, tripwire will notice the action and alert the administrator via an e-mail message.

After the text policy file is configured to meet your security requirements, you must use the twadmin command to create a new encrypted policy file from the text file:

```
twadmin --create-polfile filename
```

The *filename* is the name of the text policy file. Again, it is a good idea to delete the text file after creating the encrypted file.

Now that the configuration and policy files are created, you are ready to run the tripwire program.

Running Tripwire

The first step is to create a baseline database of files and directories. Tripwire uses this baseline database to compare with all future scans. To create the baseline database, you can use the tripwire command in database initialization mode:

```
tripwire --init
```

You will be queried to enter the database pass phrase before tripwire continues scanning the files and directories. As tripwire processes, it notifies you if any files or directories in the policy file are not found on the system. You should delete these entries from the policy file and reinitialize the database until you get a clean scan of the system.

After the baseline database is created, you should run tripwire in the checking mode on a regular basis, typically using a cron entry. The format of the checking mode is simply:

```
tripwire --check
```

This command runs tripwire to check any inconsistencies in the current system with entries in the initial database. Any inconsistencies are reported in the tripwire report, and an e-mail to the appropriate e-mail addresses is defined in the policy file.

Summary

Securing the mail server is a crucial part of the security process. You must ensure that the mail server is not vulnerable to hackers breaking in and compromising the system. There are several methods you can use to do this.

The most important job for the system administrator is to continually monitor the system log files. The syslogd program should always be running and capturing events to the log files. By monitoring the log files on a regular basis, you can quickly determine when something is wrong with the system.

Most hacker attacks are made on default system applications running on the system. Often, novice system administrators do not know about turning off network services that can be used as backdoors by hackers. It is always a good idea to disable any network services that are not needed on the server.

A more sophisticated method of blocking network access to the server is to use the Network Address Translation (NAT) tables in the kernel. The system administrator can configure the NAT table to block network access for a specific IP network or address for a specific TCP or UDP port. This procedure enables you to create a custom environment to selectively allow specific hosts to communicate with your server.

CHAPTER 8

The sendmail E-mail Package

The sendmail MTA package is one of the most popular open source MTA packages used by Internet mail servers. In the past it was plagued with backdoors and security flaws; however, it has been rewritten not only to remove the security flaws, but also to incorporate many newer MTA features, such as spam control. The newer versions of the sendmail program have proven to be secure as well as versatile.

This chapter describes the contents of the sendmail package, how to install it, and how to configure it for your e-mail environment.

What Is sendmail?

The sendmail package is composed of several different parts, each part performing a separate function of the MTA process. Figure 8.1 shows a block diagram of how these parts interact with one another.

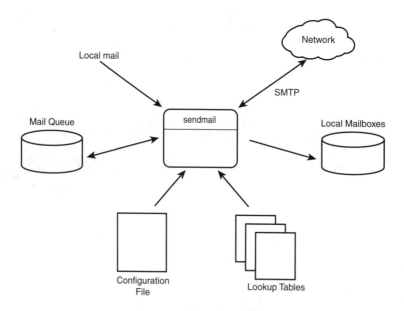

FIGURE 8.1

Block diagram of the sendmail package.

Besides the main sendmail program, a configuration file and several tables can be created to contain information that sendmail uses while processing incoming and outgoing mail messages. Table 8.1 lists the parts used in a normal sendmail installation.

TABLE 8.1 sendmail Parts

Part	Description
sendmail	Receives messages from local and remote users and determines how to deliver them
sendmail.cf	Configuration file that controls the behavior of the sendmail program
sendmail.cw	Contains a list of domain names that the sendmail program will receive messages for
sendmail.ct	Contains a list of trusted users that can control sendmail operations
aliases	Contains a list of valid local mail addresses that can redirect mail to another user, a file, or a program
newaliases	Creates a new aliases database file from a text file
mailq	Checks the mail queue and prints any messages
mqueue	The directory used to store messages waiting to be delivered
mailertable	Used to override routing for specific domains
domaintable	Used to map old domain names to new ones
virtusertable	Used to map users and domains to alternative addresses
relay-domains	Used to allow specific hosts to relay messages though the sendmail program
access	Used to allow or refuse messages from specific domains

Configuring sendmail

The sendmail program needs to be told how to handle messages as the server receives them. As an MTA, sendmail processes incoming mail and redirects it to another mail package, either on a remote system or on the local system. The configuration file instructs sendmail on how to parse the destination mail addresses to determine where and how to forward the message. The default location for the configuration file is /etc/mail/sendmail.cf.

The sendmail.cf file consists of rule sets that analyze each incoming mail message and determine what actions to take. Some rule sets are included by default in sendmail, but you can add other rule sets. Each rule set identifies certain mail formats and instructs sendmail on how to handle that message. As a message is received, sendmail parses its header and passes it through the various rule sets to determine what action to take for that message. By creating rule sets, you enable sendmail to handle mail in many different formats. Mail received from an SMTP host, for example, has different header fields than mail received from a UUCP host. Rule sets, therefore, help sendmail know how to handle a variety of mail situations.

Rules also have three different types of helper functions defined in the configuration file:

- *Classes* define common phrases used to help the rule sets identify certain types of messages.
- *Macros* are values set to simplify typing long strings in the configuration file.
- *Options* are defined to set parameters for the sendmail program's operation.

The configuration file, therefore, is made up of a series of classes, macros, options, and rule sets. Each function is defined as a single text line in the configuration file. That line begins with a single character that specifies the action to be taken. Lines that begin with a space or a tab are continued lines from a previous action line. Lines that begin with a pound sign (#) indicate comments and are not processed by sendmail.

The action defined at the beginning of the text line indicates what the line is used for. Table 8.2 shows the standard sendmail actions and what they represent.

TABLE 8.2 Characters Used in sendmail Configuration File Lines

Configuration Line	Description[Characters
C	Defines classes of text
D	Defines a macro
F	Defines files containing classes of text
H	Defines header fields and actions
K	Defines databases that contain text to search
M	Defines mailers
O	Defines sendmail options
P	Defines sendmail precedence values
R	Defines rule sets to parse addresses
S	Defines rule set groups

The following sections describe the format of the different configuration lines and what they represent to the sendmail program. These configuration lines are discussed in order of usage, not alphabetically.

D Lines

Configuration lines that start with a D define macros used in the rule sets. A *macro* is a long word or phrase represented by a single macro name, similar to environment variables. It can save a lot of typing and confusion in the rule sets.

A macro name can be a single character or a word enclosed in braces ({ }). sendmail uses lowercase letters and special symbols for predefined macros, but the mail administrator can use uppercase letters to define site-specific values.

The format of the D line is as follows:

```
Dx value
```

In this line, *x* is the macro name and *value* is the value of the macro. After you define a macro, you reference it with the command $*x* (*x* is the macro name). Whenever you see the $*x* macro, it should represent the *value* that was defined in the D line. Here is an example of a D macro line:

```
DnMAILER-DAEMON
```

This is a commonly found macro that assigns the text string MAILER-DAEMON to the macro n. The rule sets can then use the macro $n to represent the string MAILER-DAEMON.

You can also create conditional macros that test whether a macro has previously been defined. To do that, use the following format:

```
$?x value1 $| value2 $
```

In this line, *x* is the macro name to test, *value1* is the value the macro takes if the macro name has been set, and *value2* is the value the macro takes if the macro name has not been set. The $| does not have to be included in the command, but is often used to help separate the values and make the line easier to read.

As mentioned, sendmail uses some predefined macros, listed in Table 8.3, to substitute for commonly used phrases.

TABLE 8.3 sendmail D Macros

Macro	Description
$a	The date of the message from the Date: field
$b	The current date in RFC 822 format
$c	The number of message hops (the hop count) a particular message has gone through
$d	The current date in Unix format
$f	The sender address
$g	The sender address in relation to the recipient (includes hostname)
$h	The recipient host
$i	The queue ID
$j	The full domain name for the site
$k	The UUCP node name for the site
$m	The domain part of the gethostname value
$n	The name of the sendmail daemon

TABLE 8.3 Continued

Macro	Description
$p	sendmail's process ID
$q	Default format of sender address
$r	Protocol used to receive the message
$s	Sender's hostname
$t	A numeric representation of the current time
$u	The recipient user
$v	The version number of sendmail
$w	The hostname of the site
$x	The full name of the sender
$z	The home directory of the recipient
$_	The validated sender address
${bodytype}	The message body type
${client_addr}	The IP address of the SMTP client
${client_name}	The hostname of the SMTP client
${client_port}	The TCP port number of the SMTP client
${envid}	The envelope ID passed to sendmail
${opMode}	The current operation mode (using the -b parameter)
${deliveryMode}	The current delivery mode (from the DeliveryMode option)

C Lines

Configuration lines that begin with a C define classes of phrases that may be used in the rules. Classes group phrases that have something in common so that the rule sets can scan the class for matches. This method allows you to define multiple phrases with a single variable. This is the format of a C line:

Ccphrase1 phrase2 ...

In this line, c is the name of the class, and *phrase1*, *phrase2*, and so forth are phrases that will be grouped together in the class. Similar to the D line command, class names must be a single character or a word enclosed in braces. Class names consisting of a lowercase letter or a special character are reserved for internal sendmail use. You can use uppercase letters to define site-specific classes. Table 8.4 lists some predefined class names used internally in sendmail.

TABLE 8.4 sendmail C Line Classes

Class	Description
e	Content-Transfer-Encodings (can be 7-bit, 8-bit, or binary)
k	The UUCP node name
m	The domain name
n	Set of MIME body types that cannot be encoded as 7-bit
q	Set of Content-Types that cannot be encoded as base-64
s	Set of subtypes of messages that can be treated recursively
t	Set of trusted users
w	Set of all names this host is known by

A simple example is the w class, which defines all names the host is known by:

```
Cwlocalhost shadrach
```

This example assigns the phrases localhost and shadrach to the w class. When the $w variable is used in rule sets, sendmail will try substituting both the localhost and shadrach phrases for the variable.

F Lines

Configuration lines that begin with an F also define classes that can be used by rule sets, but they define classes a little differently than the C lines do. F lines point to filenames that contain the list of phrases to use in the class. This allows you to list multiple phrases in a separate file that can be used in the variable defined in the F line. This method is handy because you can then modify the file at any time without having to rebuild the configuration file. The following line shows the format of an F line:

```
Fc filename
```

In this line, c is the single-character class name, and *filename* is the full pathname of the file containing the phrases. Each phrase should be on a separate line in the file.

As with C lines, sendmail uses lowercase letters and special characters as internal class names. You can use uppercase letters to define site-specific class names.

K Lines

Configuration lines that begin with a K define special mapped databases that sendmail uses to look up different types of information. These lines use the following format:

```
Kmapname mapclass arguments
```

In this line, *mapname* is the name of the database as used in the configuration file, *mapclass* is the type of database generated, and *arguments* are passed to sendmail to help create the database. Often arguments include the location of the database and flags used to help process the database.

Maps are referenced by the rule sets, using the following syntax:

```
$(map key $@ arguments $: default $)
```

In this line, *map* is the mapname, *key* and *arguments* are passed to the mapping function to obtain the return record, and *default* is a value to use if no record is returned.

sendmail can use many different types of mapclasses. Table 8.5 lists some of the more common classes available.

TABLE 8.5 sendmail Mapclasses for K Lines

Mapclass	Description
dbm	Uses the ndbm(3) database library
btree	Uses the btree interface to the Berkeley DB library
hash	Uses the hash interface to the Berkeley DB library
nis	Uses Network Information System (NIS) lookups
ldapx	Uses Lightweight Directory Access Protocol (LDAP) x.500 directory lookups
text	Uses text file lookups
implicit	Used to get default lookups for alias files
user	Uses the getpwnam() function to look up usernames
host	Uses DNS to find hostnames
bestmx	Uses DNS to find the best Mail Exchange (MX) record for a host
sequence	Uses a list of multiple maps to use
program	Uses an external program for lookups

To create mapped databases from text files, you use the makemap command. Different Unix distributions use different default mapclasses. Currently the Linux version of makemap supports only the btree and hash types of mapclasses. Of those two, hash database maps are more commonly used for sendmail database maps. This is the format used for the makemap command:

```
makemap mapclass outputfile < textfile
```

In this command, *mapclass* is the type of database map to use, *textfile* is the text database file used for input, and *outputfile* is the converted database.

H Lines

Configuration lines that begin with an H define the format of header lines that sendmail inserts into the message. The header lines make use of macros and macro flags to determine the proper syntax for a mail message header, depending on the protocol used to transfer the message. SMTP hosts, for example, expect mail headers to be in a different format than UUCP hosts do, so they must use different H header lines. The format of the H line looks like this:

```
H[?mflags?]hname:htemplate
```

In this line, *mflags* are the macro flags that must be defined. In these macro definitions, *hname* is the name of the header line, and *htemplate* is the format of the header line using macros. The macros are expanded to their normal names before being placed in the outgoing message. Another format of the H line passes the message to a particular rule set if a specific header is present:

```
Hheader:$>Ruleset
```

In this format for H lines, *header* is the header field that should be present, and *Ruleset* is the rule set number (see the "Rule Sets" section later in this chapter). A sample of some H lines is shown in Listing 8.1.

LISTING 8.1 Sample sendmail *H* Lines

```
H?P?Return-Path: <$g>
HReceived: $?sfrom $s $.$?_($?s$|from $.$_)
    $.by $j ($v/$Z)$?r with $r$. id $i$?u
    for $u; $|;
    $.$b
H?D?Resent-Date: $a
H?D?Date: $a
H?F?Resent-From: $?x$x <$g>$|$g$.
H?F?From: $?x$x <$g>$|$g$.
H?x?Full-Name: $x
HPosted-Date: $a
H?l?Received-Date: $b
H?M?Resent-Message-Id: <$t.$i@$j>
H?M?Message-Id: <$t.$i@$j>
```

The first H line shows a simple conditional line. If the P macro is defined (earlier in this sendmail.cf, it was defined as a period), sendmail adds a Return-Path header field using the $g macro as the data value. If you remember from Table 8.3, the $g macro expands to represent the sender's address in relation to the receiver. Therefore, this H line causes sendmail to add the fully qualified username and hostname in the Return-Path header field of the message if the P macro flag is specified.

M Lines

Configuration lines that begin with an M define a mailer that sendmail uses to forward messages. Each different type of mailer must have an M line definition for sendmail to know how to use the mailer. The format for the M line looks like this:

```
Mprog,[field=value]...
```

In this line, *prog* is the name of the mailer program, and each *field=value* pair defines attributes that are required for sendmail to use the mailer. Field names, listed in Table 8.6, can use the whole field name, but sendmail uses only the first character of the field name, so they are often entered only as one-character fields.

TABLE 8.6 sendmail M Line Fields

Field Name	Description
Path	The pathname of the mailer
Flags	Flags used for the mailer
Sender	Rule sets used for the sender address
Recipient	Rule sets used for the recipient address
Argv	Any arguments passed to the mailer
Eol	The end-of-line string used by the mailer
Maxsize	The maximum message length used by the mailer
Linelimit	The maximum line length used by the mailer
Directory	The working directory of the mailer
Userid	The default user ID and group ID for running the mailer
Nice	The Unix nice() value for the mailer, used to run the mailer at a lower system priority
Charset	The default character set for 8-bit characters
Type	The Message Transport System (MTS) type information used by error messages

The Flags field is used to identify how sendmail should use the mailer. Flags define actions that sendmail may or may not use. You can use multiple values in the Flags field, and these multiple flags are written as a sequence of characters with no embedded spaces. Table 8.7 shows some flags that can be used.

TABLE 8.7 sendmail M Line Flags

Flag	Action
a	Use ESMTP
A	Use the aliases database

TABLE 8.7 Continued

b	Force a blank line at the end of the message
c	Do not include comments in addresses
C	Add the local domain name to receive addresses without an @ sign
d	Do not include angle brackets around route-address syntax addresses
D	Include a Date: header field
F	Include a From: header field
h	Preserve uppercase in hostnames
l	The mailer is local
m	The mailer can send to multiple users in one transaction
M	Include a Message-ID: header field
n	Do not insert a Unix-style "From" line
S	Don't reset the user ID before calling the mailer
u	Preserve uppercase usernames
U	Use UUCP-type "From" lines
5	If no aliases are found, use rule set 5 to find alternative resolution
9	Do limited 7- to 8-bit MIME conversion

Listing 8.2 shows some M configuration lines from a sample sendmail.cf file.

LISTING 8.2 Sample M Configuration Lines

```
###    SMTP Mailer specification    ###
Msmtp,  P=[IPC], F=mDFMuX, S=11/31, R=21, E=\r\n, L=990, T=DNS/RFC822/SMTP,
Mesmtp, P=[IPC], F=mDFMuXa, S=11/31, R=21, E=\r\n, L=990,
➡ T=DNS/RFC822/SMTP,
Msmtp8, P=[IPC], F=mDFMuX8, S=11/31, R=21, E=\r\n, L=990,
➡ T=DNS/RFC822/SMTP,
Mrelay, P=[IPC], F=mDFMuXa8, S=11/31, R=61, E=\r\n, L=2040,
➡ T=DNS/RFC822/SMTP,
###    UUCP Mailer specification    ###
Muucp,       P=/usr/bin/uux, F=DFMhuUd, S=12, R=22/42, M=100000,
Muucp-old,   P=/usr/bin/uux, F=DFMhuUd, S=12, R=22/42, M=100000,
Msuucp,      P=/usr/bin/uux, F=mDFMhuUd, S=12, R=22/42, M=100000,
Muucp-new,   P=/usr/bin/uux, F=mDFMhuUd, S=12, R=22/42, M=100000,
Muucp-dom,   P=/usr/bin/uux, F=mDFMhud, S=52/31, R=21, M=100000,
Muucp-uudom, P=/usr/bin/uux, F=mDFMhud, S=72/31, R=21, M=100000,
###    PROCMAIL Mailer specification    ###
Mprocmail, P=/usr/local/bin/procmail, F=DFMSPhnu9, S=11/31, R=21/31,
```

LISTING 8.2 Continued

```
➡ T=DNS/RFC822/X-Unix,
###   Local and Program Mailer specification   ###
Mlocal, P=/usr/local/bin/procmail, F=lsDFMAw5:/|@qSPfhn9, S=10/30, R=20/40,
Mprog,          P=/bin/sh, F=lsDFMoqeu9, S=10/30, R=20/40, D=$z:/,
```

The first group (Msmtp) defines SMTP mailers. Different SMTP mailers are defined to handle different types of SMTP connections. Each mailer uses a different combination of flags to define the type of SMTP connection.

The second group (Muucp) defines UUCP mailers. As with the SMTP mailers, different UUCP mailers are defined to allow sendmail to handle different types of UUCP connections.

The last group defines a local mailer on the host, procmail (Mproc). The mailer path is defined to point sendmail to the executable file that executes the mailer. The Mlocal mailer is defined as using procmail to make sure any message that sendmail identifies for local delivery is passed to the procmail program. Finally, the program mailer (Mprog) is defined to allow sendmail to pass messages to a shell program for processing.

P Lines

Configuration lines beginning with a P define precedence values. Each RFC 822 format-ted message can use the Precedence: header field to define the message's urgency. The P configuration lines help sendmail assign a numeric priority value based on the Precedence: field text string. This is the format of the P line:

Ptext=value

In this line, *text* is the Precedence: field string, and *value* is a numeric value that sendmail uses to rank messages. The default sendmail configuration uses the following precedence values:

```
Pfirst-class=0
Pspecial-delivery=100
Plist=-30
Pbulk=-60
Pjunk=-100
```

Higher values have higher priorities than lower values. As shown, some sendmail configu-ration implementations assign negative values to the Precedence: field values of bulk and junk to ensure that those classes of mail get lowest priority when transferring mail to remote hosts.

The actual text strings used in Precedence: header fields can vary between MTA packages. You might have to add additional values to support strings generated by MTA packages you commonly receive messages from.

O Lines

Configuration lines that begin with an O define options that control the behavior of the sendmail program. Many global options can be set with O lines. Besides specifying options in the configuration file, they can also be specified from the command line by using the -o or -O parameters when the sendmail program is started.

Older versions of sendmail used single-character option names; for these type of options, use the following format for O lines:

Oo value

In this line, o is the single-character option name, and value is the value for the option.

Version 8.7 of sendmail introduced support for long option names, which take the following format for O lines:

O option=value

In this line, option is the long option name, and value is the value for the option. Depending on the option, value can be a string, an integer, a Boolean, or a time interval.

There are lots and lots of options available to control sendmail's behavior—too many to cover in this chapter. Table 8.8 shows some of the more common options used in configuring sendmail on a standard mail server.

TABLE 8.8 sendmail Options

Option	Description
AliasFile	File to specify mail aliases
DefaultUser	Sets the user ID and group ID for sendmail to run under
DontBlamesendmail	Allows world-writable files and directories—very dangerous
HoldExpensive	Allows sendmail to queue mail for expensive mailers to process when specified
CheckpointInterval	Performs a checkpoint on the mail queue as specified
DeliveryMode	Sets delivery mode of sendmail to interactive, background, queued, or deferred
ErrorMode	Sets method for reporting errors—via print, mail, or none
SaveFromLine	Keeps all Unix-style From: header lines, even if redundant
MaxHopCount	Sets number of times messages can be processed by an MTA, and discards messages that exceed the hop count
IgnoreDots	Ignores dots in incoming messages (always disabled for SMTP)
SendMimeErrors	Sends error messages in MIME format
ConnectionCacheTimeout	Sets the maximum amount of time a cache connection can be idle

TABLE 8.8 Continued

Option	Description
LogLevel	Sets the log level (default is 9, a normal level of logging)
MeToo	Sends message to username even if it is in an alias expansion
CheckAliases	Validates aliases when rebuilding the alias database
OldStyleHeaders	Assumes headers may be in old format using spaces to delimit names
QueueDirectory	Specifies the mail queue directory
StatusFile	Logs summary statistics in a file for the mailstats program
Timeout.queuereturn	Sets how long to wait for a message
UserDatabaseSpec	Sets the user database specification
ForkEachJob	Uses a separate process to deliver each job in the queue
SevenBitInput	Strips input to 7 bits
EightBitMode	Sets method of handling 8-bit data
MinQueueAge	Processes only jobs that have been in the queue longer than a set time
DefaultCharSet	Sets character set to convert non-MIME data to MIME
DialDelay	Allows a delay time for dial-on-demand networks to establish the connection
NoRecipientAction	Sets action to take for messages that have no valid recipients
MaxDaemonChildren	Sets number of sendmail children that can process incoming mail simultaneously
ConnectionRateThrottle	Sets number of incoming daemon connections allowed concurrently

Rule Set Lines

The core of the configuration file is the rule sets, which instruct sendmail on how to parse incoming messages and determine how to deliver the message to the intended recipients. Rule sets use the R and S configuration lines, described in the following sections. R configuration lines define the actual processes to perform on the message, and S configuration lines define groups of rule sets.

R Lines

The R lines use tokens and parsing to process an incoming message to determine the proper recipients and the methods used to send the message to the recipients. Each R line represents a separate rule.

There are two parts to a rule: the left-hand side (LHS), and the right-hand side (RHS). The LHS defines what tokens (or phrases) to look for in the incoming message. The

RHS defines how to rewrite the address based on tokens found in the LHS. The format of an R line looks like this:

```
Rlhs    rhs    comments
```

Each field must be separated by at least one tab character. Any macros and classes used in the rule set are expanded to match the parsed information. The LHS defines special symbols to use to parse the messages. Table 8.9 shows the symbols used in the LHS tokens.

TABLE 8.9 LHS Symbols in sendmail Rule Sets

LHS Symbol	Description
$*	Match zero or more tokens
$+	Match one or more tokens
$-	Match exactly one token
$@	Match zero tokens
$=x	Match any item in class x
$~x	Match any item not in class x

When tokens match a symbol in the LHS, they are assigned as values to the RHS. Each new macro name is in the form $n; n is the numeric index of the token in the message. For example, if the LHS $-:$+ is applied to an input of uucp-dom:ispmail, the values passed to the RHS would be $1 equals uucp-dom and $2 equals ispmail.

If the LHS symbols do not match the message, nothing is done with the rule set. If the LHS symbols *do* match an incoming message, the input is rewritten using the format of the RHS. The RHS also uses symbols, listed in Table 8.10, as it rewrites the message.

TABLE 8.10 RHS Macros in sendmail Rule Sets

Macro	Description
$n	Substitute token n from LHS
$[name$]	The Fully Qualified Domain Name (FQDN) of the host
$(map key $@ arguments $:Default $)	Generalized key mapping function
$>n	"Call" rule set n
$#mailer	Resolve to mailer program name
$@host	Specify host
$:user	Specify user

As shown in Table 8.10, any hostnames passed to the RHS that are enclosed with $[and $] are expanded to their full hostname to include the domain name. Also, as shown in the table, one rule set can directly pass off to another rule set by using the $>*n* metasymbol; *n* is the s line identifier of the next rule set to process the tokens.

S Lines

Configuration lines that begin with an s identify a group of rules that form a rule set, which is normally identified by a numeric value. sendmail has six standard rule sets, listed in Table 8.11, for parsing mail messages to find the recipients to whom messages should be forwarded.

TABLE 8.11 sendmail Rule Set Numbers for s Lines

Rule Set	Description
0	Resolves a mailer, host, and user
1	Applied to all sender addresses
2	Applied to all recipient addresses
3	Turns addresses into FQDN form
4	Translates internal to external addresses
5	Applied to local addresses that do not have aliases

Some special rule sets begin with the string check_. These rule sets identify messages that will be forwarded to the error or discard mailers. Figure 8.2 shows the typical path a message takes through the standard rule sets.

All messages first pass through rule set 3, which "cleans up" the addresses by turning hostnames into the proper FQDN format.

After rule set 3 is finished, rule set 0 extracts the mailer, hostname, and username from the address. After rule set 0 has extracted the mailer information, it can then pass the message off to the appropriate mailer system specified in the M line definitions.

Likewise, rule set 1 is used to rewrite any sender addresses, and rule set 2 rewrites any recipient addresses. That information is then passed to rule set 4 to resolve the addresses to an external format.

You can watch the various rule sets in action by using the sendmail program with the -bt option. This option tests an intended address and shows how rule sets act, given the configuration file and the address that was entered. Listing 8.3 shows a sample sendmail session that uses the -bt option. Line numbers have been added to aid in the following discussion.

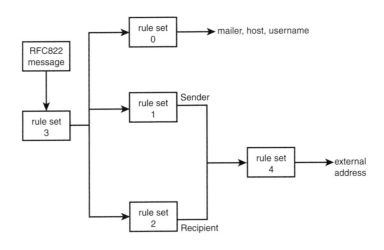

FIGURE 8.2

Sendmail rule set paths.

LISTING 8.3 Sample sendmail *-bt* Session

```
1  [rich@shadrach rich]$ /usr/sbin/sendmail -bt -C test.cf
2  ADDRESS TEST MODE (ruleset 3 NOT automatically invoked)
3  Enter <ruleset> <address>
4  > 3,0 rich
5  rewrite: ruleset   3   input: rich
6  rewrite: ruleset  96   input: rich
7  rewrite: ruleset  96 returns: rich
8  rewrite: ruleset   3 returns: rich
9  rewrite: ruleset   0   input: rich
10 rewrite: ruleset 199   input: rich
11 rewrite: ruleset 199 returns: rich
12 rewrite: ruleset  98   input: rich
13 rewrite: ruleset  98 returns: rich
14 rewrite: ruleset 198   input: rich
15 rewrite: ruleset 198 returns: $# local $: rich
16 rewrite: ruleset   0 returns: $# local $: rich
17 > 3,0 president@whitehouse.gov
18 rewrite: ruleset   3   input: president @ whitehouse . gov
19 rewrite: ruleset  96   input: president < @ whitehouse . gov >
20 rewrite: ruleset  96 returns: president < @ whitehouse . gov >
21 rewrite: ruleset   3 returns: president < @ whitehouse . gov >
22 rewrite: ruleset   0   input: president < @ whitehouse . gov >
```

LISTING 8.3 Continued

```
23 rewrite: ruleset 199   input: president < @ whitehouse . gov >
24 rewrite: ruleset 199 returns: president < @ whitehouse . gov >
25 rewrite: ruleset  98   input: president < @ whitehouse . gov >
26 rewrite: ruleset  98 returns: president < @ whitehouse . gov >
27 rewrite: ruleset 198   input: president < @ whitehouse . gov >
28 rewrite: ruleset  95   input: < uucp-dom : ispmail > president
➡ < @ whitehouse . gov >
29 rewrite: ruleset  95 returns: $# uucp-dom $@ ispmail $: president
➡ < @ whitehouse . gov >
30 rewrite: ruleset 198 returns: $# uucp-dom $@ ispmail $: president
➡ < @ whitehouse . gov >
31 rewrite: ruleset   0 returns: $# uucp-dom $@ ispmail $: president
➡ < @ whitehouse . gov >
32 >
```

Line 1 shows using the sendmail program with the -bt option to test a configuration file, specified with the -c option. In line 4, the address rich is tested using rule set 3 and then rule set 0. Lines 5 through 8 show that rule set 3 is called with rich as the input. Rule set 3 then calls rule set 96 to process the input, and then returns rich. Lines 9 through 16 show rule set 0 in action with rich as the input again. Rule set 0 calls rule sets 199, 98, and then 198. The output of rule set 0 shown in line 16 is the mailer local and the address rich. Not too exciting.

Lines 17 through 31 show a more interesting test. Again, rule sets 3 and 0 are tested using an external address: president@whitehouse.gov. Lines 18 through 21 show rule set 3 processing the input. This time the output of rule set 3 is different from the original input. Rule set 3 separated the username portion (president) from the hostname portion (whitehouse.gov) to pass on to rule set 0. Lines 22 through 31 show how rule set 0 processed the input. Many intermediate rules were called by rule set 0 before it came up with its return value. As stated earlier, rule set 0 produced the mailer required to send the message (uucp-dom), the hostname to forward the message to (ispmail), and the username of the recipient (president@whitehouse.gov). This result shows that the sample configuration file is set to forward any external mail messages via UUCP to the host ispmail. To exit this mode, press Ctrl+D.

Using the m4 Preprocessor

The m4 macro preprocessor is used to create the sendmail configuration file from a set of macro files. As a macro file is read into the input, macros are expanded before being written to an output file. Some macro definitions are included with the m4 preprocessor program; others are defined in the sendmail configuration distribution. Besides expanding macros, the m4 macro preprocessor can also contain built-in functions, such as running shell commands, manipulating text, and performing integer arithmetic. Many Linux distributions use the GNU version of the m4 macro preprocessor. The most current version of GNU m4 is version 1.4, available on most Unix distributions.

You can use the m4 preprocessor to create configuration files by defining a small set of macros instead of having to hand-code all the individual action lines in the configuration file. Table 8.12 lists some of the macros available to use in the semdmail configuration file.

TABLE 8.12 sendmail Macro Definitions

Macro	Description
divert(*n*)	Defines a buffer action for m4. When *n* = -1 the buffer is deleted; 0 starts a new buffer.
OSTYPE	Defines the operating system the macro is used on. This macro allows the m4 program to add operating system–specific macro files.
Domain	Defines what domains the MTA will be using to transfer messages.
Feature	Defines a special feature set that will be used in the configuration file.
Define	Defines specific option values in the configuration file.
MASQUERADE_AS	Defines an alternative hostname that sendmail will answer messages as.
MAILER	Defines a method of mail transport for sendmail.

The entries in the macro definition file are expanded by the m4 preprocessor to create the complete configuration file. Listing 8.4 shows a sample macro file that can be used to create a standard sendmail configuration file.

LISTING 8.4 Sample sendmail Macro File

```
divert(-1)
divert(0)dnl
include(`/usr/lib/sendmail-cf/m4/cf.m4')dnl
OSTYPE(`linux')dnl

FEATURE(`allmasquerade')dnl
FEATURE(`masquerade_envelope')dnl
FEATURE(`always_add_domain')dnl
FEATURE(`virtusertable')dnl
FEATURE(`local_procmail')dnl
FEATURE(`access_db')dnl
FEATURE(`blacklist_recipients')dnl
```

LISTING 8.4 Continued

```
MASQUERADE_AS(`ispnet1.net')dnl

MAILER(`smtp')dnl
MAILER(`procmail')dnl
```

As seen in this example, the Feature macro command can define many different features. Each feature represents a separate set of action lines in the final configuration file. Note how each line ends with the text dnl, which represents the end of a line entry in the macro file.

CAUTION

You may have noticed the odd way of quoting text strings in the m4 macro file. The m4 preprocessor uses the backtick (`` ` ``) and the single tick (') to represent quotation marks. If you do not use these characters properly, the m4 program will not create the final configuration file correctly.

After the .mc file is created, you must use the m4 preprocessor program to create the text configuration file. This procedure is discussed later in the "Creating and Installing a Configuration File" section.

The sendmail Command Line

Unlike some other MTA programs, the sendmail program performs all the MTA functions from a single executable, thus making the command-line syntax somewhat complex. This section describes the parameters and options that modify sendmail's behavior.

The format of the sendmail command looks like this:

```
sendmail [flags] [address ...]
```

By default, with no *flags* specified, sendmail reads the standard input until it reaches an end-of-file marker or a line with a single period, whichever comes first. It then considers the input text a message and attempts to mail it to the *address* listed in the command line.

Flags can be added to the command line to control sendmail's behavior. Flags are separated into two groups: parameters and options. Parameters, listed in Table 8.13, modify the way sendmail behaves when it is running.

TABLE 8.13 sendmail Command-Line Parameters

Parameter	Description
-B	Specifies the format of the message body, either 7BIT or 8BIT-MIME.
-b *mode*	Sets sendmail's mode of operation.
-C *file*	Specifies an alternative configuration file.
-d *debug*	Activates debugging flags while running sendmail.
-F *sender*	Specifies the name of the sender of the message, used in the From: header field.
-f *sender*	Allows the sender to specify an alternative sender address for the message. Can be used only by a trusted user.
-h *count*	Sets a maximum hop count for the message.
-i	Ignores single periods on a line.
-N *status*	Sets the delivery notification status of the message to what's specified in *status*.
-n	Indicates that aliasing or forwarding messages is not allowed.
-p *prot*	Defines the transport protocol used to send the message.
-q *param*	Specifies how to process the mail queue. By having *param* set to a time, sendmail will regularly process the mail queue. This parameter can also be used to process certain types of messages.
-R *mess*	Specifies what sendmail returns if a message is undeliverable; *mess* can be either full for the complete message or hdrs for just the message headers.
-t	Instructs sendmail to extract the destination addresses from the message's RFC 822 header fields.
-U	Specifies that the message was sent from an internal MUA program.
-V *val*	Sets the message envelope ID to *val*. This parameter is often used to help track messages.
-v	Specifies verbose mode.
-X *log*	Specifies a log file for sendmail to use.
--	Defines the end of the parameter section.

The -b *mode* command-line parameter defines the mode that the sendmail program runs in. Table 8.14 lists the different run modes for sendmail.

TABLE 8.14 sendmail Run Modes

Mode	Description
a	Run sendmail in ARPANET mode
d	Run sendmail as a background daemon
D	Run sendmail as a foreground daemon
h	Print the persistent host database
H	Purge the persistent host database
i	Initialize the alias database
m	Deliver mail (default)
p	Print a listing of the mail queue
s	Use the SMTP protocol on the input and output
t	Run sendmail in test mode
v	Verify names only; tells sendmail not to deliver messages

For normal operation, the -bd parameter is used to allow sendmail to work in the background as a daemon process. This setting is the one normally used for a production e-mail server. If you are testing a new configuration, you can use the -bt parameter to run sendmail in test mode. This mode attempts to deliver a single message defined on the command line and then exit.

Options, the second group of flags, modify the default values of items in the configuration file. Using options allows you to test various configurations without having to rebuild the sendmail.cf configuration file.

Installing sendmail

Over the years, the sendmail program has been through many different versions. The current production version at the time of this writing is version 8.11.4. As many of the upgrades to sendmail involve security fixes, it is often wise to install the latest version when it becomes available. After you determine your proper configuration file details, you can often upgrade the binary programs without having to re-create your configuration file.

This section describes how to install the sendmail program by downloading the sendmail source code from the sendmail Web site (www.sendmail.org) and compiling it.

Obtaining and Building the Source Code

Many Unix distributions include a binary release of the sendmail program. Unfortunately, not all Unix distributions keep their sendmail package up-to-date. It is always advisable to watch the sendmail Web site for new releases. When there is a new release, you can download the source code from the sendmail Web site. The sendmail distributions are located in the download area. Several different versions of sendmail are available for download, so be careful to pick the correct version for your needs. The most current production version at the time of this writing is sendmail.8.11.4.tar.gz, a Unix tar file that has been compressed with the GNU zip program. Alternatively, there is another version named sendmail.8.11.4.tar.Z, which uses the standard Unix compress method. Download the smallest version you can extract on your server.

After you have downloaded the distribution file to a working directory, extract the source code with the `tar` command:

```
tar -zxvf sendmail.8.11.4.tar.gz -C /usr/local/src
```

This command extracts the source code files into a directory called /usr/local/src/sendmail-8.11.4. You must have root permissions to create subdirectories in the /usr/local directory.

The next step is to compile the binary executables from the source code. You can change directories to the /usr/local/src/sendmail-8.11.4 subdirectory and use the premade script named `Build`. This script creates all the sendmail executable files using default values. You can run the `Build` script by typing the command:

```
sh ./Build
```

You specify `./Build` to make sure you're running the `Build` script in the current directory. The `Build` script uses the `uname -a` function to determine the operating system being used and creates a makefile accordingly.

To install the newly created sendmail executable files, you can use the `Build` script again, this time with the install options:

```
sh Build install
```

Make sure you are the `root` user when you do this, or you will not have the permission needed to place files in the proper directories on your Linux system.

Creating and Installing a Configuration File

After creating and installing the executable files, you create the configuration file next. The sendmail package includes a group of configuration file templates for creating a generic configuration file. The cf/cf directory under the sendmail-8.11.3 directory contains sample configuration files for many different Unix platforms and distributions.

Each configuration template is stored in two formats:

- The standard .cf format
- The m4 .mc format

The .cf version of the configuration template is the standard text format of the sendmail configuration file discussed earlier in the "Configuring sendmail" section. The .mc version is the m4 preprocessor version of the configuration file. This file is used by the m4 preprocessor to create the actual configuration file, as described earlier in the "Using the m4 Preprocessor" section.

After you determine the .mc configuration file template that is close to your e-mail environment, you can copy it to a file named config.mc, and add any site-specific information that might be necessary. Next, use the Build script to create a configuration file:

```
cp generic-linux.mc config.mc
sh Build config.cf
cp config.cf /etc/mail/sendmail.cf
```

After creating the new config.cf file, copy it to the /etc/mail/sendmail.cf file to be used as the default configuration file.

Starting and Testing sendmail

After creating a generic configuration file, you can start sendmail. The easiest method of using sendmail is as a background daemon process, having it regularly check the mail queue for new messages. To do that, use the -b and -q options, as shown in the following line:

```
sendmail -bd -q30m
```

This command runs sendmail as a background process (-bd) and instructs it to check the unsent message queue for new messages every 30 minutes (-q30m). Because this command runs sendmail in background mode, you should see a command prompt immediately after issuing the command. Remember to issue this command with root privileges. At this point, if your configuration file is correct, you should be able to send and receive messages using sendmail.

Receiving Local Mail

You can test sendmail's ability to receive messages from local users by logging in as a user and using the mail command to send yourself a message. If sendmail is working properly, the message should appear in your mailbox, as shown in Listing 8.5.

LISTING 8.5 Sending a Message from a Local User

```
[rich@test rich]$ mail rich
Subject: This is a test message
This is a test message
.
```

LISTING 8.5 Continued

```
Cc:
[rich@test rich]$ mail
Mail version 8.1 6/6/93.  Type ? for help.
"/var/spool/mail/rich": 1 message 1 new
>N  1 rich               Fri May 18 15:28   13/370    "This is a test messag"
&
Message 1:
From rich  Fri May 18 15:28:10 2001
Date: Fri, 18 May 2001 15:28:10 -0500
From: Rich Blum <rich>
To: rich
Subject: This is a test message

This is a test message

&
```

As you can see in this example, the message was successfully sent and received. Next you can test whether sendmail can receive messages from remote SMTP hosts.

Receiving Remote Mail

You can test sendmail's ability to receive messages from remote hosts by simulating an SMTP session and sending yourself a message, as shown in Listing 8.6.

LISTING 8.6 Sending a Message from a Remote User

```
[rich@test rich]$ telnet localhost 25
Trying 127.0.0.1...
Connected to localhost.
Escape character is '^]'.
220 test.ispnet1.net ESMTP sendmail 8.11.3/8.11.3; Fri, 18 May
➥ 2001 15:31:49 -0
EHLO test.ispnet1.net
250-test.ispnet1.net Hello IDENT:rich@localhost [127.0.0.1], pleased to
➥ meet you
250-ENHANCEDSTATUSCODES
250-EXPN
250-VERB
250-8BITMIME
250-SIZE
250-DSN
250-ONEX
```

LISTING 8.6 Continued

```
250-ETRN
250-XUSR
250 HELP
MAIL FROM: <rich@test.ispnet1.net>
250 2.1.0 <rich@test.ispnet1.net>... Sender ok
RCPT TO: <rich@test.ispnet1.net>
250 2.1.5 <rich@test.ispnet1.net>... Recipient ok
DATA
354 Enter mail, end with "." on a line by itself
To: rich
From: rich
Date: 18 May 2001, 15:30
Subject: Test Internet message
This is a test of sending from a remote user.
.
250 2.0.0 f4IKW2d19206 Message accepted for delivery
QUIT
221 2.0.0 test.ispnet1.net closing connection
Connection closed by foreign host.
You have new mail in /var/spool/mail/rich
[rich@test rich]$ mail
Mail version 8.1 6/6/93.  Type ? for help.
"/var/spool/mail/rich": 1 message 1 new
>N  1 rich@test.ispnet  Fri May 18 15:32  13/496   "Test Internet message"
&1
Message 1:
From rich@test.ispnet1.net  Fri May 18 15:32:47 2001
From: Rich Blum <rich@test.ispnet1.net>
To: rich
Date: 18 May 2001, 15:30
Subject: Test Internet message

This is a test of sending from a remote user.

&
```

To simulate an incoming SMTP message, you can use telnet on TCP port 25 of your local server. If the sendmail program is listening for remote connections, it will accept the connection and greet you with an opening banner, as shown in this example. Following that, you can manually enter a standard SMTP session, identifying yourself as both the sender and the recipient. After the message has been sent, the SMTP session can be closed, and the mail program can be used to read the message. As shown in the example, the message was successfully delivered to the local recipient.

Securing sendmail

Back on the old days of sendmail, the mail administrator often had to change many things in the default installation to make sendmail secure. Now sendmail's default installation has several features and default settings that make it more secure. You should not have to change too many things to ensure a secure mail environment when using sendmail.

This section describes a few of sendmail's security features and explains why they are there to protect you.

File Permissions

Proper file permissions are an important part of the sendmail system. Using improper file and directory permissions and owners can give remote hackers access to your system. sendmail uses strict file permission and ownership policies on the mail server system. If the file permission policies are violated, sendmail produces a warning message.

Many new restrictions are now placed on files and directories in sendmail. Most of them boil down to two often-overlooked scenarios:

- sendmail will not read, write, or run files that are group or world writable.
- sendmail will not read, write, or run files located in directories that are group or world writable.

These two scenarios cover the majority of problems novice mail administrators run into. As an example, if the sendmail.cf file or the /etc/mail directory have group-writable permissions, sendmail will not read the sendmail.cf configuration file located there. In sendmail version 8.11.3, a message is produced warning you of this situation:

```
[root@test mail]# sendmail -bd -q30m
/etc/mail/sendmail.cf: WARNING: dangerous write permissions
[root@test mail]#
```

If you are in an e-mail environment where you must have group- or world-writable files or directories, you can disable the sendmail warnings by using the DontBlamesendmail option parameter in the sendmail.cf configuration file:

```
O DontBlamesendmail = option
```

In this line, option is one or more parameter names that describe the level of openness you want. The default value is safe, which enforces the strict policies. To allow sendmail to process files located in group-writable directories, you can use this format:

```
O DontBlamesendmail = GroupWritableDirPathSafe
```

This option directs sendmail to ignore any directory permission settings on the system.

CAUTION

The `DontBlamesendmail` options are provided to assist you when troubleshooting or experimenting with alternative configurations. However, you should not operate a production sendmail server with these options enabled.

Sendmail Users

sendmail recognizes three categories of special users. All three are defined as option values in the sendmail.cf configuration file:

- `TrustedUser`
- `DefaultUser`
- `RunAsUser`

By default, sendmail assumes that the `root` username will be used to run sendmail and own all the special sendmail files, such as the sendmail.cf and sendmail.cw files. You can use these options as described in the following sections to modify the usernames sendmail uses.

The `TrustedUser` Option

The `TrustedUser` option allows you to specify one or more users that sendmail allows to own files accessed by sendmail. You can use this option to create a separate mail administrator account on your Unix system that is responsible for maintaining the sendmail tables, without giving that person `root` privileges. Remember that any trusted users you have specified other than `root` have the capability of hacking into `root` if sendmail is running under the `root` username.

You can use two methods to define trusted users for sendmail. You can define individual trusted users by listing them individually in the configuration file with T lines:

```
Troot
Tdaemon
Tuucp
Tsendmail
```

Alternatively, you can define an Ft line that defines a file containing a text list of the trusted usernames:

```
Ft/etc/mail/sendmail.ct
```

The `DefaultUser` Option

The `DefaultUser` option allows sendmail to run the separate mailer programs (such as procmail) under a username other than `root`. By default, sendmail attempts to run all mailers with the username `mailnull`. Only if it doesn't find this username on the system does it start the mailers as `root`.

If you create the `mailnull` username, sendmail uses it automatically. If you specify an alternative username for `DefaultUser`, sendmail uses that username instead.

The RunAsUser Option

The `RunAsUser` option specifies the username permissions that sendmail operates under after it starts. sendmail must start as the `root` user so that it can access the SMTP network port on the server. After that, it can perform a `setuid` function to change to an alternative username on the system.

This option is useful for helping minimize the effects of the sendmail system becoming compromised. By limiting the areas that the sendmail username can access, you can prevent hackers from accessing critical files on the server.

The `RunAsUser` username must have access to these sendmail-related areas on the server:

- Write access to the /var/spool/mqueue directory
- Write access to the /var/log/maillog file
- Read access to the sendmail.cf file and any other sendmail tables used

When the sendmail system operates under another username, you must also ensure that the local mail delivery program runs as `setuid` because the sendmail program will not have access to individual users' mailboxes.

Trusted Applications

As a higher level of security control, sendmail allows you to specify the executable programs it is allowed to use when forwarding mail messages based on alias or .forward files.

The smrsh program, installed as part of the sendmail package, creates a restricted shell that runs only programs found in a specified directory. By specifying the smrsh feature in the sendmail.cf configuration file, you can tightly control what programs your users can pass messages to.

To add the smrsh feature, you should specify it in the config.mc script by using the `FEATURE` command:

```
FEATURE(smrsh)
```

When the sendmail.cf file is created, it incorporates the smrsh program in the program mailer function to forward all program requests to the smrsh shell. When a request is made to forward a message to a program (such as procmail or majordomo), the smrsh shell looks for the executable in the /usr/adm/sm.bin directory.

You can control which programs are allowed to run from sendmail by restricting the programs located in the /usr/adm/sm.bin directory. Links to the actual executable program files are usually created in the /usr/adm/sm.bin directory.

Summary

The most popular open source MTA package available for the Unix platform is the sendmail package. It is composed of not only the sendmail executable program, but also a single configuration file and several lookup tables to help process messages.

The sendmail configuration file contains all the information sendmail uses to control how it processes e-mail messages (with the exception of lookup information stored in the lookup tables). This file includes rule sets that sendmail uses to determine how individual messages are processed. By comparing the message headers and body to specific rule sets, sendmail determines where and how the message should be delivered.

To simplify creating the sendmail configuration file, the sendmail developers have come up with the m4 macro preprocessor. By using macro directives, you can create a small m4 macro file that will be expanded into a full-blown configuration file. This preprocessor greatly simplifies configuring sendmail.

The sendmail program itself is extremely versatile. You can control how it is used by setting command-line options and parameters. You can also run sendmail in a multitude of ways, from processing the mail queue once to running as a daemon for continuous message processing.

Installing sendmail has become simple. Many binary distributions are available, or you can download the sendmail source code and compile it yourself on your Unix platform.

Sendmail supports several security features, such as being extremely picky about the file and directory permissions of files it uses when processing messages. You can disable this feature while testing, but following the strict permissions is recommended in a production environment. By default sendmail runs with root permissions. If you prefer not to use root, you can create a separate user ID for sendmail to run under, but remember to grant the special user ID access to all the required sendmail files. Another security feature is controlling the programs users can launch via sendmail by using a restricted shell, which limits hackers' ability to run rogue programs from their e-mail accounts.

The qmail E-mail Package

Another popular MTA package for the Unix environment is qmail, developed by Dan Bernstein. This package supports many features that make it an attractive alternative to the sendmail package for many ISPs and corporate mail administrators.

This chapter describes the different parts of the qmail package and how to install and configure qmail for a standard mail server.

What Is qmail?

The qmail package is more than a simple sendmail replacement; in fact, it differs from the sendmail package in many ways. It is composed of several executable programs that interact to transfer messages and a lot of text configuration files, each responsible for controlling the behavior of those executable programs. Figure 9.1 shows a block diagram of the core programs used by qmail.

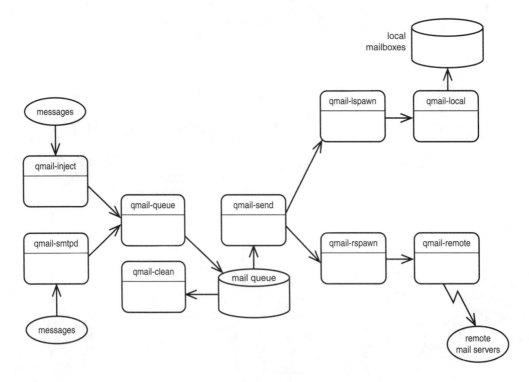

FIGURE 9.1

A qmail block diagram.

Nine core programs are used in qmail. The qmail-queue program stores messages in the mail queue. The next two programs insert a new mail message into qmail-queue—qmail-inject for messages generated locally, and qmail-smtpd for messages from remote mail servers.

After the message is successfully saved in the mail queue, the qmail-send program is called to deliver the message to the appropriate destination. Messages detected as local to the mail server are forwarded to the qmail-lspawn program, and messages destined for remote mail servers are forwarded to the qmail-rspawn program. The qmail-clean program removes any messages that have been left in the mail queue because they are in an unknown state or marked as permanently undeliverable.

Both the qmail-lspawn and qmail-rspawn programs have helper programs: qmail-local and qmail-remote, respectively. Each helper program assists in getting the mail message to the correct final destination. The qmail-local program can be used to deliver messages to a local user's qmail mailbox and can also use the defined local e-mail mailer program (often binmail for most Unix systems) to help it deliver messages in a method compatible with the existing mail system. The qmail-remote program uses the Simple Mail Transfer Protocol (SMTP) to establish a connection with the remote mail server and transfer the message.

Control Files

The qmail version of configuration files, control files, are the center of the qmail configuration. These files do what they say: They control qmail's operation and behavior. They are located in the control directory under the qmail main directory. In a default qmail installation, this directory would be located at /var/qmail/control.

One or more control files are used to determine how each core executable qmail program works. Each control file, described in the following sections, defines a different variable in the qmail executable program.

Control File Structure

The qmail control files are ASCII text files that define qmail parameters. When a control file is not present, qmail assigns default values to specifically define a parameter. The presence of a control file indicates that the qmail administrator wants to change a parameter's default value.

The Unix echo command is often used to create the qmail control file. Here is an example of using this command:

```
echo "ispnet1.net  Welcome to our server" > /var/qmail/control/smtpgreeting
```

This command sets the value of the `smtpgreeting` control file to the ASCII text string listed in the `echo` command. After creating the control file, you should always check the permissions that were set for the file. Only the `root` user should be allowed modify control files.

qmail Control Files

One or more control files control the qmail core executable programs; however, some qmail executable programs do not require a control file. Table 9.1 lists the qmail core programs and the associated control files used for each one.

TABLE 9.1 qmail Control Files

qmail Executable Program	Control Files
qmail-smtpd	badmailfrom
	databytes
	localiphost
	morercpthosts
	rcpthosts
	smtpgreeting
	timeoutsmtpd
qmail-qmqpc	qmqpservers
qmail-inject	defaultdomain
	defaulthost
	idhost
	plusdomain
qmail-send	bouncefrom
	bouncehost
	concurrencylocal
	concurrencyremote
	doublebouncehost
	doublebounceto
	envnoathost
	locals
	percenthack
	queuelifetime
	virtualdomains
qmail-remote	helohost
	smtproutes
	timeoutconnect
	timeoutremote

The following sections describe how each control file is used with its associated qmail programs.

badmailfrom

The `badmailfrom` control file supplies a list of e-mail addresses that should be blocked from sending mail to the qmail server. Each address should be listed on a separate line. Domain names can be used to indicate all senders at a particular domain. If a `badmailfrom` file is not in the control file directory, no addresses are blocked from the mail server.

bouncefrom

The `bouncefrom` control file defines a username that appears on messages bounced back to the original sender. Most often these bounced-back messages are ones that have suffered permanent delivery failure in qmail.

The default value for `bouncefrom` is the generic username `MAILER-DAEMON`, which does not represent a normal Unix username. It is often a fictitious username that points to a real username in the alias file on the mail system.

If you want the bounced messages to appear to come from a different username, you can place that name in the `bouncefrom` control file by using the following command:

```
echo postmaster > /var/qmail/control/bouncefrom
```

After the `bouncefrom` control file exists, qmail uses the username in the file as the default bounced message sender.

bouncehost

The `bouncehost` control file is related to the `bouncefrom` file in that it specifies the default hostname that appears on messages bounced back to the original sender. Again, these bounced-back messages have usually suffered permanent delivery failure in qmail.

The default value for `bouncehost` is the hostname defined in the me control file (see the "me" section later in this chapter). If the me control file does not exist, then qmail uses the hostname `bouncehost`.

The combination of `bouncefrom` and `bouncehost` define the sender e-mail address of all messages bounced by qmail for any reason. This is the format of the sender address:

```
bouncefrom@bouncehost
```

Using the default values, this address becomes `MAILER-DAEMON@hostname`; *hostname* is the local mail server hostname. The `MAILER-DAEMON` username is often used as an alias pointing to the real username of the system's mail administrator.

concurrencylocal

The `concurrencylocal` control file defines the number of simultaneous local delivery processes that qmail can run. qmail can process multiple message deliveries simultaneously, and this feature comes in extremely handy when hosting large mailing lists that must process several hundred e-mail deliveries.

The default value for this parameter is `10`, which allows up to 10 local mail delivery processes to run simultaneously. The maximum value for this control file is set by the `conf-spawn` compile parameter (see "Modifying qmail Program Parameters," later in this chapter). By default, this value is set to `120`, which limits `concurrencylocal` to a maximum of 120 processes. Its maximum value is `255`.

concurrencyremote

The `concurrencyremote` control file is similar to the `concurrencylocal` control file, but it defines the number of simultaneous *remote* delivery processes that qmail can run.

The default value for this parameter is `20`, which allows up to 20 remote mail delivery processes to run simultaneously. The maximum value for this control file is also set by the `conf-spawn` compile parameter (which, again, has a default setting of `120`).

Although it is possible to have up to 255 different local and remote mail delivery processes running, this might not necessarily be a good idea. Each mail process that's running requires memory and disk space to operate, so the mail server can become overloaded if too many mail processes are running simultaneously. It is the mail administrator's job to regulate the number of mail processes running and not overload the mail server.

defaultdomain

The `defaultdomain` control file is used to augment any e-mail addresses in the message that are not recognized as being in proper `user@host.domain` format. By default, qmail-inject adds `defaultdomain` to the host address if it does not see any dots in the host address. If the `defaultdomain` file does not exist, it is set to the value used in the `me` control file—the hostname of the local mail server.

The `defaultdomain` file is most often used when sending mail messages to local users on the same mail server. If user `rich` on host `shadrach.ispnet1.net` sends a message to the local user `jessica@shadrach`, qmail automatically assumes that the recipient should be `jessica@shadrach.ispnet1.net`, and uses that address as the recipient address.

If you set the `QMAILDEFAULTDOMAIN` environment variable in the qmail executable programs, its value will override the `defaultdomain` control file value.

defaulthost

The `defaulthost` control file defines the hostname used to augment any e-mail addresses in the message that do not have a hostname. By default, qmail-inject adds the value of `defaulthost` to the username part of the address. If the `defaulthost` control file does not exist, the string `defaulthost` is used.

The `defaulthost` control file is most often used when sending mail messages to local users on the same mail server, much like the `defaultdomain` control file. For example, if user `rich` on host `shadrach.ispnet1.net` sends a message to the local user `jessica`, qmail automatically alters the recipient address to be `jessica@shadrach.ispnet1.net`. This method allows the qmail-send executable program to identify local addresses more easily and quickly than if it had to resolve the incomplete local address.

If you set the `QMAILDEFAULTHOST` environment variable in the qmail executable programs, it will override the `defaulthost` control file value.

databytes

The `databytes` control file defines the maximum number of bytes allowed in an e-mail message received by qmail-smtpd. The default value for this parameter is 0, which indicates no limit to the message size. To specify a maximum message size, create the `databytes` control file with the text value in bytes of the message size you want. For example, the following command would restrict incoming messages to 1MB or less:

```
echo 1000000 > /var/qmail/control/databytes
```

With this command, any message larger than 1MB would cause a permanent delivery failure error message.

doublebouncehost

The `doublebouncehost` control file specifies the hostname to use for messages that suffer a *double bounce*, which occurs when both the original message and the bounced message notification bounce. In this case, qmail attempts to send another notification of the double bounce to a different e-mail address (often to the mail administrator).

The `doublebouncehost` value is used with the `doublebounceto` value described next to create a valid e-mail address that qmail-send can forward double-bounced messages to. If this control file does not exist, qmail uses the hostname value in the `me` control file. If the `me` control file does not exist, qmail uses the text string `"doublebouncehost"`, which most likely will fail on its delivery attempt.

doublebounceto

The `doublebounceto` control file specifies the username to use for messages that suffer a double bounce. As described in the previous section, a double bounce occurs when a bounced message notification as well as the original message bounce.

By default, qmail uses the username `postmaster` with the `doublebouncehost` hostname to forward the double bounce notification message. If the double bounce message also bounces, `qmail-send` gives up and does not try to forward the bounce notification again.

envnoathost

The qmail-send program uses the `envnoathost` control file to specify the hostname for mail message recipients that do not supply a hostname. By default, if this control file is not present, qmail-send uses the value defined in the `me` control file, which should be the local server hostname. If the `me` control file does not exist, qmail-send uses the string `envnoathost`, which most likely will produce an error message on the delivery attempt.

This control file allows qmail-send to change the local recipient addresses into the proper `user@host` format.

helohost

The `helohost` control file specifies the hostname used in qmail-remote SMTP sessions with remote mail servers. The SMTP `HELO` command identifies the SMTP client to the remote SMTP server (see Chapter 2, "SMTP").

If the `helohost` control file is not present, qmail-remote uses the value in the `me` control file. If the `me` control file is not present, qmail-remote refuses to run.

idhost

The `idhost` control file specifies the hostname used to produce `Message-ID:` header fields in messages. By default, qmail-inject uses the hostname in the `me` control file for the `Message-ID:` field. qmail generates a unique RFC 822 `Message-ID:` field for all messages sent via qmail-inject that do not already contain a `Message-ID:` field. If you do not want to use the hostname in the `me` control file, qmail uses the hostname specified in the `idhost` control file.

If neither the `idhost` nor `me` control files are present, qmail-inject uses a hostname of `"idhost"`. Also, qmail-inject checks for the presence of the `QMAILIDHOST` environment variable. If this variable exists, it overrides the values in the `idhost` and `me` control files.

localiphost

The `localiphost` control file specifies the local hostname for mail messages that use the dotted decimal IP address notation of the local IP address.

The qmail-smtpd program is responsible for recognizing the local IP address of the qmail server in mail messages, and replacing that address with the text hostname address specified in `localiphost`. If the `localiphost` control file is not present, qmail-smtpd uses the value in the `me` control file.

Using the actual IP address of the mail server as the hostname in an address is perfectly legal in RFC 822–formatted messages, but its use has been frowned on with the use of DNS servers. The format for using IP addresses in an e-mail address looks like:

```
user@[a.b.c.d]
```

In this line, `user` is the username of the message recipient, and `a.b.c.d` is the IP address of the recipient's mail server. Note that when using this format, you must know the IP address of the mail server able to accept mail messages for the username. The DNS method of specifying hostnames has become more popular because DNS databases can be created to allow multiple hosts to accept messages for a domain.

locals

The `locals` control file specifies mail addresses that qmail should consider as local addresses to the mail server. qmail-send processes any message whose recipient address appears in the `locals` control file as a local message by forwarding it to the qmail-lspawn program. Also, note that any hostname *not* found in the `locals` control file is assumed to be a remote host (even if it is the local mail server hostname).

If the `locals` control file does not exist, qmail-send assumes that the hostname defined in the `me` control file is the only local mail host available. If the `me` control file does not exist, qmail-send refuses to run.

me

The `me` control file, the most important control file in qmail, must be present for qmail to run. This control file specifies the hostname of the local mail server. The value defined is used as the default value for many of the other control files if they are not present.

The `me` control file is usually created by running the `config` script in the qmail configuration subdirectory. The `config` script automatically determines the DNS name of the mail server and creates the proper control files (`me`, `locals`, and `rcpthosts`). If for some reason your mail server cannot connect to the DNS server (such as on a dial-up line), you can run the `config-fast` script, manually specifying the hostname of the mail server:

```
/var/qmail/configure/config-fast shadrach.ispnet1.net
```

morercpthosts

The `morercpthosts` control file specifies additional host and domain names that the qmail server will accept messages for. The main control file used to specify hosts to receive messages for is the `rcpthosts` file (discussed later in this chapter).

The qmail documentation recommends placing no more than about 50 hostnames in the `rcpthosts` file. Any additional hosts the mail server needs to receive messages for should be placed in the `morercpthosts` file.

qmail does not directly use the morercpthosts file. The qmail-newmrh program processes hostnames in the morercpthosts file to create a binary database file based on the addresses listed in morercphosts. After running the qmail-newmrh program, qmail produces the morercpthosts.cdb file, which contains the binary database. qmail-smtpd uses the morercpthosts.cdb file to quickly search the addresses listed in the morercpthosts file.

percenthack

The percenthack control file specifies a list of domains in which usernames containing a percent symbol in the address are converted to DNS-style domain names. The older Unix-to-Unix Copy Protocol (UUCP) for e-mail used the percent symbol to separate the user and hostnames in an e-mail address (user%hostname).

The qmail-send program uses the percenthack control file to determine when to convert %-style address to DNS-style addresses. For example, if the domain test.net is in the percenthack file, an address in the form of barbara%corp1.net@test.net is converted to the mail address barbara@corp1.net.

plusdomain

The plusdomain control file specifies a domain name for any address that ends with a plus sign. qmail uses these special addresses for mail list addresses that can be added onto the end of an existing user address. For example, the address rich+bass can specify a mail list address bass controlled by the normal mail address rich.

By default, the domain name in the me control file is added to any e-mail address that ends with a plus sign. If the me control file is not present, qmail-inject adds the string plusdomain to the end of the e-mail address.

qmqpservers

The qmqpservers control file specifies the addresses of Quick Mail Queuing Protocol (QMQP) servers used by the qmail-qmqpc program. The qmail-qmqpc program is usually used to send messages from a workstation to a central mail server using the qmail protocol QMQP instead of using qmail-queue to store the message in the local qmail mail queue. Often a symbolic link is created to replace qmail-queue with qmail-qmqpc so that all messages are automatically forwarded to the QMQP server.

queuelifetime

The queuelifetime control file specifies the number of seconds a message can stay in the mail queue before it is removed. The default value for this parameter is 604,800 seconds, or one week. After the queuelifetime value expires, the qmail-send program attempts to deliver the message one final time. If the message is still undeliverable, it is removed from the mail queue.

rcpthosts

The rcpthosts control file is another important control file that should be present in the qmail configuration. The rcpthosts file defines the hosts and domains that qmail-smtpd will accept messages for. Any message destined for a recipient with a host or domain name not listed in the rcpthosts file is rejected.

If the environment variable RELAYCLIENT is present, qmail-smtpd ignores the rcpthosts file (if any) and adds the value of the RELAYCLIENT environment variable to the end of each recipient address.

smtpgreeting

The smtpgreeting control file specifies the SMTP greeting banner that qmail-smtpd uses to initiate an SMTP connection with a remote client. By default, qmail-smtpd uses the hostname in the me control file. If the me control file is not present, qmail-smtpd refuses to run.

smtproutes

The smtproutes control file specifies static SMTP routes that can be used to deliver mail to specific destinations. The format of an smtproute line is as follows:

host:relay

In this line, host can be a host or domain name that should be redirected to a specific mail host defined by relay.

timeoutconnect

The timeoutconnect control file specifies the number of seconds that qmail-remote waits for the remote SMTP server to accept a new SMTP connection before disconnecting. The default value for this parameter is 60 seconds (one minute). This parameter can be used when connecting to a remote SMTP server across a slow Internet link or with busy remote servers.

timeoutremote

The timeoutremote control file specifies the number of seconds that qmail-remote waits for each response from the remote SMTP server. By default, qmail-remote waits 120 seconds (two minutes) for a response from the remote SMTP server before disconnecting the session and logging a temporary delivery failure.

timeoutsmtpd

The timeoutsmtpd control file specifies the number of seconds that qmail-smtpd waits to receive a buffer of data from the remote SMTP client. The default value for this parameter is 120 seconds (two minutes). If qmail-smtpd receives no data by the end of the `timeoutsmtpd` period, the SMTP connection with the remote server is terminated.

virtualdomains

The `virtualdomains` control file, an important control file for ISPs, allows the qmail server to accept mail for users or domains other than for the local mail server and hold those messages in a special location for the real domain mail server to collect later.

The `virtualdomains` control file consists of entries of virtual users or domains that the mail administrator wants the qmail server to accept messages for. Each separate user or domain is listed on a separate line in the file. Two formats can be used to enter data in the file. The first format, for defining virtual users, uses the following format:

```
user@domain:prepend
```

Using this format, qmail-send watches for message recipients with the address *user@domain*. When a message destined for *user@domain* is received, qmail-send converts the address to *prepend-user@domain* and passes the message to qmail-lspawn for local delivery.

The second format, for defining virtual domains, looks like this:

```
domain:prepend
```

Using this format, qmail-send watches for any message recipients containing the domain indicated by *domain* in the address. When a message contains *domain*, it is converted to *prepend-address*; *address* is the full address of the recipient (*user@domain*).

Downloading and Compiling the qmail Source Code

If your Unix system does not have a binary distribution of the qmail software package, you must download the qmail source code and compile it on your system. The qmail source code distribution is available from the qmail Web site at `http://www.qmail.org`. Simply click the "download qmail" link to navigate to the Web page with the latest version. At the time of this writing, the latest version of qmail is version 1.03. The size of the qmail version 1.03 distribution is about 220KB. The source code distribution is packaged as a compressed tar file. After the file is downloaded, it can be uncompressed and untarred into a working directory.

It has become common practice among Unix administrators to use the /usr/local/src directory structure for a work area when downloading and compiling new software. To work in this area, you must be logged in as the `root` user. This is the command used to extract the source code into the qmail working directory:

```
tar -zxvf qmail-1.03.tar.gz -C /usr/local/src
```

This command produces a /usr/local/src/qmail-1.03 directory that contains the source code distribution and related installation documentation.

Items to Check Before Compiling

Before the source code can be compiled, you need to check a few items to prepare qmail and the Unix system for installing and running qmail. The qmail directory, user IDs, and configuration parameters must all be set according to the specific qmail installation you want before you can begin to compile the qmail program. The following sections describe these items.

Creating the qmail Directory

The qmail directory location is important because it contains all the qmail elements. The binary executables, the configuration files, and the qmail mail queue directories are all located under the qmail directory.

By default, the qmail source code distribution sets the qmail directory to /var/qmail. If you want to change it to a different location, you must edit the conf-qmail file in the /usr/local/src/qmail-1.03 directory (or whatever working qmail directory you selected) before compiling qmail. The file is a text file whose first line contains the location of the qmail directory.

After the conf-qmail file is set to the qmail directory location, you must manually create the new qmail directory by using the following command while logged in as the root user:

```
mkdir /var/qmail
```

Note that you should substitute whichever qmail directory you selected for the working directory.

Modifying qmail Program Parameters

As demonstrated in the previous section "concurrencylocal," special *conf-* files are used to specify certain parameters used in the qmail installation.

The following sections describe the individual *conf-* files and how they affect the qmail installation.

The Conf-break File

The conf-break file specifies the character delimiter for user-defined mail usernames. By default, this value is set to a hyphen (-).

qmail uses this character to enable local users to create their own separate mailboxes. By adding a hyphen and other text to the end of the username, a user can create alternative mailboxes. For example, user rich could create a mailbox called rich-list that could contain a list of other usernames—both local and remote. This list would be completely controlled by the username rich.

By changing the value of the conf-break file, the mail administrator can change the break character from a hyphen to something else.

The Conf-cc File

The conf-cc file specifies the compiler command and command-line options for compiling the qmail .c source code files. By default, this file is set to the value cc -02.

This command uses the local Unix C compiler, along with the -02 option that includes code optimization if possible. You should not have to change this parameter if your Unix system uses the GNU C compiler.

The Conf-groups File

The conf-groups file specifies the qmail groups that qmail uses to contain the usernames it creates. Two separate groups must be created. By default, these groups are set to qmail and nofiles.

The qmail group contains usernames used for controlling the qmail system. The nofiles group is used for qmail processes that are not allowed access to any files on the system, so this group increases the security of the qmail system. If a hacker compromises any of the qmail user IDs, he still does not have access to anything on the Unix system.

The Conf-ld File

The conf-ld file specifies the command used to link qmail .o object files. By default, it is set to cc -s.

This command uses the local Unix C compiler with the -s option, which is used for linking object files. You should not have to change this file for normal Unix systems that are using the GNU C compiler.

The Conf-patrn File

The conf-patrn file specifies the default umask settings for qmail files. The default value for this parameter is 002.

The Conf-qmail File

The conf-qmail file specifies the location of the qmail directory. By default, this value is set to /var/qmail. All the qmail binary, configuration, and mail queues are located under this directory.

The Conf-spawn File

The conf-spawn file specifies the maximum number of simultaneous qmail-local and qmail-remote sessions that can be running on the system. The default value for this parameter is `120`.

The actual number of sessions that can occur is controlled by an entry in the qmail control configuration files. This parameter specifies the maximum number (255) that can be set in the control file.

The Conf-split File

The conf-split file specifies the number of subdirectories that the qmail directories for mail queuing—info, local, mess, and remote—are divided into. The default value for this parameter is `23`.

On qmail servers with a large volume of mail, the OS file access speed in the qmail queue can become a limiting factor in mail delivery speed. Accessing files in directories with more than 1,000 files can become overwhelming for some OSs. To help offset this problem, qmail provides the conf-split value, which is used to divide the queued messages between multiple subdirectories in the queue, thus reducing the number of files per directory in the queue.

Each queue directory is subdivided into directories numbered from 0 to one less than the value of conf-split. As each message is received in the mail queue, it is placed in the appropriate subdirectory based on the following equation:

```
dir = msg % conf-split
```

In this equation, *msg* is the inode number assigned to the message file. The *dir* number is the subdirectory under the main queue directory where the message is placed. For large qmail servers, conf-split values as high as 3,000 have been recommended.

The Conf-users File

The conf-users file specifies the unique usernames that qmail requires on the Unix system. Each username has a separate function in qmail. Table 9.2 shows the default usernames and their purpose.

TABLE 9.2 Default qmail Usernames

Username	Description
alias	The qmail alias user account
qmaild	The qmail daemon user account
qmaill	The qmail log user account
root	The owner of the qmail binary files
qmailp	The qmail password user account

TABLE 9.2 Continued

Username	Description
qmailq	The qmail queue user account
qmailr	The qmail remote user account
qmails	The qmail send user account

The usernames shown in Table 9.2 are the default usernames that qmail looks for on the Unix system. You can change them to any usernames you like. Remember that whatever usernames are defined in the conf-users file must be present as valid users on the Unix system for qmail to install and operate properly. Also, the conf-groups file contains the two different groups qmail uses to contain the qmail usernames (see the previous section "The Conf-groups File").

Creating qmail User IDs and Group IDs

As mentioned previously, qmail uses several unique usernames and group names to control security in the mail system. Each of the group and usernames defined in the conf-groups and conf-users files must be created on the Unix system before compiling and installing qmail.

As shown earlier in the section "The Conf-groups File," two new group names must be added to the Unix system for qmail: nofiles and qmail.

These two groups contain the usernames listed in Table 9.2 with the exception of the root user.

The Unix system assigns group ID and user ID numbers to the individual group and usernames. The numbers assigned to these names are not important. What's important is that each of the specific group and usernames are created on the system.

Each Unix system has its own method used for installing new user IDs and group IDs. The qmail source code distribution includes a sample script file that can be used to automatically create these IDs for various Unix systems.

The INSTALL.ids file contains several different script files that can be used for installing the new user IDs and group IDs on the Unix system. You can uncomment the section pertinent to your Unix distribution and run the script to create the necessary users and groups.

Fixing the qmail DNS Problem

There is one annoying bug in the current version of qmail. Using the default source code, the qmail program cannot handle DNS response packets larger than 512 bytes. This limitation prevents qmail from determining the mail host for a domain, making delivery of any messages to that domain impossible.

The bug appears in the dns.c program code in qmail, where the DNS maximum packet size has been set to 512 bytes. Christopher Davis, a qmail user, has created a patch file that fixes this problem in the dns.c code and made it available on the Internet. A link to his site is on the qmail Web home page.

An easier (although not as elegant) way to fix this problem has been suggested by other qmail users. You can manually change the maximum DNS packet size value directly in the dns.c source code before compiling. The constant used to define the packet size is PACKETSZ. Line 24 of the dns.c code file should look like this:

```
static union { HEADER hdr; unsigned char buf[PACKETSZ]; } response;
```

By changing the variable PACKETSZ to the value 65536 in line 24 of the dns.c code before compiling, qmail will not choke on large DNS packets.

Compiling qmail

After all the items identified in the previous section have been checked and set according to your particular qmail installation, you can begin the process of compiling the qmail software package, which is the simplest step in the qmail installation process.

To compile the qmail software, from the /usr/local/qmail-1.03 directory, type the command:

```
make setup check
```

This command uses the prebuilt makefile from the qmail software distribution. The makefile setup section calls for both the *it* and *man* sections to be built. The *it* section builds all the qmail binary files, and the *man* section builds all the qmail man page files. After the binary files are built, the qmail directories are created, the binary files are copied to their proper location, and the installation is checked for completion.

Configuring qmail

After qmail has been installed, you must configure it to work properly in your particular e-mail environment. This section describes the basic qmail configuration requirements to support a simple e-mail environment.

Creating the Basic qmail Control Files

Only one control file is necessary for qmail to operate: the me control file, which qmail needs to determine what hostname to accept mail for. Without this control file, qmail refuses to start.

The me control file contains the fully qualified domain name for the local mail server. If your qmail server is connected to the Internet, you can use the config program in the

/var/qmail/configure directory to create the me control file automatically. You run the config program by typing this command:

```
/var/qmail/configure/config
```

The config program attempts to perform a DNS lookup on the hostname of the qmail server. If it is successful, it creates the me control file with the appropriate hostname information. If your qmail server is not connected to the Internet, or you are not using a valid DNS name for your mail server, you can manually create the me control file by using the following command:

```
echo hostname > /var/qmail/control/me
```

In this command, hostname is the fully qualified hostname of the qmail server. Remember that you must be logged in as the root user to perform this command. Also remember that permissions must be set to the 644 mode for all control files.

Although the me control file is all that is absolutely required, it is a good idea to create a couple more control files. The locals and rcpthosts control files are also used to identify hosts that qmail will accept message for. For this basic installation you can copy the me control file to both the locals and rcpthosts files.

CAUTION

If no rcpthosts control file is present, qmail will accept messages for any user, including users on remote hosts, and attempt to relay the message to the proper host. This feature has been exploited by Internet mass mail spammers, however, and should be disabled. To disable open relaying, create an rcpthosts control file using the value of the me control file.

Creating Necessary qmail Aliases

By default qmail does not accept mail messages destined for the root user. This is used as a security precaution so that no malicious messages can be sent directly to the root user to cause security problems on the mail server.

Unfortunately, many Unix systems send log reports to the root user account. If you need to receive messages for the root user, you must configure a qmail alias for the root user account. This can be done in one simple command:

```
echo user > /var/qmail/aliases/.qmail-root
```

In this command, user is the username where you want any message sent to the root user to be forwarded. It is a good idea to use the system administrator's username (your system administrator does have her own account, doesn't she?).

Two other popular mail aliases are the postmaster and MAILER-DAEMON aliases, often used in mail message administration. Bounced messages are sent from the MAILER-DAEMON account, and sometimes an ill-informed user might respond to them. Also, the postmaster username has become a common name to use as a point of contact for Web and FTP sites. These two aliases can be forwarded to the mail administrator's user account the same way as the root account was aliased. Remember to include the .qmail part of the alias filename for each new alias account.

Determining the Local Mail Delivery Method

The qmail-lspawn program is responsible for forwarding messages destined for local mail users. One of the more confusing aspects of qmail is that it can use three different methods to deliver messages destined for users on the local mail server. You must select and configure one of the three methods for qmail to be able to deliver mail to the local system users.

qmail uses a startup script to start the qmail program, and this script starts the qmail-lspawn and qmail-rspawn programs, as well as the qmail-send and qmail-clean programs. By default, the startup script is located in the file /var/qmail/rc. The qmail software installation provides several templates for creating the qmail startup script. The rc script templates are located in the /var/qmail/boot directory. Only one script can be used for the system, and is copied to the /var/qmail/rc file.

The following sections compare the three different local mail delivery methods and shows how to configure qmail to use each of them. The method you choose to support your mail server could depend on several factors, both technical and political.

Using the Existing Local Mail Method

Every Unix implementation contains at least one program that can perform local mail delivery to users on the system, and you can configure qmail to use this program to forward mail to users on the local mail system.

qmail uses the preline program to forward messages to the local mail delivery program. The preline program processes the messages before sending them to the local mail delivery program. By default, preline adds a From:, Return-Path:, and Delivered-To: header field to each message.

To complicate things further, three different local mail delivery programs are in use on Unix platforms. You must know the proper local mail delivery program that your Unix system is using to select the right qmail startup script. These are the three different mail programs:

- mail.local, which is used by BSD 4.4 Unix systems such as NetBSD.
- binmail (which is called "mail"). There are two different versions of the binmail program for V7 and SRV4 systems. Linux systems use the V7 version of binmail.

- procmail, which can be installed as an additional option on both Linux and FreeBSD systems.

Although qmail can use any of these local mail programs, it uses a different script file to implement each mail program. qmail contains several sample startup scripts in the /var/qmail/boot directory. After you determine the local mail delivery program your Unix system uses, you can select the proper startup script and copy it to the /var/qmail/rc file. Table 9.3 shows the script files as they are related to the local mail delivery systems.

TABLE 9.3 qmail Script Files and Local Mail Delivery Programs

Script	Mail Delivery System
binm1	mail.local
binm2	SRV4 binmail
binm3	V7 binmail
proc	procmail

You might notice in the /var/qmail/boot directory that each of the qmail scripts listed in Table 9.3 also has a version with a "+df" after it. These versions are for using the qmail dot-forward program, which supports sendmail .forward file processing.

Listing 9.1 shows a sample startup script template used on a FreeBSD system.

LISTING 9.1 Sample qmail Startup Script for Mail.local

```
#!/bin/sh

# Using splogger to send the log through syslog.
# Using binmail to deliver messages to /var/spool/mail/$USER by default.
# Using BSD 4.4 binmail interface: /usr/libexec/mail.local -r

exec env - PATH="/var/qmail/bin:$PATH" \
qmail-start \
'|preline -f /usr/libexec/mail.local -r "${SENDER:-MAILER-DAEMON}" -d
➥ "$USER"' \
splogger qmail&
```

The qmail startup script uses the qmail-start program to initialize the qmail core programs and to start the necessary background processes for qmail. This is the format of the qmail-start program:

```
qmail-start [ defaultdelivery [ logger arg ... ] ]
```

As shown in Listing 9.1, the startup script used for the FreeBSD Unix system uses the `preline` command with the mail.local mail delivery program as the qmail-start *defaultde-livery* parameter. The *logger* parameter is replaced with the qmail splogger program.

To use the binm1 startup script, copy it to the /var/qmail/rc script file:

```
cp /var/qmail/boot/binm1 /var/qmail/rc
```

Using the $HOME/Mailbox Method

The standard Unix local mail delivery programs listed in Table 9.3 all use a common system to store messages for users. All mail messages are stored in a common mail directory, which is usually located in one of two places: /var/spool/mail or /var/mail. Most Linux systems store mail in the /var/spool/mail directory, but FreeBSD systems use the /var/mail directory.

Each user has a separate file in the common mail directory that contains all the messages sent to that user. The filename is the same as the username. Users have access only to their mail files within the mail directory. As the MTA receives new messages for users, they are appended to the appropriate user's mail file in the mail directory.

A few problems have been identified with the standard Unix mailbox system. By placing all the user mailboxes in a single directory, the mail system is vulnerable to both security and disk access speed problems. By creating a common mail directory that every user must have access to, the standard Unix mailbox system opens a security can of worms. Because the mailbox must be user writable, the mailbox directory must be writable by everyone, also a possible security problem. Programs that read mail must carefully check permissions to allow a mailbox owner access, but refuse other users trying to access mailboxes owned by other users.

With one mailbox file for every user, systems that support thousands of users have a lot of mailbox files, thus creating quite a large mailbox directory. Large directories can slow down disk access speeds, so having many directories with a few files each is better than having a few directories that each store a lot of files.

To solve the problems identified with the standard Unix mailbox system, qmail uses two alternative mailbox systems. The first one moves the users' mailbox files to their home directories (the second one is described in the following section). When user mailboxes are moved to their home directories, both the security and disk problems are remedied. Each user's mailbox is created as a file called Mailbox in his $HOME directory.

Although this method solves some problems, it creates another problem. Most MUA software has been written to use the standard Unix mailbox format. By moving the users' mailboxes to their home directories, qmail creates a problem for MUA programs: The MUA programs do not know that the mailboxes have been moved. To solve this problem, some qmail users have written patches for some of the more common MUA programs to enable them to access the new user mailboxes.

Another solution is to create symbolic links from the new user mailboxes to the place where the standard Unix mailboxes would be located. This solution works for most of the common MUA programs and is easy to implement.

To ensure that no mail is lost in this process, the following steps should be performed with the mail MTA program disabled and with no users logged into the system:

1. As the root user, move each user mailbox found in the standard Unix system mailbox area to the user's home directory, renaming it as Mailbox:

   ```
   mv /var/mail/barbara /home/barbara/Mailbox
   ```

2. Create a link from the standard Unix mailbox location to the new mailbox location:

   ```
   ln -s /home/barbara/Mailbox /var/mail/barbara
   ```

After performing these steps for each system user, you must create the qmail startup script that uses the qmail Mailbox format. The Mailbox template script is located at /var/qmail/boot/home. Again, if you are using the qmail dot-forward program, you must use the home+df script and copy the proper startup script template to the /var/qmail/rc file. Listing 9.2 shows the qmail startup script used to support the qmail Mailbox method of storing messages.

LISTING 9.2 Sample qmail Startup Script for the Mailbox Format

```
#!/bin/sh

# Using splogger to send the log through syslog.
# Using qmail-local to deliver messages to ~/Mailbox by default.

exec env - PATH="/var/qmail/bin:$PATH" \
qmail-start ./Mailbox splogger qmail&
```

Again, the qmail startup script uses the qmail-start program to initialize and start the qmail core programs. This time the defautdelivery parameter is set to the value of ./Mailbox. This value is passed to the qmail-lspawn program to set the default message delivery method for qmail-local to the Mailbox format.

Using the $HOME/Maildir Method

The second alternative mailbox system that qmail uses is the Maildir system, which takes the qmail Mailbox format one step further. Not only is each user's mailbox moved to her home directory, but the standard Unix mailbox format is changed.

One problem with the standard Unix mailbox system is that it is highly vulnerable to data corruption. Because the mailbox contains all the users' mail messages, corrupting the mailbox could have catastrophic results. The qmail Maildir system changes the method for storing user messages. Much like other qmail files, user messages are stored as separate files in a specially formatted user mailbox directory. Therefore, even if one message becomes corrupt, the rest of the messages are safe in the mailbox directory.

If you decide to use the Maildir format, you must copy the appropriate startup script template to the /var/qmail/rc file. The Maildir startup script, shown in Listing 9.3, is located in the /var/qmail/boot/maildir file.

LISTING 9.3 Sample qmail Startup Script for the Maildir Format

```
#!/bin/sh

# Using splogger to send the log through syslog.
# Using qmail-local to deliver messages to Maildir format by default

exec env - PATH="@PREFIX@/qmail/bin:$PATH" \
qmail-start ./Maildir/ splogger qmail &
```

As normal, the startup script uses the qmail-start program to initialize and run the qmail core programs. Make sure to include the ending / on the /Maildir/ parameter, or qmail will just create a Mailbox-type mailbox but use the filename Maildir instead. The ending / is what triggers qmail to use the Maildir format.

Using the qmail sendmail Wrapper

For qmail to be a complete sendmail replacement, it must support the actual sendmail program that many programs call for sending mail. The qmail program includes an executable file that replaces the standard sendmail program. To use qmail as your mail server, you must install qmail's sendmail wrapper program.

The qmail sendmail wrapper program is just a front end to the normal qmail-inject program. It is written to accept parameters similar to the standard sendmail program, so it is 100% compatible with MUA programs that are written to use sendmail as the MTA. The qmail sendmail program is in the /var/qmail/bin directory.

The original sendmail program location depends on your Unix distribution. You must replace all occurrences of the sendmail program that are appropriate for your Unix distribution. The two most common locations are /usr/lib/sendmail and /usr/sbin/sendmail.

To replace the existing sendmail programs with qmail's sendmail wrapper program, you should first move the existing program to a different filename (in case you ever want to remove qmail and go back to sendmail):

```
mv /usr/sbin/sendmail /usr/sbin/sendmail.old
```

NOTE

The original sendmail program uses the Unix `setuid` bit to allow users to run the sendmail program as the `root` user. For security purposes, you might want to remove it from the sendmail program you copied. You can use the chmod program to do that; `chmod 555 sendmail.old` will do the trick.

After moving the original sendmail programs, you can create a link from the original sendmail file location to the qmail sendmail wrapper program:

```
ln -s /var/qmail/bin/sendmail /usr/sbin/sendmail
```

Receiving SMTP Messages

The qmail-smtpd program, used to accept mail messages from remote mail hosts using SMTP, does not run in background mode as the other qmail programs do. It is started by the inetd program when an incoming SMTP session is detected.

To configure inetd to know about qmail-smtpd, you must add a line to the /etc/inetd.conf configuration file. The inetd.conf configuration file is divided by IP port names as described in the /etc/services file. The keyword for the SMTP service is `smtp`. The line added to the /etc/inetd.conf file should look like this:

```
smtp    stream tcp    nowait  qmaild  /var/qmail/bin/tcp-env tcp-env
➥ /var/qmail/bin/qmail-smtpd
```

Because qmail needs to know information about the network connection passed to it by inetd, a helper program is used. The tcp-env program is a qmail utility that converts the network information received from the inetd program to Unix environment variables. When the qmail-smtpd program runs, it can check the appropriate environment variables to find the network information about the remote mail client.

To allow inetd to recognize the new configuration, you must send it a HUP signal. To do that, determine the inetd process ID (PID) and use the Unix kill program with the `-HUP` command line option. First, to find the PID of the inetd program, you can use the `ps` command with the `ax` command-line options:

```
$ ps ax | grep inetd
  184  ??  Is     0:00.48 inetd -wW
```

As shown in these code lines, the PID for the inetd process would be 184. To restart the inetd process, you can issue the command:

```
kill -HUP 184
```

This command forces the inetd process to reread the /etc/inetd.conf file, which should now pass any SMTP connections to the qmail-smtpd program. You can test it by using telnet on port 25 of the mail server, as shown in Listing 9.4.

LISTING 9.4 Sample SMTP Connection to the qmail Server

```
$ telnet localhost 25
Trying 127.0.0.1...
Connected to localhost.ispnet1.net.
Escape character is '^]'.
220 shadrach.ispnet1.net ESMTP
QUIT
221 shadrach.ispnet1.net
Connection closed by foreign host.
$
```

If the /etc/inetd.conf file is configured properly for qmail-smtpd, you should get the qmail smtpgreeting banner when you use `telnet` on the SMTP port. If there is no `smtp-greeting` control file, then qmail defaults to the contents of the `me` control file (as shown in the 220 SMTP response line in Listing 9.4). To exit the SMTP session, you type `QUIT`.

qmail and Security

The default qmail configuration supports several security and reliability features:

- qmail programs run using several separate user IDs.
- qmail minimizes the use of the root `setuid`.
- Messages are stored immediately in split message queues to avoid overcrowded directories and messages lost because of system failure.
- qmail uses detailed message delivery logging.

These features are standard qmail features, so no additional configuration is necessary . The novice mail administrator can easily configure a secure qmail MTA package, and this ease of configuration has made qmail an attractive MTA package for many mail administrators.

Summary

The qmail MTA package has quickly become a popular choice for mail administrators. Its incorporation of reliability and security features has made it an attractive alternative to the sendmail package. Instead of one monolithic program controlling all the MTA functions, qmail uses several smaller programs that interact to perform the functions. Each program controls a core piece of the total MTA functionality.

The qmail program is not controlled by a single configuration file, as sendmail is. Instead, qmail uses many smaller individual control files. Each control file is responsible for controlling a single part of the qmail functionality. This method helps simplify configuration for the mail administrator.

The qmail mail package is not normally found on most Unix distributions. You must download the source code and compile it yourself. Before compiling, however, you must configure several items, one of which is the separate user and group IDs used to control the qmail processes.

qmail can also use different methods of local mail delivery. One unique method is the Maildir mailbox format, which uses a separate directory in each user's $HOME directory. Each incoming message is created as a separate file in the mailbox directory. This method increases the reliability and integrity of received messages.

To help replace the sendmail functionality, qmail uses a sendmail wrapper program, thus allowing other programs to continue making function calls to a sendmail program to send messages. qmail then intercepts those messages and processes them in its normal fashion. qmail also incorporates an SMTP server that can send and receive messages from the Internet using standard SMTP.

The qmail package incorporates several security features by default. With these features, a novice mail administrator can configure a secure mail server without too much pain or effort.

CHAPTER 10

The Postfix E-mail Package

The Postfix software package is quickly becoming one of the more popular e-mail packages available for Unix systems. Postfix was developed by Wietse Venema to provide an alternative Mail Transfer Agent (MTA) for standard Unix servers. The Postfix software is capable of turning any Unix system into a fully functional e-mail server.

The Postfix Web site is at http://www.postfix.org. You can subscribe to several different mailing lists described on the Web site. By subscribing to a Postfix mailing list, you can keep up-to-date on the latest information about Postfix, including important patches and software improvements.

It is the responsibility of the MTA package to manage messages that come into or leave the mail server. Postfix accomplishes this message tracking by using several different modular programs and a system of mail queue directories. Each program processes messages through the various message queues until they are delivered to their final destination. If the mail server crashes during a message transfer, Postfix can determine what queue the message was last successfully placed in and attempt to continue the message processing.

This chapter details the features and components that make up the Postfix software package.

What Is Postfix?

The Postfix system consists of several mail queue directories and executable programs, all interacting with each other to provide mail service. Figure 10.1 shows a block diagram of the core Postfix components.

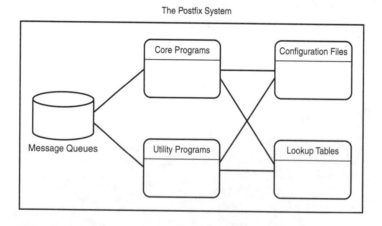

FIGURE 10.1

Block diagram of Postfix.

Each component in the Postfix block diagram provides a different function for the whole e-mail process. The following sections describe these components in more detail.

Postfix Core Programs

The Postfix package uses a master program that runs as a background process at all times. The master program enables Postfix to spawn programs that scan the mail queues for new messages and send them to the proper destinations. The core programs can be configured to remain running for set times after they are used. This configuration allows the master program to reuse a running helper program if necessary, saving processing time. After a set time limit, the helper program quietly stops itself. Listing 10.1 shows the Postfix processes running on a normal Unix system.

LISTING 10.1 Postfix Background Programs

```
232 con- I+  0:00.34 /usr/sbin/postfix/master
236 con- I+  0:00.07 qmgr
237 con- I+  0:00.05 pickup
```

These processes run continuously in the background to control mail delivery on the Postfix system. The master program, used to control the overall operation of Postfix, is responsible for starting other Postfix processes as needed. The queue manager (qmgr) and pickup programs are also configured to remain as background processes. The pickup program determines when messages are available to be routed by the Postfix system. The qmgr program is responsible for the central message routing system for Postfix.

Besides the qmgr and pickup programs, Table 10.1 shows other core programs that Postfix uses to transfer mail messages.

TABLE 10.1 Core Postfix Mail Processing Programs

Program	Description
bounce	Returns bounced messages to the sender and posts a log in the bounce message queue
cleanup	Processes incoming mail headers and places messages in the incoming queue
error	Processes message delivery requests from qmgr, forcing messages to bounce
flush	Processes messages waiting to be retrieved by a remote mail server
local	Delivers messages destined for local users
pickup	Waits for messages in the maildrop queue and sends them to the cleanup program to begin processing
pipe	Forwards messages from the qmgr program to external programs
postdrop	Moves an incoming message to the maildrop queue when that queue is not writable by normal users

TABLE 10.1 Continued

Program	Description
qmgr	Processes messages in the incoming queue, determining where and how they should be delivered, and spawns programs to deliver them
sendmail	Provides a sendmail-compatible interface for programs to send messages to the maildrop queue
showq	Reports Postfix mail queue status
smtp	Forwards messages to external mail hosts using SMTP
smtpd	Receives messages from external mail hosts using SMTP
trivial-rewrite	Receives messages from the cleanup program to ensure header addresses are in a standard format for the qmgr program, and used by the qmgr program to resolve remote host addresses

Postfix Message Queues

Unlike some other MTA packages, Postfix uses several different message queues for managing e-mail messages as they are processed. Each message queue (listed in Table 10.2) contains messages in a different message state in the Postfix system.

TABLE 10.2 Postfix Message Queues

Queue	Description
maildrop	New messages waiting to be processed; received from local users
incoming	New messages waiting to be processed; received from remote hosts, as well as processed messages from local users
active	Messages ready to be delivered by Postfix
deferred	Messages that have failed on an initial delivery attempt and are waiting for another attempt
flush	Messages destined for remote hosts that will connect to the mail server to retrieve them
mail	Delivered messages stored for local users to read

If the Postfix system shuts down at any time, messages remain in the last queue where they were placed. When Postfix is restarted, the individual components automatically begin processing messages from the queues.

Message queues are often a bottleneck on busy mail servers. As new messages are received, they are placed in separate files in the message queues. As more files are stored in the message queues, file-handling performance decreases.

Accessing files in a Unix directory with many files is slower than accessing fewer files in multiple subdirectories. As such, Postfix was created so that the message queue directories can be divided into separate subdirectories.

Each of these message queues divides the main queue directory into two levels of subdi-rectories. Each message is placed into a subdirectory based on the first two characters of its filename. Figure 10.2 illustrates this layout.

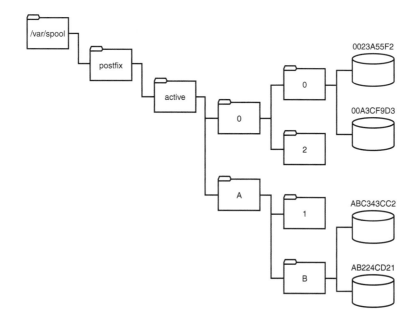

FIGURE 10.2

New message queue directory format.

As new messages are received in the message queues, new subdirectories are created. As files are retrieved from the directories, the newly created subdirectories remain behind to be used by other messages. Although this structure seems more complicated, it actually does a more efficient job of retrieving messages from the message queue than the old structure did.

Postfix Utility Programs

Besides the Postfix core programs, several utilities are used by both Postfix processes and local Postfix users to help manipulate and transfer messages. Table 10.3 shows the utilities available on a Postfix system.

TABLE 10.3 Postfix Utility Programs

Program	Description
mailq	Checks the Postfix mail queues for messages and displays the results
postfix	Controls starting, stopping, and reloading the Postfix system
postalias	Creates, updates, or queries the Postfix alias database
postcat	Displays the contents of Postfix queue files
postconf	Displays and modifies parameter entries in the main.cf configuration file
postkick	Sends command requests to running Postfix services
postlock	Locks specified Postfix files and issues a specified command
postlog	Logs a message to the system logging facility using Postfix-style log messages
postmap	Creates or queries a Postfix lookup table
postsuper	Performs maintenance on specified Postfix queue directories

Each Postfix utility program plays a different role in processing mail messages or querying the Postfix system for status information. Postfix core programs use some of the utilities to process mail; other utilities can be used by the Postfix administrator to manipulate messages and get statistics about the running system.

Postfix Configuration Files

The next block in the diagram is the Postfix configuration files, which contain information the Postfix programs use when processing messages. Unlike some other MTA programs, it is possible to change configuration information while the Postfix server is running and issue a command to have Postfix load the new information without completely shutting down the mail server.

There are three Postfix configuration files, which are located in a common Postfix directory. The default location for this directory is /etc/postfix. Usually, all users have access to view the configuration files, but only the root user has the ability to change values within the files. Of course, these access rights can be modified for your own security situation. Table 10.4 lists the Postfix configuration files.

TABLE 10.4 Postfix Configuration Files

File	Description
install.cf	Contains information from the install parameters used when Postfix was installed
main.cf	Contains parameters used by the Postfix programs when processing messages
master.cf	Contains parameters used by the Postfix master program when running core programs

You can control the operation of the core Postfix programs by using the master.cf configuration file. Each program is listed in a separate line along with the parameters to control its operation. Listing 10.2 shows a sample master.cf file with default settings.

LISTING 10.2 Sample master.cf Configuration File

```
# ==========================================================================
# service type  private unpriv  chroot  wakeup  maxproc command + args
#               (yes)   (yes)   (yes)   (never) (50)
# ==========================================================================
smtp     inet   n       -       n       -       -       smtpd
pickup   fifo   n       n       n       60      1       pickup
cleanup  unix   -       -       n       -       0       cleanup
qmgr     fifo   n       -       n       300     1       qmgr
rewrite  unix   -       -       n       -       -       trivial-rewrite
bounce   unix   -       -       n       -       0       bounce
defer    unix   -       -       n       -       0       bounce
smtp     unix   -       -       n       -       -       smtp
showq    unix   n       -       n       -       -       showq
error    unix   -       -       n       -       -       error
local    unix   -       n       n       -       -       local
```

The Postfix operational parameters are set in the main.cf configuration file. Postfix parameters have a default value that is implied within the Postfix system. If a parameter value is not present in the main.cf file, Postfix presets its value. However, if a parameter value *is* present in the main.cf file, its contents override the default value.

Each Postfix parameter is listed on a separate line in the configuration file along with its value, in the following form:

parameter = *value*

Both *parameter* and *value* are plain ASCII text strings that the mail administrator can easily read. The Postfix master program reads the parameter values in the main.cf file when Postfix is first started, and again whenever a Postfix `reload` command is issued.

Two examples of this process are the `myhostname` and `mydomain` parameters. If they are not specified in the main.cf configuration file, the `myhostname` parameter assumes the results of a `gethostname()` command, and the `mydomain` parameter assumes the domain part of the default `myhostname` parameter. If the mail administrator does not want to use these values for the mail server, he can specify different values in the configuration file using these parameters:

```
myhostname = mailserver.smallorg.org
mydomain = smallorg.org
```

When Postfix starts, it recognizes the local mail server as `mailserver.smallorg.org` and the local domain as `smallorg.org`, and ignores any system-set values.

Postfix Lookup Tables

The mail administrator can also create several lookup tables, listed in Table 10.5, for Postfix to use. Each lookup table defines parameters that control the delivery of mail in the Postfix system.

TABLE 10.5 Postfix Lookup Tables

Table	Description
access	Maps remote SMTP hosts to an accept/deny table for security purposes
alias	Maps alternative recipients to local mailboxes
canonical	Maps alternative mailbox names to real mailboxes for message headers
relocated	Maps an old user mailbox name to a new mailbox name
transport	Maps domain names to delivery methods for remote host connectivity and delivery
virtual	Maps recipients and domains to local mailboxes for delivery

The mail administrator creates each lookup table as a plain ASCII text file. After the text file is created, you use the `postmap` command to create a binary database file. Postfix uses the binary database file when searching the lookup tables, which helps speed up the lookup process.

Downloading and Compiling Postfix

If your Unix distribution does not include a binary Postfix package, or if you want to install the most current version of Postfix, you have to use a source code distribution. You can find the Postfix source code distributions on many Postfix mirror sites described on the `www.postfix.org` Web page. At the time of this writing, the most current production release is version 20010228, patch level 3; it can be downloaded from `ftp://ftp.porcupine.org`. This is the current release distribution file:

```
/mirrors/postfix-release/official/postfix-20010228-pl03.tar.gz
```

There are also experimental releases available for downloading. Experimental releases are denoted by the term "snapshot" instead of the normal "postfix" heading. Remember to use caution when installing an experimental Postfix release on a production mail server. Although the experimental releases are considered stable, they have not been fully tested on different types of Unix systems.

Download the distribution file to a work area using the FTP BINARY mode. This file is a GNU-zipped tar file that must be uncompressed and expanded. You should pick a common directory for extracting source code distributions so they don't clutter up your workspace. It has become a fairly common practice among Unix users to extract source code into the /usr/local/src directory.

CAUTION

Remember that you must be logged in as the root user to write to the /usr/local/src directory.

To extract the source code into a working directory, you can use the tar command with the -C parameter:

```
tar -zxvf postfix-20010228-pl03.tar.gz -C /usr/local/src
```

This command creates the directory /usr/local/src/postfix-20010228-pl03 and places the source code distribution there. The Postfix source code distribution has several subdirectories that contain documentation and source code for the release.

Creating the Postfix User ID and Group ID

For Postfix to work properly, you must create a specific Postfix user and group name. The postfix username is required to own the Postfix message queue directories. The actual user ID and group ID (the numerical identifiers) assigned by the Unix system are not important, but the user and group names must be postfix.

In Linux you can create a new user and group ID using the useradd command:

```
useradd -M postfix
```

This command creates a user account with the next available user ID for the system. The postfix user does not need a home directory, or a login shell, so the -M option is used to avoid creating a home directory for the postfix user.

Compiling Postfix

After creating the Postfix user and group names, you can compile the executable programs. The Postfix source code distribution includes a makefile that attempts to use the standard compiler for the Unix system being used. For many Unix systems, this is the GNU C compiler—gcc.

CAUTION

You should ensure that you have some type of C development programs and libraries loaded on your Unix system before attempting to compile from the source code distribution. As a quick test, you can try to use the command cc --version. It should return the version of the C compiler used on your system.

To compile the source code files, from the top-level Postfix distribution directory (/usr/local/src/postfix-20010228-pl03), logged in as root, type the following:

```
make
```

This command uses the make program to process the makefile and build the individual executable programs. As the make program runs, it produces messages indicating its progress. The make program traverses subdirectories for each Postfix executable program and compiles the programs. When it finishes compiling the programs, it returns to the command-line prompt.

Installing Postfix

After the Postfix executables have been created, you must run the INSTALL.sh script to install everything in its proper place. Before you do this, however, you might have to do a little housekeeping.

The Postfix system uses copycat commands to replace the sendmail program functionality. The Postfix sendmail, mailq, and newaliases commands are direct replacements for the same sendmail commands. If your Unix system previously had the sendmail program installed, you might want to copy these files to an alternative location in case you need to "fall back" to the original sendmail system to process mail messages in the sendmail mail queue. These programs can be moved to a safe area by using the Unix mv command (as the root user):

```
mv /usr/sbin/sendmail /usr/sbin/sendmail.OLD
mv /usr/bin/mailq /usr/bin/mailq.OLD
mv /usr/bin/newaliases /usr/bin/newaliases.OLD
```

It is important to remember that the sendmail program uses the Unix setuid to grant its programs root privileges when they run. Therefore, even though you have moved the programs, they could still be a security risk. To alleviate this problem, it is wise to change the permission settings on these files as shown here to remove the setuid privileges:

```
chmod 755 /usr/sbin/sendmail.OLD
chmod 755 /usr/bin/mailq.OLD
chmod 755 /usr/bin/newaliases.OLD
```

After the sendmail programs are moved out of the way, the Postfix install script can be run from the source code distribution directory as the `root` user:

```
sh INSTALL.sh
```

The install script asks several questions to determine where to place specific executables, the mail queues, the configuration files, and the man pages. Listing 10.3 shows the questions asked by the install script, with the default values shown in brackets.

LISTING 10.3 Postfix Install Script Questions

```
install_root: [/]
tempdir: [/usr/local/src/snapshot-20001005]
config_directory: [/etc/postfix]
daemon_directory: [/usr/libexec/postfix]
command_directory: [/usr/sbin]
queue_directory: [/var/spool/postfix]
sendmail_path: [/usr/sbin/sendmail]
newaliases_path: [/usr/bin/newaliases]
mailq_path: [/usr/bin/mailq]
mail_owner: [postfix]
setgid: [no]
manpages: [/usr/local/man]
```

During the install process, the Postfix install script suggests default values for the file paths. To use the default values, simply hit the Enter key. By default, Postfix is installed with the less secure writable maildrop message queue (the `setgid` option line). The "Postfix and Security" section later in this chapter describes how to use this `setgid` option for a more secure mail server. The install options that were selected are written to the /etc/postfix/install.cf configuration file for future reference.

NOTE

You might notice that when you install with the source code distribution, the Postfix message queue directories are not created. This omission is remedied, however, as soon as the Postfix master program is started. The master program scans the Postfix message queue directory (/var/spool/postfix) and determines what (if any) subdirectories are missing. The master program then creates any missing message queue directories.

At this point Postfix should be installed using the default operating parameters. Of course, it still needs to be configured to meet the requirements of your particular e-mail environment.

Configuring Postfix

There are several steps necessary to configure the Postfix server, as shown here:

- Edit the master.cf file
- Determine local mail delivery method
- Edit the main.cf file
- Create an alias table
- Create any user-defined files

The following sections describe these steps in more detail.

Editing the master.cf File

The master.cf file controls the operational behavior of the core Postfix programs. Before you configure this file, however, you need to determine how you want your Postfix server to operate.

There should be a skeleton master.cf file created in the /etc/postfix directory during the installation process. You can then edit this file and make any changes necessary. Listing 10.4 shows the sample skeleton master.cf file installed by the Postfix source code installation.

LISTING 10.4 Sample master.cf Configuration File

```
smtp       inet  n   -   n   -    -    smtpd
pickup     fifo  n   n   n   60   1    pickup
cleanup    unix  -   -   n   -    0    cleanup
qmgr       fifo  n   -   n   300  1    qmgr
#qmgr      fifo  n   -   n   300  1    nqmgr
rewrite    unix  -   -   n   -    -    trivial-rewrite
bounce     unix  -   -   n   -    0    bounce
defer      unix  -   -   n   -    0    bounce
flush      unix  -   -   n   1000? 0   flush
smtp       unix  -   -   n   -    -    smtp
showq      unix  n   -   n   -    -    showq
error      unix  -   -   n   -    -    error
local      unix  -   n   n   -    -    local
lmtp       unix  -   -   n   -    -    lmtp
cyrus      unix  -   n   n   -    -    pipe
➥ flags=R user=cyrus argv=/cyrus/bin/deliver -e -m
➥ ${extension} ${user}
uucp       unix  -   n   n   -    -    pipe
➥ flags=F user=uucp argv=uux -r -n -z -a$sender - $nexthop!rmail
```

LISTING 10.4 Continued

```
➥ ($recipient)
ifmail   unix  -     n     n       -      -      pipe
➥   flags=F user=ftn argv=/usr/lib/ifmail/ifmail -r $nexthop
➥ ($recipient)
bsmtp    unix  -     n     n       -      -      pipe
➥ flags=F. user=foo argv=/usr/local/sbin/bsmtp -f $sender $nexthop
➥ $recipient
```

The skeleton file values should be fine for a simple Postfix server, but you can make any changes necessary for your particular e-mail environment in the master.cf file. You might choose to run Postfix in a chroot environment for security purposes (described in the "Postfix and Security" section).

Determining Local Mail Delivery

In Postfix, you can use four different methods of local mail delivery. Before you start Postfix, you must decide which one of the methods will work in your e-mail environment. These are the four delivery methods:

- sendmail-style delivery
- $HOME/Mailbox delivery
- $HOME/Maildir delivery
- External MDA delivery

The following sections describe the delivery methods and can help you decide which method may be right for your environment.

Using sendmail-Style Mailboxes

The most basic form of local mail delivery is to allow Postfix to deliver messages directly to sendmail-style mailboxes. These mailboxes place all messages for a user in a single text file located in a common mailbox directory. Each user has a separate mailbox file that is accessible only to that user.

Configuring Postfix for using sendmail-style mailboxes is simple. No configuration parameters are required, and Postfix will deliver mail for local users to sendmail-style mailboxes by default. If your Unix system is using a non-standard mailbox directory, you can specify the location using the `mail_spool_directory` parameter in the main.cf configuration file:

```
mail_spool_directory = /var/spool/testing/mail
```

$HOME/Mailbox Delivery

Despite the ease of use of the sendmail-style mailbox system, a few problems have been identified. By placing all the user mailboxes in a single directory, the mail system is vulnerable to both security risks and disk access speed problems.

By creating a common mail directory that every user must have access to, the sendmail-style mailbox system opens a security can of worms. Because the mailbox must be user writable, the mailbox directory must be writable by everyone, a possible security problem. Programs that read mail must carefully check permissions to allow the owner of a mailbox access, but refuse other users trying to access mailboxes owned by other users.

With one mailbox file for every user, systems that support thousands of users have lots of mailbox files, which creates quite a large mailbox directory. Large directories slow down disk access speeds, so it is much better to have many directories with one file each than one directory with a lot of files.

For Postfix to deliver messages for local users to their $HOME/Mailbox file, you need to set one parameter in the main.cf configuration file:

```
home_mailbox = Mailbox
```

Postfix will then use the $HOME/Mailbox method to deliver messages. The mail administrator can use any mailbox name instead of Mailbox as the value. Whatever text is used becomes the name of the mailbox located in the users' $HOME directory where Postfix will store messages.

CAUTION

Be very careful not to include a / at the end of the mailbox name. You will find out why in the next section.

$HOME/Maildir Delivery

Another alternative Postfix mailbox system is the Maildir system, which takes the $HOME/Mailbox method one step further. Not only is each user's mailbox moved to her home directory, but the sendmail-style mailbox format is changed, too.

Dan Bernstein, creator of the qmail MTA package, designed the Maildir mailbox method. One problem with the sendmail-style mailbox system is that it is highly vulnerable to data corruption. Because the mailbox file contains all the users' mail messages, corrupting the mailbox could mean loosing all the mail messages.

The Maildir system changes the method used for storing user messages. User messages are stored as separate files within a specially formatted user mailbox directory. This method ensures that even if one message becomes corrupt, the rest of the messages are safe in the mailbox directory. Figure 10.3 shows how the Maildir mailbox format works.

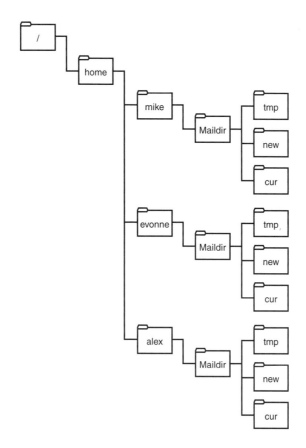

FIGURE 10.3

The Maildir mailbox system.

New messages are first created in the tmp directory. When the message is complete, it is transferred to the new directory. After the user reads the message in the new directory, it is transferred to the cur directory. For Postfix to deliver messages to the local users' Maildir directory, the main.cf configuration file must include one parameter:

```
home_mailbox = Maildir/
```

Note the slash / at the end of the mailbox name. This character is required to indicate a Maildir-type mailbox. The mailbox name can be anything the mail administrator wants, but the trailing slash must be present.

External MDA Delivery

The last method of mail delivery that Postfix supports is the use of external Mail Delivery Agents (MDAs). With this method, Postfix passes the message to the MDA program for delivery. After the message is passed to the MDA program, Postfix assumes that it will be delivered and deletes it from any internal queue.

For Postfix to use an external MDA program to deliver local mail, the main.cf configuration file must be set accordingly. The parameter used to define the MDA program is the `mailbox_command` parameter:

```
mailbox_command = /usr/sbin/procmail
```

The full pathname should be used so that Postfix can find the MDA program on the system. Postfix can also pass environment variables to the MDA program as command-line parameters, which enables Postfix to call the MDA program with information about the message to deliver. Table 10.6 lists the different environment variables that Postfix can use.

TABLE 10.6 Postfix MDA Environment Variables

Variable	Description
$HOME	The user's home directory
$SHELL	The user's Unix shell
$LOGNAME	The user's Unix username
$USER	The recipient's username
$EXTENSION	The address extension
$DOMAIN	The domain part of the address
$LOCAL	The local part of the address

The procmail program can use command-line options to indicate how to deliver the message, so the main.cf parameter for using procmail would be the following:

```
mailbox_command = /usr/sbin/procmail -a "$EXTENSION" -d "$USER"
```

Editing the main.cf File

The next step in starting Postfix is to determine what parameters are needed in the main.cf configuration file. For a basic configuration, you might not need any parameters. However, it is a good idea to go over the basic parameters before starting the Postfix server. The following sections describe the basic parameters that should be checked to ensure proper mail delivery on the mail server.

Determining Interfaces

The Postfix server has the capability of receiving messages on any or all interfaces running on the mail server. You can elect to receive messages on just a single interface if you are in a multi-network environment.

To determine the interfaces available on your system, use the Unix `ifconfig` command:

```
$ /sbin/ifconfig
eth0      Link encap:Ethernet  HWaddr 00:E0:7D:74:DF:C7
          inet addr:192.168.1.1  Bcast:192.168.1.255  Mask:255.255.255.0
          UP BROADCAST RUNNING MULTICAST  MTU:1500  Metric:1
          RX packets:681 errors:0 dropped:0 overruns:0 frame:0
          TX packets:604 errors:0 dropped:0 overruns:0 carrier:0
          collisions:0 txqueuelen:100
          Interrupt:10 Base address:0x6400

lo        Link encap:Local Loopback
          inet addr:127.0.0.1  Mask:255.0.0.0
          UP LOOPBACK RUNNING  MTU:3924  Metric:1
          RX packets:37193 errors:0 dropped:0 overruns:0 frame:0
          TX packets:37193 errors:0 dropped:0 overruns:0 carrier:0
          collisions:0 txqueuelen:0

$
```

Each interface is listed along with the IP address and interface statistics. If you are using a dial-up connection to the Internet, remember that the PPP interface will not be present unless you are currently dialed into the ISP.

By default, Postfix receives messages on all the interfaces available on the mail server. You can specify an individual interface by using the `inet_interfaces` parameter:

```
inet_interfaces = localhost.$mydomain
```

This example restricts Postfix to receiving messages only on the localhost loopback interface, l0.

Determining Recipient Addresses

You must also determine what hostnames Postfix will use to receive messages for the local mail server. The `mydestination` parameter is used to define the hostnames Postfix will accept messages for.

By default, Postfix receives messages addressed to the hostname of the local mail server, as well as messages sent to the special hostname `localhost`. To configure the hostnames, you use the `mydestination` parameter:

```
mydestination = $myhostname, localhost.$mydomain
```

These values assume that the mail server hostname and domain names are properly set on the system. The Postfix `mydomain` parameter can also be used to specify the domain name:

```
mydomain = ispnet1.net
```

Alternatively, you might want the Postfix server to receive mail messages sent to alias hostnames of the mail server, such as www.ispnet1.net. This can be accomplished by adding the alias name value to the `mydestination` parameter:

```
mydestination = $myhostname, localhost.$mydomain, www.$mydomain
```

This example assumes that the DNS entries for your domain include a canonical name (CNAME) entry for the www address, which points the www address to the original host address.

Finally, you might want the Postfix server to receive mail messages addressed to your domain name instead of using the full mail server hostname. This method has become popular for companies that just want to use their company name in the e-mail address, such as prez@ispnet1.net. The format for the `mydestination` parameter would then need to include the domain variable:

```
mydestination = $myhostname, localhost.$mydomain, $mydomain
```

Determining the Origin Address

The last basic item to configure in the configuration file is determining what address Postfix will use as your origin address. This parameter affects the format your address appears in when sending messages to users on remote mail servers.

By default, the `myorigin` parameter is set to the local mail server's hostname:

```
myorigin = $myhostname
```

If you are using an alias hostname, such as a www address, you might want your messages to be sent out as, for example, webmaster@www.ispnet1.net so that remote users have your alias hostname to use as the return address. This can be accomplished by using the following parameter:

```
myorigin = www.$mydomain
```

Alternatively, you might decide to use just your domain name in your mail messages. This method requires that Postfix use just the domain name in all header addresses sent out. To do that, use the following parameter:

```
myorigin = $mydomain
```

Creating the Aliases Table

After you have finished working with the main.cf configuration file, you should check the aliases lookup table to make sure all the system usernames are configured and the root username points to a normal user who logs into the system on a daily basis.

Most Unix systems contain several usernames that are configured in the /etc/passwd file, but are not necessarily used as logins. These usernames include addresses for the ftp server, the uucp server, and shutting down the system. Although these usernames are normally set not to allow logins, it is a good idea to forward their mail messages to a common place so that it's easier to watch for hacker attempts via the mail system. The best place to forward these usernames to is the root user. Listing 10.5 shows a listing of the system usernames on a Mandrake Linux system.

LISTING 10.5 System Usernames on a Mandrake System

```
root:x:0:0:root:/root:/bin/bash
bin:x:1:1:bin:/bin:
daemon:x:2:2:daemon:/sbin:
adm:x:3:4:adm:/var/adm:
lp:x:4:7:lp:/var/spool/lpd:
sync:x:5:0:sync:/sbin:/bin/sync
shutdown:x:6:0:shutdown:/sbin:/sbin/shutdown
halt:x:7:0:halt:/sbin:/sbin/halt
mail:x:8:12:mail:/var/spool/mail:
news:x:9:13:news:/var/spool/news:
uucp:x:10:14:uucp:/var/spool/uucp:
operator:x:11:0:operator:/root:
games:x:12:100:games:/usr/games:
gopher:x:13:30:gopher:/usr/lib/gopher-data:
ftp:x:14:50:FTP User:/home/ftp:
nobody:x:99:99:Nobody:/:
lists:x:500:500:BeroList:/dev/null:/dev/null
xfs:x:100:238:X Font Server:/etc/X11/fs:/bin/false
```

Besides these usernames, there are several other well-known mail addresses used on the Internet:

- The MAILER-DAEMON generic account
- The postmaster generic account
- The Webmaster generic account

It is a good idea to ensure that these addresses are included in the aliases file and point to a real address of the responsible administrator. If any mail is sent to these addresses, you will be able to read and respond to it.

Finally, you should always redirect messages sent to the root user to a normal user account. It is never a good idea to regularly log in to the mail server using the root account. Accidents do happen, and accidentally deleting system files is not a good thing. It is a much safer practice to perform as many tasks as possible as a normal system user. Also, some MDA programs (such as procmail) refuse to deliver messages to the root account for security reasons.

The Postfix source code distribution creates a skeleton aliases file in the /etc/postfix directory. You can edit this file with any Unix text editor to add your specific changes. A completed aliases file might look similar to the example shown in Listing 10.6.

LISTING 10.6 Sample Aliases File

```
# Basic system aliases — these MUST be present
MAILER-DAEMON:  postmaster
postmaster: root
webmaster: root

# General redirections for pseudo accounts
bin:        root
daemon:     root
named:      root
nobody:     root
uucp:       root
www:        root
ftp-bugs:   root
postfix:    root

# Put your local aliases here.
Rich.Blum rich
Richard.Blum rich

# Well-known aliases
manager:    root
dumper:     root
operator:   root
abuse:      postmaster

# trap decode to catch security attacks
decode:     root
```

LISTING 10.6 Continued

```
# Person who should get root's mail
#root:      you
root:    rich
```

After creating the text aliases file, you must convert it to an indexed binary database file by using the postalias command:

```
postalias /etc/postfix/alias
```

This command creates either the aliases.db or aliases.dbm file that is used by Postfix, depending on the database type your system uses. You should make sure the main.cf file contains the proper pointer to the new aliases table by using the alias_maps parameter:

```
alias_maps = hash:/etc/postfix/aliases
```

This entry not only points to the location of the aliases file, but also defines what type of database file it is.

Starting Postfix

To start the Postfix software, you must be logged in as the root user, and use this command:

```
postfix start
```

The first time you start Postfix, it checks the /var/spool/postfix directory and creates any message queue directories as needed:

```
postfix-script: warning: creating missing Postfix pid directory
postfix-script: warning: creating missing Postfix incoming directory
postfix-script: warning: creating missing Postfix active directory
postfix-script: warning: creating missing Postfix bounce directory
postfix-script: warning: creating missing Postfix defer directory
postfix-script: warning: creating missing Postfix deferred directory
postfix-script: warning: creating missing Postfix flush directory
postfix-script: warning: creating missing Postfix saved directory
postfix-script: warning: creating missing Postfix corrupt directory
postfix-script: warning: creating missing Postfix public directory
postfix-script: warning: creating missing Postfix private directory
```

You should be able to check the log where your mail logs are kept (often the /var/log/maillog file) to see if Postfix started properly:

```
Jun  2 05:49:56 shadrach postfix-script: starting the Postfix mail system
Jun  2 05:49:56 shadrach postfix/master[864]: daemon started
```

You should not see any warning or error messages (other than the ones for creating the missing directories). If so, compare the messages with your configurations to determine what could be wrong.

If Postfix started properly, you should see three new processes running in background mode on the mail server. Use the ps command to list all the processes running on the server. Different Unix systems use different options for the ps command. Most Linux systems can use the ax command to display all processes running. These are the Postfix processes you should look for:

```
864 ?          S       0:00 /usr/libexec/postfix/master
865 ?          S       0:00 pickup -l -t fifo
866 ?          S       0:00 qmgr -l -t fifo -u
```

The first field (864, for example) is the process ID of the running program. The programs are shown in the last field. The master program should run at all times. The pickup and qmgr programs should be configured in the master.cf configuration file to wake up at predetermined intervals, so they should also remain running.

The Postfix install method outlined earlier in the "Installing Postfix" section replaces the /usr/sbin/sendmail file with the Postfix version. If you do that, any messages sent should use the Postfix system to send the message. You can test this method by sending a test message to a remote user and watching the Postfix processes:

```
864 ?          S       0:00 /usr/libexec/postfix/master
865 ?          S       0:00 pickup -l -t fifo
866 ?          S       0:00 qmgr -l -t fifo -u
885 ?          S       0:00 cleanup -t unix -u
886 ?          S       0:00 trivial-rewrite -n rewrite -t unix -u
896 ?          S       0:00 smtp -t unix -u -c
```

If Postfix is installed properly, it should call the cleanup, trivial-rewrite, and smtp programs to help it deliver the message to the final destination. These programs will stay active in background mode until they reach their timeout limit set in the master.cf file, and then they will quietly go away. Of course, the best way to determine whether Postfix worked is to see if the message actually made it to the remote user.

Postfix and Security

By default, Postfix has several security and reliability features. Postfix also supports two additional features that you can configure separately from the default installation. This section describes these two features and how to configure them.

Determine Postfix Maildrop Security

As the mail administrator, you must decide at what level of security you want your Postfix system to operate. The default installation of the Postfix source code distribution creates a maildrop message queue directory that is writable by all local users. This setup allows users to place messages directly in the message queue.

If you are not comfortable with having a maildrop directory writable by all system users, you can create a separate group name to own the maildrop message queue. The maildrop message queue directory is then writable only by the special maildrop group. This configuration restricts local users from inserting their own messages (or attempting any trickery with the maildrop message queue).

You can create a separate system group for maildrop by using the Linux `groupadd` command:

```
groupadd maildrop
```

This command creates the group `maildrop` that Postfix uses to control the maildrop message queue. When the maildrop message queue is restricted, the Postfix sendmail core program automatically detects this situation and calls on the postdrop program to insert new messages into the maildrop message queue.

You must rerun the INSTALL.sh installation script file to reconfigure how Postfix will run:

```
sh INSTALL.sh
```

You should enter the maildrop group name when the install script prompts you for the `setgid` name:

```
setgid: [no] maildrop
```

This line instructs Postfix to use the `postdrop` command when attempting to insert messages into the maildrop message queue. Any other attempt by normal system users to place messages in the maildrop message queue will be denied.

Installing Postfix in a Chroot Environment

As an extra security precaution, the Postfix system can be run in a restricted area on the mail server. This method ensures that even if a mail program is compromised, the attacker will not be able to access files in the mail server system directories.

The method that Postfix uses to accomplish this goal is the Unix `chroot` command. The Unix chroot program forces a command to run with a specified directory acting as the root directory. By specifying a subdirectory on the Unix system, the command is limited in its ability to modify any normal system files outside the specified subdirectory on the server. All of the Postfix core programs, except the local and pipe programs, can be run in the chroot environment. This chroot environment sets the /var/spool/postfix directory as the root directory for the Postfix programs to operate in.

To run the Postfix core programs in a chroot environment, you must configure two settings. First, the /var/spool/postfix directory must be modified to accommodate being used as the root directory for Postfix, and second, the master.cf file must be modified to indicate which Postfix programs should be run in the chroot environment.

When running Postfix core programs, certain files must be present for the core programs to operate properly. If the /var/spool/postfix directory is used as the chroot directory, those programs are hidden from view. To compensate for this, the mail administrator must copy these files to the /var/spool/postfix directory using the same directory paths.

To help facilitate running in a chroot environment, the Postfix source code distribution includes sample script files for various operating systems. These script files are located in the examples/chroot-setup subdirectory under the source code working directory. The script file in Listing 10.7, LINUX2, is used to set up a chroot environment on a Linux server.

LISTING 10.7 Sample Linux Chroot Script

```
CP="cp -p"

cond_copy() {
  # find files as per pattern in $1
  # if any, copy to directory $2
  dir=`dirname "$1"`
  pat=`basename "$1"`
  lr=`find "$dir" -maxdepth 1 -name "$pat"`
  if test ! -d "$2" ; then exit 1 ; fi
  if test "x$lr" != "x" ; then $CP $1 "$2" ; fi
}

set -e
umask 022

POSTFIX_DIR=${POSTFIX_DIR-/var/spool/postfix}
cd ${POSTFIX_DIR}

mkdir -p etc lib usr/lib/zoneinfo
# find localtime (SuSE 5.3 does not have /etc/localtime)
lt=/etc/localtime
if test ! -f $lt ; then lt=/usr/lib/zoneinfo/localtime ; fi
if test ! -f $lt ; then lt=/usr/share/zoneinfo/localtime ; fi
if test ! -f $lt ; then echo "cannot find localtime" ; exit 1 ; fi
rm -f etc/localtime

# copy localtime and some other system files into the chroot's etc
$CP -f $lt /etc/services /etc/resolv.conf /etc/nsswitch.conf etc
$CP -f /etc/host.conf /etc/hosts /etc/passwd etc
ln -s -f /etc/localtime usr/lib/zoneinfo

# copy required libraries into the chroot
cond_copy '/lib/libnss_*.so*' lib
```

LISTING 10.7 Continued

```
cond_copy '/lib/libresolv.so*' lib
cond_copy '/lib/libdb.so*' lib

postfix reload
```

To run the script, you must first use the Unix `chmod` command to make the script executable:

```
chmod 755 /usr/local/src/postfix-20010228-pl03/examples/chroot-setup/LINUX2
```

After changing the permission of the script, you can run it from the chroot-setup directory by typing:

```
./LINUX2
```

The chroot-setup script for Linux creates the etc and lib subdirectories under the /var/spool/postfix directory. Files necessary for the Postfix core programs are copied from the real locations on the system to the new chroot location. After the chroot files have been copied to the Postfix directory, the master.cf configuration file must be modified to indicate which core programs should be run in the chroot environment. You can select any core programs except the local and pipe programs to be run in the chroot environment.

To activate the chroot environment, in the master.cf file place a y character in the chroot field of the Postfix program you want to run in the chroot environment:

```
smtp      inet  n   -   y   -   -   smtpd
```

Programs that communicate with remote hosts, such as smtpd and smtp, are the most susceptible to attacks by outside hackers, and should be run in the chroot environment.

Summary

The Postfix package is an alternative MTA package for Unix platforms. It has gained popularity because it uses a simple text-based configuration file that is easier to configure than the standard sendmail configuration files.

Two separate configuration files are used with Postfix. The master.cf configuration file defines how Postfix processes interact with each other. The main.cf configuration file defines how Postfix behaves in a particular e-mail environment. Postfix also has several lookup tables you can create to control how Postfix delivers messages.

Some Linux packages include a binary distribution of Postfix. If your Unix platform does not include a binary distribution, or if you want to install the latest version of Postfix, you can download the source code from the http://www.postfix.org Web site and compile it yourself. After compiling and installing Postfix, you must configure the main.cf configuration file and create any required lookup tables, such as the alias table, to meet your particular e-mail environment's needs.

Although by default Postfix offers a high level of security, you can configure two additional options to offer even more security. The maildrop message queue is where users place new messages for processing by Postfix. You can restrict access and allow only Postfix to place messages in the queue. This method requires a separate group ID that Postfix uses to control access to the maildrop message queue. A second security option is running several of the Postfix core programs in a chroot environment. This option "locks" the programs into a specific directory. If a hacker should compromise the programs, he would not be able to access other directories on the mail server.

Preventing Open Relays

Relaying messages was once a common SMTP function. SMTP provides a means for clients to send messages destined for remote Internet users to a common mail server, which in turn could relay the message via SMTP to the appropriate destination mail server. This process is called *open relaying*.

With the increase of unsolicited commercial e-mail (UCE), open relaying has become an ugly subject. Forwarding mail from server to server without any degree of selectivity isn't considered smart these days. Instead, some degree of intelligence is required to selectively forward e-mail messages. This process is called *selective relaying*.

This chapter describes open and selective relaying, provides methods for configuring your e-mail MTA package to avoid being an open relay, and demonstrates how to avoid receiving messages from known open relays.

Open and Selective Relaying

Mail relaying has become a complicated issue on the Internet. In the early days of the Internet, mail relaying was a common courtesy extended to other mail servers on the network. If a mail server attempted to deliver a mail message to your mail server for a user on a different mail server, you gladly accepted the message and forwarded it to the appropriate remote mail server for the user. Unfortunately, with the popularity of the Internet came abuse of the Internet and of e-mail systems.

Mass marketers are constantly looking for ways to flood unsuspecting users' mailboxes with advertisements. A key to the successful mass marketer is the ability to hide the message's originating e-mail address (otherwise people might be able to track it down and complain); enter mail relaying. By using some SMTP trickery, a mass marketer can bounce e-mail messages off an Internet mail relay using a phony originating mail address. The current SMTP does not enable validating the mail address of incoming messages, so the mail relay happily forwards the messages to the recipients using the phony originating e-mail address. Figure 11.1 illustrates this procedure.

A message originating somewhere on the Internet is sent through the shadrach.ispnet1.net mail server to get to the mailhost.ispnet2.net mail server. The shadrach.ispnet1.net server forwards the message to the remote host with no complaints.

There has been much discussion on how to control UCE on the Internet. The most obvious methods involve improving SMTP to validate information sent in the message headers. This improvement would ensure that mass marketers could not falsify the mail addresses in their messages (see Chapter 6, "Reading E-mail Headers").

The new SMTP extensions have made many improvements to the security of Internet e-mail. However, there are still many (if not most) Internet mail servers that are either not using software that takes advantage of the new SMTP extensions or have not configured their software properly to use the features.

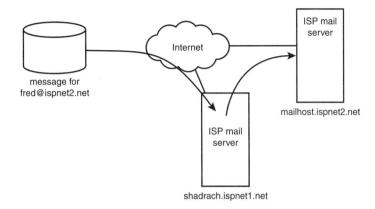

FIGURE 11.1

Using an open mail relay for UCE.

To compensate for these problems, most e-mail software packages include a method of screening SMTP connection attempts. There are basically two approaches to relaying on the Internet. The first and most obvious solution is for the MTA mail program to refuse all relayed messages and accept only messages destined for users on the local mail server. This is the safest and easiest solution.

Unfortunately, most ISPs have users who dial into the ISP and use some type of MUA program on their PCs to receive mail. These programs must also be able to send messages to remote users on the Internet. The method that almost all MUA programs use to send messages is forwarding the messages via SMTP to a *smart host*, which is an MTA server that the MUA program assumes can relay the message to the appropriate destination mail server. This is where the problem is.

If you are a conscientious mail administrator and have disabled relaying on your mail server, none of your customers will be able to use your mail server as a smart host to send messages to the Internet. That would not be good for business. To address the smart host problem, the second solution—selective relaying—uses the best of both worlds.

Figure 11.2 illustrates the process of selective relaying. By allowing the MTA mail program to check a local database, it can determine on a case-by-case basis what messages to relay and what messages to refuse.

By placing all the local IP addresses assigned to your customers in the relaying database, the MTA program can allow those addresses to use it as a smart host and forward any messages destined for remote Internet users. However, any message coming from an IP address not in the database and destined for a remote user will be refused.

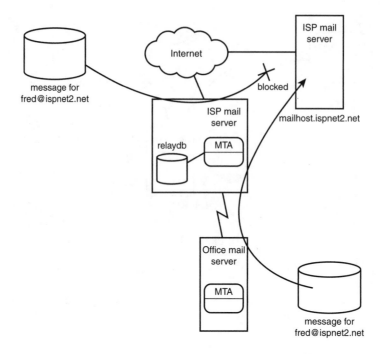

FIGURE 11.2

Using selective relaying on a mail server.

Configuring Selective Relaying

Most popular MTA packages now use default configurations that avoid being an open relay. However, if you want to use selective relaying, you must specifically configure it. The following sections describes how to configure selective relaying for the three most popular open source MTA packages: sendmail, qmail, and Postfix.

Sendmail Configuration

The early versions of sendmail were notorious for allowing open relays in default configurations. Fortunately, as of version 8.9, sendmail prevents open relaying by default. Instead, you must specify which hosts, networks, or domains are permitted to relay messages through your e-mail server. This section describes how to configure sendmail for selective relaying.

Using an Access Table

Sendmail versions 8.9 and higher allow you to create an *access table*, a table of hosts that are allowed access to your e-mail server. The sendmail access table matches host, subnet, and domain addresses with a specific action for sendmail to follow. Each entry is in the following form:

```
host    action
```

The *host* variable specifies a specific hostname, IP address, subnet, or domain that you want to control. The *action* variable determines the action sendmail performs when a message from the listed host is received:

- OK—The remote host can send messages to your e-mail server.
- RELAY—The remote host can relay messages through your e-mail server to other remote hosts.
- REJECT—The remote host is not allowed to send messages either to or through your e-mail server.
- DISCARD—Incoming messages from the remote host are discarded, and no error messages are returned to the sender.
- *nnn text*—Incoming messages from the remote host are discarded, but sendmail returns an error message to the sender using the SMTP code specified by *nnn* and a text description (the *text* variable).

A sample access table would look like this:

```
192.168. RELAY
ispnet1.net OK
spammer.net REJECT
mail1.anotherspammer.com REJECT
badguy.net 550 Sorry, we don't allow spammers here
nuisance.trouble.com DISCARD
```

Each entry in this access table defines a specific category of hosts. The first entry allows sendmail to relay messages coming from the 192.168.0.0 network. The second entry allows sendmail to accept messages coming from the ispnet1.net network. The next two entries specifically reject messages coming from any host in the spammer.net domain and from the specific host mail1.anotherspammer.com. The next entry not only refuses messages from any host in the badguy.net domain with the SMTP code 550, but instructs sendmail to send a specific error message back to the host (Sorry, we don't allow spammers here). The final entry demonstrates the DISCARD action. Any messages received from the nui-sance.trouble.com host will be discarded, but the remote host will not be notified of this action. This action differs from REJECT in that the remote host does not know that sendmail discarded the message.

Adding an Access Table to the Configuration

If you are building your sendmail.cf configuration file using the m4 macro preprocessor, this is the command you must add to your configuration script:

```
FEATURE(`access_db')
```

This command creates an access table in the default location using the system default binary database type. For sendmail version 8.9, the default location is /etc/access. For sendmail versions 8.10 and higher, the default location is /etc/mail/access. The default binary database type varies depending on the Unix distribution you are using. For Linux systems the standard hash database function is used.

If you are not using the m4 macro preprocessor, you must manually add a K configuration line to define the access table:

```
Kaccess hash /etc/mail/access
```

This example uses the default access database location of /etc/mail/access with the hash binary database format. You can change either of these parameters to suite your particular e-mail environment.

Creating an Access Table

You must create the binary access table database by using the Unix makemap command. This command reads an ASCII-formatted text file and creates a binary database using the default system database type. This is the easiest method for creating the database from a text file:

```
makemap /etc/mail/access < /etc/mail/access.txt
```

This command reads the text file /etc/mail/access.txt and creates the binary database /etc/mail/access, which sendmail will use for selective relaying.

Other Relaying Options

sendmail offers other methods of selective relaying besides the access table. These other methods can be configured in the m4 macro file by using the FEATURE command. Table 11.1 lists the FEATURE commands that implement these other methods.

TABLE 11.1 Alternative sendmail Relaying Methods

FEATURE *Command*	*Description*
relay_hosts_only	Permits only hosts to be listed in the access table
relay_entire_domain	Permits relaying from any remote server claiming to be in your domain
relay_based_on_MX	Permits relaying for domains that the host maintains

TABLE 11.1 Continued

FEATURE *Command*	*Description*
relay_local_from	Permits relaying from any host on your local network
loose_relay_check	Turns off checking for explicit routing through the e-mail host
promiscuous_relay	Enables open relaying

Each of these different FEATURE commands enables sendmail to permit relaying for a different type of remote host.

CAUTION

Be careful if using the relay_entire_domain and relay_local_from features. It is not difficult for a hacker to masquerade the SMTP session addresses to impersonate a server on your network.

---

qmail Configuration

By default, qmail acts as an open relay only if the rcpthosts control file is missing. In a normal installation (see Chapter 9, "The qmail E-mail Package"), placing the contents of the me control file in the rcpthosts control file prevents your e-mail server from being an open relay. The trick is if you want to use your qmail package as a selective relay.

In qmail, the qmail-smtpd program is used to receive messages from remote mail servers using SMTP. The rcpthosts control file is used to control what addresses qmail-smtpd can receive messages for. If a remote host attempts to send a message for a user on a host not defined in the rcpthosts file, qmail-smtpd rejects the message.

There is one exception to this rule. If the Unix environment variable RELAYCLIENT is set, qmail-smtpd ignores the values in the rcpthosts file and forwards all messages to the remote address specified by the RELAYCLIENT variable.

You can "trick" qmail-smtpd into relaying messages by exploiting this feature. If you set the RELAYCLIENT environment variable to an empty string, qmail-smtpd attempts to forward the message to the destination remote mail server automatically. The trick is to set the RELAYCLIENT variable to an empty string only for the clients you want to relay messages for.

This section describes two methods that can be used to set the RELAYCLIENT Unix environment variable for certain IP addresses, thus implementing selective relaying on a qmail mail server.

Using the Tcpwrapper Program

The tcpwrapper program is a common Unix program used as a "middle man" program along with the inetd program. It provides additional functionality to the inetd program in that it enables the following:

- Creating a database of IP address to allow or deny
- Adding additional logging capabilities for connections
- Verifying hostname and IP addresses via DNS

If you are using the inetd program to monitor the network for SMTP connections, you can use the tcpwrapper program to give the qmail-smtpd program selective relaying functionality. The following sections describe how this is done.

Configuring Tcpwrapper

To implement selective relaying using the tcpwrapper program, you must set up an access control database for tcpwrapper. The tcpwrapper tcpd program uses a standard host access text file as the access control database. The host access text file has the following format:

```
daemon_list : client_list [ : shell_command ]
```

The *daemon_list* field defines the Unix application program that the access rule should match. Remember that the qmail tcp-env program always precedes the qmail-smtpd program (see Chapter 9), so that is the entry that must be made in the access control database.

The *client_list* field defines the addresses that should be matched for the access rule. Addresses can be defined using hostnames, IP addresses, or wildcard patterns.

The *shell_command* field is where you can enter the shell command to set the RELAYCLIENT environment variable to trigger the qmail-smtpd relay function.

The access control database is contained in a file called hosts.allow. The location of this file varies depending on the Unix distribution. Linux systems often place this file in the /etc directory. FreeBSD systems place it in the /usr/local/etc directory. Listing 11.1 shows a sample hosts.allow access control database file.

LISTING 11.1 Sample hosts.allow File

```
tcp-env: 192.168.: setenv = RELAYCLIENT
tcp-env: localhost: setenv = RELAYCLIENT
```

The first line in Listing 11.1 is an example of setting the RELAYCLIENT environment variable for any connection originating from the 192.168.0.0 network. The second line demonstrates how to set the RELAYCLIENT environment variable for any connection originating from the local mail server. This could be required for some MUA programs to work properly. After the hosts.allow file is created, you must let the inetd program know about the tcpwrapper. The next section describes this process.

Configuring the /etc/inetd.conf File

For the inetd program to pass connection attempts to the tcpwrapper program, you must configure inetd in the /etc/inetd.conf configuration file. Adding the tcpwrapper program makes for a messy configuration line, but it works.

The format of the line for the qmail tcp-env program in /etc/inetd.conf should look like this:

```
smtp    stream tcp    nowait qmaild /usr/local/libexec/tcpd
➥ /var/qmail/bin/tcp-env  /var/qmail/bin/qmail-smtpd
```

Remember that this must all be entered on a single line in the /etc/inetd.conf file. The inetd protocol tag should be set to smtp for all SMTP connections. The program that inetd passes the connection to now becomes the tcpwrapper tcpd program. This example is from a FreeBSD system. The location of the tcpd program for other Unix systems could (and probably will) vary.

Using the Tcpserver Program

Dan Bernstein, the author of qmail, developed the tcpserver program as a replacement for the inetd program. The tcpserver program offers the following advantages over inetd:

- Can record all input and output from the server in a file
- Can provide access control features to deny or allow connections from select clients
- Contains concurrency limits to prevent overloading the Unix system

The tcpserver program provides access control by utilizing a hash database of rules configured by the administrator. This section describes installing and configuring the tcpserver program for selective relaying.

Installing the Tcpserver Program

The tcpserver program is part of the ucspi-tcp package created and maintained by Dan Bernstein, and you must install the ucspi-tcp package to get tcpserver.

Dan has provided the source code for the ucspi-tcp package as a compressed tar file. At the time of this writing, the current version of ucspi-tcp is version 0.88. You can download it at this Web site:

```
http://cr.yp.to/ucspi-tcp/ucspi-tcp-0.88.tar.gz
```

After downloading the source code, you can untar it into a working directory. A common place for source code working directories is the /usr/local/src directory. To untar the source code into its own directory, you can use the following command:

```
tar -zxvf ucspi-tcp-0.88.tar.gz -C /usr/local/src
```

This command creates the directory /usr/local/src/ucspi-tcp-0.88 and untars the bundled source code into that directory.

NOTE

Remember, you must be the root user to create files in the /usr/local directory.

After the source code is untarred, you can use the GNU make program to compile the source code. The command used to create the new programs from the source code is make.

Next, you will most likely want to place the executable programs created by the source code in a location where you can easily run them from boot scripts. A common location for executable programs is the /usr/local/bin directory. The ucspi-tcp package automatically installs the executable programs in this directory if you rerun the GNU make program using the setup and check options:

```
make setup check
```

This command copies the executable programs to the /usr/local/bin directory and checks to ensure that the installation was successful. After doing that, the tcpserver package should be successfully installed on your Unix system.

The Tcpserver Command Line

The ucspi-tcp tcpserver program is used to replace the Unix inetd program. It accepts incoming TCP connections from remote clients and passes them to an application program defined in the command. The tcpserver command line uses this format:

```
tcpserver options host port application
```

The *host* and *port* parameters define the hostname and TCP port number of the local server that the application will accept connections on. The *host* parameter can be local-host to specify the local server, an IP address of the host, or the host's full domain name. The *port* parameter can be a numerical value or the name of a TCP port as defined in the /etc/services file on the server.

The *application* parameter defines the application that the connection will be passed to after it is established. Any command-line parameters needed for the application should also be included on the tcpserver command line.

The *options* parameter defines the behavior of the tcpserver program. There are three types of options that can be used:

- General options control how the tcpserver displays messages
- Connection options define how tcpserver handles incoming connection requests
- Data-gathering options defines how tcpserver gets information to use in the Unix environment variables passed to the application program

Table 11.2 shows the connection options that can be used in tcpserver.

TABLE 11.2 Tcpserver Connection Options

Option	Description
-b *n*	Allow a backlog of n connection requests
-B banner	Write banner to the network connection after the connection has been established
-c n	Do not accept more than n simultaneous connections
-d	Delay sending data to remote hosts when host is responding slowly
-D	Never delay in sending data to remote hosts
-g gid	Change the active group ID to gid after preparing to receive connections
-l	Print the local port number to stdout
-o	Do not change IP options in the connection packets
-O	Delete IP options to route packets (default)
-u uid	Change the active user ID to uid after preparing to receive connections
-U	Equivalent to -g $GID -u $UID
-x db	Use the rules in the hash database specified by *db* to accept/deny remote clients
-X	Allow connections if the database specified by the -x option does not exist

The data-gathering options that can be used with the tcpserver program are shown in Table 11.3.

TABLE 11.3 Tcpserver Data-Gathering Options

Option	Description
-h	Look up remote hostname using DNS (default).
-H	Do not look up remote hostname using DNS. You must use this option for port 53 (the DNS service).
-l *localname*	Do not look up the local server hostname using DNS; instead, use *localname*.
-p	Stands for "paranoid." Look up the remote host IP address using reverse DNS and compare it to the hostname. If they do not match, remove the environment variable $TCPREMOTEHOST.
-P	Not paranoid. Do not look up the remote host IP address using reverse DNS (default).
-r	Attempt to obtain $TCPREMOTEINFO from the remote host (default).
-R	Do not attempt to obtain $TCPREMOTEINFO data from the remote host. You must use this option for ports 53 and 113.
-t *n*	Stop trying to get $TCPREMOTEINFO data after *n* seconds (default = 26).

As shown in Table 11.3, there are several Unix environment variables that tcpserver attempts to receive data for. These environment variables help the application program process information about the network connection. Table 11.4 shows the environment variables used.

TABLE 11.4 Tcpserver Unix Environment Variables

Environment Variable	Description
$PROTO	The protocol used (default TCP)
$TCPLOCALIP	The IP address of the local host in dotted decimal notation
$TCPLOCALPORT	The local TCP port number in decimal notation
$TCPLOCALHOST	The DNS lookup value of the local host
$TCPREMOTEIP	The IP address of the remote client
$TCPREMOTEPORT	The TCP port number of the remote client in decimal notation
$TCPREMOTEHOST	The DNS lookup value of the remote host
$TCPREMOTEINFO	An information string provided by the remote client using the RFC931 or RFC1413 protocols

When tcpserver accepts a connection from a remote client, it attempts to provide the environment variables listed in Table 11.4 to the application. When it cannot receive information for a particular variable, it does not set the variable.

Configuring the Tcpserver Program

The tcpserver program uses an access control database similar to the tcpwrapper program. One improvement Bernstein made is having tcpserver use a hashed cdb (binary) database that it can access more quickly than accessing a text file. This feature improves the time required for the server to determine whether the connection should be accepted.

You must first create a text version of the database and use the tcprules program (also in the ucspi-tcp package) to create a binary database. This is the format of the text database file:

address:action

In this line, *address* is used to match incoming addresses from the network, and *action* is a predefined tcprule action.

The tcprules *action* field indicates whether the address should be allowed or denied, along with any environmental variables that should be set for the connection. Listing 11.2 shows an example of an access control database.

LISTING 11.2 Sample Tcpserver Access Control Database

```
192.168.:allow,RELAYCLIENT=""
192.168.1.10:deny
```

The first rule allows connections from the 192.168.0.0 network and sets the RELAYCLIENT environment variable to an empty string. This rule would allow relaying from any client within this network. The second rule demonstrates selectively denying an SMTP connection from the IP address 192.168.1.10. Any other connection originating from any other IP address not specifically mentioned in the rules will be allowed to connect via SMTP to transfer messages to the mail server, but will be blocked from relaying messages to another remote mail server.

After configuring the text access control database, you must create the binary database using the tcprules program:

```
tcprules database tmpfile
```

The *database* parameter defines the output filename for the binary database. The *tmpfile* parameter defines a temporary file that will be deleted when the tcprules program finishes.

The tcprules program accepts input from the Unix standard input. To convert a text access control database file to a binary database file, you must send the text file to the tcprules program:

```
tcprules /etc/tcp.smtp.cdb /etc/tcp.smtp.tmp < /etc/tcp.smtp.txt
```

There is no set location for the tcpserver access control database. The tcpserver program uses the -x parameter to determine the location of the database. A standard has been adopted by Dan Bernstein to use the filename:

```
/etc/tcp.protocol.format
```

In this standard, *protocol* is the TCP protocol the rules were created for, and *format* is the format of the database (either text or cdb).

Running the Tcpserver Program

When the database has been created, the tcpserver command must point to the location of the binary database and can be inserted into the normal system boot scripts. A sample tcpserver command that listens to the SMTP TCP port, uses the access database for blocking relaying, and passes the accepted connections to the qmail-smtpd program should look like this:

```
tcpserver -v -p -x /etc/tcp.smtp.cdb 0 smtp /var/qmail/bin/qmail-smtpd
```

After you start the tcpserver program, it monitors the SMTP port for incoming connections and passes them to the qmail-smtpd program, along with any environment variables set in the tcp.smtp.cdb database. Hosts that have the RELAYCLIENT environment variable set will be allowed to use the qmail server as an SMTP relay.

Postfix Relaying Parameters

Postfix has several parameters you can use to control how mail is delivered on the mail server. The most common and easiest method of restricting mail relaying is to control how Postfix delivers (or refuses to deliver) messages received from external hosts. The parameter best suited for this job is the smtpd_recipient_restrictions parameter in the main.cf configuration file.

Postfix uses the smtpd_recipient_restrictions parameter to restrict the recipients that the Postfix smtpd server will accept messages for. By carefully setting this parameter, you can successfully block mail-relaying attempts from unknown remote hosts, while allowing customers to continue using the Postfix server as a mail relay.

The format of the smtpd_recipient_restrictions parameter is just like any other parameter in the main.cf configuration file:

```
smtpd_recipient_restrictions = value
```

You can add multiple values to the parameter by separating them with a comma or with whitespace. Restrictions are added in the value list and applied from left to right.

One thing that does make this parameter different from most other Postfix parameters is that if the parameter is used, it must have at least one of three essential values listed in the value list:

- check_relay_domains—Checks if the message is intended for a recipient address in the $mydestination, $inet_interfaces, $virtual_maps, or $relay_domains parameter values.
- reject—Refuses all messages, even local ones.
- reject_unauth_destination—Refuses all messages unless they meet the check_relay_domains criteria.

The following sections define the values that can be used with the smtpd_recipient_restrictions parameter and how they can be combined to prevent mail relay abuse on your Postfix server.

Default Values

The default behavior of the smtpd_recipient_restrictions parameter assumes that the permit_mynetworks and check_relay_domains values are set.

The `permit_mynetworks` value allows any client with a host IP address on your local sub-net to use the Postfix server as a mail relay. If you assign addresses to your customers based on a set subnetwork number that the Postfix server is in, this is a good feature. It allows any client on your subnet to use the Postfix server as a mail relay, while blocking any external mail servers.

If you assign IP addresses outside the subnetwork the Postfix server is in to your clients, then you must use an additional value to specify them. This method requires one of the database-check values described later in the "Database Checks" section.

The `check_relay_domains` value enables additional clients to use the mail relay based on other Postfix parameters. These are the additional clients:

- Any client listed in the `$relay_domains` parameter, which by default includes the `$mydestination` parameter
- Any destination address in the `$relay_domains` parameter list
- Any destination address listed in the `$inet_interfaces` parameter
- Any destination address listed in a virtual lookup table

Notice that by default Postfix allows relaying from any client as long as the message is destined for a recipient host that the Postfix server is configured to accept messages for. Although you might not consider this process relaying, technically it is (the Postfix server is relaying the message to itself).

Reject Values

You can also specifically prevent remote sites from using the Postfix mail server as a mail relay by including several different reject values in the `smtp_recipient_restrictions` para-meter. Reject values deny relaying to hosts or clients that meet certain defined criteria. Table 11.5 lists the reject values and their descriptions.

TABLE 11.5 Reject Values

Value	Requests Restricted
`reject`	All requests, even local
`reject_invalid_hostname`	Invalid HELO hostnames
`reject_maps_rbl`	Client is listed in `$maps_rbl_domains`, the Realtime Blackhole List database
`reject_non_fqdn_hostname`	Non-FQDN (Fully Qualified Domain Name) HELO host-names
`reject_non_fqdn_recipient`	Non-FQDN recipient addresses
`reject_non_fqdn_sender`	Non-FQDN sender addresses
`reject_unauth_destination`	Mail not sent to `$mydestination`, `$inet_interfaces`, `$virtual_maps`, or `$relay_domains`

TABLE 11.5 Continued

Value	Requests Restricted
reject_unauth_pipelining	Mail sent from pipelining software
reject_unknown_client	Client hostname is not known
reject_unknown_hostname	HELO hostname that does not have a DNS A (Address) or MX (Mail Exchange) entry
reject_unknown_recipient_domain	Mail sent to domains without a DNS A or MX record
reject_unknown_sender_domain	Mail sent from domains without a DNS A or MX record

By specifying particular reject values, the Postfix server can prevent relaying either from or to particular domains. You can enter multiple values separated by commas or spaces for the parameter.

As an example, you can add the following parameter line in the main.cf file:

```
smtpd_recipient_restrictions = reject_non_fqdn_hostname,
    reject_unauth_destination
```

After issuing the Postfix reload command, the Postfix server should now reject mail from hosts that do not properly identify themselves in the HELO statement:

```
shadrach# telnet localhost 25
Trying 127.0.0.1...
Connected to localhost.ispnet1.net.
Escape character is '^]'.
220 shadrach.ispnet1.net ESMTP Postfix
HELO dude
250 shadrach.ispnet1.net
MAIL FROM: <rich@shadrach.ispnet1.net>
250 Ok
RCPT TO: <rich@shadrach.ispnet1.net>
504 <dude>: Helo command rejected: need fully-qualified hostname
QUIT
221 Bye
Connection closed by foreign host.
$
```

As shown, the attempt to send a message to a remote host through the Postfix server is blocked after the SMTP RCPT TO: command is issued. Any attempts from mass marketers to send mail using a phony HELO SMTP command (as they often try to do) will be rejected.

Permit Values

Alternatively, you can configure settings in which remote users are permitted to relay mail messages through the Postfix server. Three values explicitly permit mail relaying:

- `permit`
- `permit_auth_destination`
- `permit_mx_backup`

The `permit` value works similarly to its cousin, `reject`. It permits any client to send mail to any host (open relaying). It is usually used as a final action in a list of restrictive values, where by default the mail server permits mail relaying.

The `permit_auth_destination` value is used to allow Postfix to accept mail for any of the local host designations (`$mydestination`, `$inet_interfaces`, `$virtual_maps`, and `$relay_domains`). This value can be used in combination with a list of reject values to ensure that local mail is accepted.

The `permit_mx_backup` value is a handy value to use for a domain's backup mail server. When the Postfix server is a backup mail server, it is given a lower MX value for the DNS record:

```
othercompany.com   IN SOA   host1.ispnet1.net. postmaster.host1.ispnet1.net (
                   20001105001      ;unique serial number
                   8H               ; refresh rate
                   2H               ;retry period
                   1W               ; expiration period
                   1D)              ; minimum

           MX      10 host1.ispnet1.net. ; defines primary mail server
           MX      20 host2.ispnet1.net. ; defines secondary mail server
```

All mail messages for the `othercompany.com` domain will be sent to the `host1.ispnet1.net` mail server. If that server is down, the `host2.ispnet1.net` mail server must be able to accept mail messages for the domain. The `permit_mx_backup` value allows Postfix to accept messages for the domains defined in DNS records that point to the Postfix server.

Database Checks

Similar to sendmail and qmail, Postfix can read relaying information from a lookup table. Four values can be used to define lookup tables to restrict mail relay behavior:

- `check_client_access`
- `check_helo_access`
- `check_recipient_access`
- `check_sender_access`

Each of these four values points to a database type and name used for the lookup table, such as:

```
check_client_access hash:/etc/postfix/clients
```

The lookup table must be created using the database type listed in the parameter. The format of the database records looks like this:

```
address action
```

The *address* field can be an individual hostname, IP address, domain name, or IP network range. This value is matched against the object represented in the value name (client, HELO, recipient, or sender). The *action* field describes the action Postfix takes when a message is received that matches the address.

The action phrase REJECT is used to force Postfix to refuse messages that match the *address* field. Alternatively, the mail administrator can place an SMTP error code (4*xx* for temporary errors, or 5*xx* for permanent errors) along with descriptive text in the *action* field. This code and text are returned to the remote host in the SMTP reply statement.

Any other text used for *action* allows the host address that matches the *address* field to relay messages through the Postfix server.

Here is an example of building a tight mail relay domain by using the check_client_access value along with a specific lookup table:

```
ispnet1.net OK
ispnet2.net OK
ispnet3.net OK
```

By configuring the smtpd_recipient_restrictions parameter to reject by default, only domains listed in the check_client_access value are permitted to send messages to the Postfix server.

The main.cf configuration parameter line should look like this:

```
smtpd_recipient_restrictions = check_client_access hash:/etc/access, reject
```

After running the postmap utility on the access lookup table and issuing the Postfix reload command, the Postfix server should now accept mail messages only from hosts that identify themselves as being in one of the three domains listed in the access lookup table. Listing 11.3 shows some sample SMTP sessions using this configuration.

LISTING 11.3 Sample SMTP Sessions Using check_client_access

```
$ telnet localhost 25
Trying 127.0.0.1...
Connected to localhost.
Escape character is '^]'.
220 shadrach.ispnet1.net ESMTP Postfix
HELO dude
250 shadrach.ispnet1.net
MAIL FROM: <spammer>
250 Ok
RCPT TO: <rich@shadrach.ispnet1.net>
554 <rich@shadrach.ispnet1.net>: Recipient address rejected: Access denied
QUIT
221 Bye
Connection closed by foreign host.
$ telnet localhost 25
Trying 127.0.0.1...
Connected to localhost.
Escape character is '^]'.
220 shadrach.ispnet1.net ESMTP Postfix
HELO ispnet3.net
250 shadrach.ispnet1.net
MAIL FROM: <rich@ispnet3.net>
250 Ok
RCPT TO: <rich@othercompany.com>
250 Ok
DATA
354 End data with <CR><LF>.<CR><LF>
From: <rich@ispnet3.net>
To: <rich@othercompany.com>
Date: 11 Nov 2000 10:50
Subject: Mail Relay blocking
Rich -

    This is a test of mail blocking using the SMTP client address.
.
250 Ok: queued as 4C3533B11A
QUIT
221 Bye
Connection closed by foreign host.
$
```

As seen in the first example in Listing 11.3, the remote SMTP server did not identify itself properly in the SMTP MAIL FROM: command. When it tried to send a message through the Postfix server, it was blocked. In the second example, the remote SMTP server did identify itself correctly, and its domain was listed in the lookup table configured for the check_client_access value. It was allowed to send a message to a recipient on a third host. The Postfix server accepted the message, and will now try to forward that message to the appropriate mail server.

Avoiding Open Relays

Not only is it a good practice to not be an open relay server, it is also a good practice not to accept incoming messages from known open relays. This practice can significantly reduce the number of UCE messages your users receive.

Several Internet sites compile information about open relays on the Internet. Most of the sites get their information by actively querying e-mail hosts and testing whether they would forward a message. Unfortunately, this method has met with increased resistance from many mail administrators on the Internet. Equally unfortunately, many open relay information sites have practiced questionable ethics in posting violators.

Because of the controversial nature of their business, many open relay information sites have pending legal disputes, and some have even been taken off of the network. Possibly the most popular site was the Open Relay Blacklist System (ORBS). At the time of this writing, the ORBS site has been shut down because of pending legal action in New Zealand.

Another well-known open relay information site is the Mail Abuse Prevention System (MAPS). MAPS maintains several different lists you can access to look up UCE information. One such list is the MAPS Realtime Blackhole List (RBL), which lists addresses of known open relays on the Internet. The Web site for MAPS is at http://mail-abuse.org.

Many MTA packages have methods for enabling the mail server to connect to the MAPS RBL server to determine whether a remote mail server is listed as a known open relay. If the remote mail server address is found, the incoming message is assumed to be spam mail, and is blocked from entering the server.

The following sections describe how to configure sendmail, qmail, and Postfix to use the MAPS RBL server.

CAUTION

When you configure your MTA package to use an Internet blacklist server, you are at the mercy of the administration of that server. All e-mail from sites listed in the server's blacklist will be blocked. There is no way to distinguish valid messages from spam messages from a particular site. There are many cases of sites complaining that they were improperly listed in the blacklists. Be prepared to have the blacklist filter cause your MTA package to block some valid e-mail messages. Depending on your particular e-mail environment, you might have to weigh the pros and cons of using a blacklist service.

Sendmail Configuration

The sendmail configuration allows you to use the MAPS RBL to prevent open relays from sending messages to your mail server. If you use the m4 macro preprocessor to create your sendmail.cf file, you must add this entry:

```
FEATURE(`dnsbl', `host')
```

The *host* parameter allows you to point to an alternative RBL server. If you want to use the standard MAPS RBL server, you can omit the *host* parameter.

If you are not using the m4 macro preprocessor, you must add additional rules to the Basic_check_relay rule set section in the sendmail.cf configuration file. These are the rules to add:

```
# DNS based IP address spam list blackholes.mail-abuse.org
R$*           $: $&{client_addr}
R::ffff:$-.$-.$-.$-  $: <?> $(host $4.$3.$2.$1.blackholes.mail-abuse.org. $:
➥ OK $)
R$-.$-.$-.$-          $: <?> $(host $4.$3.$2.$1.blackholes.mail-abuse.org. $:
➥ OK $)
R<?>OK         $: OKSOFAR
R<?>$+         $#error $@ 5.7.1 $: "550 Mail from " $&{client_addr} " refused
➥ by blackhole site blackholes.mail-abuse.org"
```

This example uses the standard MAPS RBL server located at blackholes.mail-abuse.org. If you want to use a different RBL server, just replace that address with the alternative server's address.

qmail Configuration

qmail uses a specific program to connect with the RBL server to verify client addresses: the rblsmtpd program, which is part of the ucspi-tcp package (described earlier in the "Installing the Tcpserver Program" section).

The rblsmtpd program can query an RBL database server to determine whether an address has been blacklisted on the Internet. If it has, rblsmtpd denies the SMTP connection attempt. This is the format of the rblsmtpd command:

```
rblsmtpd options program
```

The *program* parameter is used to specify the application program that the connection is passed to if the RBL database does not block the connection. For a qmail server, it would be the qmail-smtpd program.

The *options* parameter specifies various options that modify the behavior of the rblsmtpd program. Table 11.6 shows the available options.

TABLE 11.6 Rblsmtpd Options

Option	Description
-a address	Use address as the source of the anti-RBL database. If address is found in the database, messages are accepted.
-b	Use a 553 return error code if an address is listed in the RBL.
-B	Use a 451 return error code if an address is listed in the RBL (default).
-c	Block the connection if the RBL lookup fails.
-r address	Use address as the source of the RBL database.
-t n	Use a timeout of n seconds.

The -a and -r options can be used multiple times, defining more than one database to check. The anti-RBL database does what it says; it is a database of good e-mail source addresses. If you want to limit your e-mail to only specific hosts, this is one way to do it. The -r option can be used to define your own RBL database of specific spammers that have not yet been caught by the official RBL database.

If you are using the tcpserver program to start qmail-smtpd, you can substitute the rblsmtpd program in place of the normal qmail-smtpd program in the tcpserver startup script:

```
/usr/local/bin/tcpserver -v -R -H -l 0 -x /etc/tcp.smtp.cdb -c "$MAXSMTPD"
➥ -u $QMAILDUID -g $NOFILESGID 0 smtp /var/qmail/bin/rblsmtpd
➥ /var/qmail/bin/qmail-smtpd
```

This entry passes all SMTP connections to the rblsmtpd program for verification. Addresses that pass the RBL verification are then forwarded to the normal qmail-smtpd program for processing.

Postfix Configuration

Similar to its selective relaying configuration, Postfix also has a method for blocking SMTP clients wanting to send messages to the mail server. The smtpd_client_restrictions command line in the main.cf configuration file defines what clients Postfix should refuse messages from.

The smtpd_client_restrictions command line can use several different parameter values to define restricted hosts. One of the available parameters is reject_maps_rbl:

```
smtpd_client_restrictions = reject_maps_rbl
```

By default, Postfix uses the standard blackholes.mail-abuse.org RBL server.

If you want to use an alternative server, you must specify it with the `maps_rbl_domains` command line in the main.cf configuration file:

```
maps_rbl_domains = altserver.ispnet1.net
```

Postfix then rejects any messages received from an address listed in the specified RBL server.

Summary

Relaying messages on the Internet has become a hot topic. What was once a common courtesy has become a nightmare. If your e-mail server is freely relaying messages from other sites, there is a good possibility your site will become blacklisted by other sites that will then refuse to accept mail from your site and users.

The idea of using selective relaying allows you to support users who need to relay messages through your e-mail server to the Internet, while still blocking attempts from remote e-mail servers to relay. All open source MTA packages now support some form of selective relaying.

The sendmail, qmail, and Postfix packages enable you to configure a database file containing addresses of clients you will allow to use your e-mail server as a mail relay. All other attempts by hosts not in the database will be refused by the MTA package. Additionally, with the sendmail and Postfix packages, you can create alternative conditions, such as blocking misidentified hosts.

Several different servers on the Internet create lists of known e-mail servers that have been used as open relays to forward spam. You can use these servers to block messages received by a known spam source. The Mail Abuse Prevention System (MAPS) is one site you can configure in sendmail, qmail, and Postfix to look up addresses of connecting remote e-mail servers. If the connecting address is in the MAPS database, the MTA package will refuse all messages from that site.

CHAPTER 12

Blocking Spam

Chapter 11, "Preventing Open Relays," described how to avoid being an open relay and how to avoid accepting messages received from open relays, where most spam mail comes from. One of the problems with using this type of spam blocking is that spammers often use commonly used hosts to send their mail messages. By blocking a known open relay host, you could also inadvertently block good messages from other users of that mail host.

This chapter discusses how to use advanced features of your MTA to block specific spam hosts or filter specific spam messages to fine-tune your spam filtering.

Methods Used to Block Spam

In the short lifetime of the Internet, many different techniques have been tried to attempt to block spam messages. Of the different techniques, three have become the most popular:

- Refusing to accept messages from known spam hosts
- Validating SMTP session information provided by the remote host
- Filtering incoming messages looking for tell-tale spam signs

All these methods have their pros and cons when used on production mail servers. The following sections explain how these methods work and describe their benefits and drawbacks.

Refusing Mail from Known Spam Hosts

Similar to the method of refusing mail from known open relay hosts described in Chapter 11, you can configure your MTA package to refuse mail from known spam hosts while allowing messages from other remote mail servers. Figure 12.1 illustrates this.

To use this method, you need some type of address lookup system to check the address of each remote host requesting to send a message to your mail server. For the MTA package to know which hosts to reject messages from, there must be some mechanism for listing known spam hosts. There are two commonly used methods to implement this feature:

- Create your own list of spam hosts that the mail server can check against.
- Connect to an Internet server that provides a list of known spam hosts.

These two methods of blocking messages from known spam hosts are described in more detail in the following sections.

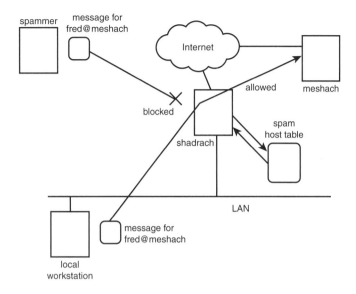

FIGURE 12.1

Blocking incoming messages from known spam hosts.

Creating Your Own Spam Host List

Many mail administrators prefer to create their own list of known spam sites. In this method, as mail server users receive spam messages, the mail administrator places the originating addresses in a local file. The MTA package is then configured to refuse any further messages from the addresses in that file. The addresses can be complete user@host e-mail addresses or simply the hostname of the offending spammer.

This method requires feedback from the users on your mail server. As each individual user receives a spam message, he needs to manually forward the message to you or to a common administrator mail account. As you receive forwarded spam messages from your users, you need to examine the messages and determine their originating e-mail addresses (see Chapter 6, "Reading E-mail Headers").

You must then decide how you want to enter the information into your lookup table. Using complete e-mail addresses, including the username, will block specific spammers, but be careful because many (if not most) spammers forge their return addresses. Also, most spammers frequently change the username portion of the address just to confuse spam-blocking software. You can instead choose to block spammers by the originating host address. This method is more effective, but be careful, as you can also block any valid e-mail messages originating from the same host.

The downside to this method is that you cannot block a spam site until one of your users has been hit by the spammer. Although this method does minimize spam mail for your users, it does not provide protection from new spam addresses.

Alternatively, you can harvest known spam host addresses from Internet servers that track spam sites. As discussed in Chapter 6, the SpamCop Web site (www.spamcop.net) supplies lists of known spam hosts submitted by people who have already received spam messages. To use these lists, however, you need to manually extract the host information from SpamCop and place it in your local spam host list.

This method has the advantage of using someone else's spam experience, allowing you to effectively block spam before it gets to your users. However, it still requires manual intervention on your part to keep your spam host list updated regularly.

To automate the process, several Internet sites have provided a service that can automatically check host addresses against known spam sites. The next section describes this process.

Using a Spam Host List Provider

Similar to the known open relay servers described in Chapter 11, there are Internet servers containing lists of known spam hosts that can be automatically queried by most MTA packages. Figure 12.2 demonstrates how this works.

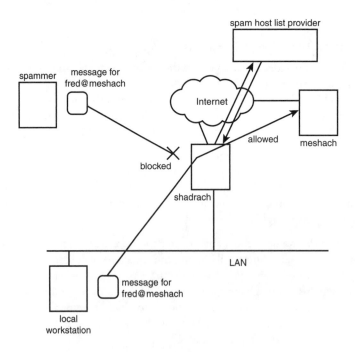

FIGURE 12.2

Using an Internet server to determine known spam hosts.

For each incoming mail message, the MTA package obtains the address of the remote mail server and queries a remote Internet server to validate the address. If the remote server's address is listed as a known spam host, the MTA package refuses to accept the incoming mail message.

The Mail Abuse Prevention System (MAPS) project (described in Chapter 11) maintains a list of known spam sites as well as open relay sites. The Relay Spam Stopper (RSS) feature at MAPS allows remote mail servers to send address queries for validation as incoming mail messages are received. If the address is found in the MAPS RSS database, the mail server can assume it is a known spam host and refuse the incoming message.

Requiring Valid SMTP Information

Another effective method used to block spam is validating the SMTP information used by the remote host during the SMTP session. This information is commonly referred to as the *message envelope*, as it is not part of the actual message. It is, however, vital in ensuring that the message is delivered properly.

As discussed in Chapter 6, many spam hosts attempt to use forged or invalid information when transferring spam messages to your e-mail server. The sooner the mail server can recognize and reject a spam host, the less resources it wastes on processing spam.

Many MTA packages allow you to configure either strict or loose checking of incoming SMTP information. The two SMTP commands most often checked are HELO (or EHLO for ESMTP) and MAIL FROM:.

The HELO command is used to find the identity of the remote mail server. As discussed in Chapter 2, "SMTP," this command is often forged by spammers. The proper form of the HELO command should look like this:

```
HELO hostname
```

The *hostname* parameter should identify the full name of the remote host that established the SMTP session. Many spammers forge this information, either by providing false information or not giving a hostname at all. With some MTA packages, you can require that the information entered by the remote mail server in the HELO command is accurate. Performing a DNS hostname lookup often screens invalid information supplied in the HELO command.

The MAIL FROM: command is used to identify the sender of the e-mail message. A normal MAIL FROM: command should contain the Fully Qualified Domain Name (FQDN) format of the recipient's mail address:

```
MAIL FROM: <rich@shadrach.ispnet1.net>
```

Again, many MTA packages allow you to verify the information provided by the remote host in this command by performing DNS hostname lookups of the supplied hostname.

Filtering Spam Mail

The last method of blocking spam is using the filtering capabilities of your MTA package to search for phrases often found in spam messages. If a message does contain a known spam phrase, the mail server will not accept it. The trick to this method is determining what phrases to validate and filter.

Two different parts of the incoming mail message can be checked for spam phrases. The message header contains separate fields that can be scanned individually for known phrases. As discussed in Chapter 6, many spam hosts use forged message headers to propagate their advertisements. You can use this information to help filter out future spam messages from that site.

As an example, your users often get spam messages that contain this header field:

```
From: yourfriend@gooddeals.com
```

Even if the From: header field is forged (which it most likely is), you can scan the From: fields of each incoming message for the known phrase yourfriend@gooddeals.com. Any messages containing this phrase will be assumed to be spam and rejected by the mail server.

Alternatively, you can configure some MTA packages to search for specific phrases in the body of the message. This method is more intensive than just scanning the header fields, as there could be many lines of message body data for the mail server to scan. Also, scanning the entire message body for a phrase is riskier than scanning header fields because there is a higher likelihood that the phrase will appear in the body of a valid e-mail message. This could prevent a user from receiving valid (and possibly important) e-mail. However, often it can be the easiest (and sometimes the only) way to filter out spam messages.

Implementing Spam Blocking

Now that you have seen the different types of spam blocking, it is time to see how to configure the different MTA packages to implement it. This section describes how to implement spam blocking using sendmail, qmail, and Postfix mail servers.

sendmail

The sendmail MTA package has had a checkered past with spam. In early versions of sendmail, the administrator could not control any spam features, thus leaving users at the mercy of spammers. Since version 8.9.3, sendmail has included extensive spam control features that makes blocking spam much easier. This section describes the spam control features that current versions of sendmail use.

Creating Your Own Spam Host List

As described in the "Configuring Selective Relaying" section in Chapter 11, you can add an access table to sendmail to list hosts that are allowed or denied access to your mail server. Each entry can reflect an individual host or an entire domain. If you specify REJECT as the action, the host (or hosts) will not be allowed to send messages to users on your mail server.

Also, instead of just specifying REJECT in the access table, you can also specify an SMTP error code and text that is returned to the remote mail server. This feature is used to ensure that the remote host knows you are rejecting the messages because it is suspected of being spam. The format of the access table entry looks like this:

```
address     code text
```

A sample access table used for spam blocking is shown in Listing 12.1

LISTING 12.1 Sample Spam Access Table

```
spamco.com      550 We do not like spammers
badhost.ispnet1.net     550 Your host has been caught spamming
gooddeals.com    REJECT
192.168.1.20     550 This host has been caught spamming
```

The access table matches domain addresses as well as individual hostnames and addresses. By entering a domain name, any host within the domain will match the entry. When a matching address is found in the access table, sendmail returns the SMTP error code and text associated with the address.

After the text table is created, it must be converted into a binary database format with the Unix makemap command:

```
makemap hash /etc/mail/access < /etc/mail/access
```

This command creates the access.db binary database file. Every time the access database is modified, the binary database needs to be re-created, and sendmail should be restarted. Listing 12.2 shows a sample spam session that is blocked by the access database.

LISTING 12.2 Sample Blocked Spam Session

```
$ telnet localhost 25
Trying 127.0.0.1...
Connected to localhost.
Escape character is '^]'.
220 shadrach.ispnet1.net ESMTP sendmail 8.11.3/8.11.3; Fri, 22 Jun 2001
➡ 07:02:27 -0
```

LISTING 12.2 Continued

```
EHLO spamco.com
250-shadrach.ispnet1.net Hello IDENT:root@localhost [127.0.0.1], pleased to
➥ meet you
250-ENHANCEDSTATUSCODES
250-EXPN
250-VERB
250-8BITMIME
250-SIZE
250-DSN
250-ONEX
250-ETRN
250-XUSR
250 HELP
MAIL FROM: <rich@spamco.com>
550 5.0.0 <rich@spamco.com>... We do not like spammers
QUIT
221 2.0.0 shadrach.ispnet1.net closing connection
Connection closed by foreign host.
$
```

As soon as the offending address is received in the MAIL FROM: command, sendmail returns a 550 error message to the remote mail server. This error message informs the remote host that the message will never be accepted by the sendmail server. This method intercepts the potential spam message before the actual message body is received and processed, saving valuable processor time on the mail server.

Using the MAPS RSS Server

Again, similar to the open relay blocking implementation described in Chapter 11, sendmail can use the dnsbl FEATURE command to connect to the MAPS RSS server (blackholes.mail-abuse.org). The FEATURE command used in the m4 macro file looks like this:

```
FEATURE(dnsbl, `blackholes.mail-abuse.org', `Rejected - see
➥ http://www.mail-abuse.org/rbl/')dnl
```

Not only does the dnsbl FEATURE use the blackholes.mail-abuse.org server to look up spam host addresses, it also allows entering customized text in the SMTP return message. If you are modifying the sendmail.cf file by hand, you must add the following rule sets to the Basic_check_relay S group:

```
# DNS based IP address spam list blackholes.mail-abuse.org
R$*         $: $&{client_addr}
R::ffff:$-.$-.$-.$- $: <?> $(host $4.$3.$2.$1.blackholes.mail-abuse.org. $:
➥ OK $)
```

```
R$-.$-.$-.$-          $: <?> $(host $4.$3.$2.$1.blackholes.mail-abuse.org. $:
➥ OK $)
R<?>OK          $: OKSOFAR
R<?>$+          $#error $@ 5.7.1 $: Rejected - see
➥ http://www.mail-abuse.org/rbl/
```

If a message is blocked from a known spam host, sendmail indicates the remote host in the mail log file. If you want to also see the message's intended recipient, you can add an additional FEATURE command:

```
FEATURE(`delay_checks')dnl
```

This command delays checking incoming SMTP connections until after the RCPT TO: command is issued, allowing sendmail to also log the value in the RCPT TO: command—the intended recipient of the spam message. Although this method helps you by adding more explanatory text in the log file, it does allow the SMTP session to proceed two more steps before deciding to terminate the session, wasting some additional network bandwidth and system processor time on the spam message.

Validating SMTP Information

Since version 8.9.3, sendmail has enforced the following strict SMTP validation restrictions on all sessions by default:

- Refuse mail if the MAIL FROM: parameter is an unresolved domain
- Refuse mail if the MAIL FROM: parameter is not in FQDN format
- Refuse mail from hosts that send an empty HELO or EHLO command

Although these are default actions, sendmail provides configuration parameters that enable you to override these settings. The first two defaults can be changed by using FEATURE commands. To accept messages with MAIL FROM: parameters from an unresolved domain, you can use this m4 command:

```
FEATURE(`accept_unresolvable_domains')dnl
```

To accept messages with MAIL FROM: parameters that are not in FQDN format you can use the m4 command:

```
FEATURE(`accept_unqualified_senders')dnl
```

Finally, if you want to accept messages from hosts that send an empty HELO or EHLO command, you can use this m4 command:

```
define(`confALLOW_BOGUS_HELO', `True')dnl
```

If you include any of these commands in your original m4 macro file, the sendmail.cf configuration file is configured to override the default behavior.

Each of these m4 commands can be manually entered into the sendmail.cf configuration file. The `accept_unresolvable_domains` feature adds an additional rule set in the `Basic_check_mail` S group:

```
R<?> $* < @ $+ >      $: <OK> $1 < @ $2 >
```

In the case of the `accept_unqualified_senders` feature, you must remove a rule set that is used by default. The rule set to remove is again in the `Basic_check_mail` S group:

```
R<? $+> $*      $#error $@ 5.5.4 $: "501 Domain name required for sender
➥ address " $&f
```

Finally, the `confALLOW_BOGUS_HELO` m4 command inserts an O line that defines the `AllowBogusHELO` option. By default it is set to `False`. To change this behavior, you can set the value to `True`:

```
O AllowBogusHELO=True
```

CAUTION

These features have been incorporated into sendmail to help prevent spam. Removing any of these features should be done with caution and with the understanding that it is decreasing the server's spam protection.

Using Message Filters

As described in Chapter 8, "The sendmail E-mail Package," the sendmail configuration file contains rule sets that each incoming message is checked against. You can specify special rules that filter incoming messages searching for spam phrases in message header fields.

The H configuration lines define actions for sendmail to take on specific message header fields. You can specify new H lines that instruct sendmail to run the special rule sets based on particular types and values of header fields.

A common method to use is creating a file that contains spam phrases found in message `Subject:` header fields. For this example, take a look at creating a file called /etc/mail/bad_subjects that contains interesting spam `Subject:` fields phrases. Listing 12.3 shows the sample file.

LISTING 12.3 Sample /etc/mail/bad_subjects File

```
Make more money
An important offer from
From your friends at
How to be a millionaire
```

As your users get spam messages, you can add new phrases to the file. Remember that you will have to restart sendmail for the new phrases to take effect (but more on that later).

Next, you must configure the sendmail.cf configuration file to check the header fields for spam phrases. First you add the spam-checking H line at the end of the existing H lines defined in the configuration file. The new H line will look for the phrase Subject:, and run the special rule set you create. This line should do the trick:

```
HSubject: $>Check_Subject
```

The next step is to create the rule set, which requires three separate lines in the configuration file: an S line to identify the rule set, an F line to define the location of the bad_subjects file you created, and an R line to define the actual rule that will be run. Listing 12.4 shows an example of what this rule set should look like.

LISTING 12.4 Sample Spam Rule Set

```
SCheck_Subject
F{Header}/etc/mail/bad_subjects
R$={Header} $*    $#error $: 553 We don't like spam here.
```

This rule set can be added anywhere in the default rule sets in the configuration file, but usually it is easier to tack it onto the end of the rule sets. The S line must use the same tag name as the H line that references it. The F line defines the variable {Header} that points to your text file containing the spam phrases. Finally, the actual rule is defined in the R line. Any message with a Subject: header field that matches one of the phrases in your bad_subjects file will be rejected with a 553 error, as well as your customized error text.

After saving the modifications in the sendmail.cf configuration file, you must restart sendmail. The easiest method is to send a SIGHUP signal to the running sendmail process. You can do that by listing the sendmail process, obtaining the process ID (PID), and performing a kill -HUP command on that PID:

```
# ps -ax | grep sendmail
191  ??  Is   0:18.24 sendmail: accepting connections on port 25 (sendmail)
# kill -HUP 191
```

After you restart sendmail it should be on the watch for spam phrases in received messages. Listing 12.5 demonstrates what this looks like to the remote spam host.

LISTING 12.5 Sample Spam Session

```
$ telnet localhost 25
Trying 127.0.0.1...
Connected to localhost.
Escape character is '^]'.
220 test.ispnet1.net ESMTP sendmail 8.11.3/8.11.3; Wed,
➡ 20 Jun 2001 13:35:52 -0
EHLO test.ispnet1.net
250- test.ispnet1.net Hello IDENT:rich@localhost [127.0.0.1], pleased to
➡ meet you
250-ENHANCEDSTATUSCODES
250-EXPN
250-VERB
250-8BITMIME
250-SIZE
250-DSN
250-ONEX
250-ETRN
250-XUSR
250 HELP
MAIL FROM: rich@test.ispnet1.net
250 2.1.0 rich@test.ispnet1.net... Sender ok
RCPT TO: rich
250 2.1.5 rich... Recipient ok
DATA
354 Enter mail, end with "." on a line by itself
From: rich
To: rich
Subject: From your friends at spamco

This is a test spam message.
.
553 5.0.0 We don't like spam here.
QUIT
221 2.0.0 test.ispnet1.net closing connection
Connection closed by foreign host.
$
```

As shown in the listing, the mail server refused to accept the message that failed the spam filter test (note the "From your friends at" phrase in the message). Unfortunately, the mail server did have to wait until the complete message was received from the remote host before realizing that it was spam.

qmail

The qmail MTA package has limited spam controls built into the default qmail programs. Several qmail users have created add-on programs that enhance qmail's ability to control spam messages. The following sections describes the built-in qmail spam features, as well as one add-on spam package that can be used with qmail.

Creating Your Own Spam Host List

The `badmailfrom` control file is used to provide qmail with a list of e-mail addresses that the qmail server should refuse messages from. Each address should be listed on a separate line. Domain names can be used to indicate all hosts in a particular domain. If a `badmailfrom` file is not present in the control file directory, no addresses are blocked from the mail server.

The `badmailfrom` list contains the ASCII text of the list of addresses you want barred from sending e-mail messages to your local qmail users, as shown in this example:

```
nuisance@advert.corp1.com
@mail.hq.corp.com
@evildomain.net
```

The first line shows restricting a specific username at a specific hostname— `nuisance@advert.corp1.com`. Any other user at the `advert.corp1.com` mail server would be able to send mail messages to recipients on the local qmail server. The second line shows restricting all users on a single remote mail server, and the third line shows restricting mail from all hosts in an entire domain. Note that when defining host and domain names in the `badmailfrom` file, you must use the @ sign before the host or domain name. Addresses can be added and deleted from the `badmailfrom` file without having to restart qmail.

Listing 12.6 shows a sample SMTP connection from a host whose domain is listed in the `badmailfrom` file.

LISTING 12.6 Sample `badmailfrom` Host Session

```
$ telnet localhost 25
Trying 127.0.0.1...
Connected to localhost.ispnet1.net.
Escape character is '^]'.
220 shadrach.ispnet1.net ESMTP
HELO evildomain.net
250 shadrach.ispnet1.net
MAIL FROM: <badguy@evildomain.net>
250 ok
RCPT TO: <rich@ispnet1.net>
```

LISTING 12.6 Sample `badmailfrom` Host Session

```
553 sorry, your envelope sender is in my badmailfrom list (#5.7.1)
QUIT
221 shadrach.ispnet1.net
Connection closed by foreign host.
$
```

This listing shows a sample Telnet session to the local qmail server's SMTP port. Immediately after the message recipient is identified, qmail responds with a negative SMTP response (code 553) indicating that it will not allow the offending message sender access to local e-mail recipients.

Using the MAPS RSS Server

The qmail program can check incoming connections with the MAPS RSS server by using the rblsmtpd program described in Chapter 11. The same format should be used as when checking for open relays, except that the RSS server should be specified in the command line with the -r option:

```
/usr/local/bin/tcpserver -v -R -H -l 0 -x /etc/tcp.smtp.cdb -c "$MAXSMTPD"
➥ -u $QMAILDUID -g $NOFILESGID 0 smtp /var/qmail/bin/rblsmtpd
➥ -r "blackholes.mail-abuse.org: Your
➥ site has been listed in the MAPS RSS database"
➥ /var/qmail/bin/qmail-smtpd
```

Note that you can include the SMTP error text returned to the remote host within the -r option.

NOTE

At the time of this writing, the rblsmtpd program is having difficulty retrieving records from the MAPS RSS site because of a DNS issue. It is not known when or if this issue will be resolved. In the meantime, a qmail user has created a patch that allows the rblsmtpd program to work with the RSS server. It can be found at `http://www.qmail.org/ucspi-rss.diff`.

Validating SMTP Information

At the time of this writing, the current version of qmail, version 1.03, did not support any type of SMTP information checking by default. Some qmail users have created patches to incorporate checking SMTP information, but so far none have been extensively tested and used. The qmail Web site (`www.qmail.org`) contains a list of user-contributed qmail patches, but it is hoped that this feature will be added in future releases of the qmail package.

Using Message Filters

Version 1.03 of qmail also does not include any spam message filtering techniques by default. However, given the importance of spam-filtering controls, qmail users have created several packages that add message-filtering techniques to the standard qmail package. One of the more popular solutions is the qmail-qfilter package created by Bruce Guenter.

The qmail-qfilter program allows you to place a Perl-based filter script before the qmail-queue program. The filter script intercepts the incoming message and scans it before it is placed in the message queue. The script can define multiple filters that can be configured to scan any data in the message, both in the message headers and the message body.

Downloading and Installing qmail-qfilter

The current version of qmail-qfilter at the time of this writing is version 1.5 and can be downloaded from:

```
http://untroubled.org/qmail-qfilter/qmail-qfilter-1.5.tar.gz
```

After downloading the source code, you should unpack it into a working directory using this command:

```
tar -zxvf qmail-qfilter-1.5.tar.gz -C /usr/local/src
```

This command creates the directory /usr/local/src/qmail-qfilter-1.5 (remember to perform the tar command as root). After creating the directory, you must make a few edits to the programs, described in the next section, to support your qmail environment.

Configuring qmail-qfilter

You need to modify two lines in the qmail-qfilter.c program so that it works properly in your qmail environment. First you indicate a temporary directory that the qmail-qfilter program can use as a workspace while it is filtering mail messages. This is specified as the variable TMPDIR using a #define statement:

```
#define TMPDIR "/tmp"
```

The default value of /tmp should work for most Unix systems.

Next you must define an alternative program name for the qmail-queue program. The premise behind qmail-qfilter is that you replace the original qmail-queue file with a script that calls your Perl mail filter program, and then returns to the original qmail-queue program. This method requires that you move the original qmail-queue program to an alternative location, specified by using the #define statement in the qmail-qfilter.c file:

```
#define QMAIL_QUEUE "/var/qmail/bin/qmail-queue-old"
```

After saving the changes made in the qmail-qfilter.c file, you can compile the executable with the `make` command.

Using qmail-qfilter

After the executable program has been created, you must create a Perl script for filtering all incoming mail messages. qmail-qfilter takes advantage of Perl exit codes to block messages. If you want the filter to block an incoming message, the filter script must use an exit code of 31, which causes qmail-smtpd to exit and report an error to the remote host. If the filter script exits with an exit code of 99, qmail-smtpd silently drops the message without sending a response to the remote host. Any other exit code allows the message to pass to the alternative qmail-queue program for processing.

This example creates a deny-spam script, used to block messages containing known spam phrases. First, you create the Perl script in the /var/qmail/bin directory. Listing 12.7 shows a sample deny-spam script.

LISTING 12.7 Sample deny-spam Perl Script

```perl
#!/usr/bin/perl

while(<>) {
    print;
    exit 31 if /^Subject: Make more money/;
    exit 31 if /^Subject: An important offer from/;
    exit 31 if /^Subject: From your friends at/;
    exit 31 if /^Subject: How to be a millionaire/;
    exit 31 if /^From: 1234\@spamco.com/;
}
```

This sample script blocks a few different known spam `Subject:` header field phrases, as well as a known spam `From:` header file phrase. Note how the @ sign must be preceded by a backslash character. Copy the script to the /var/qmail/bin/ directory, and ensure that the script is readable and executable by all users:

```
chmod 755 /var/qmail/bin/deny-spam
```

After the Perl mail filter script has been installed, you create the phony qmail-queue script that points to it. First, you copy the existing qmail-queue program to the alternative location you specified in the qmail-qfilter.c program:

```
mv /var/qmail/bin/qmail-queue /var/qmail/bin/qmail-queue-old
```

With the original qmail-queue program out of the way, you then create the phony qmail-queue script. The script should look like the following:

```
#!/bin/sh
exec /var/qmail/bin/qmail-qfilter /var/qmail/bin/deny-spam
```

This script calls the qmail-qfilter program with the name of your Perl filter script. This script should be owned by the `qmailq` user, be executable by all users, and not have the `setuid` bit set. Basically, the new programs should look like this:

```
-rwxr-xr-x   1 qmailq    qmail        1753 Jun 21 11:03 deny-spam
-rwxr-xr-x   1 qmailq    qmail        6404 Jun 22 07:38 qmail-qfilter
-rwxr-xr-x   1 qmailq    qmail          74 Jun 21 11:04 qmail-queue
-rws—x—x     1 qmailq    qmail       12944 Jun 21 10:05 qmail-queue-old
```

After you restart qmail, your filter script becomes active. The server will then reject any messages that meet the filter rules. You can add new rules to the deny-spam script file without having to restart qmail.

Listing 12.8 shows a sample SMTP session that was blocked by the qmail-qfilter script.

LISTING 12.8 Sample Blocked Spam SMTP Session

```
$ telnet localhost 25
Trying 127.0.0.1...
Connected to localhost.
Escape character is '^]'.
220 shadrach.ispnet1.net ESMTP
EHLO spamco.com
250-shadrach.ispnet1.net
250-PIPELINING
250 8BITMIME
MAIL FROM: 1234@spamco.com
250 ok
RCPT TO: rich@shadrach.ispnet1.net
250 ok
DATA
354 go ahead
From: 1234@spamco.com
To: rich@shadrach.ispnet1.net
Subject: Sample spam session

This session should be blocked by our spam script!
.
554 mail server permanently rejected message (#5.3.0)
QUIT
221 shadrach.ispnet1.net
Connection closed by foreign host.
$
```

The sample message was permanently rejected with a 554 SMTP error code by the qmail server. Note that the From: message header contained a return address that matched a rule in the deny-spam Perl script.

Postfix

The Postfix MTA package includes several layers of spam protection that can be used. The following sections describe these spam controls and how to implement them.

Creating Your Own Spam Host List

As described in Chapter 11, Postfix enables you to create an access table defining hosts to refuse messages from. You use the smtpd_client_restrictions parameter in the main.cf configuration file, as shown in the following line, to check the access table for blocking known spam hosts from sending messages to the mail server:

```
smtpd_client_restrictions = check_client_access hash:/etc/postfix/badclients
```

Similar to the sendmail access table, each spam host or domain should be listed in the /etc/hash/badclients file, along with the SMTP error code and text you want returned to the spam host:

```
spamco.com      550 We do not like spammers
badhost.ispnet1.net     550 Your host has been caught spamming
192.168.1.20     550 This host has been caught spamming
```

After creating the text access table, you use the postmap utility to create the binary database file used by Postfix:

```
postmap hash /etc/postfix/badclients
```

After restarting Postfix, the new access table is used to block incoming messages from the hosts and domains listed.

Using the MAPS RSS Server

Also as described in Chapter 11, Postfix uses the smtpd_client_restrictions parameter in the main.cf configuration file to use the MAPS RSS server to block known spam sites by adding the line:

```
smtpd_client_restrictions = reject_maps_rbl
maps_rbl_domains = blackholes.mail-abuse.org
```

Note that you can also specify both the MAPS RBL and RSS servers in the maps_rbl_domains parameter to check remote mail server addresses against the MAPS open relay and known spam lists.

Validating SMTP Information

Postfix offers one of the most robust methods of checking the SMTP information provided by remote hosts. You can configure Postfix to perform several different types of checks, described in the following sections, on the remote host information.

Verifying HELO Addresses

With Postfix, the mail administrator can restrict remote hosts that do not properly identify themselves in the HELO command. To do that, you use the smtpd_helo_restrictions parameter in the main.cf configuration file.

By default Postfix does not do any checking of the value submitted by the HELO command, but the mail administrator can configure Postfix to check this value in several different ways. Table 12.1 shows the HELO restrictions that can be configured for Postfix.

TABLE 12.1 Postfix HELO Restriction Values

Value	Description
check_helo_access	Check hostname in specified lookup table
check_client_access	Check client address in specified lookup table
permit	Allow any HELO hostname
permit_mynetworks	Allow if client address is included in the mynetworks parameter
reject	Reject all HELO hostnames
reject_unknown_client	Reject if client address is unknown
reject_maps_rbl	Reject if the client address is included in the $maps_rbl_domain value
reject_invalid_hostname	Reject invalid hostnames
reject_unknown_hostname	Reject hostnames without a DNS A or MX record
reject_non_fqdn_hostname	Reject hostnames not in FQDN format

You can select multiple values for the parameter to be as specific as needed when trying to block remote servers. This is the format of the parameter:

```
smtpd_helo_restrictions = reject_unknown_hostname, permit_mynetworks
```

You can list multiple values for the parameter, separated by a comma or a space. Postfix checks the values in the order entered in the list. Listing 12.9 shows an example using these values.

LISTING 12.9 Sample SMTP Session with Bad HELO Hostname

```
$ telnet localhost 25
Trying 127.0.0.1...
Connected to localhost.
Escape character is '^]'.
220 shadrach.ispnet1.net ESMTP Postfix
HELO dude
250 shadrach.ispnet1.net
MAIL FROM: <spammer@badguy.com>
250 Ok
RCPT TO: <rich@shadrach.ispnet1.net>
450 <dude>: Helo command rejected: Host not found
QUIT
221 Bye
Connection closed by foreign host.
$
```

In Listing 12.9, the remote host failed to identify itself properly in the HELO command. Although Postfix did not complain about it then, it did refuse to accept a message destined for a local user from the remote host.

Similar to the open relay and spam address access tables, you can also configure a HELO access table of known bad HELO addresses. The table can then be referenced in the main.cf configuration file by using the smtpd_helo_restrictions parameter:

```
smtpd_helo_restrictions = check_helo_access hash:/etc/postfix/bad_helo
```

The format of the /etc/postfix/bad_helo table is exactly the same as the other access tables used by Postfix. Again, you use the postmap command to convert the table into a binary database.

After saving the new configuration file and issuing the Postfix reload command, you can test the restrictions. Listing 12.10 shows an example of the new restrictions.

LISTING 12.10 Sample HELO Access Restrictions

```
[haley@shadrach haley]$ telnet localhost 25
Trying 127.0.0.1...
Connected to localhost.
Escape character is '^]'.
220 shadrach.ispnet1.net ESMTP Postfix
HELO spammer.org
250 shadrach.ispnet1.net
MAIL FROM: <rich@spammer.org>
```

LISTING 12.10 Continued

```
250 Ok
RCPT TO: <rich@shadrach.ispnet1.net>
554 <spammer.org>: Helo command rejected: Access denied
QUIT
221 Bye
Connection closed by foreign host.
[haley@shadrach haley]$
```

As shown in Listing 12.10, Postfix refused to allow the remote host listed in the lookup table to send messages to local users.

Verifying MAIL FROM: Addresses

The smtpd_sender_restrictions parameter defines restrictions that can be placed in the information the Postfix server accepts in the MAIL FROM: command. Table 12.2 shows the possible values for this parameter.

TABLE 12.2 Postfix MAIL FROM: Restriction Values

Value	Description
check_client_access	Check client address in specified lookup table
check_helo_access	Check HELO address in specified lookup table
check_sender_access	Check sender address in specified lookup table
permit	Allow any sender hostname
permit_mynetworks	Allow any sender address listed in the mynetworks parameter
reject	Reject all sender hostnames
reject_invalid_hostname	Reject invalid HELO hostnames
reject_maps_rbl	Reject if client is listed in the $maps_rbl_domains parameter
reject_non_fqdn_hostname	Reject HELO hostname if not in FQDN format
reject_non_fqdn_sender	Reject sender hostname if not in FQDN format
reject_unknown_client	Reject if the client hostname is not known
reject_unknown_hostname	Reject HELO hostnames without a DNS A or MX record
reject_unknown_sender_domain	Reject sender hostname without a DNS A or MX record

As with the HELO restrictions, you can list multiple values for the parameter to specifically define how you want Postfix to examine the incoming messages, as shown in this example:

```
smtpd_sender_restrictions = reject_unknown_sender_domain, permit_mynetworks
```

In Listing 12.11, the restrictions in the preceding example are used to prevent Postfix from receiving messages from an unknown sender.

LISTING 12.11 Sample Bad MAIL FROM: Example

```
$ telnet localhost 25
Trying 127.0.0.1...
Connected to localhost.ispnet1.net.
Escape character is '^]'.
220 shadrach.ispnet1.net ESMTP Postfix
HELO dude
250 shadrach.ispnet1.net
MAIL FROM: <badguy@spammer.com>
250 Ok
RCPT TO: <rich@shadrach.ispnet1.net>
450 <badguy@spammer.com>: Sender address rejected: Domain not found
QUIT
221 Bye
Connection closed by foreign host.
$
```

The Postfix server rejected the attempt from the remote mail server to use a fictitious address in the MAIL FROM: command.

Using Message Filters

The header_checks parameter in the main.cf configuration file can be used to scan message headers, looking for particular phrases contained in the message. Messages that include a phrase are blocked from delivery. This is the format of the header_checks parameter:

```
header_checks = regexp:/etc/postfix/bad_header
```

The header_checks parameter uses either a regular expression table or a Posix Common Regular Expression (pcre) table to use wildcard text matching of the defined phrase. The text lookup table is created in this form:

```
pattern action
```

In this format, *pattern* is a regular expression to match in the header fields, and *action* is the action to take if the pattern is matched. There are three possible actions:

- REJECT—Rejects the message
- OK—Accepts the message
- IGNORE—Discards the header line from the message

Each line in the lookup table is compared against the message header fields until one line matches. If no lines match, the message is accepted. A sample `header_checks` lookup table would look like this:

```
/^subject: more money$/ REJECT
/^subject: I LOVE YOU$/ REJECT
/^to: our valued customer$/ REJECT
/^from: your friend$/ REJECT
```

Each line in the lookup table contains a different regular expression that is matched against the text in the message header lines. The expressions are not case sensitive, so you do not have to worry about matching different possible case situations. The start of the text expression is denoted by the ^ character, and the end of the text expression is denoted by the $ character. Listing 12.12 shows an example of how Postfix rejects a message that matches a pattern in the lookup table.

LISTING 12.12 Sample `header_checks` Session

```
$ telnet localhost 25
Trying 127.0.0.1...
Connected to localhost.ispnet1.net.
Escape character is '^]'.
220 shadrach.ispnet1.net ESMTP Postfix
HELO goodguy.com
250 shadrach.ispnet1.net
MAIL FROM: <spammer@goodguy.com>
250 Ok
RCPT TO: <rich@shadrach.ispnet1.net>
250 Ok
DATA
354 End data with <CR><LF>.<CR><LF>
From: spammer@goodguy.com
To: rich@shadrach.ispnet1.net
Date: 20 Nov 2000 19:40
Subject: more money

How would you like to make more money?
Just call us to find out our secret method.
.
552 Error: content rejected
QUIT
221 Bye
Connection closed by foreign host.
$
```

Postfix allows the remote mail server to send the message, as the envelope portion did not match any of the other anti-spam methods. However, once the message is received, Postfix applies the header_checks lookup table to the values sent in the message header. One line in the lookup table matches the contents in the Subject: header field (more money, in this case), and the message is rejected. Postfix then notifies the remote mail server that the message was rejected.

Similar to the header_checks parameter, Postfix also provides the body_checks parameter. This parameter is used the same way as the header_checks parameter, except it is used to scan the entire body of the incoming message for a match to phrases listed in a file. Although this feature can be useful in stopping specific spam messages, it can consume a lot of processor time on the mail system. Care should be taken when using the body_checks parameter.

Summary

Stopping spam mail has become one of the most important jobs of the mail administrator, and several different methods are used to accomplish it. The three most common are refusing mail from known spam hosts, requiring valid SMTP information, and filtering messages for spam phrases.

Most open source MTA packages can be configured to refuse mail from remote hosts appearing in a list of known spam sites. You can create your own spam list, filling in new addresses as you become aware of them, or you can configure your MTA package to connect to an Internet spam host list provider, such as MAPS. Each incoming message request should have the originating host's address matched against the spam host list.

Requiring valid SMTP information helps prevent the spammer from using forged information to hide his identity. By requiring proper addresses in the HELO and MAIL FROM: SMTP commands, you can reduce some of your spam traffic.

A third method is filtering messages based on known phrases commonly used in spam messages. Scanning each incoming message to look for the phrases does require extra processing on the mail server, but it can greatly reduce the amount of spam your users receive.

The sendmail, qmail, and Postfix open source MTA packages all provide methods for implementing each of these methods of stopping spam.

CHAPTER 13

Filtering Viruses

Spam mail is a huge nuisance on the Internet, but viruses have become a dangerous element. Their destructive behavior has prompted many a mail administrator to look for ways to stop them. Although few viruses affect the mail server directly, it is usually the mail administrator's job to attempt to block them from entering the corporation's work-stations via the mail system.

This chapter describes methods for blocking viruses from being propagated via open source mail servers on the Internet. First, some common methods used to block viruses are discussed, and then implementing those methods on common open source MTA packages is explained.

Methods Used to Block Viruses

Similar to handling spam messages, different methods have been tried to help prevent viruses from being transmitted by the mail server. Two particular methods of blocking viruses have proved useful and thus become quite popular:

- Filtering based on known phrases
- Scanning individual attachments

This section describes the pros and cons of these two virus-blocking methods.

Virus Filtering

Similar to the spam-filtering methods described in Chapter 12, "Blocking Spam," many mail administrators have used MTA filtering techniques to attempt to block known viruses. This method is based on the concept that most viruses use some kind of known phrase within the message header or body. Incoming messages can, therefore, be filtered by searching for known virus phrases. Messages that match the phrase (whether they are viruses or not) are blocked.

There are some drawbacks to this method, however. First, it depends on being able to find phrases that consistently turn up in individual viruses. Some virus creators have been kind enough to provide this kind of consistency for mail administrators. The famous "ILOVEYOU" virus, for example, was known to contain this phrase in the Subject: header field of all messages it spawned. Stopping this virus was as simple as creating a Subject: header field rule that blocked the "ILOVEYOU" phrase.

Given the widespread use of mail filtering, many virus creators have gone to great lengths to make sure they produce random text in the message header fields. Of course, this randomness makes it more difficult for mail administrators to detect virus messages. Instead, other indicators are checked, such as the file size of the attachment.

NOTE

Virus filtering has created sort of a cat-and-mouse game between hackers and mail administrators. Hackers constantly seek clever ways to try to hide their viruses, and administrators are always on the lookout for methods to filter them out of the mail stream, even going to such lengths as checking the size of attachment files.

Filtering incoming messages to check for viruses has some inherent dangers, too. There is always the possibility that your users will receive valid mail messages that accidentally contain text being filtered for a virus.

As a last resort, some mail administrators have taken virus filtering one step further—by configuring filters that stop all messages containing any type of executable attachment. This is done by filtering on file types in the MIME `Content-Type:` and `Content-Disposition:` fields.

Although this method certainly does prevent viruses from entering your e-mail system, it also prevents people from sending valid attachments to your users. Depending on your e-mail environment, it might not be a good method to use.

NOTE

Of course, more advanced users quickly realize the trick of changing an executable file extension to a non-blocked extension name and changing it back to the original name after it is received.

The drawback to virus filtering is that you are dependent on outside information to determine whether a message contains a virus. You must constantly keep abreast of the latest virus news and manually update the filter table your particular MTA package uses. The advantage to virus filtering is that it is relatively easy on system resources. Usually, you simply have to scan the message header fields to quickly find a virus.

Virus Scanning

Using commercial anti-virus software is the second method of stopping viruses on your mail server. Although your mail server platform is Unix, there are still anti-virus software packages you can run on the server that scan Microsoft DOS and Windows programs for known viruses.

Scanning mail messages for viruses is more complicated than filtering for known phrases. It is usually a multistep process:

1. Determine whether the mail message contains a MIME or uuencoded attachment.

2. Extract the MIME or uuencoded files to their binary forms.

3. Determine whether the binary files are compressed (in the .zip or self-extracting .exe formats for Microsoft Windows workstations and .sit or self-extracting .sea formats for Apple Macintosh workstations). If so, uncompress the files.

4. Scan all uncompressed files, searching for known viruses.

5. If the file attachments do not contain viruses, allow the message to be delivered as normal. If they do, notify the sender, the local mail administrator, and possibly the recipient.

As you can tell, lots of processing is involved in scanning mail message attachments. This function is not recommended for low-end mail servers or mail servers that handle a large volume of messages.

The advantage of virus scanning is that all commercial virus-scanning software offers virus signature update files. The *virus signature file*, the heart of virus-scanning software, supplies the information the scanner uses to search for and detect viruses. By downloading new virus signature files as they become available, you are guaranteed to be up to date on the latest known viruses wandering around the Internet. Most Unix anti-virus packages allow you to create a batch job that can be run by the Unix cron program to automatically check the anti-virus software's FTP site for new signature files on a regular basis.

Implementing Virus Filtering

Almost all open source MTA packages have methods that enable you to filter incoming messages for specific phrases. Chapter 12 detailed how to configure sendmail, qmail, and Postfix to filter messages based on specific spam phrases, and the technique for filtering viruses is exactly the same. In fact, with sendmail, qmail, and Postfix, you can use the same filter configurations to filter for both spam and virus phrases. As mentioned, the most difficult part of filtering viruses is detecting common phrases in the virus message. Table 13.1 lists some recent virus phrases found in the `Subject:` header field.

TABLE 13.1 Common Virus Phrases

Phrase	Virus
Subject: Homepage	VBS.VBSWG2.X@mm
Subject: Where are you?	VBS.Loveletter.CN@mm
Subject: Snow White and the Seven Dwarfs	W95.Hybris.gen
Subject: What is the seven sins?	VBS.Copy@mm
Subject: WindowsXP Betatest	VBS.Merlin.A@mm
Subject: Fw: Great & New Stuff 4 You!	VBS.Catfish@mm
Subject: Miss World	W32.MsWorld@mm

You can add these phrases to the filtering configuration of your particular MTA package. For sendmail and Postfix, these phrases can be added to the phrase file read by the MTA software. For qmail, these phrases can be added to the qmail-qfilter Perl script. You can get current virus phrases from many of the commercial anti-virus product Web sites, such as `http://www.symantec.com/avcenter/`.

Alternatively, you can block messages with particular types of attachments using the same filtering techniques. By searching the message headers for files that end with known executable file types, you can prevent all executable attachments from entering your mail system. Table 13.2 lists some of the more popular file types that have been used by viruses.

TABLE 13.2 Possible Executable Virus File Types

File Type	Description
.com	Microsoft executable files
.exe	Microsoft executable files
.vbs	Visual Basic script
.hlp	Microsoft help files
.pif	Microsoft Program Information File
.reg	Microsoft Registry file
.scr	Microsoft screen capture binary file
.shs	Shell automation code
.wsf	Microsoft Windows Scripting File
.sit	Apple Macintosh StuffIt format
.sea	Apple Macintosh self-extracting file

Implementing Virus Scanning

Implementing virus scanning in open source MTA packages is a more complicated procedure. Besides the normal MTA software, two additional pieces of external software are required:

- Software to detect and extract binary file attachments from mail messages
- Software to scan the binary files for known viruses

A few different open source packages are available that can detect and extract binary file attachments. The A Mail Virus Scanner (AMaViS) package is a well-known and widely used open source package that can extract attachment files from messages, uncompress any compressed files, and pass them to anti-virus software for virus scanning. AMaViS works well with most open source MTA software packages, including sendmail, qmail, and Postfix, and the examples in this chapter use this package.

The second software piece required is the anti-virus scanner. Unfortunately, at the time of this writing, there are no open source virus-scanning packages available for the Unix platform. However, there are many commercial packages that can be purchased. Some commercial software packages have been made available for a free trial basis, usually for 30 days. During the 30-day trial period, the software is fully functional, so you can configure and use it with AMaViS to determine whether it works for your particular e-mail environment. After the trial period expires, you can often purchase the appropriate licenses without having to reinstall the software package.

The AMaViS package can be configured to work with many different commercial Unix anti-virus packages. Table 13.3 lists the different anti-virus software packages that AMaViS supports.

TABLE 13.3 Unix Anti-Virus Software Packages

Package	Notes
Network Associates Virus Scan	Version 3.x is available for free use, but is not supported. No new virus signature files are being created for this release (http://www.nai.com).
DrSolomon	This product has been discontinued; it is now part of the Network Associates product that has merged with McAfee (http://www.nai.com).
H+BEDV AntiVir/X	Free for noncommercial use, but requires registration (http://www.hbedv.com).
Sophos Sweep	30-day trial versions available (http://sophos.com).
Kaspersky Lab AVP	Supports only Linux systems (http://avp.ru).
Cybersoft Vfind	Standard Edition available for Unix systems (http://cyber.com).
Trend Micro FileScanner	Interscan Viruswall available for purchase for Unix systems (http://antivirus.com).
Computer Associates (CA) InoculateIT	30-day trial versions available (http://www.cai.com).

For the examples in this chapter, the CA InoculateIT package is used. This package offers a free 30-day trial period for evaluation. If you decide to use InoculateIT, you can purchase the license without having to reinstall the software. Updated virus signature files are available from the InoculateIT FTP server, and can be automatically downloaded using a script file included with the distribution package.

The following sections describe the steps necessary to configure the AMaViS software with the InoculateIT anti-virus scanner for sendmail, qmail, and Postfix.

The AMaViS Package

The AMaViS package provides e-mail scanning support for any Unix platform that supports the Perl programming language. It is available in three different distributions:

- As an executable program that runs in background mode
- As a Perl script run separately for each file scan
- As a daemonized Perl script that runs in background mode

Each version of the AMaViS software performs the same function, but does it a little bit differently. At the time of this writing the Perl script version has developed into the current stable release of the software; for production systems, this version is recommended. The daemonized Perl script is the current development branch and will most likely be used in future stable releases. This version increases performance because it doesn't require running a new Perl script for each file scan.

The examples in this chapter uses the stable Perl script release, which at the time of this writing is currently at version 11.

Downloading AMaViS

You can get the current release of AMaViS from the AMaViS Web site (`http://www.amavis.org`). The current Perl script version can be downloaded at this URL:

```
http://www.amavis.org/dist/perl/amavis-perl-11.tar.gz
```

After downloading the distribution file, you unpack it into a working directory with this command:

```
tar -zxvf amavis-perl-11.tar.gz -C /usr/local/src
```

This command creates the directory /usr/local/src/amavis-perl-11 and places the source code distribution there. Before you can compile the AMaViS package, you must first ensure that several different utilities are loaded onto your Unix system.

Installing Utilities Used by AMaViS

AMaViS requires that several different packages be installed on your system. Obviously, the most important package is the Perl package, created by Larry Wall. Because of its popularity, most Unix distributions include a Perl package, and some even install it by default. If you do not have a version of Perl on your Unix distribution, you can download the source code from the Comprehensive Perl Archive Network (CPAN) Web site at `http://www.cpan.org`.

Besides the standard Perl installation, AMaViS requires several additional Perl modules, which can also be downloaded from the CPAN Web site. The easiest way to find these modules is to use the CPAN modules listing Web site (`http://www.cpan.org/modules/01modules.index.html`). Table 13.4 lists the required Perl modules and their current version filenames at the time of this writing.

TABLE 13.4 Required Perl Modules for AMaViS

Module	File
IOStringy	IO-stringy-1.220.tar.gz
Syslog	Syslog-0.95.tar.gz
MailTools	MailTools-1.15.tar.gz
MIME-Base64	MIME-Base64-2.12.tar.gz
MIME-tools	MIME-tools-5.411.tar.gz

TABLE 13.4 Continued

Module	File
Convert–Uulib	Convert-UUlib-0.2.tar.gz
Convert–TNEF	Convert-TNEF-0.12.tar.gz
Compress–Zlib	Compress-Zlib-1.13.tar.gz
Archive–Tar	Archive-Tar-0.22.tar.gz
Archive–Zip	Archive-Zip-0.11.zip
libnet	libnet-1.0703.tar.gz

After downloading the additional Perl modules, you install them into the Perl configuration by following these steps (a somewhat tedious process):

1. Uncompress the distribution file.
2. Unpack the file into a working directory.
3. Build the module.
4. Run the install script.

Each module should be unpacked into a separate working directory, as they all contain an individual Makefile.PL Perl script. This script is run to create the makefile used to create the module. After unpacking the module package, you create the module using these commands:

```
perl Makefile.PL
make
make test
make install
```

The make test command is used to perform premade tests on the module. If the module passes all the tests, you can install it. You must have root privileges to perform the install step. Listing 13.1 shows an example of how this process works on the IOStringy module.

LISTING 13.1 Sample Perl Module Installation

```
$ perl Makefile.PL
Checking if your kit is complete...
Looks good
Writing Makefile for IO-stringy
$ make
mkdir blib
mkdir blib/lib
mkdir blib/arch
mkdir blib/arch/auto
```

LISTING 13.1 Continued

```
mkdir blib/arch/auto/IO-stringy
mkdir blib/lib/auto
mkdir blib/lib/auto/IO-stringy
mkdir blib/man3
cp lib/IO/Wrap.pm blib/lib/IO/Wrap.pm
cp lib/IO/Lines.pm blib/lib/IO/Lines.pm
cp lib/IO/WrapTie.pm blib/lib/IO/WrapTie.pm
cp lib/IO/InnerFile.pm blib/lib/IO/InnerFile.pm
cp lib/IO/AtomicFile.pm blib/lib/IO/AtomicFile.pm
cp lib/IO/Stringy.pm blib/lib/IO/Stringy.pm
cp lib/IO/ScalarArray.pm blib/lib/IO/ScalarArray.pm
cp lib/IO/Scalar.pm blib/lib/IO/Scalar.pm
Manifying blib/man3/IO::Wrap.3
Manifying blib/man3/IO::Lines.3
Manifying blib/man3/IO::InnerFile.3
Manifying blib/man3/IO::WrapTie.3
Manifying blib/man3/IO::AtomicFile.3
Manifying blib/man3/IO::Stringy.3
Manifying blib/man3/IO::ScalarArray.3
Manifying blib/man3/IO::Scalar.3
$ make test
PERL_DL_NONLAZY=1 /usr/bin/perl -Iblib/arch -Iblib/lib
➥ -I/usr/lib/perl5/5.00503/i386-linux -I/usr/lib/perl5/5.00503 -e
➥ 'use Test::Harness qw(&runtests $verbose)
; $verbose=0; runtests @ARGV;' t/*.t
t/IO_Lines..........ok
t/IO_Scalar.........ok
t/IO_ScalarArray....ok
t/IO_WrapTie........ok
All tests successful.
Files=4,  Tests=63,  2 wallclock secs ( 1.62 cusr +  0.15 csys =  1.77 CPU)
$ su
Password:
# make install
Installing /usr/lib/perl5/site_perl/5.005/IO/Wrap.pm
Installing /usr/lib/perl5/site_perl/5.005/IO/Lines.pm
Installing /usr/lib/perl5/site_perl/5.005/IO/WrapTie.pm
Installing /usr/lib/perl5/site_perl/5.005/IO/InnerFile.pm
Installing /usr/lib/perl5/site_perl/5.005/IO/AtomicFile.pm
Installing /usr/lib/perl5/site_perl/5.005/IO/Stringy.pm
Installing /usr/lib/perl5/site_perl/5.005/IO/ScalarArray.pm
Installing /usr/lib/perl5/site_perl/5.005/IO/Scalar.pm
```

LISTING 13.1 Continued

```
Installing /usr/lib/perl5/man/man3/IO::Wrap.3
Installing /usr/lib/perl5/man/man3/IO::Lines.3
Installing /usr/lib/perl5/man/man3/IO::InnerFile.3
Installing /usr/lib/perl5/man/man3/IO::WrapTie.3
Installing /usr/lib/perl5/man/man3/IO::AtomicFile.3
Installing /usr/lib/perl5/man/man3/IO::Stringy.3
Installing /usr/lib/perl5/man/man3/IO::ScalarArray.3
Installing /usr/lib/perl5/man/man3/IO::Scalar.3
Writing /usr/lib/perl5/site_perl/5.005/i386-linux/auto/IO-stringy/.packlist
Appending installation info to /usr/lib/perl5/5.00503/i386-linux/perllocal.pod
$
```

Note that for the final make install step, you must have root privileges for the Perl modules to install properly.

Besides installing additional Perl modules, you must also make sure your Unix system has some popular file-handling software packages installed. AMaViS requires these packages to ensure that it can determine the attachment file types and unpack any compressed attachments. Here is a list of the Unix packages that must be installed for AMaViS, along with their download locations:

file: ftp://ftp.gw.com/pub/unix/file/file-3.35.tar.gz

arc: ftp://metalab.unc.edu/pub/Linux/utils/compress/arc521.tar.Z

bunzip2: ftp://sourceware.cygnus.com/pub/bzip2/v100/bzip2-1.0.1.tar.gz

lha (at least version 1.14g): http://www2m.biglobe.ne.jp/~dolphin/lha/prog/
➥lha-114g.tar.gz

unarj: ftp://metalab.unc.edu/pub/Linux/utils/compress/unarj-2.43.tar.gz

uncompress: ftp://metalab.unc.edu/pub/Linux/utils/compress/compress.tar.Z

unrar: ftp://metalab.unc.edu/pub/Linux/utils/compress/unrar-2.71.tar.gz

zoo: ftp://metalab.unc.edu/pub/Linux/utils/compress/zoo-2.10-3.src.rpm

Many Unix systems already include binary distributions of each of these packages. If your system does, use those distributions. If not, you can download source code distributions of each of the packages from the sites listed and install them on your system according to the installation instructions for each package. Most can simply be unpacked into a working directory and compiled by using the make command. After the executable program file is created, you should copy it to a common location on your system, such as /usr/local/bin.

Installing an Anti-Virus Package

Before you can compile AMaViS, you must also install one of the supported anti-virus software packages. This example uses the Computer Associates InoculateIT anti-virus package. Here is the URL for downloading the software's Linux version:

```
ftp://ftp.ca.com/pub/getbbs/linux.eng/inoctar.LINUX.Z
```

The distribution package does not automatically create a directory for the software, so it is best to create one yourself before unpacking the software:

```
mkdir /usr/local/inoculateit
chmod 755 /usr/local/inoculateit
tar -zxvf inoctar.LINUX.Z -C /usr/local/inoculateit
```

For security, you should ensure that the root user owns the inoculateit directory and that no one else has write access to it. Listing 13.2 shows the contents of the new directory.

LISTING 13.2 The inoculateit Directory Listing

```
# ls -al /usr/local/inoculateit
total 3740
drwxr-xr-x   2 root     root        4096 Jun 19 08:52 .
drwxr-xr-x  17 root     root        4096 May  9 14:55 ..
-r--r--r--   1 root     root        9396 Jan 12 09:57 README.txt
-r-xr-xr-x   1 root     root        4177 May 29 08:44 ftpdownload
-rw-r--r--   1 root     root     1918771 Jun 19 08:51 inoctar.LINUX.Z
-rwxr-xr-x   1 root     root      861976 May 25 20:04 inocucmd
-rw-r--r--   1 root     root          43 Jun 19 08:51 linux.txt
-r-xr-xr-x   1 root     root        2010 May 29 11:56 update_signature
-r-xr-xr-x   1 root     root      994431 May 23 16:32 virsig.dat
#
```

The inocucmd file is the anti-virus scanning program. AMaViS uses it to scan file attachments for known viruses. The virsig.dat file is the virus signature file that defines the known viruses InoculateIT will detect. The update_signature script can be used as a cron job to automatically connect to the ftp.ca.com FTP server and update the virsig.dat file with new virus signatures. Downloading the latest virus signature file is recommended before implementing your virus scanner.

Now that you have installed an anti-virus package, you can compile AMaViS for your e-mail environment.

Compiling and Installing AMaViS

The first step of compiling the AMaViS package is to run the configure program to set the configuration for your particular e-mail and Unix environment. You can set several different parameters, listed in Table 13.5, for the config program.

TABLE 13.5 AMaViS Config Parameters

Parameter	Description
--with-perl=*PERL_PROG*	Location of Perl binary
--with-file=*FILE_PROG*	Location of file binary
--with-sendmail-wrapper=*PROG*	Location of sendmail or wrapper
--with-sendmail-source=*DIR*	Location of sendmail source
--enable-qmail	Use qmail as MTA
--enable-postfix	Use Postfix as MTA
--enable-exim	Use exim as MTA
--enable-relay	Enable relay configuration for Postfix/sendmail
--with-origconf=*FILE*	Original sendmail config file
--enable-smtp	Deliver scanned mails via SMTP (default = no)
--with-smtp-port=*PORT*	Port to deliver scanned mails to (default = 10025)
--enable-all	Include code for all scanners (default = no)
--with-sophos-ide=*DIR*	Where Sophos IDE files are installed (default = /usr/local/lib)
--with-runtime-dir=*DIR*	Directory for runtime files (default = /var/amavis)
--enable-syslog	Use syslog (default is MTA-specific)
--with-syslog-level=*FAC.LVL*	Facility and level used for logging (default = mail.info)
--with-logdir=*DIR*	Log directory if not using syslog (default = /var/amavis)
--with-amavisuser=*USER*	Username to run AMaViS as (default is MTA-specific)
--disable-virusbackup	Don't back up infected mails (default = backup)
--with-virusdir=*DIR*	Quarantine directory for infected mail (default = /var/virusmails)
--with-maxlevel=*VALUE*	Maximum depth of recursive unpacking (default = 20)
--with-warnsender=*FILE*	Customized notification text sent to the message sender (default = yes)
--with-warnrecip=*FILE*	Send notification to receivers (default = no)
--with-warnadmin=*FILE*	Send notification to administrator (default = yes)
--with-mailfrom=*USER*	Username mail is sent from (default = postmaster)
--with-mailto=*USER*	Username that virus alerts are sent to (default = virusalert)
--enable-credits	Display AMaViS credits to users (default = no)
--disable-x-header	Don't add X-Virus-Scanned header (default = add)

You use only the configure parameters necessary to change the default values for your particular environment. By default, the configure program attempts to detect which MTA package you have installed. If you have more than one MTA installed, you might have to explicitly use the --enable parameter for your MTA package, along with a special --disable parameter used for the other MTA packages:

```
./configure --enable-postfix --disable-sendmail --disable-qmail
```

The configure program proceeds by determining whether all the required components are installed for AMaViS and shows a completion message when it is done:

```
** Configuration summary for amavis perl-11 2001-04-07:


   Install amavis as:          /usr/sbin/amavis
   Configured for use with:    sendmail
   Relay configuration:        no
   Original sendmail.cf:
   Use virus scanner(s):   CAI InoculateIT Inocucmd command line utility 4.0
   Scanner runs as:            root
   Logging to syslog:          yes
   Quarantine directory:       /var/virusmails
   Max. recursion depth:       20
   Add X-Virus-Scanned header: yes
   Display AMaViS credits:     no
   Warn sender:                yes
   Reports sent to:            virusalert
   Reports sent by:            postmaster


To accept the above, type "make"
```

After the configure script is done, you compile the AMaViS executable script with the make command, check it with the make check option, and, finally, install it with the make install option:

```
make
make check
make install
```

You must have root privileges when you run the make install command so the AMaViS programs are placed in the proper directories with the proper permissions.

NOTE

At the time of this writing, the amavis-perl-11 package does not pass all the make check tests when compiled for the qmail MTA package. This is a known bug and does not necessarily mean there are problems with the installation.

CAUTION

Remember that the AMaViS script is dependent on the MTA package you are using. If you later change your MTA package, you must rebuild AMaViS using the appropriate --enable parameter.

NOTE

The AMaViS package uses the mail address virusalert to send warning messages to when viruses are received. You should add an entry in your aliases file to redirect those messages to a standard system account that is checked daily.

Configuring the MTA for AMaViS

After the AMaViS package is installed, you can configure your particular MTA package to use virus scanning. Three different options can be used when scanning for viruses.

The most popular configuration (and the one demonstrated in this chapter) option is scanning all incoming mail messages. This method gives your users maximum protection from known viruses transmitted via the e-mail system. It includes scanning messages received from local users to other local users, as well as messages received via the Internet from users on remote mail hosts.

A second configuration option is scanning all outbound messages as well as inbound messages. This option adds a safety precaution to make sure none of your users are transmitting viruses in their e-mail messages. Although it is a helpful feature, often it can be too resource consuming to be practical.

A third configuration option is scanning not only all inbound and outbound mail messages, but also any messages the MTA package allows to be relayed through the mail server to a remote mail server. Again, this option consumes lots of processor resources on the mail server and should not be used unless you are confident that your mail server can handle the additional mail processing load.

The following sections describe how to configure sendmail, qmail, and Postfix to use AMaViS for scanning all inbound mail messages received by the mail server. This option provides maximum protection for your users receiving mail messages from any source, while minimizing the load on your mail server caused by virus scanning.

sendmail

To use AMaViS with the sendmail MTA package, you must configure sendmail to pass all messages destined for local users to AMaViS. AMaViS scans any attachments and delivers the message to the normal local mailer if it passes the virus scan. The local mailer should then deliver the message as normal.

This configuration requires changing the local mail delivery definition in the sendmail.cf configuration file. To do that, use the m4 macro preprocessor definitions or manually make edits directly in the sendmail.cf configuration file.

If you created your sendmail.cf configuration file using the m4 macro preprocessor, you can add the following statements to your normal configuration macro file before any MAILER definitions:

```
define(`LOCAL_MAILER_PATH', `/usr/sbin/amavis')dnl
define(`LOCAL_MAILER_ARGS', CONCAT(`amavis $f $u /usr/bin/',
➥LOCAL_MAILER_ARGS))dnl
MODIFY_MAILER_FLAGS(`LOCAL', `-m')dnl
```

These commands replace the local mailer that is normally configured with the AMaViS program and adds the local mailer commands to the end of the AMaViS command line.

If you manually create your sendmail.cf configuration file, you must manually replace the local mailer definition. Similar to the m4 method, you replace the local mailer with the AMaViS program and add the complete local mailer with command-line options at the end of the AMaViS command line.

The simplest way to explain this is to show an example. On my Linux system using sendmail 8.11.3, the sendmail.cf local mailer configuration lines were as follows:

```
Mlocal,     P=/usr/bin/procmail, F=lsDFMAw5:/|@qSPfhn9,
            S=EnvFromL/HdrFromL, R=EnvToL/HdrToL,
            T=DNS/RFC822/X-Unix,
            A=procmail -Y -a $h -d $u
```

The Mlocal tag defines the local mailer definition (see the "Configuring sendmail" section in Chapter 8, "The sendmail E-mail Package"). The procmail mail delivery program is defined as the local mailer. After inserting the AMaViS program configuration, the local mailer definition looks like this:

```
Mlocal,     P=/usr/sbin/amavis, F=lsDFMAw5:/|@qSPfhn9,
            S=EnvFromL/HdrFromL, R=EnvToL/HdrToL,
            T=DNS/RFC822/X-Unix,
            A=amavis $f $u /usr/bin/procmail -Y -a $h -d $u
```

Note how the P parameter value has changed to point to the location of the AMaViS program instead of to procmail, and the A parameter has added the full procmail command line from the original configuration as a parameter to the AMaViS program. Also note that the full pathname of the procmail program was included.

After creating the new sendmail.cf configuration file, you must restart sendmail to enable AMaViS virus scanning.

qmail

To use AMaViS with qmail, you must first make sure you have compiled AMaViS with the qmail option enabled. The output from the configure program should look like this:

```
** Configuration summary for amavis perl-11 2001-04-07:


    Install amavis as:          /usr/sbin/amavis
    Configured for use with:    qmail
    Use virus scanner(s):   CAI InoculateIT Inocucmd command line utility 4.0
    Scanner runs as:            qmailq
    Log file directory:         /var/amavis
    Quarantine directory:       /var/virusmails
    Max. recursion depth:       20
    Add X-Virus-Scanned header: yes
    Display AMaViS credits:     no
    Warn sender:                yes
    Reports sent to:            virusalert
    Reports sent by:            postmaster


To accept the above, type "make"
```

After compiling and installing the AMaViS script, you must then do some qmail file manipulation. The technique used to run AMaViS with qmail is to replace the standard qmail-queue program file with the AMaViS script file. This method ensures that all messages received by qmail are passed to AMaViS. After the messages are scanned, they must be passed back to the real qmail-queue program. To do that, you need to rename the original qmail-queue file so it is still available for use. By default, AMaViS tries to use the filename qmail-queue-real for the real qmail-queue file.

These are the commands necessary to configure qmail to use AMaViS:

```
mv /var/qmail/bin/qmail-queue /var/qmail/bin/qmail-queue-real
cp /usr/sbin/amavis /var/qmail/bin/qmail-queue
chown qmailq.qmail /var/qmail/bin/qmail-queue
chmod 4711 /var/qmail/bin/qmail-queue
```

The only command you have not seen used yet in previous chapters is the chmod 4711 command. It is used to assign the setuid of the qmail-queue program to the root user, allowing the program to run with root privileges. Also, you must ensure that the AMaViS log and quarantine directories are writable by the qmailq user. The quarantine directory is used to hold copies of infected messages for the administrator to examine. The directories are /var/amavis and /var/virusmails. You can use the chown command for this:

```
chown qmailq.qmail /var/amavis
chown qmailq.qmail /var/virusmails
```

After the changes are made, you must restart qmail to enable the AMaViS anti-virus scanning.

CAUTION

Some Unix distributions do not install Perl with the root `setuid` set. Without this setting, AMaViS cannot work with qmail, as qmail does not run as the `root` user. To fix this, you must set the Perl program `setuid` for the qmail group:

chown root:qmail /usr/bin/perl

chmod 4710 /usr/bin/perl

Postfix

Much like using AMaViS with qmail, you must use some trickery to get it to work with Postfix. The idea with Postfix is to use its `content_filter` option to pass messages to AMaViS. To inject scanned messages back into Postfix for delivery, you must configure an alternative SMTP channel in Postfix to listen for scanned messages and send them directly to the local delivery mailer.

First, you need to make sure AMaViS has been compiled with the `postfix` and `smtp` options (because AMaViS uses SMTP to reinsert the scanned messages back into Postfix):

```
./configure --enable-postfix --enable-smtp --disable-qmail
➥ --disable-sendmail
```

The result of the configure program should look like this:

```
** Configuration summary for amavis perl-11 2001-04-07:


    Install amavis as:          /usr/sbin/amavis
    Configured for use with:    postfix
    Relay configuration:        no
    Enable SMTP:                yes
    Use SMTP port:              10025
    Use virus scanner(s):   CAI InoculateIT Inocucmd command line utility 4.0
    Scanner runs as:            vscan
    Logging to syslog:          yes
    Quarantine directory:       /var/virusmails
    Max. recursion depth:       20
    Add X-Virus-Scanned header: yes
    Display AMaViS credits:     no
    Warn sender:                yes
    Reports sent to:            virusalert
    Reports sent by:            postmaster


To accept the above, type "make"
```

Note that in this configuration AMaViS is run as the user vscan. You must create this user account before installing AMaViS. Different Unix distributions use different commands to add new users. For Linux, you can use the command useradd -M vscan, which creates the user vscan without creating a $HOME directory. After creating the vscan user, you can run the make, make check, and make install commands for AMaViS as normal.

Next you must modify Postfix to use AMaViS. To do that, you need to add configuration lines in both of the Postfix configuration files. First, in the main.cf configuration file, you add the content_filter line:

```
content_filter = vscan:
```

This line points the content filter to the name of a process to run. Next you configure the vscan process in the master.cf configuration file, along with the additional SMTP process AMaViS uses to send the scanned message back to Postfix. These are the two entries:

```
vscan    unix  -     n     n     -      10      pipe user=vscan
➡ argv=/usr/sbin/amavis ${sender} ${recipient}
localhost:10025    inet n   -    n   -    -      smtpd -o content_filter=
```

The first entry defines the vscan process and points it to the AMaViS program, along with the message sender and recipient values. The second entry instructs Postfix to listen to port 10025 on the localhost interface and pass any connections to the Postfix smtpd process. The key to this is that the content_filter parameter is overridden with an empty value, which tells Postfix not to use the configured content_filter value (AMaViS) for this message. By default AMaViS is configured to send the scanned message back to Postfix using port 10025, but this value can be changed by using the --with-post configure parameter when compiling AMaViS.

After modifying the main.cf and master.cf configuration files for AMaViS, you must restart Postfix for AMaViS to start scanning viruses.

Testing for Virus Scanning

Once you have installed AMaViS into your MTA package, you should test it to make sure it's doing what you want it to do. There are two different tests you should perform. The first test determines whether normal messages are getting delivered. The second test checks that the anti-virus software is catching viruses. The following sections describe these two tests.

Testing the AMaViS Software

To test the AMaViS script, you can send a simple text message from a local user to any other local user on the system. You can then watch the running processes by using the

Unix ps command to see if the MTA package invokes AMaViS and if AMaViS starts the anti-virus software. Listing 13.3 shows a partial ps command output during a local message delivery, showing the relevant mail processes.

LISTING 13.3 Mail Processes During a Message Delivery

```
$ ps ax
  PID TTY       STAT    TIME COMMAND
30284 ?         S       0:00 sendmail: accepting connections
31391 ?    S       0:00 send-mail -i rich
31392 ?    S       0:09 perl -T /usr/sbin/amavis rich rich /usr/bin/procmail
31398 ?    D       0:00 /usr/local/inoculateit/inocucmd -sec -nex /var/amavis
31399 pts/0   R       0:00 ps ax
$
```

Note that both the amavis and inocucmd programs have been called by the MTA package to process the message. This extra processing does add a delay to receiving the new message.

After the message is received, you should look at it. By default, AMaViS adds a header field indicating that the message has been virus scanned. By looking at the message headers, you can verify that the test message has been scanned. Listing 13.4 shows a sample scanned message.

LISTING 13.4 Sample Scanned Message

```
Date: Tue, 26 Jun 2001 20:29:18 -0500
From: Rich Blum <rich>
To: rich
Subject: test
X-Virus-Scanned: by AMaViS perl-11

This is a test message.
```

Note the X-Virus-Scanned: header field added to the test message. This field proves that AMaViS has indeed scanned the test message.

Scanning text messages is fine for testing AMaViS, but it does nothing for proving that the anti-virus software is working. The next test determines whether the installed anti-virus software is working properly.

Testing the Anti-Virus Software

To test the anti-virus software, you might be tempted to find a copy of a virus and send it to yourself. This is a dangerous practice, however, and should not be performed on a production mail server. Anti-virus software companies realized that a safe method of testing software installations is necessary, so they have agreed on a test virus pattern. The virus pattern itself is harmless to workstations, but can be recognized by anti-virus software as a virus and processed accordingly. This test pattern is configured into all the commercial virus signature files.

The test pattern is called the eicar.com file, named after the eicar organization (http://www.eicar.org), a group of individuals committed to anti-virus research ("eicar" is not an acronym; it is a name). You can either download the eicar.com program from their Web site, or create the eicar.com file manually with a standard text editor, such as Microsoft Notepad. The eicar.com file contains a single line of text:

```
X5O!P%@AP[4\PZX54(P^)7CC)7}$EICAR-STANDARD-ANTIVIRUS-TEST-FILE!$H+H*
```

After the test file is created, it can then be e-mailed through your mail server as a normal file attachment.

CAUTION

Use caution when handling the test virus file. If your workstation uses anti-virus auto-protection (which it should), the test virus file automatically trips your anti-virus software, which will gladly remove the "virus" for you. Of course, this can also be a good way to test your workstation anti-virus software.

When you e-mail the virus test file, be performed the anti-virus software should detect it as a virus and notify AMaViS. AMaViS then generates two different e-mail messages. The first message is sent to the message's original sender, informing him that his message contained an infected attachment. Listing 13.5 shows a sample return message.

LISTING 13.5 Sample Return Virus Warning

```
From: <postmaster>
To: <rich@meshach.ispnet1.net>
Subject: VIRUS IN YOUR MAIL
Date: Wednesday, June 27, 2001 7:27 AM


                V I R U S   A L E R T

Our viruschecker found the

    4294967295


virus(es) in your email to the following recipient(s):

-> rich
```

LISTING 13.5 Continued

Please check your system for viruses, or ask your system administrator
to do so.

For your reference, here are the headers from your email:

```
---------------------- BEGIN HEADERS ----------------------------
Return-Path: <rich@meshach.ispnet1.net>
Received: from meshach ([192.168.1.10])
    by shadrach.ispnet1.net (8.11.3/8.11.3) with SMTP id f5RCRWw32117
    for <rich@shadrach.ispnet1.net>; Wed, 27 Jun 2001 07:27:32 -0500
Message-ID: <000e01c0ff05$87e62460$0201a8c0@meshach>
From: "Rich Blum" <rich@meshach.ispnet1.net>
To: <rich@shadrach.ispnet1.net>
Subject: Test message with a "Virus"
Date: Wed, 27 Jun 2001 07:34:22 -0500
MIME-Version: 1.0
Content-Type: multipart/mixed;
    boundary="----=_NextPart_000_000A_01C0FEDB.953D7660"
X-Priority: 3
X-MSMail-Priority: Normal
X-Mailer: Microsoft Outlook Express 5.00.2615.200
X-MimeOLE: Produced By Microsoft MimeOLE V5.00.2615.200
----------------------- END HEADERS ----------------------------
```

The complete message header fields are returned to the sender to help identify the individual message that was infected. The second message is sent to the special mail alias virusalert, warning that a message with a virus was received, who received it, and where it is stored on the mail server. You should use your MTA package's alias file to redirect those messages to the mail administrator account.

The AMaViS software retains a copy of the original message in the /var/virusmails directory. The message sent to virusalert lists the filename of the quarantined virus message. You can then analyze the stored virus messages later. Listing 13.6 shows a sample of the administrator message generated by AMaViS.

LISTING 13.6 Sample Administrator Warning Message

```
From: <postmaster>
To: <virusalert>
Subject: FOUND VIRUS IN MAIL from rich@meshach.ispnet1.net
Date: Wednesday, June 27, 2001 7:27 AM
```

LISTING 13.6 Continued

```
A virus was found in an email from:

rich@meshach.ispnet1.net

The message was addressed to:

-> rich

The message has been quarantined as:

/var/virusmails/virus-20010627-072748-32119

Here is the output of the scanner:

4294967295

Here are the headers:

---------------------- BEGIN HEADERS ----------------------------
Return-Path: <rich@meshach.ispnet1.net>
Received: from meshach ([192.168.1.10])
    by shadrach.ispnet1.net (8.11.3/8.11.3) with SMTP id f5RCRWw32117
    for <rich@shadrach.ispnet1.net>; Wed, 27 Jun 2001 07:27:32 -0500
Message-ID: <000e01c0ff05$87e62460$0201a8c0@meshach>
From: "Rich Blum" <rich@meshach.ispnet1.net>
To: <rich@shadrach.ispnet1.net>
Subject: Test message with a "Virus"
Date: Wed, 27 Jun 2001 07:34:22 -0500
MIME-Version: 1.0
Content-Type: multipart/mixed;
    boundary="----=_NextPart_000_000A_01C0FEDB.953D7660"
X-Priority: 3
X-MSMail-Priority: Normal
X-Mailer: Microsoft Outlook Express 5.00.2615.200
X-MimeOLE: Produced By Microsoft MimeOLE V5.00.2615.200
---------------------- END HEADERS ----------------------------
```

As mentioned, the full pathname of the quarantined virus message is listed, along with the sender and recipient. This information can be invaluable when trying to track down who is sending viruses into your mail system.

If your configuration has passed these two tests, it should be ready to accept and scan mail messages for your users. Remember, though, that virus security is an ongoing effort. You must update the virus signature file on a regular basis, either manually or automatically.

Summary

Viruses have plagued workstations for many years, and the Internet has "helped" by providing a mechanism for quickly sending viruses to multiple workstations via the e-mail system. As the mail administrator, it may be your job to attempt to stop viruses from entering your company through the e-mail system.

Two popular methods have been used to help block viruses in the e-mail system. The first method uses standard filtering techniques. By scanning message headers, you can often detect viruses that use certain phrases in their message headers. Also, some mail administrators use filtering to stop all messages containing executable file attachments, but this extreme action often is not possible in a corporate environment. A second method uses commercial anti-virus packages. By extracting the message file attachments and scanning them for viruses, you can help stop viruses before they get to your users.

All the open source MTA packages described in this book support some form of virus detection. Filtering viruses can be performed in the same manner discussed in Chapter 12 for filtering spam messages. By creating a list of common virus phrases, the MTA package can compare incoming message headers to the virus list to filter out known viruses.

You can use the AMaViS package as an add-on to the MTA packages as a method for extracting file attachments from messages and forwarding them to an anti-virus program. After the anti-virus program scans the file attachments, the message can be delivered to the recipient.

PART III

E-mail Service Security

CHAPTER 14

Using E-mail Firewalls

Hackers and spammers use several different methods to gain information about your e-mail system and the users on your e-mail system, but techniques have been created to help you combat this problem. By disabling some of the SMTP commands, you can prevent others from discovering valid usernames on your mail server. Also, you can create a separate e-mail firewall to effectively shield your normal e-mail servers from prying and attacks.

This chapter describes different methods for creating a more secure e-mail environment to protect your internal e-mail servers from possible prying and tampering by external hackers.

The SMTP VRFY and EXPN Commands

Although the idea behind the SMTP VRFY and EXPN commands (described in Chapter 2, "SMTP") was good, hackers and spammers have misused these commands to gain information from unsuspecting mail administrators. Using both of these commands, a hacker or spammer can determine valid e-mail addresses (and thus system accounts) on your server. The following sections describe the VRFY and EXPN commands in more detail, and why they should not be enabled on your mail server.

The VRFY Command

The VRFY command (short for "verify") is used to query remote mail servers for an e-mail address. If the mail server is configured to respond to the VRFY command, it returns an SMTP code depending on the status of the queried address. RFC 821 lists several different SMTP return codes that the mail server could return in response to a VRFY command. These are the most common VRFY return codes used by MTA packages:

- 250   The address exists and the server will accept messages for it.
- 252   The address may exist and the server will accept messages for it and attempt to deliver them.
- 550   The address does not exist and the server will refuse any messages for it.

By sending large quantities of VRFY commands for various e-mail addresses, a remote attacker can guess valid accounts on your system based on the SMTP return codes the mail server returns. When a spammer has a list of valid e-mail addresses, he not only uses them for his own purposes, but can also sell them to other spammers. Or worse, if a hacker determines valid system accounts, he can begin attacking their passwords to break into the mail server. Listing 14.1 shows an example of how a normal VRFY session with an SMTP server behaves.

LISTING 14.1 Sample VRFY Session

```
$ telnet localhost 25
Trying 127.0.0.1...
Connected to localhost.
Escape character is '^]'.
220 shadrach.ispnet1.net ESMTP sendmail 8.11.3/8.11.3; Tue, 3 Jul 2001
➡ 06:59:12 -00
EHLO shadrach.ispnet1.net
250-shadrach.ispnet1.net Hello IDENT:rich@localhost [127.0.0.1], pleased
➡ to meet you
250-ENHANCEDSTATUSCODES
250-EXPN
250-VERB
250-8BITMIME
250-SIZE
250-DSN
250-ONEX
250-ETRN
250-XUSR
250 HELP
VRFY rich
250 2.1.5 Rich Blum <rich@shadrach.ispnet1.net>
VRFY mike@shadrach.ispnet1.net
250 2.1.5 Mike Pierce <mike@shadrach.ispnet1.net>
VRFY evonne@meshach.ispnet2.net
252 2.1.5 <evonne@meshach.ispnet2.net>
VRFY alex
550 5.1.1 alex... User unknown
QUIT
221 2.0.0 shadrach.ispnet1.net closing connection
Connection closed by foreign host.
$
```

The SMTP server responds to the VRFY command depending on the status of the requested username. The first two examples show the response for local users. Note that the mail server returns not only the complete e-mail address, but also any identification text listed in the system /etc/passwd file. If you do enable the VRFY command, you should be careful what information you include in your /etc/passwd file.

The third VRFY example in the Listing shows using a VRFY query for an address on a remote mail server. The mail server returns the 252 status code, indicating that although the address is not local to the server, it will attempt to relay the message to the indicated address. The final example shows the 550 return code, used for a nonexistent address on the mail server.

Alternatively, most MTA packages allow you to disable the VRFY command. Instead of returning a response code that depends on the status of the requested address, the SMTP server returns a consistent response for all queries. Listing 14.2 shows an example of an MTA package with the VRFY command disabled.

LISTING 14.2 Sample Disabled VRFY Session

```
$ telnet localhost 25
Trying 127.0.0.1...
Connected to localhost.
Escape character is '^]'.
220 shadrach.ispnet1.net ESMTP sendmail 8.11.3/8.11.3; Tue, 3 Jul 2001
➥ 07:05:47 -00
EHLO shadrach.ispnet1.net
250-shadrach.ispnet1.net Hello IDENT:rich@localhost [127.0.0.1],
➥ pleased to meet you
250-ENHANCEDSTATUSCODES
250-8BITMIME
250-SIZE
250-DSN
250-ONEX
250-ETRN
250-XUSR
250 HELP
VRFY rich
252 2.5.2 Cannot VRFY user; try RCPT to attempt delivery (or try finger)
VRFY mike@shadrach.ispnet1.net
252 2.5.2 Cannot VRFY user; try RCPT to attempt delivery (or try finger)
VRFY evonne@meshach.ispnet1.net
252 2.5.2 Cannot VRFY user; try RCPT to attempt delivery (or try finger)
VRFY alex
252 2.5.2 Cannot VRFY user; try RCPT to attempt delivery (or try finger)
QUIT
221 2.0.0 shadrach.ispnet1.net closing connection
Connection closed by foreign host.
$
```

With the VRFY command disabled, the mail server returns the same SMTP code no matter what the actual status of the address is. Not only is the VRFY attempt refused, but it is also recorded as an entry in the mail system log file:

```
Jul 2 08:43:11 shadrach sendmail[15478]: f62Dgrk15478: IDENT:rich@localhost
➥ [127.0.0.1]: VRFY rich [rejected]
```

This entry enables you to discover who is attempting to use the VRFY command on your mail server.

The EXPN Command

Another often abused command is the SMTP EXPN command (short for "expand"). As mentioned in Chapter 2, its purpose is to allow a remote host to request a listing of alias and mailing list addresses. This listing would enable a remote mail server to determine the actual mail addresses used by a message sent to an alias or a mailing list. Unfortunately, spammers and hackers have exploited this command to pry into mail servers. Listing 14.3 shows an example of the EXPN command on a mail server that does not block the command.

LISTING 14.3 Sample EXPN Command

```
$ telnet localhost 25
Trying 127.0.0.1...
Connected to localhost.
Escape character is '^]'.
220 shadrach.ispnet1.net ESMTP sendmail 8.11.3/8.11.3; Tue, 3 Jul 2001
➡ 07:19:13 -00
EHLO shadrach.ispnet1.net
250-shadrach.ispnet1.net Hello IDENT:rich@localhost [127.0.0.1],
➡ pleased to meet you
250-ENHANCEDSTATUSCODES
250-EXPN
250-VERB
250-8BITMIME
250-SIZE
250-DSN
250-ONEX
250-ETRN
250-XUSR
250 HELP
EXPN blumfamily
250-2.1.5 Rich Blum <rich@shadrach.ispnet1.net>
250-2.1.5 Barbara Blum <barbara@shadrach.ispnet1.net>
250-2.1.5 Katie Jane Blum <katie@shadrach.ispnet1.net>
250 2.1.5 Jessica Blum <jessica@meshach.ispnet2.net>
EXPN postmaster
250 2.1.5 Rich Blum <rich@shadrach.ispnet1.net>
QUIT
221 2.0.0 shadrach.ispnet1.net closing connection
Connection closed by foreign host.
$
```

The first example shows using the EXPN command with the blumfamily mailing list name. The mail server returns the full address and local system identification information for all the recipients in the mailing list. The second example shows the EXPN command results for an alias name. It indicates that the postmaster mail alias is resolved to the rich username.

If you do not want this information available for remote mail servers, most MTA packages allow you to disable the EXPN command. If the EXPN command is disabled, no information is returned to the remote host about the mailing list or alias names. Instead, an error code is returned indicating that the command has been disabled on the mail server. Listing 14.4 shows an example of this.

LISTING 14.4 Sample Disabled EXPN Session

```
$ telnet localhost 25
Trying 127.0.0.1...
Connected to localhost.
Escape character is '^]'.
220 shadrach.ispnet1.net ESMTP sendmail 8.11.3/8.11.3; Tue, 3 Jul 2001
➥ 07:25:45 -00
EHLO shadrach.ispnet1.net
250-shadrach.ispnet1.net Hello IDENT:rich@localhost [127.0.0.1],
➥ pleased to meet you
250-ENHANCEDSTATUSCODES
250-8BITMIME
250-SIZE
250-DSN
250-ONEX
250-ETRN
250-XUSR
250 HELP
EXPN blumfamily
502 5.7.0 Sorry, we do not allow this operation
EXPN postmaster
502 5.7.0 Sorry, we do not allow this operation
QUIT
221 2.0.0 shadrach.ispnet1.net closing connection
Connection closed by foreign host.
$
```

When the EXPN command is disabled, the mail server returns a 502 error code to indicate that the EXPN command is not implemented. Note that when the VRFY command was disabled, the mail server returned a 252 SMTP error code, indicating that the address might be on the server.

Similar to the VRFY command, when the mail server receives an EXPN command, it is logged as an entry in the mail log file:

```
Jul 3 07:25:59 shadrach sendmail[18094]: f63CPjA18094: IDENT:rich@localhost
➥ [127.0.0.1]: EXPN postmaster [rejected]
```

Getting Around the VRFY Restriction

Unfortunately, many mail administrators think they are safe from prying eyes by just disabling the VRFY and EXPN commands. This is far from the truth. Spammers and hackers can also determine valid local system usernames by using the standard RCPT TO: SMTP command. Take a look at Listing 14.5.

LISTING 14.5 Sample RCPT TO: Session

```
$ telnet localhost 25
Trying 127.0.0.1...
Connected to localhost.
Escape character is '^]'.
220 shadrach.ispnet1.net ESMTP sendmail 8.11.3/8.11.3; Tue, 3 Jul 2001
➥ 07:09:14 -00
EHLO shadrach.ispnet1.net
250-shadrach.ispnet1.net Hello IDENT:rich@localhost [127.0.0.1],
➥ pleased to meet you
250-ENHANCEDSTATUSCODES
250-8BITMIME
250-SIZE
250-DSN
250-ONEX
250-ETRN
250-XUSR
250 HELP
MAIL FROM: <badguy@otherplace.com>
250 2.1.0 <badguy@otherplace.com>... Sender ok
RCPT TO: rich
250 2.1.5 rich... Recipient ok
RCPT TO: mike@shadrach.ispnet1.net
250 2.1.5 mike... Recipient ok
RCPT TO: evonne@meshach.ispnet2.net
250 2.1.5 evonne@meshach.ispnet2.net... Recipient ok
RCPT TO: alex
550 5.1.1 alex... User unknown
QUIT
221 2.0.0 shadrach.ispnet1.net closing connection
Connection closed by foreign host.
$
```

Notice that the mail server has to return a specific SMTP return code for each individual address in the different RCPT TO: commands. This convention enables valid remote mail servers to determine whether a recipient address is correct.

By exploiting the return codes from the RCPT TO: command, a remote host can determine which e-mail addresses are valid user accounts on the remote system. If you want to hide the valid e-mail accounts on your mail system, you must create an e-mail firewall, discussed later in this chapter in the "Using an E-mail Firewall" section.

Disabling the VRFY and EXPN Commands

With most MTA packages, you can disable the VRFY and EXPN commands. In fact, most MTA packages have these features disabled by default. This section describes how to configure the sendmail, qmail, and Postfix MTA packages to ignore VRFY requests from remote mail servers.

sendmail

Since version 8.9.3, the sendmail MTA package can be configured to ignore VRFY and EXPN commands by using an option statement in the sendmail.cf configuration file. The PrivacyOptions option allows you to configure several different flags, listed in Table 14.1, that control security features on the sendmail server. The individual SMTP commands listed in this table were described in Chapter 2.

TABLE 14.1 PrivacyOptions Flags

Flag	Description
public	Allows open access.
needmailhelo	Requires that a HELO or EHLO command be sent before a MAIL FROM: command is accepted.
needexpnhelo	Requires that a HELO or EHLO command be sent before an EXPN command is accepted.
noexpn	Disables the EXPN command.
needvrfyhelo	Requires that a HELO or EHLO command be sent before a VRFY command is accepted.
novrfy	Disables the VRFY command.
noetrn	Disables the ETRN command.
noverb	Disables the SMTP VERB command, which is used to enable verbose return messages.
restrictmailq	Restricts the mailq command to trusted users.
restrictqrun	Restricts the sendmail -q command-line flag to only trusted users.

TABLE 14.1 Continued

Flag	Description
noreceipts	Don't return delivery status notification requests.
nobodyreturn	Don't return the body of a message in a delivery status notification request.
goaway	Disables all SMTP query commands.
authwarnings	Inserts an X-Authentication-Warning: header field in messages and log warnings.

By specifying the novrfy and noexpn flags, you disable the VRFY and EXPN commands on the mail server. If you are using the m4 macro preprocessor to create the sendmail.cf configuration file, you must add the following line to your configuration:

```
define(`confPRIVACY_FLAGS', `novrfy,noexpn')dnl
```

This command enables the PrivacyOptions configuration file option and sets the novrfy and noexpn flags. Instead of disabling both features, however, you can set only the flag that you want disabled and keep the other option enabled.

If you are creating the sendmail.cf configuration file by hand, you need to add the following option line:

```
O PrivacyOptions=novfy,noexpn
```

Again, you can enable or disable whichever feature you want. After you restart sendmail, the new restrictions should apply. Listings 14.2 and 14.4 showed the results of the novrfy and noexpn options.

qmail

The qmail MTA package was designed with security in mind, so its default configuration refuses VRFY and EXPN queries. Listing 14.6 shows a sample SMTP session with a qmail server.

LISTING 14.6 Sample VRFY Session with qmail

```
$ telnet localhost 25
Trying 127.0.0.1...
Connected to localhost.
Escape character is '^]'.
220 shadrach.ispnet1.net ESMTP
EHLO shadrach.ispnet1.net
250-shadrach.ispnet1.net
250-PIPELINING
250 8BITMIME
```

LISTING 14.6 Continued

```
VRFY mike@shadrach.ispnet1.net
252 send some mail, i'll try my best
VRFY evonne@meshach.ispnet2.net
252 send some mail, i'll try my best
VRFY alex
252 send some mail, i'll try my best
EXPN maillist
502 unimplemented (#5.5.1)
QUIT
221 shadrach.ispnet1.net
Connection closed by foreign host.
$
```

By default, qmail returns a 252 SMTP return code for any VRFY query received, no matter what the actual address status is. The EXPN command returns a 502 (command not implemented) code, indicating that the command is not enabled on this server. You cannot modify the behavior of these commands in qmail.

Postfix

The Postfix MTA package offers an option of defining how it handles VRFY queries. By default, Postfix responds to all VRFY queries with a 252 return code, indicating that it will attempt to deliver mail to all addresses. Listing 14.7 shows an example of this behavior.

LISTING 14.7 Sample Postfix VRFY Responses

```
$ telnet localhost 25
Trying 127.0.0.1...
Connected to localhost.
Escape character is '^]'.
220 shadrach.ispnet1.net ESMTP Postfix
EHLO shadrach.ispnet1.net
250-shadrach.ispnet1.net
250-PIPELINING
250-SIZE 10240000
250-ETRN
250 8BITMIME
VRFY rich
252 <rich>
VRFY mike@shadrach.ispnet1.net
252 <mike@shadrach.ispnet1.net>
```

LISTING 14.7 Continued

```
VRFY evonne@meshach.ispnet2.net
252 <evonne@meshach.ispnet1.net>
VRFY alex
252 <alex>
QUIT
221 Bye
$
```

As you can see, each of the different categories of addresses returned a 252 SMTP return code. One problem that has been noted with this behavior is that many spam address-harvesting programs interpret this return code as a valid address and begin sending spam messages to invalid addresses on your mail server. Your mail server would then be stuck processing hundreds (or even thousands) of bounce messages, thus taking up processing time.

To avoid this problem, Postfix allows the mail administrator to completely disable the VRFY response by using the `disable_vrfy_command` parameter in the main.cf configuration file. This parameter allows you to completely disable VRFY queries by returning a 502 SMTP error code, indicating that the VRFY command has been disabled.

To have the Postfix server ignore VRFY queries, set the `disable_vrfy_command` parameter in the main.cf configuration file to yes:

```
disable_vrfy_command = yes
```

Listing 14.8 shows an example of how the Postfix server responds to VRFY queries with this parameter set.

LISTING 14.8 Sample Postfix VRFY Deny Session

```
[root@indytest snapshot-20010610]# telnet localhost 25
Trying 127.0.0.1...
Connected to localhost.
Escape character is '^]'.
220 indytest.dfas.mil ESMTP Postfix
EHLO shadrach.ispnet1.net
250-indytest.dfas.mil
250-PIPELINING
250-SIZE 10240000
250-ETRN
250 8BITMIME
VRFY rich
502 VRFY command is disabled
VRFY mike@indytest.dfas.mil
502 VRFY command is disabled
```

LISTING 14.8 Continued

```
VRFY evonne@meshach.ispnet2.net
502 VRFY command is disabled
VRFY alex
502 VRFY command is disabled
QUIT
221 Bye
Connection closed by foreign host.
$
```

Postfix responds to all EXPN commands with a 502 (command not implemented) return code. You cannot enable this command via the configuration files.

Using an E-mail Firewall

As mentioned earlier, to avoid the RCPT TO: attack you can create a separate e-mail firewall. An e-mail *firewall* is an e-mail server with the sole purpose of passing incoming and outgoing messages to and from your internal e-mail server. The e-mail firewall is configured to accept messages for your domain, and then pass them directly to the real domain mail server, usually located on the internal network.

Likewise, the e-mail firewall is also used to pass all outbound messages from the internal mail server(s) to the Internet. Ideally, the e-mail firewall should not accept any messages for any users configured on it and should not hold any messages for any internal mail servers. If the e-mail firewall becomes compromised, hackers still would not have access to users' mailboxes. Not all MTA packages allow you to configure these features, though.

If you decide to implement an e-mail firewall, you have three different possibilities for its location on your network. The following sections describe the pros and cons of each location.

Inside the Network Firewall

The simplest method is to place the e-mail firewall on the same server as the network firewall. Of course, this method is available only if your network firewall is implemented on a Unix server that can also support the MTA package. This method is illustrated in Figure 14.1.

This method has the advantage of using fewer servers than the other methods do, because a single server is used as both the network firewall and the e-mail firewall. Often commercial network firewall products include an e-mail firewall option that can be configured to pass SMTP traffic to the internal mail server.

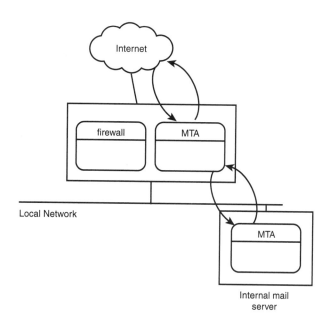

FIGURE 14.1

Placing the e-mail firewall on the network firewall server.

If you are using a standard Unix server to provide both network and e-mail firewall functions, you should make sure it's powerful enough to handle the load of both packet filtering and mail delivery. Often, this requirement is difficult to assess. Many network administrators have to use the trial-and-error method of determining whether the firewall server has enough processing capacity. Of course, this testing period could be an annoying process for network users.

Within a DMZ

A compromise solution to the one-server setup is to place the mail server in a *Demilitarized Zone (DMZ)*. The DMZ is a special network configured in the firewall that is separate from both the external network and the normal internal network. The firewall is responsible for allowing specific network traffic into and out of the DMZ. Usually the firewall is configured to allow external access to hosts in the DMZ area, while restricting access to the normal internal network. Servers that are frequently accessed by external users, such as Web servers, FTP servers, and mail servers, are often placed in the DMZ. Figure 14.2 shows this method.

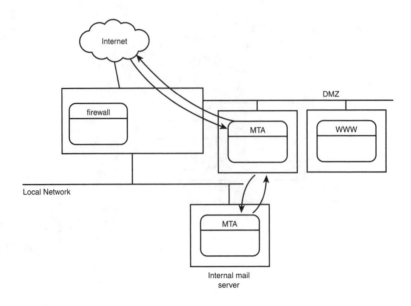

FIGURE 14.2

Placing the e-mail firewall server in a DMZ.

Although this method allows for tight security on the mail server, it creates a very complicated configuration environment for the firewall server. The DMZ must be strictly monitored to ensure that network traffic from the Internet does not compromise the local network.

As an Internal Mail Server

Another method simply places the dedicated mail firewall on a separate server in the normal local network along with the internal mail server. The network firewall must be configured to allow the appropriate network traffic into the local network to connect with the e-mail firewall, while blocking access to the internal mail server. Figure 14.3 illustrates this method.

In this method, the firewall server must be carefully configured to allow SMTP, POP3, and IMAP traffic from the Internet only to the e-mail firewall, not to any other hosts on the internal network.

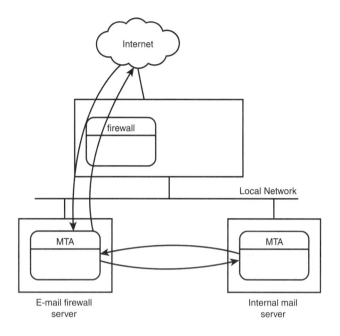

FIGURE 14.3

Using an internal mail server.

NOTE

You might have noticed that all three e-mail firewall setups do not take into account a backup mail server. This is often a problem with e-mail firewall environments. Usually it's best to use a mail server completely outside the network (such as an ISP server) as the backup mail server, and just retrieve messages in bulk when the real mail server is back online.

Creating an E-mail Firewall

No matter where the e-mail firewall is located, its configuration remains the same. It must receive messages for the domain and pass them along to the internal mail server where the real user mailboxes are located. In turn, the internal mail server must be configured to pass all outbound messages to the e-mail firewall for forwarding to the Internet.

This section describes configurations for sendmail, qmail, and Postfix to support an e-mail firewall. All these examples assume an e-mail firewall named `firewall.ispnet1.net` and an internal e-mail server named `mailserver.ispnet1.net` that contains the real user mailboxes. The domain that's used is `ispnet1.net`.

The following sections show the e-mail firewall and the internal mail server configurations in detail.

The sendmail Firewall

The sendmail e-mail firewall configuration uses the table called virtusertable to map the local domain e-mail addresses to the internal mail server. The virtusertable is created as a text file that contains the address mappings you require for your e-mail environment. The internal mail server must be configured to use the e-mail firewall as the relay host. The following sections describe these configurations.

Configuring the sendmail E-mail Firewall

To configure sendmail to use the virtusertable, you must add an entry to the standard sendmail.cf configuration file (described in Chapter 8, "The sendmail E-mail Package") pointing to the new table. If you use the m4 macro preprocessor to create the sendmail.cf configuration file, you must add a new FEATURE line defining the virtusertable:

```
FEATURE(`virtusertable', `db [options]')
```

In this command, *db* is the database map type, and *options* are any options required to create and access the database. The default database map type is the Berkeley hash database, and the default database file location in *options* is /etc/mail/virtusertable. You can specify an alternative database type or file location in the FEATURE macro line, however.

When the sendmail.cf configuration file is created, an additional K line is added to the file. If you manually create the sendmail.cf configuration file, you must add the K line defining the virtuser variable along with the database type and filename:

```
Kvirtuser hash /etc/mail/virtusertable
```

After modifying the sendmail.cf configuration file, you create the virtusertable database text file using this format:

```
alias    location
```

In this file, *alias* is the virtual alias that the e-mail firewall will receive messages for, and *location* is the hostname or e-mail address of the internal mail server that sendmail will send messages to.

To redirect all messages destined for users in the ispnet1.net domain to the same username on the internal mail server, you use this table entry:

```
@ispnet1.net    %1@mailserver.ispnet1.net
```

Any message received for any user in the ispnet1.net domain is then forwarded to the same username on the mailserver.ispnet1.net host. No messages are stored on the e-mail firewall.

After the text virtusertable file is created, it must be converted to a binary database file:

```
makemap hash /etc/mail/virtusertable < /etc/mail/virtusertable
```

To complete the configuration, you should add the domain name that you will be receiving messages for (ispnet1.net for this example) to the /etc/mail/local-host-names file, which defines the hostnames that sendmail will receive messages for.

Configuring the sendmail Internal Mail Server

In a standard sendmail configuration, the sendmail server attempts to deliver outbound messages directly to the mail host for the message recipient. The internal mail server should instead be configured to pass all outbound messages to the e-mail firewall for processing. This procedure is implemented using sendmail's smart host feature.

A *smart host* is a remote mail server where all outbound messages are passed for delivery. The smart host determines the destination of each individual message and delivers it to the appropriate remote mail server on the Internet.

The smart host feature is configured in the m4 macro preprocessor configuration file by using the define command, specifying the address of the smart host:

```
define(`SMART_HOST', `firewall.ispnet1.net')dnl
```

Alternatively, you can define an IP address as the smart host if your internal e-mail server does not use DNS to resolve address names.

If you manually create the sendmail.cf configuration file, you must add a variable definition using a D configuration line. The S variable specifies the smart host:

```
DSfirewall.ispnet1.net
```

If no smart host is defined, the S variable is set to null, so the DS line might already appear in your sendmail.cf configuration file with no hostname defined. All you need to do is add the hostname and restart sendmail.

After the smart host feature is configured, one more feature still needs to be added. Although the messages will properly be sent to the smart host, you need to make sure the return addresses on the messages point to the domain name instead of the internal mail server. You do that by using the sendmail masquerade feature.

The masquerade feature tells sendmail to change the return address of all outbound messages to an alternative hostname or, in this case, a domain name. These are the m4 macro preprocessor commands you need:

```
MASQUERADE_AS(domain)
FEATURE(`masquerade_envelope')
```

Using these values ensures that the return addresses of all outbound mail match the *domain* value supplied.

The qmail Firewall

Similar to sendmail, the qmail e-mail firewall configuration also uses a virtual table to map addresses. Unfortunately, the qmail method gets a little more complicated, as the virtual table cannot use variables as sendmail does. There are three steps required to configure the qmail e-mail firewall:

- Add the domain mapping to the `virtualdomains` control file.
- Add the domain name to the `rcpthosts` control file so qmail will accept messages for the domain.
- Create a separate local username with separate .qmail files for each domain username.

The following sections describe the configuration requirements for these steps.

Configuring the qmail Firewall

The `virtualdomains` control file consists of entries of virtual users or domains that the qmail server should accept messages for. Each separate user or domain is listed on a separate line in the file. Two formats can be used to enter data in the file. The first format is for defining individual virtual users:

user@domain:prepend

Using this format, qmail watches for message recipients with the address *user@domain*. When a message destined for *user@domain* is received, qmail converts the To: address to *prepend-user@domain*, and processes the message for local delivery. The *prepend* value should be the name of a local user on the mail server.

The second format is used for defining entire virtual domains:

domain:prepend

Using this format, qmail watches for any message recipients that contain the address *user@domain* in the address. When a message contains *domain*, it is converted to *prepend-user*; *user* is the original user address of the message recipient.

If this sounds confusing, it is. Here's an example to help clear this up. Add the following line to the `virtualdomains` control file, with `ispnet1.net` representing the *domain* variable and `mymail` representing *prepend*:

`ispnet1.net:mymail`

After this line is added, qmail scans all message recipients for anything addressed to a user in the `ispnet1.net` domain. If a message is received for `prez@ispnet1.net`, qmail converts the recipient address to `mymail-prez@ispnet1.net` and processes the message for local delivery.

For the second step of configuring the qmail e-mail firewall, you must add the ispnet1.net domain name to the rcpthosts control file to enable qmail to accept messages for this domain. If you do not want the firewall to accept any messages sent to the local users on the firewall, you can leave out the local hostname in the rcpthosts file.

You must also create the mymail user account (along with a $HOME directory) by using the standard useradd program for your Unix distribution. All messages for the ispnet1.net domain will be forwarded to the mymail user account.

Now that all the messages destined for the ispnet1.net domain are sent to the mymail user account, you must create rules to parse the messages and forward them to the internal mail server addresses.

For the third step of configuring the qmail e-mail firewall, qmail uses .qmail files in local users' $HOME directories to control how messages are handled by the local user. Each local user can create his own .qmail files to handle received messages. By prepending the local username to the original message recipient, the message I sent to the local user uses the corresponding .qmail file. For example, the qmail file .qmail-prez in the mymail user $HOME directory controls the delivery of any messages sent to the mymail-prez mail address, which is exactly what the virtualdomains control file converts the message sent to prez@ispnet1.net to. Each .qmail file must contain the valid e-mail address that the received message should be forwarded to.

Now all the pieces are fitting together. The virtualdomains control file points the ispnet1.net domain to a common local user account, mymail:

```
ispnet1.net:mymail
```

The rcpthosts control file contains the domain name to instruct qmail to accept messages for the domain:

```
ispnet1.net
```

Messages received by the qmail firewall server are sent to the mymail local account with the original message recipient added to the local username:

```
frankie@ispnet1.net - mymail-frankie
melanie@ispnet1.net - mymail-melanie
nicholas@ispnet1.net - mymail-nicholas
```

Next the mymail user account is configured with each of the possible recipients for the ispnet1.net domain. A separate .qmail file is created to forward the message to the mailserver.ispnet1.net internal mail server:

```
/home/mymail/.qmail-frankie
/home/mymail/.qmail-melanie
/home/mymail/.qmail-nicholas
```

The individual .qmail files contain the delivery address for the individual username. For example, the /home/mymail/.qmail-frankie file will contain this single text line:

```
frankie@mailserver.ispnet1.net
```

This line instructs qmail to forward any messages received for `frankie@ispnet1.net` to the address `frankie@mailserver.ispnet1.net`.

Configuring the qmail Internal Mail Server

On the internal mail server, you must configure qmail to send all outbound messages to the `firewall.ispnet1.net` mail server. Unlike other MTA packages that perform this feature internally, qmail uses an external program to accomplish this.

The serialmail package, also written by Dan Bernstein, contains several utility programs that qmail can use. One of them is the maildirsmtp program, which attempts to transfer all messages contained in a Maildir-style mailbox to a remote SMTP relay server. The following sections describe how to use maildirsmtp to configure the qmail internal mail server to forward all outbound messages to the e-mail firewall.

Downloading and Compiling the Maildirsmtp Program

As mentioned, the maildirsmtp program is part of the serialmail package, which can be downloaded from a link on the serialmail Web site:

```
http://cr.yp.to/serialmail.html
```

At the time of this writing, the most current version of serialmail is version 0.75, and can be downloaded at `http://cr.yp.to/software/serialmail-0.75.tar.gz`. The serialmail source code is distributed as a compressed tar file. As with other software distributions, you must unpack it into a working directory, as shown here:

```
tar -zxvf serialmail-0.75.tar.gz -C /usr/local/src
```

Before compiling and installing serialmail, you must verify that the serialmail configuration files properly reflect your compiler and qmail environment. Four configuration files are used to compile serialmail:

- conf-cc
- conf-home
- conf-ld
- conf-qmail

The conf-cc configuration file is used to define the C compiler on your Unix distribution and any necessary command-line parameters. By default, serialmail uses the GNU C compiler with optimizing tuned on.

The conf-home configuration file defines where the serialmail home directory will be located. Serialmail places all the executable files in the $HOME/bin directory; $HOME is defined in the conf-home file. By default, serialmail uses the /usr/local directory, thus placing the serialmail executable programs in the /usr/local/bin directory.

The conf-ld configuration file defines the C linker that is used to create the executable programs. By default, serialmail uses the GNU C compiler with the -s option to link object files into executable files. This should be fine for systems using the GNU C compiler.

Finally, the conf-qmail configuration file defines where the qmail home directory is located on the qmail server. The default setting points to the default location of the qmail home directory, the /var/qmail directory.

After the configuration files are modified to reflect the setup of the mail server, the serialmail program can be compiled and installed. Compiling and installing serialmail is a two-step process. From the serialmail working directory, type the following:

```
make
make setup check
```

The first make command should compile the source code and man pages for serialmail. The second make command installs and checks the installation of the serialmail program. If both commands are completed successfully, the serialmail executable programs should be installed in the $HOME/bin directory. $HOME is defined by the conf-home configuration file, which by default is the /usr/local/bin directory.

Configuring qmail to Use a Relay Host

The internal mail server must first be configured to use a relay host for all outbound messages. First, you need to create the virtualdomains control file to pass all messages external to the mail server to a common user account:

```
:firewall
```

By not specifying a domain name, this entry instructs qmail to deliver all messages not destined for local users to the local user named firewall. Next, you must ensure that there really is a local user named firewall, that the user has a Maildir-style mailbox, and that the default delivery method for the firewall user is the Maildir mailbox. This is accomplished using three commands:

```
useradd firewall
maildirmake /home/firewall/Maildir
echo ./Maildir/ > /home/firewall/.qmail-default
```

The useradd command creates the firewall user with a default $HOME directory (usually /home/firewall). You should also make sure your Unix system does not assign a default password to this user account. Most Unix systems assign a null password by default, making it impossible for anyone to log in to the system using this username.

The `maildirmake` command is a standard qmail utility program that creates a Maildir-style mailbox, and the `echo` command sets the default mail delivery method to the local Maildir mailbox in the .qmail-default file for the firewall user.

Now all messages sent from local users to external recipients are stored in the /home/firewall/Maildir mailbox. The final step is to pass these messages to the e-mail firewall to relay them to the Internet.

Using the Maildirsmtp Progam

The maildirsmtp program is used to read a Maildir-style mailbox and send any messages to a remote mail server via SMTP. This is the format for the `maildirsmtp` command:

```
maildirsmtp dir prefix host helohost
```

The maildirsmtp command-line parameters are defined in Table 14.2.

TABLE 14.2 Maildirsmtp Command-Line Parameters

Parameter	Description
dir	A Maildir-style mailbox
prefix	An envelope address prefix
host	Hostname or IP address of the remote SMTP relay host
helohost	The hostname used by maildirsmtp in the SMTP HELO command when connecting to the remote SMTP host

The *prefix* parameter is used to filter messages in the Maildir mail directory. Any messages that contain recipient addresses beginning with *prefix* are forwarded to the remote SMTP host defined in the *host* parameter. Before they are sent, *prefix* is removed from the recipient address. Any messages accepted by *host* for delivery are removed from the Maildir directory. Any messages rejected by *host* are bounced back to the original message sender.

The next step is to run the maildirsmtp program to transfer any messages waiting in the Maildir directory to the ISP mail server. The command should look like this:

```
maildirsmtp /home/firewall/Maildir firewall- firewall.ispnet1.net
➥ mailserver.ispnet1.net
```

The `maildirsmtp` command line tells maildirsmtp to check the /home/firewall/Maildir mailbox for messages. The *prefix* that it should look for is the `firewall-` prefix that is added to all messages forwarded to the account. The next two parameters define the e-mail firewall address (`firewall.ispnet1.net`) and the internal mail server name (`mailserver.ispnet1.net`). You should configure a cron script to run the `maildirsmtp` command at regular intervals on the internal mail server.

The Postfix Firewall

The Postfix configuration for the firewall mail server is similar to the sendmail and qmail configurations. Instead of the virtual table, Postfix provides a transport table that defines how to deliver messages for a given domain. As a side bonus, Postfix can be configured to refuse to accept any messages for the e-mail firewall server. You can use this feature to completely "lock down" the e-mail firewall.

Configuring the Postfix E-mail Firewall

To configure Postfix so that it won't accept any messages, you must trick it a little. Normally, the `relay_domains` parameter is used to inform Postfix what hosts it should receive messages for. If you set this value to nothing, Postfix refuses to accept messages for any host, including itself:

```
relay_domains =
```

Now that the Postfix server will not accept mail messages, you must configure it to pass along messages to the internal mail gateway server configured for the network. This can be done by using a transport table with a single line:

```
ispnet1.net smtp:mailserver.ispnet1.net
```

This line configures the Postfix transport table to receive messages for the `ispnet1.net` domain. When messages are received, they are immediately sent using the SMTP transport to the `mailserver.ispnet1.net` mail server inside the firewall.

After creating the transport table, you need to create an indexed binary database file using the postmap utility:

```
postmap hash:/etc/postfix/transport
```

Next, modify the main.cf configuration file to point to the new transport lookup table:

```
transport_maps = hash:/etc/postfix/transport
```

After issuing the Postfix `reload` command, the new e-mail firewall should accept messages for the `ispnet1.net` domain and forward them to the internal mail server. You can then configure the `mailserver.ispnet1.net` mail server to receive messages for the `ispnet1.net` domain.

Configuring the Postfix Internal Mail Server

The internal mail server must be configured to pass all outbound messages to the e-mail firewall. Postfix implements this feature with the `relayhost` parameter in the main.cf configuration file. The `relayhost` parameter defines the smart host that receives all outbound messages and forwards them to the appropriate recipient. The format of the `relayhost` parameter looks like this:

```
relayhost = address
```

The *address* variable can be a hostname or an IP address specified in brackets. If you specify the IP address in brackets, Postfix does not attempt to perform a DNS name lookup on the address. This is helpful for mail servers located on networks that do not have DNS lookup capabilities. If your network supports DNS, you can simply enter the following:

```
relayhost = firewall.ispnet1.net
```

Using the `relayhost` parameter, all messages destined for recipients on remote mail servers will be automatically forwarded to the e-mail firewall for delivery to the appropriate remote mail server.

Finally, as with the sendmail example, the Postfix internal mail server must use masquerading to ensure that the proper return addresses are used on outbound messages. The `myorigin` parameter in the main.cf configuration file can be set to the domain name so that all addresses are set to the domain name instead of the internal mail server hostname:

```
myorigin = ispnet1.net
```

This value overrides the hostname value for all outbound messages.

Summary

With the increase in Internet attacks on mail servers, you should use caution when implementing an Internet mail server. Many different methods are used to attack mail servers, but fortunately there are configurations you can use to avoid these attacks.

The SMTP VRFY and EXPN commands can be exploited to gain valuable information about valid e-mail and system accounts on the mail server, so you should disable these commands if possible. Most MTA packages allow you to disable them within the configuration file. However, even if these commands are disabled, a resourceful hacker or spammer can get information about your mail server just by trying to send messages to various usernames on your system.

To help prevent this problem, you can configure an e-mail firewall that is responsible for communicating with the outside world. The purpose of the e-mail firewall is to accept messages destined for users on the local domain and forward them to an internal mail server. The actual user accounts reside on the internal mail server, safe from the prying of hackers and spammers. If the e-mail firewall is attacked, the users' mailboxes are safely hidden on the internal mail server.

Each of the MTA packages discussed in this book—sendmail, qmail, and Postfix—allow you to configure e-mail servers to act as the e-mail firewall or the internal mail server. The e-mail firewall should be configured to accept any messages for local system users and should forward all messages to the internal mail server. The internal mail server should in turn be configured to accept messages for local users and forward all outbound messages to the e-mail firewall for processing to remote mail servers.

CHAPTER 15

Using SASL

Chapter 11, "Preventing Open Relays," described methods you can use to selectively allow remote SMTP hosts to relay messages through your e-mail server. Those methods allow relaying based on specific IP addresses or hostnames. Unfortunately, it is not always practical to assume that all your remote users use a specific IP address that can be defined in the relay table.

Another popular method of allowing remote hosts to relay messages through the e-mail server is to use an authentication method. The authentication method can uniquely identify the remote mail server so that your mail server can determine whether it is allowed to relay messages.

One of the most popular methods of authenticating network connections is the Simple Authentication and Security Layer (SASL). This protocol defines a set of authentication mechanisms that any network application can use to authenticate remote users. Many open source MTA packages use SASL to implement the AUTH command, which allows SMTP hosts to use client authentication within a standard SMTP session.

This chapter describes the SASL protocol and the SMTP AUTH authentication command. Cyrus-SASL, a popular open source SASL library package, is also discussed, along with how it is used in open source MTA packages to provide SASL support.

What Is SASL?

RFC 2222 describes how SASL can be used to provide an authentication mechanism for network applications that use client/server commands, such as POP3, IMAP, and SMTP. SASL itself is not a complete application; it just provides authentication support for existing applications and is intended to be used as a plug-in for network applications.

The following sections describe SASL and how it is used to authenticate SMTP users with the SMTP AUTH command.

How SASL Operates

SASL support must be compiled into the network application program. It operates within the network application, providing an Application Programming Interface (API) that can be called on to validate remote clients' authentication attempts. Figure 15.1 illustrates how this works.

The network application must provide a method to accept an authentication token from the remote network client. This is usually done in the form of a text command, such as the SMTP AUTH command described later in the "Using SASL in SMTP" section. The authentication token is passed to the SASL layer for verification.

If the authentication token is verified, SASL returns a positive response to the application, and the remote network client is allowed to continue using the network application as normal. If the authentication token is rejected, SASL returns a negative response and the remote client is denied access to the application.

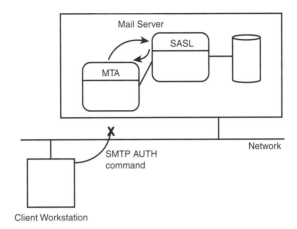

Client Workstation

FIGURE 15.1

Using SASL in a network application.

It should be noted that SASL does not offer a way to encrypt the network session. All SASL provides is a means to authenticate the remote user. In fact, it is possible to choose a SASL authentication method that sends the authentication data in clear text, providing no security at all.

An alternative is the use of encrypted SMTP sessions using the Secure Socket Layer (or SSL, discussed in Chapter 16, "Secure POP3 and IMAP Servers"). Unfortunately, support for this feature is not widespread, as it requires both SMTP servers to support SSL.

SASL Authentication Mechanisms

Each authentication session must take place using a specific authentication mechanism. The *authentication mechanism* is an underlying protocol used to send authentication tokens to the server. Many different mechanisms can be used to authenticate the user within the SASL framework. RFC 2222 defines these three specific mechanisms:

- KERBEROS_V4   Host sends a ready response with a random 32-byte number, and the client responds with a Kerberos ticket and authenticator for the username.
- GSSAPI   Client sends a Generic Security Service Application Interface (GSSAPI) encoded username and password.
- SKEY   Client sends a base-64 encoded username and one-time password combination.

Each of these mechanisms has already been discussed in Chapter 3, "POP3," as they are standard encryption techniques also used in encrypting data in POP3 and IMAP sessions. A username and password pair is encoded with the encryption technique. Obviously, both the client and the server must use the same encryption technique for the SASL session.

Since the publishing of RFC 2222, several other mechanisms have been defined for SASL. The CRAM-MD5 and DIGEST-MD5 mechanisms are other common encryption techniques that use the challenge/response model, similar to the KERBEROS_V4 and SKEY methods. They have become common mechanisms for secure mail clients.

The PLAIN mechanism allows the client to send clear text ASCII user IDs and passwords to the server. This method by itself provides no security, as the tokens can be intercepted on the network and compromised. Therefore, the PLAIN mechanism should be used only in secure (encrypted) network connections.

Possibly the most popular mechanism is LOGIN. This mechanism uses base-64 encoding of the user ID and the password. Although the user ID and password are encoded, as you saw in Chapter 5, encoding itself does not mean secure communication. If the encoded user ID and password are captured, it's a simple exercise to decode them to their text equivalents.

NOTE

Although the LOGIN mechanism is not recommended by most SASL software packages, if you need to support Microsoft Outlook and Netscape Messenger clients, you must include support for the LOGIN mechanism in your SASL environment, as both of these clients use the LOGIN mechanism to encode user IDs and passwords.

Using SASL in SMTP

RFC 2554 provides an additional command for SMTP servers to support SASL authentication: A remote client can send an authentication token by using the SMTP AUTH command. The AUTH command can be used as a standalone command or as an option to the MAIL FROM: command to indicate that a trusted host has already authenticated the message.

As a standalone command, this is the format of the AUTH command:

```
AUTH mechanism
```

The mechanism parameter defines what authentication mechanism the remote client wants to use for the SASL session. The local server and the remote client must be able to agree on a common mechanism for the authentication to work. To help this process, ESMTP enables the server to advertise its supported authentication mechanisms in the EHLO greeting banner. Listing 15.1 shows the start of a sample ESMTP session.

LISTING 15.1 Sample ESMTP Session

```
$ telnet localhost 25
Trying 127.0.0.1...
Connected to localhost.
Escape character is '^]'.
220 shadrach.ispnet1.net ESMTP sendmail 8.11.3/8.11.3; Thu, 5 Apr 2001
➥ 09:12:36 -00
EHLO shadrach.ispnet1.net
250-shadrach.ispnet1.net Hello IDENT:rich@localhost [127.0.0.1], pleased
➥ to meet you
250-ENHANCEDSTATUSCODES
250-EXPN
250-VERB
250-8BITMIME
250-SIZE
250-DSN
250-ONEX
250-ETRN
250-XUSR
250-AUTH LOGIN DIGEST-MD5
250 HELP
```

The EHLO greeting banner lists the ESMTP commands that the mail server accepts. The AUTH command is listed, along with the authentication mechanisms it supports. The remote client must determine which common authentication mechanism is appropriate for the network environment. Obviously, in this example, if the remote client also supports both the LOGIN and DIGEST-MD5 mechanisms, it would be better to select the DIGEST-MD5 mechanism because it is more secure.

After the client sends the AUTH command, the server responds with an authentication challenge phrase. The phrase differs depending on the authentication mechanism used. Listing 15.2 shows a sample SMTP session using the LOGIN mechanism.

LISTING 15.2 Sample SMTP Authentication Session

```
$ telnet localhost 25
Trying 127.0.0.1...
Connected to localhost.
Escape character is '^]'.
220 shadrach.ispnet1.net ESMTP sendmail 8.11.3/8.11.3; Thu, 5 Apr 2001
➥ 09:12:36 -00
EHLO shadrach.ispnet1.net
250-shadrach.ispnet1.net Hello IDENT:rich@localhost [127.0.0.1],
➥ pleased to meet you
```

LISTING 15.2 Continued

```
250-ENHANCEDSTATUSCODES
250-EXPN
250-VERB
250-8BITMIME
250-SIZE
250-DSN
250-ONEX
250-ETRN
250-XUSR
250-AUTH LOGIN DIGEST-MD5
250 HELP
AUTH LOGIN
334 VXNlcm5hbWU6
cmljaA==
334 UGFzc3dvcmQ6
cHJsbmpn
235 2.0.0 OK Authenticated
MAIL FROM: rich@shadrach.ispnet1.net
250 2.1.0 rich@[158.18.1.153]... Sender ok
RCPT TO: richard.blum@meshach.ispnet2.net
250 2.1.5 richard.blum@meshach.ispnet2.net... Recipient ok
DATA
354 Enter mail, end with "." on a line by itself
Subject: test
From: rich@shadrach.ispnet1.net
To: richard.blum@meshach.ispnet2.net

This is a test message.
.
250 2.0.0 f35EDFB04406 Message accepted for delivery
QUIT
221 2.0.0 shadrach.ispnet1.net closing connection
Connection closed by foreign host.
$
```

The server accepts the AUTH LOGIN command sent by the client, and a challenge phrase is returned. The client then responds to the challenge phrase using the negotiated mechanism (LOGIN in this example). The encoded username and password pair are sent to the server for authentication. At the end of the challenge/response, the server indicates whether the authentication attempt has been successful. If it has, the SMTP session can continue as normal.

RFC 2554 also provides a method of identifying authenticated messages relayed through mail servers. If a mail server receives a message using the SMTP AUTH command, but must relay it on to another mail server, it should indicate to the receiving host that the message has already been authenticated.

RFC 2554 provides an extension to the standard MAIL FROM: SMTP command to add authentication notification. The command format looks like this:

```
MAIL FROM: reverse-path AUTH=address
```

The AUTH parameter identifies the address of the host that has previously authenticated the messages and vouches for its authenticity. If *address* is set, the listed host has already authenticated the message using the AUTH command, and no further authentication is required (assuming that the receiving host trusts the sending host listed in the AUTH parameter). If *address* is set to an empty set (<>), the sending host has not authenticated the message.

The Cyrus-SASL Library

As mentioned earlier, SASL support must be compiled into network applications. To support this, Carnegie Mellon University has developed the Cyrus-SASL library, a C library that standard network applications can use to easily add SASL support.

The following sections describe how to download and install the Cyrus-SASL library on your Unix system, along with how to configure it to be used with open source MTA packages that support SASL by using the Cyrus-SASL library API.

Downloading and Installing Cyrus-SASL

Many Unix systems include the Cyrus-SASL package as a binary distribution. If your Unix system includes a binary distribution, you should determine—by observing the EHLO greeting banner—whether it has been compiled supporting the authentication mechanisms your e-mail environment requires. If not, you must download the source code and compile it yourself with the required options.

The Cyrus-SASL package can be downloaded from the Carnegie Mellon FTP site at ftp://ftp.andrew.cmu.edu/pub/cyrus-mail. At the time of this writing, the most current production version is 1.5.24, which can be download as cyrus-sasl-1.5.24.tar.gz.

After downloading the distribution package, you extract it to a working directory using this command:

```
tar -zxvf cyrus-sasl-1.5.24.tar.gz
```

CAUTION

Unlike the other source code distribution packages discussed in this book, the Cyrus-SASL package requires a specific method of unpacking the source code. You should not be logged in as the root user, or as a user with root privileges, to unpack the distribution. Because of this requirement, you cannot use the standard /usr/local/src working directory that has been used in other examples in this book.

After unpacking the source code, you can change to the distribution directory, cyrus-sasl-1.5.24. The Cyrus-SASL package uses the standard configure program to create the necessary makefile for compiling the source code on your Unix system. You can change many features with the configure options, including the authentication mechanisms supported by the SASL libraries. If you know which authentication mechanisms you will use in your e-mail environment, it is best to specifically enable the ones you will use and disable the ones you won't use. Table 15.1 lists the more popular configure options used with the `configure` command.

TABLE 15.1 Cyrus-SASL Configure Options

Option	Description
--with-pam	Use the system Pluggable Authentication Module (PAM) (default = yes)
--with-pwcheck	Use the Cyrus-SASL pwcheck program to authenticate users. (default = no)
--enable-cram	Enable CRAM-MD5 authentication (default = yes)
--enable-digest	Enable DIGEST-MD5 authentication (default = yes)
--enable-krb4	Enable KERBEROS_V4 authentication (default = yes)
--enable-gssapi	Enable GSSAPI authentication (default = yes)
--enable-plain	Enable PLAIN authentication (default = yes)
--enable-login	Enable LOGIN authentication (default = no)

Each of the --enable options has a corresponding --disable option; if you do not want to include a specific authentication mechanism, you can indicate it in the --disable option.

After you have decided on the configuration options required for your e-mail environment, you can run the configure program:

```
./configure —enable-login —disable-gssapi —disable-cram —with-pwcheck
```

This command enables the SASL LOGIN authentication method to allow Microsoft Internet Explorer and Netscape Navigator clients to authenticate; it also disables the GSS-API and CRAM-MD5 authentication methods. The --with-pwcheck option is used to create the separate pwcheck program for authenticating clients.

The configure program creates the appropriate makefiles for the options you selected. After the configure program finishes, you use the make command to create the executable programs. Remember that you cannot be the root user when running this command. The next step is installing the libraries and utility files by using the make install command. This command must be issued as a user with root privileges.

CAUTION

The Cyrus-SASL package requires that the gdbm, Berkeley db, or ndbm database library be loaded on your Unix system. My Linux Mandrake 8.0 system had the Berkeley db binary package installed, but I had to manually install the Berkeley db developer RPM package as well to compile Cyrus-SASL. Make sure your Unix system includes one of these database packages as well as the header files to compile support for these packages.

The installation process places the new SASL library files in the /usr/local/lib and /usr/local/lib/sasl directories. Some open source MTA programs cannot access the SASL libraries in these locations, however. To make life easier for yourself, you should perform the following two steps as the root user:

1. Copy the SASL libraries located in the /usr/local/lib directory to the /usr/lib directory:

   ```
   cp /usr/local/lib/libsasl* /usr/lib
   ```

2. Create a soft link from the /usr/local/lib/sasl directory to the /usr/lib/sasl directory:

   ```
   ln -s /usr/local/lib/sasl /usr/lib/sasl
   ```

Now Cyrus-SASL should be installed and ready for use. The next step is to create a configuration file so that the MTA application can use Cyrus-SASL authentication.

Cyrus-SASL Database Methods

For Cyrus-SASL to be able to authenticate users, it must connect to some type of database system that contains the usernames and passwords. Cyrus-SASL can use several different database methods, listed in Table 15.2.

TABLE 15.2 Cyrus-SASL Authentication Database Methods

Method	Description
passwd	The standard Unix /etc/passwd file
shadow	The Unix /etc/shadow password file
sia	Security Integration Architecture used on Digital Unix systems
kerberos_v4	The Unix Kerberos password system

TABLE 15.2 Continued

Method	Description
pam	The Unix Pluggable Authentication Module (PAM)
sasldb	A separate username/password database created for SASL
pwcheck	A separate program running in background mode that verifies user-names/passwords

Do not confuse these username validation methods with SASL authentication mechanisms. The SASL library uses these database methods to validate the username/password pair received from the user with an SASL authentication mechanism. In the rest of this chapter, I will use the term *authentication method* to refer to the client sending usernames/passwords to be authenticated by the server, and *validation method* to refer to the Cyrus-SASL library looking up the usernames/passwords in the database.

The specific database validation method used by SASL can vary, based on the network application using SASL. The database method must be configured in the SASL configuration file for the application. The next section describes this process.

Configuring Cyrus-SASL

After you've compiled and installed the Cyrus-SASL libraries, you don't need to change a lot of configurations to start using the libraries. The following sections describe the configuration files and the username validation methods used by Cyrus-SASL.

Application Configuration File

With Cyrus-SASL, each individual application can control how it uses the SASL libraries for authentication. Each application has its own configuration file that defines which SASL authentication method it will use. The individual configuration files are stored using this format:

/usr/lib/sasl/*application*.conf

The *application* value is the name of the executable program that uses the SASL library. For example, the sendmail program would use an SASL configuration file of /usr/lib/sasl/sendmail.conf, but the Postfix smtpd program would use a configuration file of /usr/lib/sasl/smtpd.conf.

CAUTION

You might have noticed the uppercase *S* in the sendmail.conf file. The Cyrus-SASL documentation specifies this exact method of defining the sendmail configuration file.

The SASL configuration file can contain these three parameters:

- srvtab
- pwcheck_method
- auto_transition

The srvtab parameter is used for installations using the KERBEROS_V4 authentication mechanism. It points to the location of the srvtab file used to authenticate the KERBEROS-V4 session:

```
srvtab: /var/srvtab
```

The pwcheck_method parameter, used for all installations, defines the database method Cyrus-SASL uses to validate the authentication request from the network application:

```
pwcheck_method: method
```

The method value determines the method that Cyrus-SASL uses to validate the received username and password (more on that in the next section).

The auto_transition parameter switches users from a PLAIN database to a more secure database by adding the shared secrets that the user uses when authenticating to the database. To enable this feature, you must specify the value true, like this:

```
auto_transition: true
```

Setting the Database Method

The pwcheck_method parameter in the configuration file controls how Cyrus-SASL validates usernames and passwords it receives. To do that, you need to set method to one of the seven different values listed earlier in Table 15.2.

Of these methods, the pam, sasldb, and pwcheck methods are the most commonly used. This section describes how to use these methods in more detail.

Using the pam Method

The pam method of validating system usernames is popular with Sun Solaris, FreeBSD, and Linux system administrators. Cyrus-SASL can use the existing system's PAM database to validate SASL usernames and passwords.

For this method to work, you must create an entry for the service name in the PAM configuration database. For MTA packages, the service name is smtp. On Linux systems, the PAM configuration files are located in the /etc/pam.d directory. You must create a file named smtp in that directory, and the file should contain the following two lines:

```
auth       required    /lib/security/pam_pwdb.so shadow nullok
account    required    /lib/security/pam_pwdb.so
```

The name and location of the PAM libraries specified in the smtp file might be different on your particular Linux distribution. Also, some Linux distributions use the library name pam_unix.so instead of pam_pwdb.so. You can compare the entries in the /etc/pam.d/passwd configuration file to determine the values used on your system.

Another format of the PAM configuration on some Unix systems is to use a single configuration file that contains all the allowed applications. The /etc/pam.conf file contains separate lines that define each individual application. You must edit this file to insert two lines for the smtp application:

```
smtp auth     required pam_pwdb.so shadow nullok
smtp account required pam_pwdb.so shadow nullok
```

The /etc/pam.conf file is used for BSD-based systems, such as Sun Solaris and FreeBSD, although on FreeBSD the PAM library is located in the pam_unix.so file, so the pam.conf entries should be modified accordingly.

After creating the PAM files, you should be able to use the pam authentication method to validate SASL requests.

CAUTION

The pam method expects the calling program to have root privileges. If this is not the case with your MTA package (such as with qmail and Postfix), this method might not be the best one for you to use. Changing the permissions on the pam files to match your MTA package could be a security risk. You should use an alternative database method, such as pwcheck, described next.

Using the pwcheck Method

The pwcheck method uses a separate program supplied with Cyrus-SASL to validate users. It is available only if you configure the Cyrus-SASL package with the --with-pwcheck configure option. It runs in background mode and waits for an SASL authentication request. The pwcheck program then connects to the system's shadow password file to verify the request.

By using the pwcheck method rather than the normal shadow password method, MTA programs that do not run with root privileges (such as qmail and Postfix) can access the shadow password file without having to change the permissions of the shadow password file. Changing these permissions can result in a security problem for the system.

If your Unix system uses a shadow password file, you can configure Cyrus-SASL to use the pwcheck method to verify authentication requests. To use pwcheck, you need to create a /var/pwcheck directory for the pwcheck program to share with the MTA program:

```
mkdir /var/pwcheck
chmod 700 /var/pwcheck
```

The directory should be owned by the user account that will access it. If your MTA program runs with root privileges (such as sendmail), you can allow root to own the directory. If not, you must change the directory owner to the username that your MTA program runs under. For example, for Postfix, you would issue this command:

```
chown postfix /var/pwcheck
```

After creating and modifying the /var/pwcheck directory, you can start the pwcheck program:

```
/usr/local/sbin/pwcheck
```

Once started, the program automatically runs in background mode and waits for authentication requests from the MTA program. As SASL requests are made by the MTA program, the pwcheck method validates them based on the entries in the standard /etc/shadow password file.

Using the sasldb Method

The Cyrus-SASL package also offers a way for you to create a standalone database to track authentication usernames and passwords. If you select the sasldb authentication method, however, you must manually add each username and password to the SASL database.

The SASL database is located by default in the file /etc/sasldb. You can add users to the database by using the saslpasswd utility installed in the /usr/local/sbin directory by default. This is the format of the saslpasswd command:

```
saslpasswd [-a appname] [-p] [-c] [-d] [-u DOM] userid
```

The -a option equates the username to a specific application name, appname. The username created will apply only to the specified application. By default, usernames created apply to all applications that use the SASL sasldb authentication method. Likewise, the -u option equates the username to a specific domain, DOM. By default the username created will apply to any application running on the host server. By specifying a domain, you can run separate SASL databases on the same server.

The -p option allows the saslpasswd command to read passwords from the STDIN connection on the command line. By default, saslpasswd prompts you for the password. By using the -p option, you can create a text file with saslpasswd commands and passwords that's used to mass-create users.

The -c option creates the account in the database, and the -d option disables an active account in the database. A sample saslpasswd session would look like this:

```
# /usr/local/sbin/saslpasswd -c matthew
Password:
```

```
Again (for verification):
#
```

You can use the `sasldblistuser` command to display a list of users entered into the `sasldb` database file:

```
# /usr/local/sbin/sasldblistusers
user: rich realm: shadrach.ispnet1.net mech: PLAIN
user: rich realm: shadrach.ispnet1.net mech: CRAM-MD5
user: matthew realm: shadrach.ispnet1.net mech: PLAIN
user: matthew realm: shadrach.ispnet1.net mech: CRAM-MD5
user: chris realm: shadrach.ispnet1.net mech: DIGEST-MD5
user: rich realm: shadrach.ispnet1.net mech: DIGEST-MD5
user: matthew realm: shadrach.ispnet1.net mech: DIGEST-MD5
user: chris realm: shadrach.ispnet1.net mech: PLAIN
user: chris realm: shadrach.ispnet1.net mech: CRAM-MD5
#
```

As with the `pwcheck` method, you must ensure that the username your MTA program runs with has privileges to read the /etc/sasldb file.

NOTE

The obvious downside to using the `sasldb` method is that you must maintain a separate database of usernames and passwords. For some e-mail environments, this could prove to be a huge task.

Implementing SASL

Now that the Cyrus-SASL is installed and configured properly, the next step is to configure the MTA package to use it to validate SMTP AUTH requests. The following sections describe how to configure sendmail, qmail, and Postfix to use the SASL authentication database.

sendmail

Versions 8.10 and later of sendmail include support to use the Cyrus-SASL libraries to support the SMTP AUTH command. This section describes how to compile and configure SASL support for sendmail.

Compiling SASL Support

After installing the Cyrus-SASL libraries, you need to recompile your sendmail software to use them. This requires modifying the site configuration file in the sendmail source code distribution.

The site configuration file, named site.config.m4, is located in the devtools/Site sub-directory under the sendmail source code directory tree. If you have not specified any special configuration parameters, your sendmail distribution might not include this file, so you must create it.

In the site.config.m4 file, you define the SASL support parameters as well as the location of the SASL libraries and header files. The site.config.m4 file should look like this (or have these lines added to any existing lines):

```
APPENDDEF(`confENVDEF', `-DSASL')
APPENDDEF(`conf_sendmail_LIBS', `-lsasl')
APPENDDEF(`confLIBDIRS', `-L/usr/local/lib')
APPENDDEF(`confINCDIRS', `-I/usr/local/include')
```

The first two lines instruct sendmail to include SASL support in the executable programs, and the last two lines define where the SASL libraries and header files are located. After creating (or modifying) the site.config.m4 file, you can compile sendmail by using the Build script in the main source code distribution directory (see Chapter 8, "The sendmail E-mail Package). The normal command should be sh Build, which creates the new executable programs for sendmail, including SASL support. The next step is to add SASL support to the sendmail configuration file.

NOTE

If you have previously created the sendmail executable programs by using the Build script, you have to include the -c option to re-create the Build directories. Otherwise, the new site.config.m4 parameters will not be implemented.

If you are using the m4 macro preprocessor to create your sendmail.cf configuration file, you can add the following two lines to your macro configuration file (*.mc):

```
TRUST_AUTH_MECH(`LOGIN PLAIN CRAM-MD5')dnl
define(`confAUTH_MECHANISMS', `LOGIN PLAIN CRAM-MD5')dnl
```

Both lines define the SASL authentication mechanisms that sendmail will support. Make sure you specify only the methods that your SASL installation supports. Each authentication mechanism is separated in the list by a space. After adding the additional SASL lines to the .mc macro file, you can run the m4 macro preprocessor to create the new configuration file.

If you are manually creating the sendmail.cf configuration file, add the following lines:

```
C{TrustAuthMech}LOGIN PLAIN CRAM-MD5
O AuthMechanisms=LOGIN PLAIN CRAM-MD5
```

Again, list only the authentication mechanisms, separated by a space, that your sendmail environment uses.

The sendmail Cyrus-SASL Configuration File

To ensure that the Cyrus-SASL libraries know how to validate received SASL authentication requests, you must create a Cyrus-SASL configuration file to define the sendmail MTA package as an SASL application.

The configuration file should be named sendmail.conf and located in the /usr/lib/sasl directory. In it, you must define the authentication database method that you want to use:

```
pwcheck_method: PAM
```

This example demonstrates using the PAM system username database to validate SASL authentication requests.

NOTE

Even if you do not use the `sasldb` validation method, you must create the /etc/sasldb file or sendmail will complain when it is started. Hopefully, this "feature" will be fixed in future releases of sendmail.

---

qmail

At the time of this writing, the most current version of qmail (version 1.03) does not support SASL. However, several qmail users have created patches for SASL support in qmail 1.03. The following sections describe how to install and use one of the more popular qmail SASL patches.

Compiling SASL support

A qmail user known as Mrs. Brisby has modified the standard qmail-smtpd.c file to include SMTP authentication support. Instead of using the Cyrus-SASL libraries, the method she uses incorporates another software package created by Dan Bernstein, the checkpassword package.

The checkpassword package allows any program to validate a username/password pair from the system password database (either /etc/passwd or /etc/shadow). By passing SASL validation requests to the checkpassword program, Mrs. Brisby's SASL implementation for qmail does not require the Cyrus-SASL libraries.

You can download the new qmail-smtpd.c file at the URL http://www.minh.org/hacks/qmail-smtpd.c. After it's downloaded, you can replace the original qmail-smtpd.c program with the new version, and recompile the qmail package as normal (described in Chapter 9, "The qmail E-mail Package").

After installing qmail, you download and install the checkpassword package from the qmail Web site. At the time of this writing, the package can be downloaded here:

```
http://cr.yp.to/software/checkpassword-0.81.tar.gz
```

After downloading the file, unpack it into a working directory:

```
tar -zxvf checkpassword-0.81.tar.gz -C /usr/local/src
```

This command creates the directory /usr/local/src/checkpassword-0.81 and places the source code distribution there. You can compile and install the checkpassword program with these commands:

```
make
make install
```

These commands install the checkpassword program in the /bin directory. Next, you must modify the standard qmail installation to support the new SASL requirements.

Configuring qmail for SASL Support

Since the qmail SASL solution uses the qmail checkpassword program, no Cyrus-SASL configuration file is required. Instead, you configure the smtpd entry in the /etc/inetd.conf configuration file to support the checkpassword program. To do that, add the checkpassword program as a parameter to the qmail-smtpd program in the /etc/inetd.conf file:

```
smtp    stream tcp nowait  qmaild  /var/qmail/bin/tcp-env  tcp-env
➥ /var/qmail/bin/qmail-smtpd /bin/checkpassword /bin/true
```

When connections are received on the qmail-smtpd program, they are passed to the checkpassword program for validation. If the username/password pair match the system's user database, the SMTP connection is allowed to continue.

NOTE

This authentication method supports only the LOGIN authentication mechanism, which, although it's the least secure of the choices, is the only one supported by both Microsoft Outlook and Netscape Messenger.

Postfix

Postfix includes support for SASL, but it must be compiled into the executable programs at install time. The following sections describe how to add and configure SASL support for Postfix.

Compiling SASL Support

If you have already compiled Postfix from the source code distribution, you must first remove all the old object code files from the directory by using the `make tidy` command.

To compile SASL support into Postfix, you must add the appropriate compiler and linker parameters to the Postfix configuration. This can be done by using the `make makefiles` command, along with the appropriate parameters.

Because the command is long, the Postfix documentation suggests using the Unix line-continuation character, the backslash. This character allows you to continue a long command on multiple lines:

```
make makefiles CCARGS="-DUSE_SASL_AUTH -I/usr/local/include" \
   AUXLIBS="-L/usr/local/lib -lsasl"
```

The CCARGS option adds the `-DUSE_SASL_AUTH` parameter, along with the `-I` parameter to include the SASL header files directory. The AUXLIBS option adds the SASL library to the library search parameter (`-L`) and adds the SASL library to the linker command (`-l`).

After entering this command, you can compile Postfix using the normal method outlined in Chapter 10, "The Postfix E-mail Package." After Postfix is installed, you must add SASL support to the main.cf configuration file.

To enable SASL support, first you need to define it in the main.cf configuration file by using this line:

```
smtpd_sasl_auth_enable = yes
```

This command enables SASL authentication, but you must further define how Postfix uses it. To enable the SMTP AUTH command, add another parameter to the `smtpd_recipient_restrictions` line. As described in Chapter 11, "Preventing Open Relays," the `smtpd_recipient_restrictions` line defines hosts that the Postfix server will accept messages from. If you compile Postfix with SASL support, an additional parameter is available: `permit_sasl_authenticated`. This parameter can be added to the existing `smtpd_recipient_restrictions` line.

If you were not using the `smtpd_recipient_restrictions` line, you can create a new one by using the `permit_sasl_authenticated` parameter. As mentioned in Chapter 11, you must also include one of the following required `smtpd_recipient_restrictions` parameters to the end of the line:

- `check_relay_domains`
- `reject`
- `reject_unauth_destination`

Therefore, a complete `smtpd_recipient_restrictions` line should look like this:

```
smtpd_recipient_restrictions = permit_sasl_authenticated, reject
```

This configuration line allows only remote hosts that have been SASL-authenticated to relay messages through the Postfix mail server. If you want local network hosts to be able to send messages without authenticating, you can add the `check_relay_domains` parameter as well.

The Postfix Cyrus-SASL Configuration File

Again, for Cyrus-SASL to know how to validate authentication requests received by Postfix, you must create the Cyrus-SASL configuration file. The file should be called smtpd.conf and located in the /usr/lib/sasl directory.

Because the Postfix smtpd program does not run with `root` privileges, you are limited in how Cyrus-SASL can validate authentication requests. The easiest method is to use the pwcheck program and assign the Postfix user ID as the owner of the /var/pwcheck directory. This method allows you to use the system's shadow password file without having to change any ownership privileges of the password files.

The /usr/lib/sasl/smtpd.conf file contains a single line:

```
pwcheck_method: pwcheck
```

Remember to start the pwcheck program (located in the /usr/local/sbin directory) before any remote host attempts to use SASL authentication.

Testing the SASL Server

After installing the new MTA programs and configuration files, you can test the installation by issuing `telnet` on port 25 and sending the `EHLO` command. If the SASL support has been successfully compiled into the MTA program, you should see the `AUTH` command listed in the response from the `EHLO` command, as demonstrated in Listing 15.3.

LISTING 15.3 Testing SASL Support

```
$ telnet localhost 25
Trying 127.0.0.1...
Connected to localhost.
Escape character is '^]'.
220 shadrach.ispnet1.net ESMTP sendmail 8.11.3/8.11.3; Mon, 16 Jul 2001
➡ 13:02:24 -0
EHLO test
250-shadrach.ispnet1.net Hello IDENT:rich@localhost [127.0.0.1], pleased
➡ to meet you
```

LISTING 15.3 Continued

```
250-ENHANCEDSTATUSCODES
250-EXPN
250-VERB
250-8BITMIME
250-SIZE
250-DSN
250-ONEX
250-ETRN
250-XUSR
250-AUTH LOGIN PLAIN DIGEST-MD5 KERBEROS
250 HELP
QUIT
221 2.0.0 shadrach.ispnet1.net closing connection
Connection closed by foreign host.
$
```

After sending the EHLO command, the mail server responds with the ESMTP commands it accepts. Note that the AUTH command is now accepted, along with a list of the authentication mechanisms that the mail server supports.

Summary

This chapter described the Simple Authentication and Security Layer (SASL), and how it can be used in an SMTP session to provide authentication for remote users. SASL offers several different authentication mechanisms for validating remote users to the mail server.

ESMTP provides the AUTH command to allow remote users to authenticate SMTP sessions with the mail server. Remote users must be assigned valid username and password pairs to identify themselves to the mail server. The SMTP AUTH session negotiates an SASL authentication mechanism to validate the remote user's identity.

The Cyrus-SASL implementation of SASL can be used with many MTA packages to support SMTP authentication. The Cyrus-SASL package contains an API library that can be compiled into the MTA package. The MTA package can then use the Cyrus-SASL library to validate authentication attempts. The Cyrus-SASL library supports several different methods of validating users, including using the existing system's user database as well as its own separate database.

CHAPTER 16

Secure POP3 and IMAP Servers

Most e-mail environments require users to communicate across a network with the e-mail server to send and receive messages, a process that's usually done with POP3 and IMAP (see Chapter 3, "POP3," and Chapter 4, "IMAP"). The problem with these protocols is that they transfer messages across the network using plain ASCII text, which could leave your users vulnerable to network snooping by others.

To help alleviate the problem of sending plain text across the network, the Secure Socket Layer (SSL) family of protocols has been developed. SSL allows network hosts to encrypt data before sending it across the network and allows the receiving host to decrypt the data back into its normal form. By using SSL, you can create a more secure environment for your users to send and receive their mail messages.

This chapter describes the SSL protocols and how they are used with common mail protocols. Next, this chapter describes the open source SSL package OpenSSL and explains how it can be used along with the University of Washington's IMAP and POP3 server packages to provide an encrypted environment for your users to remotely read their mail messages.

The SSL Family of Protocols

SSL started out as a proprietary protocol developed by the Netscape Corporation for use on its Internet Web servers and browsers. Netscape realized the importance of ensuring secure communications between clients and servers across the Internet, and SSL provided a method for encrypting sensitive information to prevent unauthorized viewing by anyone other than the intended recipient.

After two versions of SSL had been released with mixed reviews, Netscape released the SSL specification to the public for comments. Feedback from the public resulted in SSL version 3.0, an open specification for secure communications across network connections.

The SSL specification, while now open and widely used, is not an official Internet standard. The Internet Engineering Task Force (IETF), which is responsible for setting Internet standards, has taken the SSL version 3.0 protocol and modified it to create the Transport Layer Security (TLS) protocol. TLS is fully backward-compatible with SSL, and is accepted as the Internet standard for encrypting network communications.

The following sections describe the SSL and TLS protocols and how they are used to make standard POP3 and IMAP connection secure.

The SSL Protocol

The SSL protocol was designed to fit between the standard TCP/IP protocol and the application data placed in the network packet. It does not infringe on the standard TCP/IP packets, nor does it affect the application data. Figure 16.1 illustrates how SSL fits in the network layer diagram.

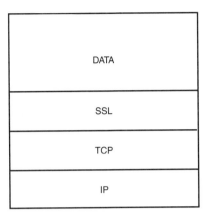

FIGURE 16.1

The SSL protocol in relation to TCP/IP.

The SSL protocol differentiates between *connections* and *sessions*. A client can initiate a single SSL session with a remote server, and then initiate multiple connections, or network applications, within the single session.

The SSL session is responsible for establishing and maintaining a secure environment for the connections, as well as authenticating the data sent by the sender. Table 16.1 lists the elements included in an SSL session.

TABLE 16.1 SSL Session Elements

Element	Description
identifier	An arbitrary byte sequence that identifies the session state.
certificate	An X.509 certificate that identifies the server.
compression	A method of compressing application data before encryption.
cipher	A data encryption algorithm and Message Authentication Code (MAC) that authenticates the application data placed in the SSL packet.
secret	A 48-byte code that is shared between the client and server for the encryption algorithm.
resumable	A flag indicating whether the session is a continuation of a previous session.

The connection is responsible for establishing and maintaining the individual application's network state. Table 16.2 lists the elements included in an SSL connection.

TABLE 16.2 SSL Connection Elements

Element	Description
server and client random	The byte sequences chosen by the server and client for each connection.
server write MAC secret	The code used in MAC operations on data sent by the server.
client write MAC secret	The code used in MAC operations on data sent by the client.
server write key	The bulk cipher key for data encrypted by the server and decrypted by the client.
client write key	The bulk cipher key for data encrypted by the client and decrypted by the server.
initialization vectors	Flags that identify the Cipher Block Chaining (CBC) mode for the connection.
sequence numbers	Flags that identify the sequence of SSL packets transmitted. The client and server maintain their own sets of sequence numbers.

The SSL protocol itself consists of two separate parts:

- A core protocol to transmit and receive SSL data
- A set of control packets used to control the SSL session

The SSL specifications define the core protocol as the Record Protocol. This is where the security and data integrity functions are performed.

The control packets are used to help establish, manage, and close the SSL session. Three separate types of control packets are used in SSL:

- Handshake Protocol
- Change Cipher Specification Protocol
- Alert Protocol

The following sections describe the SSL Record Protocol as well as the various control protocol packets.

The SSL Record Protocol

Each SSL packet transmitted across the network is considered a *record*. The SSL Record Protocol supplies five functions for the SSL session:

- **Fragmentation**   Breaks long packets into 16,384-byte packets. Client message boundaries are not preserved in the fragments.
- **Compression**   A compression algorithm can be applied to the client message fragment.
- **Message authentication**   A MAC is calculated for the compressed data by using a shared secret key. The MAC enables the client to validate the original server message.

- **Message encryption**   The resulting compressed data and MAC packet are encrypted to ensure security across the network.
- **Header bytes**   A 40-bit SSL packet header is prepended to the encrypted message. The packet header consists of an 8-bit Content-Type identifier, an 8-bit Major Version identifier, an 8-bit Minor Version identifier, and the 16-bit length of the compressed data fragment.

Figure 16.2 illustrates these functions within the SSL Record Protocol.

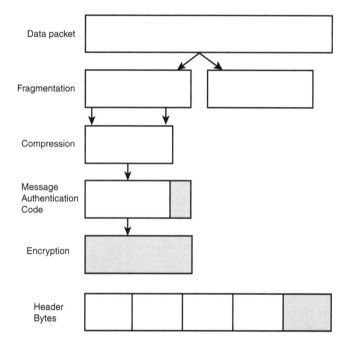

FIGURE 16.2

The SSL Record Protocol.

Besides normal data packets, the Record Protocol can also contain one of the three control packets to the remote host. Each control packet is handled in the same way as a normal data packet, using all five functions listed previously.

The SSL Handshake Protocol

The SSL Handshake Protocol enables the server and client to negotiate session parameters, using 10 different types of handshake packets. Table 16.3 lists the handshake packets and their descriptions.

TABLE 16.3 SSL Handshake Protocol Types

Type	Description
hello_request	Sent by the server to inform the client to initiate the handshake protocol.
client_hello	Sent by the client to initiate the SSL session. Identifies a list of cipher and compression methods that the client can use for the session.
server_hello	Sent by the server in response to the client_hello packet. It identifies the cipher and compression methods that the server selects to use from the client's list.
certificate	Sent by the server to authenticate itself to the client.
server_key_exchange	If the server does not have a certificate to authenticate itself, it can send its public key used for decrypting encrypted messages.
certificate_request	The server can request that the client send its certificate to authenticate the client.
server_hello_done	Indicates the end of the server hello messages.
client_certificate	Sent by the client if the server sends a certificate_request handshake packet.
client_key_exchange	Sent by the client to identify its public key used for decrypting encrypted messages sent by the client.
certificate_verify	Sent by the client to verify the client certificate sent.
finished	Sent after a Change Cipher Specification Protocol packet to verify that the key exchange and authentication processes were successful.

The SSL Change Cipher Specification Protocol

The SSL Change Cipher Specification Protocol is used to signal transitions in the cipher type used during an active SSL session. This method is often used to increase the connection's security. Changing cipher types during the connection makes it more difficult for a third party to decode the message transmission.

The SSL Alert Protocol

The SSL Alert Protocol enables the client or server to notify its peer of a problem with the SSL session. The alert message conveys the severity of the error and a description of the problem. Table 16.4 lists the alert types that can be sent.

TABLE 16.4 SSL Alert Protocol Alert Types

Alert	Description
bad_certificate	A received certificate was corrupt.
bad_record_mac	A record was received with a bad MAC.
certificate_expired	A certificate has expired or is not currently valid.
certificate_revoked	A certificate was revoked by its signer.
certificate_unknown	A certificate was rejected for some other reason.
close_notify	The connection is about to be closed.
decompression_failure	Could not decompress the compressed packet.
handshake_failure	Unable to negotiate an acceptable set of security parameters in the handshake protocol.
illegal_parameter	A field in the handshake protocol was out of range or inconsistent with other fields.
no_certificate	No certificate is available for the certificate request.
unexpected_message	An inappropriate message was received.
unsupported_certificate	A certificate was of an unsupported type.

The TLS Protocol

As mentioned, the TLS protocol is a modification of the SSL version 3.0 protocol. In fact, in the header bytes it's identified as version 3.1. All the features described for the SSL protocol apply to the TLS protocol. The TLS protocol extends the SSL features by adding several extra capabilities to the existing SSL structure.

TLS improves on several detail features, such as the algorithm used to calculate the MAC values and the way it uses padding to help defeat attacks that try to decrypt TLS packets. Several other SSL features have been expanded, such as alert types. The TLS Alert Protocol uses all the alert types defined in the SSL specification, but adds 12 more alert types. Table 16.5 lists the additional alert types used in TLS.

TABLE 16.5 TLS Alert Protocol Additional Alert Types

Alert	Description
access_denied	A valid certificate was received but the sender is denied access.
decode_error	A message could not be decoded because of an error in a field.
decrypt_error	A handshake cryptographic function failed.
decryption_failed	The receiver could not decrypt the encrypted message.
export_restriction	An encryption negotiation not in compliance with export restrictions was detected.
insufficient_security	The server requires a cipher with a higher level of security.

TABLE 16.5 Continued

Alert	Description
internal_error	An internal error unrelated to the peer was detected.
no_renegotiation	The sender is not able to renegotiate the session.
protocol_version	The protocol version negotiated is not supported.
record_overflow	A TLS record was received with a length that exceeded the maximum allowed (18,432 bytes).
unknown_ca	A valid certificate was received, but the certificate authority's (CA's) certificate did not match a known trusted CA.
user_canceled	The handshake is being canceled because of an unrelated protocol failure.

The OpenSSL Package

The OpenSSL package has become the most popular method used by open source programs to supply SSL functionality. OpenSSL provides an open source set of libraries and utilities that enables a network application to incorporate SSL version 1.0, 2.0, and 3.0 as well as TLS.

The following sections describe how to download and install the OpenSSL package and how to configure it for use with network applications.

Downloading and Compiling OpenSSL

You can download the OpenSSL package from the OpenSSL Project Web site (http://www.openssl.org). At the time of this writing, two versions of the package are available for downloading. The main package (openssl-0.9.6b) is used to add SSL capabilities to network applications by supplying a set of C APIs and header files. Alternatively, a package that contains only the OpenSSL engine that can be interfaced to external cryptographic hardware can be downloaded (openssl-0.9.6b-engine). The OpenSSL Project expects these two versions to merge when version 0.9.7 is released.

You can also download the latest version of OpenSSL from the OpenSSL FTP server at ftp://ftp.openssl.org/source/.

At the time of this writing, the latest production version available is openssl-0.9.6b.tar.gz. After downloading the source code distribution, you unpack into a working directory by using this tar command:

```
tar -zxvf openssl-0.9.6b.tar.gz -C /usr/local/src
```

This command creates the directory /usr/local/src/openssl-0.9.6b and places the source code there. You must change to the working directory to complete the rest of the installation.

As with other open source packages, the first step is to run the config program, which determines the operating environment of your Unix system and prepares the necessary makefiles for the make program.

By placing parameters on the config command line, you can configure special features and modify default values of the OpenSSL package. Table 16.6 lists the options that can be used with the config program.

TABLE 16.6 OpenSSL Config Options

Option	Description
--prefix=*DIR*	Defines the directory of the OpenSSL libraries, binary files, and certificates (default = /usr/local/ssl).
--openssldir=*DIR*	Defines the directory for the OpenSSL certificates. If no prefix is defined, library and binary files are also placed here (default = /usr/local/ssl).
no-threads	Doesn't include support for multithreaded applications.
threads	Includes support for multithreaded applications.
no-shared	Doesn't create shared libraries.
shared	Creates shared libraries.
no-asm	Doesn't use assembler code.
386	Uses the 386 instruction set code only (default = 486 code).
no-*cipher*	Does not include support for specified encryption type.

After you determine which (if any) options are required for your environment, you can run the config program:

```
./config
```

The config program attempts to automatically determine the type of Unix system you are compiling OpenSSL on and creates the OpenSSL makefiles accordingly. If for some reason the config program has difficulty determining your Unix system type, you can manually define it by using the Configure program. The Configure program performs the same function as the config program, but it also allows you to manually define your Unix system from a long list of possibilities. You can run the Configure program without parameters to see the system types defined.

After running the config (or Configure) program, you can issue the make command to create the binary files and libraries, make test to test the created files, and make install to install the OpenSSL files in the location specified in the config program.

CAUTION

You must have **root** privileges to run the make install command to install OpenSSL in the appropriate directories.

Using Certificates

Certificates are digital files that identify an entity to a remote client by a digital signature that's normally signed by an authorization entity (see the "S/MIME" section in Chapter 5, "MIME," for more information about digital signatures). The most popular certificates use the X.509 standard to implement digital signatures.

The certificate authority (CA) is a company that validates your identity (either as a person or a corporation) and creates a digital certificate verifying that you are who you say you are. You can then use that certificate to authenticate yourself to any remote client that recognizes the CA as valid.

Usually a private encryption key is included along with the certificate as a single package. The receiving client uses your public key to validate any data you encrypt with your certificate.

Each application that uses OpenSSL must have a valid X.509 certificate file that uniquely identifies itself to all potential clients. This certificate file must be installed in the OpenSSL certs directory, which by default is /usr/local/ssl/certs.

The different certificate files are identified by application name, as shown here:

`app.pem`

For OpenSSL to match certificates with applications, the name `app` must match the application's executable filename. For example, the OpenSSL certificate for the imapd program is named `imapd.pem`.

You can purchase a digital certificate from a commercial CA company that allows your server to be uniquely authenticated to other remote servers and clients. The benefit of using a commercial certificate is that most users will recognize the certificate's validity if a respected company has validated its authenticity. Many companies, such as Verisign and RSA Data Security, Inc., offer certificates.

You can also create your own certificate and validate it yourself. If you do this, your users must know you and trust that your certificate is valid. This method could be enough for many small local networks, but if you are building your mail server for an e-mail environment that includes external users, it is strongly suggested that you purchase a valid digital certificate.

For testing purposes, or if you are using your mail server in a small network environment, OpenSSL has a method for creating your own digital certificate file. This certificate does not necessarily uniquely identify your server to any user in the world, but it will serve its purpose for your local network.

The openssl program, which is included in the OpenSSL distribution, can be used for a variety of different functions:

- Creating RSA, Diffie-Hulman (DH), and Digital Signature Algorithm (DSA) key parameters
- Creating X.509 certificates
- Calculating Message Digests
- Encrypting and decrypting with ciphers
- Testing SSL/TLS clients and servers
- Handling S/MIME signed or encrypted messages

This is the format for the `openssl` command:

```
openssl command [command_opts] [command_args]
```

Many *command* options can be used to determine how the openssl program operates. To create a new X.509 digital certificate, you should use the `req` command, which starts the X.509 Certificate Signing Request (CSR) Management for handling X.509 certificates.

To control the certificate, several command arguments, listed in Table 16.7, are used with the `req` command.

TABLE 16.7 OpenSSL req Arguments

Argument	Description
-inform *arg*	Set the input format to *arg*.
-outform *arg*	Set the output format to *arg*.
-in *file*	Use the input file specified by *file*.
-out *file*	Use the output file specified by *file*.
-text	Text form of the request.
-noout	Do not display req.
-verify	Verify the signature of the req.
-modulus	RSA modulus.
-nodes	Do not encrypt the output key.
-key *file*	Use the private key found in *file*.
-keyform *arg*	Define the format of the private key.
-keyout *file*	File to send the key to.
-rand *file:file:...*	Load the file(s) into the random number generator.
-newkey rsa:*bits*	Generate a new RSA key of the size specified by *bits*.
-newkey dsa:*file*	Generate a new DSA key using the parameters found in *file*.
-[*digest*]	Use *digest* to sign the certificate.
-config *file*	Use the template file specified by *file*.
-new	Create a new request.
-x509	Create an X.509 certificate.
-days *days*	Set the certificate to be valid for the number of days specified by *days*.

TABLE 16.7 Continued

Argument	Description
-newhdr	Display "NEW" in the header lines.
-asn1-kludge	Display the certificate in a format that is wrong but some CAs report as requiring.
-extensions	Specify a certificate extension section.
-reqexts	Specify a request extension section.

You can use any combination of these command arguments to create, view, or modify your certificates. The common format for creating a new certificate looks like this:

```
openssl req -new -x509 -nodes -out imapd.pem -keyout imapd.pem -days 3650
```

This command creates a new X.509 certificate named imapd.pem (remember that the certificate name must match the application name), places both the certificate and the private key in the same file, and makes it valid for 3,650 days (about 10 years).

When you run this command, the openssl program asks you several questions that you must answer to create the certificate. The answers are used to place information about the certificate issuer (you) into the certificate. Listing 16.1 shows a sample openssl session.

LISTING 16.1 Sample Openssl Session

```
#openssl req -new -x509 -nodes -out imapd.pem -keyout imapd.pem -days 3650
Using configuration from /usr/local/ssl/openssl.cnf
Generating a 1024 bit RSA private key
.....++++++
...................++++++
writing new private key to 'imapd.pem'
-----
You are about to be asked to enter information that will be incorporated
into your certificate request.
What you are about to enter is what is called a Distinguished Name or a DN.
There are quite a few fields but you can leave some blank
For some fields there will be a default value,
If you enter '.', the field will be left blank.
-----
Country Name (2 letter code) [AU]:US
State or Province Name (full name) [Some-State]:Indiana
Locality Name (eg, city) []:Indianapolis
Organization Name (eg, company) [Internet Widgits Pty Ltd]:E-mail book
Organizational Unit Name (eg, section) []:Chapter 16
Common Name (eg, YOUR name) []:shadrach.ispnet1.net
Email Address []:postmaster@shadrach.ispnet1.net
#
```

One important item is the Common Name query. You should use your hostname for this value. If you don't, some SSL clients will either warn the user that the certificate was not issued to the server or refuse to accept the certificate altogether.

The openssl program creates the certificate file imapd.pem in the current directory. The certificate file should contain a private key as well as the certificate. Listing 16.2 shows the certificate created using the information from Listing 16.1.

LISTING 16.2 Sample X.509 Certificate File

```
-----BEGIN RSA PRIVATE KEY-----
MIICWwIBAAKBgQCe6FJRP5YPtuZylFy3FDaRNShvrZUJzjsGH9SaiGLG1+Zoq42f
fwlvJV6+cijTaMBENt59g9LRtPoLZo0DyLuXCXjfTKdNQ7Yre0/GBvUmzfR/IUtQ
U7ovCL4QLEerorp4AydFDmaROgeQ5oJf4sbZ8nWTKo3byXg0y5sj0D2oiQIDAQAB
AoGAWHtsOql5WU6yiuJprdenertqxKSW9FrNKt/WdiWzOp1FQssjlMgb7LOWSd0v
NmiBhno28RTR8sse3/I+WvkO2m5hQO9HtjBFaA03ndWn15Dp6C8scb/mXmx35Ttz
dsNuCPe8z+1PwEhXOris/Rmsxu+XEdYBouJWwpwOeULrygECQQDK2tNiQxzvTMwD
evaYX89KRm2iWWwI/WnBvuMR9tzoWogIwbHFfOF/waj+f3NL7sXSSUvujXGbWKQ3
qS5a2RN5AkEAyIoEDgYzzzWKxpnG1h3SXCG6VLygKFV2RA/qqLhWPfmYqwcnESFD
lIGneqHDxRp3bkfS+GgQzmVYfgzNzHVpkQJAYC0fy5bGQS7IC15hTB0gyrZZhH+h
GSIM4i7+uaWxVviVRpGPF3L99vR6iy8iGv46DFl0BsZI9r4wHbO4ppoFAQJABQfR
SjjFm/EP5iN9ZWmiGUWPUwjYS6q5KMPtcwYMw8k7Fy86v6dB9ru5482jB5K+ZDnR
BQI3SbYpHiBcGUDowQJASOvZywhfRi4KudIVXP0uuu1GB214YwJE/UkrbB0xEJXG
lPlWuGlclFop/9RDAiIVWWvyFwleyU2iUIU7lgUcIw==
-----END RSA PRIVATE KEY-----
-----BEGIN CERTIFICATE-----
MIID6zCCA1SgAwIBAgIBADANBgkqhkiG9w0BAQQFADCBsDELMAkGA1UEBhMCVVMx
EDAOBgNVBAgTB0luZGlhbmExFTATBgNVBAcTDEluZGlhbmFwb2xpczEUMBIGA1UE
ChMLRS1tYWlsIGJvb2sxEzARBgNVBAsTCkNoYXB0ZXIgMTYxHTAbBgNVBAMTFHNo
YWRyYWNoLmlzcG5ldDEubmV0MS4wLAYJKoZIhvcNAQkBFh9wb3N0bWFzdGVyQHNo
YWRyYWNoLmlzcG5ldDEubmV0MB4XDTAxMDcxOTEyMzYwNloXDTExMDcxNzEyMzYw
NlowgbAxCzAJBgNVBAYTAlVTMRAwDgYDVQQIEwdJbmRpYW5hMRUwEwYDVQQHEwxJ
bmRpYW5hcG9saXMxFDASBgNVBAoTC0UtbWFpbCBib29rMRMwEQYDVQQLEwpDaGFw
dGVyIDE2MR0wGwYDVQQDExRzaGGFkcmFjaC5pc3BuZXQxLm5ldDEuMCwGCSqGSIb3
DQEJARYfcG9zdG1hc3RlckBzaGFkcmFjaC5pc3BuZXQxLm5ldDCBnzANBgkqhkiG
9w0BAQEFAAOBjQAwgYkCgYEAnuhSUT+WD7bmcpRctxQ2kTUob62VCc47Bh/Umohi
xtfmaKuNn38JbyVevnIo02jARDbefYPS0bT6C2aNA8i7lwl430ynTUO2K3tPxgb1
Js30fyFLUFO6Lwi+ECxHq6K6eAMnRQ5mkToHkOaCX+LG2fJ1kyqN28l4NMubI9A9
qIkCAwEAAaOCAREwggENMB0GA1UdDgQWBBQIvRzPo76c2yJMfIEqOIC1ggh3bzCB
3QYDVR0jBIHVMIHSgBQIvRzPo76c2yJMfIEqOIC1ggh3b6GBtqSBszCBsDELMAkG
A1UEBhMCVVMxEDAOBgNVBAgTB0luZGlhbmExFTATBgNVBAcTDEluZGlhbmFwb2xp
czEUMBIGA1UEChMLRS1tYWlsIGJvb2sxEzARBgNVBAsTCkNoYXB0ZXIgMTYxHTAb
BgNVBAMTFHNoYWRyYWNoLmlzcG5ldDEubmV0MS4wLAYJKoZIhvcNAQkBFh9wb3N0
-----
```

LISTING 16.2 Continued

bWFzdGVyQHNoYWRyYWNoLmlzcG5ldDEubm0ggEAMAwGA1UdEwQFMAMBAf8wDQYJ
KoZIhvcNAQEEBQADgYEAjP2rcXaKTbG5W7loXPooEaHVHo8iJvne0HeOuF5wvSvy
ohJSEMvHq5x+jmYcS7lWbakIGGHLHhVRMN5rhEZYiCiQZoUxCEs4wgk3JPORdbH4
Mdu882f+E5060kOP/7P/KmJhRiX/aK0kZC/aKor2Iq0oBsZAVoP//Aq2Le8pH5Q=
-----END CERTIFICATE-----

Note that the certificate just defines your organization and server, not individual applications. You can use the same certificate for all of your applications that use OpenSSL. Remember to copy the certificate file to the /usr/local/ssl/certs directory, and create a copy for each application that will use it:

```
cp imapd.pem /usr/local/ssl/certs/imapd.pem
cp imapd.pem /usr/local/ssl/certs/ipop3d.pem
```

After the certificate files have been created and moved to the OpenSSL certificate directory (or if you purchased a commercial certificate, after you have renamed it and moved it to the certificate directory), you are ready to modify your network application to use SSL. The next section describes using POP3 and IMAP servers with the OpenSSL libraries.

Using UW IMAP with SSL

One of the most popular open source POP3 and IMAP server packages is the UW IMAP package, developed at the University of Washington. It includes POP3 as well as IMAP server software and can be compiled to use the OpenSSL libraries to provide SSL connectivity for standard POP3 and IMAP sessions.

The following sections describe how to download, install, and configure UW IMAP to use the OpenSSL libraries.

Downloading and Compiling UW IMAP

Many Unix distributions already come with a UW IMAP binary package. You can choose to install UW IMAP from the distribution that came with your UNIX system, or you can download the current source code file and build it yourself.

The University of Washington currently supports a Web site for the IMAP software project at http://www.washington.edu/imap/. This site contains information about the UW IMAP project at the university as well as links to the current release of UW IMAP. The current release at the time of this writing is version 2001.

NOTE

Note that before the imap-2000 release, the version name for UW IMAP was in a different format. The version before the 2000 release was version 4.0.7.

There are also many development versions you can download as new features and patches are developed. The development versions are marked with the phrase BETA.SNAP-*yymmddhhmm* (*yymmddhhmm* represents the year, date, and time of the development release).

You can download the source code distribution with the link supplied at the Web site, or you can connect directly to the FTP site at ftp.cac.washington.edu and check the /imap directory for the current release version. A link named imap.tar.Z is always set to the current release version. At the time of this writing, it is imap-2001.BETA.SNAP-0107112053. Remember to use FTP binary mode when retrieving the file.

After downloading the source code distribution file, unpack into a working directory using this command:

```
tar -zxvf imap.tar.Z -C /usr/local/src
```

This command produces a subdirectory named after the release version and places the source code in subdirectories underneath it.

The UW IMAP program does not use the config program, as it does not have any feature options that are necessary to add at compile time. Instead, features are defined as make command-line options.

One feature that must be included, however, is the type of password method you are using on your Unix system. The UW IMAP makefile uses a three-character code to define different types of Unix systems and password methods.

Many Unix distributions offer only one password method. If your system is one of these, all you need to do is find the three-character code for your Unix system to use on the make command line. For Unix distributions that offer multiple password authentication methods (such as Linux), you must determine the password method your system uses and include the appropriate three-character code. All the codes can be found in the makefile's comments section. Table 16.8 shows a few common system codes for various Unix systems.

TABLE 16.8 UW IMAP make Options

Option	Description
bsd	Generic BSD-based systems
bsf	FreeBSD systems
gso	GCC Solaris
gsu	GCC Sun
hpx	HP-UX 10.x systems
lnx	Traditional Linux systems
lnp	Linux with Pluggable Authentication Modules (PAMs)
neb	NetBSD systems

TABLE 16.8 Continued

Option	Description
s40	Sun 4.0
sl4	Linux using -lshadow for passwords
sl5	Linux using shadow passwords
slx	Linux using -lcrypt for passwords

Each code represents a different makefile section used to compile IMAP for your system. For Linux systems that use shadow passwords, for example, you can use the slx option.

After the password method code, you must include options to instruct UW IMAP to include SSL support in the programs. This is done using several different variables, listed in Table 16.9, in the command line.

TABLE 16.9 UW IMAP SSL Variables

Variable	Description
SSLTYPE	Defines whether SSL support is included (default = none)
SSLDIR	Defines the base OpenSSL directory (default = /usr/local/ssl)
SSLCERT	Defines the OpenSSL certificates directory (default = SSLDIR/certs)
SSLINCLUDE	Defines the OpenSSL header file directory (default = SSLDIR/include)
SSLLIB	Defines the OpenSSL library file directory (default = SSLDIR/lib)
SSLCRYPTO	Defines the OpenSSL crypto library (default = -lcrypto)

For default OpenSSL installations, the only option you need to set is the SSLTYPE option. It should be set to unix to enable SSL support in the executable programs.

After determining the options required to compile UW IMAP in your environment, you can run the make program:

```
make slx SSLTYPE=unix
```

This command compiles the source code and produces the IMAP executables located in the distribution's subdirectories. The next step is to install and configure the individual IMAP pieces.

Three executable programs are produced by UW IMAP:

- **ipop2d**   Aa POP2 server
- **ipop3d**   A POP3 server
- **imapd**   An IMAP server

The two POP servers are located in the ipopd directory, and the imapd server is located in the imapd directory. You should copy these files to a common location on the mail server so that it's easier to protect the file permissions for the inetd program, as shown here:

```
cp ipopd/ipop2d /usr/sbin
cp ipopd/ipop3d /usr/sbin
cp imapd/imapd /usr/sbin
```

These commands should be issued as the root user, thus protecting the ipopd and imapd servers from tampering. This completes the installation of the UW IMAP package. The ipop3d and imapd programs use the inetd program to detect incoming POP3 or IMAP sessions and start the server. The next section describes how to configure inetd to support UW IMAP.

Configuring Inetd for UW IMAP

The inetd program uses two separate configuration files. The /etc/services file defines TCP and UDP ports that can be monitored for network connections. All Unix distributions include this file with the most common network application ports defined. The second configuration file, /etc/inetd.conf, tells inetd which application a received network connection should be forwarded to.

The following sections describe the changes required for the /etc/services and /etc/inetd.conf files for secure POP3 and IMAP.

Modifying the /etc/services File

As mentioned in Chapter 2, the standard TCP port used for POP3 connections is port 110. The inetd program monitors TCP port 110, waiting for incoming network connections. As new connections are received, they are passed to the ipop3d program.

The /etc/services file defines the port name, the IP protocol type (TCP or UDP), and the port number in this form:

```
app     port/type
```

For POP3 the entry should look like this:

```
pop3    110/tcp
```

Many Unix distributions also include a separate entry for POP3 that defines the UDP port 110. UW IMAP does not use this entry, however.

A separate TCP port has been defined for use with SSL POP3 sessions. TCP port 995 has been designated for SSL POP3 connections. Not all /etc/services files include this definition, though. If your services file does not include an entry for SSL POP3, you must add it:

```
pop3s    995/tcp
```

Note that the application entry is pop3s. According to the UW IMAP documentation, this value must be set to pop3s for UW IMAP to work properly. My Mandrake Linux system originally defined this port as spop3, so it needed to be changed.

Similarly, SSL IMAP uses a different port than normal IMAP does. As described in Chapter 3, the standard IMAP TCP port is 143. The SSL IMAP TCP port is 993, so again, make sure the appropriate entries are listed in the /etc/services file, as shown here:

```
imap      143/tcp
imaps     993/tcp
```

Again, the UW IMAP documentation specifies that the application name must be set to imaps for SSL IMAP to work properly. My Mandrake Linux system originally defined this port as simap, so it needed to be changed, too.

Modifying the /etc/inetd.conf File

After modifying the /etc/services file, you need to make entries in the /etc/inetd.conf file for the SSL POP3 and IMAP servers. Inetd uses the /etc/inetd.conf file to determine which network ports to monitor and what applications to forward incoming network connection attempts to.

The /etc/inetd.conf entry consists of several fields separated by a tab or a space. Table 16.10 lists the fields used in the /etc/inetd.conf file.

TABLE 16.10 inet.conf Entry Fields

Field	Description
service	The name of the service, related to the /etc/services entry name.
socket type	The type of network socket used for data transport: stream, dgram, raw, or rdm (reliably delivered message).
protocol	The network protocol used for communication (tcp or udp).
dgramstate[.max]	The state of the datagram socket (wait or nowait). For stream sockets, it should be set to nowait. max defines the maximum number of server instances allowed to start in a 60-second interval (default = 40)
user.[group]	The username and optional group name that the server process runs under.
program	The full path of the server program.
arguments	Any command-line parameters used for the server program.

Separate /etc/inetd.conf entries need to be made for pop3, pop3s, imap, and imaps. The pop3 and pop3s entries both use the ipop3d program, and the imap and imaps entries both use the imapd program. Listing 16.3 shows sample entries.

LISTING 16.3 SSL POP3 and IMAP inetd.conf Entries

```
pop3    stream  tcp nowait  root    /usr/sbin/ipop3d    ipop3d
pop3s   stream  tcp nowait  root    /usr/sbin/ipop3d    ipop3d
imap    stream  tcp nowait  root    /usr/sbin/imapd     imapd
imaps   stream  tcp nowait  root    /usr/sbin/imapd     imapd
```

If you are running a high-volume mail server, you might want to increase the number of new sessions allowed above the 40 per minute default. To do so, add a period and then the new number after the `nowait` parameter, as shown here:

```
pop3s   stream  tcp nowait.100  root    /usr/sbin/ipop3d    ipop3d
```

Remember that increasing this value puts additional strain on your mail server. You might have to experiment with this value to determine what your particular mail server can handle without becoming overloaded.

After adding the entries to the /etc/inetd.conf file, you must restart the inetd program for them to take effect. To do that, use the Unix `kill` command with the `-HUP` option, but first determine the process ID (PID) of the currently running inetd program:

```
# ps ax | grep inetd
  349 ?        S       0:00 inetd
  707 pts/0    S       0:00 grep inetd
# kill -HUP 349
#
```

After restarting the inetd process, you should be ready to test the new UW IMAP installation. The next section describes a technique for doing this.

Testing UW IMAP

The newly installed inetd configuration should now allow the mail server to accept network connections on all of the POP3 and IMAP ports. As shown in Chapters 2 and 3, you can issue `telnet` on ports 110 and 143 to test the normal POP3 and IMAP servers. Listing 16.4 demonstrates this simple test.

LISTING 16.4 Testing the Normal POP3 and IMAP Servers

```
$ telnet localhost 110
Trying 127.0.0.1...
Connected to localhost.
Escape character is '^]'.
+OK POP3 localhost v2001.76 server ready
USER rich
+OK User name accepted, password please
```

LISTING 16.4 Continued

```
PASS guitar
+OK Mailbox open, 1 messages
QUIT
+OK Sayonara
Connection closed by foreign host.


$ telnet localhost 143
Trying 127.0.0.1...
Connected to localhost.
Escape character is '^]'.
* OK [CAPABILITY IMAP4REV1 LOGIN-REFERRALS STARTTLS AUTH=LOGIN] localhost
➡ IMAP4rev1 2001.309 at Thu, 19 Jul 2001 20:06:42 -0500 (EST)
a001 LOGIN rich guitar
* CAPABILITY IMAP4REV1 IDLE NAMESPACE MAILBOX-REFERRALS SCAN SORT
➡ THREAD=REFERENCES THREAD=ORDEREDSUBJECT MULTIAPPEND
a001 OK LOGIN completed
a002 LOGOUT
* BYE shadrach.ispnet1.net IMAP4rev1 server terminating connection
a002 OK LOGOUT completed
Connection closed by foreign host.
$
```

Although testing the normal POP3 and IMAP servers does not help you determine whether the SSL servers are running, it does allow you to make sure the UW POP3 and IMAP servers can validate your username and password properly. If you can connect to the ports but not log in to the servers, you must examine the password validation method compiled into the servers and determine that it's valid for your Unix system.

Next, you can perform a test to determine whether the SSL POP3 and IMAP servers are running properly. The openssl program included with OpenSSL can also be used as a test client to establish an SSL connection with a server. The s_client command option is used to establish a session with an SSL server, so the command used to test the SSL POP3 server would be the following:

```
openssl s_client -host localhost -port 995
```

This command connects to the SSL POP3 server on the host and establishes the SSL session. All the detailed SSL handshaking information is displayed, enabling you to debug any problems that you might encounter. After the SSL session is established, the standard POP3 session banner appears. Listing 16.5 shows the last few lines of the openssl POP3 session.

LISTING 16.5 Testing the SSL POP3 Server

```
$ /usr/local/ssl/bin/openssl s_client -host localhost -port 995
CONNECTED(00000003)
depth=0 /C=US/ST=Indiana/L=Indianapolis/O=E-mail book/OU=Chapter 16/
➥CN=shadrach.ispnet1.net
verify error:num=18:self signed certificate
verify return:1
depth=0 /C=US/ST=Indiana/L=Indianapolis/O=E-mail book/OU=Chapter 16/
➥CN=shadrach.ispnet1.net
verify return:1
--
Certificate chain
 0 s:/C=US/ST=Indiana/L=Indianapolis/O=E-mail book/OU=Chapter 16/
➥CN=shadrach.ispnet1.net
   i:/C=US/ST=Indiana/L=Indianapolis/O=E-mail book/OU=Chapter 16/
➥CN=shadrach.ispnet1.net
--
Server certificate
--BEGIN CERTIFICATE-----
MIIDPzCCAqigAwIBAgIBADANBgkqhkiG9w0BAQQFADB5MQswCQYDVQQGEwJVUzEQ
MA4GA1UECBMHSW5kaWFuYTEVMBMGA1UEBxMMSW5kaWFuYXBvbGlzMRYwFAYDVQQK
--END CERTIFICATE-----
subject=/C=US/ST=Indiana/L=Indianapolis/O=E-mail book/OU=Chapter 16/
➥CN=shadrach.ispnet1.net
issuer=/C=US/ST=Indiana/L=Indianapolis/O=E-mail book/OU=Chapter 16/
➥CN=shadrach.ispnet1.net
--
No client certificate CA names sent
--
SSL handshake has read 989 bytes and written 320 bytes
--
New, TLSv1/SSLv3, Cipher is DES-CBC3-SHA
Server public key is 1024 bit
SSL-Session:
    Protocol  : TLSv1
    Cipher    : DES-CBC3-SHA
    Session-ID: 8AC70E01DDBF80E5027D110C490D3BDAAE8031312AC8CC01904A58471AE
    Session-ID-ctx:
    Master-Key: F276BD43CE6293E1E93390E9426F0940B83C1A0F0E8488C3C7B72BCB604
    Key-Arg   : None
    Start Time: 995731589
    Timeout   : 300 (sec)
    Verify return code: 18 (self signed certificate)
```

LISTING 16.5 Continued

```
- -

+OK POP3 localhost v2001.76 server ready
USER rich
+OK User name accepted, password please
PASS guitar
+OK Mailbox open, 0 messages
LIST
+OK Mailbox scan listing follows
.
QUIT
DONE
$
```

When the SSL service accepts the network connection, it begins the SSL handshake negotiations. Note that the openssl client notices the self-signed test certificate, but allows the SSL session to continue. After the SSL session has been validated and started, the normal POP3 session begins. You can exit the session by using the standard POP3 QUIT command.

You can similarly test the SSL IMAP server with the openssl command, but you must connect to port 993.

This test proves that the SSL POP3 and IMAP servers are running and responding to network connection requests. Your e-mail users should now be able to use their workstation MUA software in SSL mode to connect to the mail server.

Testing UW IMAP with a network client

Now that the UW IMAP server is configured and has been tested, you should be able to configure a network IMAP client to access the server using the SSL protocol. Most Windows-based POP3 and IMAP clients have an easy way of enabling SSL support. Figure 16.3 shows an example of how to set the SSL option for the Microsoft Outlook Express mail client package.

If you select the This Server Requires a Secure Connection (SSL) check box in the Properties dialog box, Outlook Express will connect to the remote mail server using the SSL protocol on TCP port 995 for the POP3 connection.

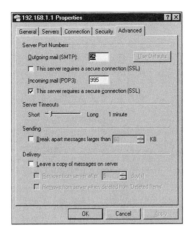

FIGURE 16.3

Enabling SSL support in Microsoft Outlook Express.

Summary

With the SSL protocol, users can read their mailboxes from remote workstations securely. The SSL protocol uses an encryption technique to ensure that communications between the mail server and the remote workstation are secure.

The OpenSSL package is open source software that provides SSL support for many network applications. The package consists of several C API libraries that network applications can use to validate authentication tokens used in the SSL protocol. After the server validates a remote workstation, the secure communication can begin.

One such network application is the UW IMAP server software. The UW IMAP server can be compiled with the OpenSSL software to give you an IMAP server that uses the SSL protocol for security. This server allows remote users to use IMAP workstation software to read their mail messages across a secure network connection.

CHAPTER 17

Secure Webmail Servers

The previous chapter described using secure POP3 and IMAP servers to allow remote users to securely read their messages on the mail server. Another alternative for remote users is reading their mail using a secure Web connection.

This chapter describes the new phenomenon of Webmail and how to build a secure Webmail server for your users using The Web Interface Gateway (TWIG) open source software package.

What Is Webmail?

The increase in popularity of the World Wide Web has spawned a new line of software products in many areas. Programmers are finding that using a Web-based interface increases the usability of their programs. Most users already know how to navigate around Web pages, so little if any user training is needed to use standard Web page controls such as hot links, drop-down lists, and control buttons.

E-mail client software is no different. Many companies have realized that by using Web-based e-mail client software, users can access their mail messages with little training and are able to access their mailboxes from a wider variety of computers (such as laptops for mobile users). There are many popular Internet Webmail implementations, such as Hotmail and Yahoo!, where users can connect to the mail server using only their Web browsers. Figure 17.1 shows how the Web-based e-mail client software interacts with the standard mail server.

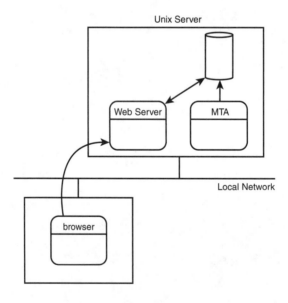

FIGURE 17.1

Using Web-based e-mail client software.

Users can use any standard Web browser to access messages stored in their mailboxes. Additionally, with most Web-based e-mail packages, users can create folders and store messages on the mail server in separate folders. By maintaining mailbox messages on the server, users can read all their messages from any computer, almost anywhere.

Several popular Web-based e-mail client packages are available for the Unix platform. Most of these packages require that both an MTA package and a Web server package be installed on the server (refer back to Figure 17.1). The following sections compare some of the Web-based e-mail packages available to mail administrators.

TWIG

Christopher Heschong developed the TWIG e-mail client package, which was originally released under the name Muppet. It is written using the PHP programming language and can be used with any Web browser that supports PHP programs. It uses the PHP IMAP programming interfaces, so it must connect to a running IMAP server on the mail server to read the mailbox messages.

TWIG also supports other features, such as scheduling, contact management, newsgroups, to-do lists, and bookmarks. It supports these extra features by incorporating an external database system, such as MySQL or Postgresql.

SqWebMail

The SqWebMail package is part of a complete MTA package called Courier. The Courier mail server package contains a complete MTA, an IMAP server, and a Web-based e-mail client solution for a mail server.

The Courier package is written in modular form, so each piece can be used independently of the others. The SqWebMail Web interface to Maildir-formatted mailboxes is popular with both Postfix and qmail MTA administrators. The SqWebMail program directly interfaces with Maildir mailboxes without the help of any MUA servers (that is, no POP3 or IMAP servers need to be running on the mail server).

IMHO

The IMHO Web-based e-mail client package was developed by the Roxen Internet Software corporation. It is based on the Roxen Unix Web server software and works only on that platform. IMHO was written using the Pike programming language, which is supported only by the Roxen server.

Like TWIG, IMHO connects to user mailboxes with a standard IMAP connection, thus requiring a separate IMAP server to be running on the mail server.

WebMail

Sebastian Schaffert created the WebMail package as a Web-based Java interface to standard mailboxes. Although it utilizes Java scripts in the Web browser, Java support is not required on the client computer browser. WebMail uses standard HTTP 1.1 Java support or can be run as a standard Java servlet on Web servers that support servlets. Sebastian claims that using a Java-based program is much faster than the normal CGI Web-based e-mail clients, such as SqWebMail.

The TWIG Webmail Server

The TWIG Webmail server uses the PHP programming language to create dynamic Web pages that enable users to read and send messages from the mail server. It also incorporates many additional features found in commercial e-mail packages, such as calendars, schedules, and newsgroups.

To support these additional features, TWIG must interface with a database, and can use any database that has PHP support. The two most popular open source databases used on the Unix platform are the MySQL and PostgreSQL packages.

The TWIG package requires that an IMAP server be running on the mail server. It connects to the mail server using IMAP to read and modify messages in users' mailboxes. Of course, the advantage of this feature is that the TWIG server does not have to be on the same system as the mail server. You can create a separate Web server to use for TWIG and even use the SSL IMAP protocol to securely transfer messages between the two servers. Figure 17.2 illustrates this method.

The TWIG package requires lots of support software to support all of the features on the server. You'll need the following list of packages:

- A Unix MTA package, such as sendmail, qmail, or Postfix
- The UW IMAP server package
- The Apache Web server
- The PHP language Apache plug-in
- The MySQL database server

Each package must be installed and configured on the server to support TWIG. Also, if you want to run the TWIG Webmail server in a secure environment, you need the OpenSSL and Apache mod_ssl packages to support secure SSL HTTP connectivity.

The following sections describe how to install and configure all the software required for a standard TWIG installation.

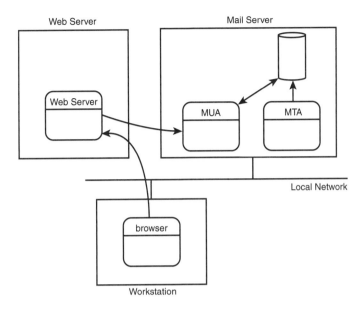

Web Server

Mail Server

FIGURE 17.2

Using TWIG on a separate server.

The MySQL Database

To start things off, you should install the database package that TWIG uses to store user information. The most popular open source database package on the Unix platform is MySQL.

The MySQL database package is available in both binary and source code distributions. Many Unix systems include a binary distribution for MySQL. If your distribution has one, you can install it and skip this section. Otherwise, continue on.

Using a Source Code Distribution

If your Unix system does not include a binary distribution of the MySQL database package, or you want to try the latest version, you can download the source code from the MySQL Web site and compile it yourself.

The MySQL software source code is distributed in several different versions of binary and source distributions for various Unix platforms. At the time of this writing, the latest stable release of MySQL is version 3.23.39. The source code can be downloaded from the MySQL download page at http://www.mysql.org.

After downloading the distribution of your choice, extract it into a working directory, as shown here:

```
tar -zxvf mysql-3.23.39.tar.gz -C /usr/local/src
```

After extracting the source code into a working directory, you can begin the steps for compiling and installing the source code. The following sections describe these steps.

Create the MySQL Username and Group Name

The MySQL database system must have a dedicated username and group name that it runs under. Using these names helps prevent security problems with the MySQL server software as it runs in background mode. Most database administrators create a group and user called mysql. On Linux systems, this can be accomplished by using these commands:

```
groupadd mysql
useradd -g mysql mysql
```

These commands create a new group and user using the next available user ID and group ID on the system.

Compile and Install MySQL

After creating the MySQL user and group names, you can begin compiling. The source code should already be extracted into a working directory, and all the compiling commands should be performed from this directory. This is the directory used for this example:

```
/usr/local/src/mysql-3.23.39
```

Two steps are required to compile the MySQL source code into the executable programs used for the database system. First, you must use the configure program to configure the MySQL makefile with any options necessary for your particular MySQL installation. Lots of options can be included with the MySQL installation. You can display a list of the available ones by using this command:

```
./configure —help
```

Table 17.1 lists a few of the options that can be used with the configure command.

TABLE 17.1 MySQL Configure Options

Option	Description
--prefix=*PREFIX*	Install architecture-independent files in *PREFIX*
--exec-prefix=*EPREFIX*	Install architecture-dependent files in *EPREFIX*
--bindir=*DIR*	Install user executables in *DIR*
--sbindir=*DIR*	Install system admin executables in *DIR*
--libexecdir=*DIR*	Install program executables in *DIR*

TABLE 17.1 Continued

Option	Description
--enable-shared	Build shared libraries (default)
--enable-static	Build static libraries
--with-raid	Enable RAID support
--with-mysqld-user=*USER*	Run the mysqld daemon as *USER* (default = mysql)
--with-low-memory	Compile using less memory
--without-server	Compile only the client programs
--without-docs	Do not install documentation
--without-bench	Do not install MySQL benchmark tests
--with-berkely-db[=*DIR*]	Use Berkeley db located in *DIR*

Not including an option assumes that MySQL will compile with the default value for
that option. After deciding which (if any) configure options are required for your
MySQL installation, you can use the configure command to create the new makefile:

```
./configure —without-bench —with-low-memory
```

The configure program performs various checks on the Unix system and creates the
makefile that directs the C compiler on how to properly compile the source code on
your system.

After running the configure program, the second required step for compiling the source
code is to use the GNU make command, which you simply issue like this:

```
make
```

The make command compiles all the executable programs MySQL requires. Depending on
the speed of your server, this could take quite a while. After the make program finishes,
you can install the newly created executable programs. To do this, you must be logged in
as the root user or perform the su command to change to the root user. To install the
executable programs, you can use the make command with the install option:

```
make install
```

The program files required for MySQL are installed in either the default directories or
the directories you specified when running the configure program. At this point, the
MySQL server should be ready to be started and configured.

Start the MySQL Server

After the MySQL software has been installed, you must start the MySQL server to access
the MySQL databases. Before starting the MySQL server, though, you need to take care

of two items. First, you must run a MySQL script that creates the system tables, and second, change the database directory permissions to allow the newly created mysql system user to access the system database tables.

The system tables control the database user ID table and access control list (ACL), which controls access to databases and tables within the MySQL server. A script is provided to perform this task. The mysql_install_db script should be located in the executable directory defined by the RPM distribution or the `configure` command. You must run this script as the `root` user:

```
mysql_install_db
```

This script produces the following output as it creates the necessary system tables:

```
Creating db table
Creating host table
Creating user table
Creating func table
Creating tables_priv table
Creating columns_priv table


To start mysqld at boot time you have to copy support-files/mysql.server
to the right place for your system

PLEASE REMEMBER TO SET A PASSWORD FOR THE MySQL root USER !
This is done with:
/usr/local/bin/mysqladmin -u root -p password 'new-password'
/usr/local/bin/mysqladmin -u root -h shadrach.ispnet1.net
➥-p password 'new-password'
See the manual for more instructions.


Please report any problems with the /usr/local/bin/mysqlbug script!


The latest information about MySQL is available on the web at
http://www.mysql.com
Support MySQL by buying support/licenses at https://order.mysql.com
```

Note that six tables are created for the MySQL system database. MySQL uses these tables to keep track of databases, user-created tables, and user IDs within the MySQL system.

Following the table creations, the script reminds the administrator to change the default password for the MySQL root user. The MySQL root user has all privileges to all databases and tables within the MySQL server. It is imperative that you change the default password, or risk your database being compromised by a hacker. You cannot do this, though, until after starting the server.

The second step mentioned previously—changing database directory permissions—must be done before starting the server to ensure that the `mysql` user is the owner of the MySQL data directories. This step allows the MySQL server to run under the `mysql` user ID and help prevent problems with hackers breaking into the server and obtaining `root` privileges. To change the ownership of the directories, you must use the Unix `chown` and `chgrp` commands:

```
chown -R mysql /usr/local/var
chgrp -R mysql /usr/local/var
```

The MySQL installation creates the /usr/local/var directory by default. It contains all the files necessary to support the MySQL databases on the system. The directory used as the data directory can vary depending on your Unix system and on whether you made any changes to the default values used in the `configure` command.

After the directory permissions are set, you can start the MySQL server software by using a simple canned script file:

```
/usr/local/bin/safe_mysqld —user=mysql &
```

This script uses the `--user` option to enable the MySQL server programs to run as the created `mysql` user. The `&` symbol is used to place the MySQL server software in background mode. To check whether the MySQL server is running, you can use the Unix `ps` command:

```
$ ps ax | grep mysqld
21147 pts/0   S    0:00 sh /usr/local/bin/safe_mysqld --user=mysql
21163 pts/0   S    0:00 /usr/local/libexec/mysqld --basedir=/usr/local --data
21166 pts/0   S    0:00 /usr/local/libexec/mysqld --basedir=/usr/local --data
21167 pts/0   S    0:00 /usr/local/libexec/mysqld --basedir=/usr/local --data
$
```

Note that the original safe_mysqld script as well as the mysqld program run continually in background mode. The presence of the mysqld programs indicates that the server is running and waiting for connections.

Server Housekeeping Tasks

MySQL tracks users by both username and location. To make sure no one can use the default `root` password, you must change the `root` password for two different locations: the localhost address and your system's DNS address (as shown in the script output). You can accomplish this with the following two commands:

```
mysqladmin -u root -p password 'guitar'
mysqladmin -u root -h shadrach.ispnet1.net -p password 'guitar'
```

When you enter these commands, MySQL prompts you for the root password, which by default is a null password. Just hit the Enter key to enter a null password. Of course, after you enter these commands, the password is changed to what was selected.

As a final test, you can use the mysqladmin command to display the version of the running MySQL server:

```
$ /usr/local/bin/mysqladmin -u root -p version
Enter password:
/usr/local/bin/mysqladmin  Ver 8.12 Distrib 3.23.39, for
➥ pc-linux-gnu on i686
Copyright (C) 2000 MySQL AB & MySQL Finland AB & TCX DataKonsult AB
This software comes with ABSOLUTELY NO WARRANTY. This is free software,
and you are welcome to modify and redistribute it under the GPL license

Server version          3.23.39
Protocol version        10
Connection              Localhost via UNIX socket
UNIX socket             /tmp/mysql.sock
Uptime:                 3 min 53 sec

Threads: 1  Questions: 7  Slow queries: 0  Opens: 7  Flush tables: 1
➥ Open tables: 1 Queries per second avg: 0.030
$
```

Remember to use the new password that you entered in the previous step when MySQL queries you for the password.

The Apache Web Server with PHP Support

The most important ingredient for a secure Webmail server is, of course, a secure Web server. The Apache open source Web server software is the most popular Web server software available for the Unix platform.

The Apache project has also produced quite a number of plug-in modules that add functionality to the basic Web server product. One of these modules is mod_ssl. It is used for incorporating the SSL protocol (discussed in Chapter 16, "Secure POP3 and IMAP Servers") into the standard Web server software, providing a secure method to transfer data between the client and the Web server.

The PHP programming language is another popular plug-in feature for the Apache Web server. Many applications (including TWIG) use PHP programming to create dynamic Web pages. The PHP organization supplies the PHP software package, which gives you PHP language support for Apache Web servers.

The following sections describe installing the Apache Web server with the Apache mod_ssl module, along with the PHP software package to create a secure Web server for the TWIG package.

Downloading Apache, mod_ssl, and PHP

The Apache Web server software can be downloaded from the Apache Web site at `http://www.apache.org`. At the time of this writing, the current version of the basic Apache Web server is version 1.3.20, which can be downloaded at:

```
http://httpd.apache.org/dist/httpd/apache_1.3.20.tar.gz
```

You need to download the mod_ssl module, too, to incorporate SSL support into the Apache server. The mod_ssl group has its own Web site at `http://www.modssl.org`, where you can download this module. At the time of this writing the current version of mod_ssl is version 2.8.4-1.3.20, available at:

```
http://www.modssl.org/source/mod_ssl-2.8.4-1.3.20.tar.gz
```

NOTE

Note that the version of mod_ssl incorporates the Apache Web server version it was made for (that is, mod_ssl version 2.8.4-1.3.20 is for Apache version 1.3.20). Make sure you download the proper version of mod_ssl for your version of the Apache Web server.

Next you must download the PHP package to plug into the Apache software. The PHP package is available at the PHP Web site at `http://www.php.net`. At the time of this writing, the current version is 4.0.6, which can be downloaded at:

```
http://www.php.net/downloads.php
```

After downloading it, unpack the packages into working directories using these commands:

```
tar -zxvf apache_1.3.20.tar.gz -C /usr/local/src
tar -zxvf mod_ssl-2.8.4-1.3.20 -C /usr/local/src
tar -zxvf php-4.0.6.tar.gz -C /usr/local/src
```

With all the required packages downloaded and unpacked, you can begin the installation process.

Installing Apache, mod_ssl, and PHP

Because the Apache, mod_ssl, and PHP packages are all interrelated, the installation process gets somewhat tricky. The mod_ssl and PHP packages modify the Apache installation, so they must be configured before you install the Apache package.

Each of the packages contains lots of options that modify the Apache package's behavior. It is not the intention of this section to describe all the possible configuration parameters for these packages, just the ones necessary to install them to use with the TWIG server. If you are interested in exploring other configuration options for these packages, consult the individual package documentation.

Preparing mod_ssl

Before compiling Apache, you must set the mod_ssl package configuration parameters. The mod_ssl package requires that OpenSSL be installed on the system. If you have been following along in the book, this was done in Chapter 16. If you have not installed OpenSSL, you can follow the directions in the section "The OpenSSL Package" in Chapter 16.

To use the SSL Web server feature, you must have a valid digital certificate (as described in Chapter 16). You can purchase a certificate from a commercial vendor, or you can create your own certificate using the Apache software. If you are supporting external users, it is best to obtain a commercial certificate that your users can trust and verify that your Web server is authentic.

If you purchase a certificate, you must modify the `configure` command line to point to the location of your certificate and key, as well as point to the location of the basic Apache server software working directory. This command line can be very long, so you should use the Unix line-continuation character (the backslash) to break the command into two separate lines. This command line would look like this:

```
./configure —with-apache=/usr/local/src/apache_1.3.20 \
 —with-crt=/path/to/server.crt —with-key=/path/to/server.key
```

The `/path/to/server.crt` and `/path/to/server.key` values should point to the location of the purchased certificate and public key files.

If you choose to create your own certificate, these options do not need to be included in this step. They are included later on in the installation process. In that case, the command line would look like this:

```
./configure —with-apache=/usr/local/src/apache_1.3.20
```

Next you prepare the basic Apache server software for installation.

Preparing Apache

After setting the mod_ssl configuration parameters, you configure the Apache installation files for PHP. At this time, you should not compile Apache; just run the configure program. The only option that's necessary is the final installation directory that Apache will use:

```
./configure —prefix=/usr/local/apache
```

This command sets the Apache installation directory to /usr/local/apache.

Installing PHP

The next step is to compile and install the PHP software for the Apache Web server. You must change to the /usr/local/src/php-4.0.6 directory to run the PHP software configure program. The configure program must include options to specify the PHP modules that are required by TWIG:

- Apache (--with-apache)
- IMAP (--with-imap)
- MySQL (--with-mysql)

TWIG uses the IMAP module in PHP to connect to an IMAP server to read users' mailboxes (see "The TWIG Webmail Server" section earlier in this chapter). The IMAP server can be located on the same host as the Apache Web server, or it can be on a remote host.

The IMAP PHP module is loaded into PHP using the —with-imap option. It uses the c-client IMAP client software included in the UW IMAP software package. The c-client software provides a C API interface to the UW IMAP software, allowing other programs (such as the IMAP PHP module) to communicate with the IMAP server. The option must point to the working directory for the UW IMAP software. Installing and configuring the UW IMAP server was discussed in Chapter 16. You can refer to the "Using UW IMAP with SSL" section in Chapter 16 for detailed instructions on how to download and install the UW IMAP software package.

NOTE

The IMAP PHP module is used for standard IMAP TCP connections. You can also configure PHP to communicate with remote IMAP servers by using the SSL IMAP protocol discussed in Chapter 16. The option for this configuration is --with-imap-ssl. Unfortunately, at the time of this writing, the current imap-2001 software did not work properly with the PHP 4.0.6 package for SSL IMAP support. If you want to use this feature, you must use the older imap-2000 version of the UW IMAP c-client software. You can check the IMAP PHP module documentation files in your release to determine whether this has changed.

Besides the module options, you must also modify the CFLAGS environment variable to specify the OpenSSL include directory for PHP. With all these things in the command line, it can get messy. To help make the command line easier to read, again, you can use the Unix line-continuation character to place each option on a separate line:

```
$ CFLAGS='-O2 -I/usr/local/ssl/include' \
>./configure \
>--with-apache=/usr/local/src/apache_1.3.20 \
>--with-imap=/usr/local/src/imap-2001.BETA.SNAP-0107110253 \
>--with-mysql \
>--enable-track-vars --enable-debug=no
```

The pathnames shown reflect the locations used in the examples in this book. If you have installed the MySQL package in the default location, you do not have to specify it. If not, you need to specify the MySQL directory as well. After running the configure program, issue the `make` command to create the PHP libraries used by Apache. To install the finished PHP libraries, use the `make install` command with `root` privileges to install PHP.

Installing Apache

With the mod_ssl and PHP packages installed, you are ready to tackle the Apache Web server package. First, change to the Apache working directory to install Apache, and run the configure program to identify the modules required for the TWIG installation. You must also define the `SSL_BASE` environment variable to point to the OpenSSL directory. You can perform both tasks by using a single command line with the Unix continuation character:

```
$ SSL_BASE=/usr/local/ssl \
>./configure \
>--prefix=/usr/local/apache \
>--enable-module=ssl \
>--activate-module=src/modules/php4/libphp4.a
```

Don't bother trying to check whether the libphp4.a file exists—it doesn't. It's created as part of the installation process.

After the configure program is finished, you can issue the `make` command without options to create the binary executable files for Apache.

Before you can install the Apache Web server software, however, you must create a certificate for the SSL connectivity.

Using an SSL Certificate

If you did not purchase a commercial SSL certificate and specified using one in the mod_ssl installation, you must create your own certificate now. As with the self-created certificate used with the OpenSSL program in Chapter 16, when you create your own certificate for the Apache Web server, your users must trust that your certificate is valid.

If you decide to create your own certificate, you use the make certificate program from the Apache installation directory:

```
make certificate
```

This program then queries you for several values used to identify your system in the certificate. Listing 17.1 shows the queries and sample responses for creating a certificate.

LISTING 17.1 Sample Make Certificate Session

```
$ make certificate
make[1]: Entering directory `/home/rich/apache_1.3.20/src'
SSL Certificate Generation Utility (mkcert.sh)
Copyright (c) 1998-2000 Ralf S. Engelschall, All Rights Reserved.

Generating test certificate signed by Snake Oil CA [TEST]
WARNING: Do not use this for real-life/production systems
_____

STEP 0: Decide the signature algorithm used for certificate
The generated X.509 CA certificate can contain either
RSA or DSA based ingredients. Select the one you want to use.
Signature Algorithm ((R)SA or (D)SA) [R]:R
_____

STEP 1: Generating RSA private key (1024 bit) [server.key]
45775 semi-random bytes loaded
Generating RSA private key, 1024 bit long modulus
.++++++
...................................................++++++
e is 65537 (0x10001)
_____

STEP 2: Generating X.509 certificate signing request [server.csr]
Using configuration from .mkcert.cfg
You are about to be asked to enter information that will be incorporated
into your certificate request.
What you are about to enter is what is called a Distinguished Name or a DN.
There are quite a few fields but you can leave some blank
For some fields there will be a default value,
If you enter '.', the field will be left blank.
-----
1. Country Name           (2 letter code) [XY]:US
2. State or Province Name  (full name)     [Snake Desert]:Indiana
3. Locality Name           (eg, city)      [Snake Town]:Indianapolis
4. Organization Name       (eg, company)   [Snake Oil, Ltd]:E-mail Book
5. Organizational Unit Name (eg, section)  [Webserver Team]:Chapter 17
6. Common Name        (eg, FQDN)       [www.snakeoil.dom]:shadrach.ispnet1.net
7. Email Address   (eg, name@FQDN) [www@snakeoil.dom]:webmaster@ispnet1.net
8. Certificate Validity    (days)          [365]:3650
_____
```

LISTING 17.1 Continued

```
STEP 3: Generating X.509 certificate signed by Snake Oil CA [server.crt]
Certificate Version (1 or 3) [3]:3
Signature ok
subject=/C=US/ST=Indiana/L=Indianapolis/O=E-mailBook/OU=Chapter17/
CN=shadrach.ispnet1.net/Email=webmaster@ispnet1.net
Getting CA Private Key
Verify: matching certificate & key modulus
read RSA key
Verify: matching certificate signature
../conf/ssl.crt/server.crt: OK
```

```
STEP 4: Enrypting RSA private key with a pass phrase [server.key]
The contents of the server.key file (the generated private key) has to be
kept secret. So we strongly recommend you to encrypt the server.key file
with a Triple-DES cipher and a Pass Phrase.
Encrypt the private key now? [Y/n]: y
read RSA key
writing RSA key
Enter PEM pass phrase:test certificate
Verifying password - Enter PEM pass phrase:
Fine, you're using an encrypted RSA private key.
```

```
RESULT: Server Certification Files

o  conf/ssl.key/server.key
   The PEM-encoded RSA private key file which you configure
   with the 'SSLCertificateKeyFile' directive (automatically done
   when you install via APACI). KEEP THIS FILE PRIVATE!

o  conf/ssl.crt/server.crt
   The PEM-encoded X.509 certificate file which you configure
   with the 'SSLCertificateFile' directive (automatically done
   when you install via APACI).

o  conf/ssl.csr/server.csr
   The PEM-encoded X.509 certificate signing request file which
   you can send to an official Certificate Authority (CA) in order
   to request a real server certificate (signed by this CA instead
   of our demonstration-only Snake Oil CA) which later can replace
   the conf/ssl.crt/server.crt file.
```

LISTING 17.1 Continued

```
WARNING: Do not use this for real-life/production systems

make[1]: Leaving directory `/home/rich/apache_1.3.20/src'
$
```

The pass phrase entered in step 4 is important. You will need to enter this pass phrase every time you start the Apache Web server software.

NOTE

You might have noticed the warning at the end of the certificate creation script. Again, using self-signed certificates is not a good idea in an Internet production environment. If, however, you are just testing the server, or using it in a small network environment, self-signed certificates could work just fine for you.

After the certificate is created, you can install the Apache software using the `make install` command. The software should be installed in the directory specified in the `--prefix` option of the Apache configure program. For this example, it was /usr/local/apache. After installing the software, you need to configure Apache and PHP to work properly on your system.

Configuring Apache and PHP

The Apache and PHP programs both require configuration files that define how the software packages operate. The PHP program uses a php.ini file that you copy into the /usr/lib directory. The default php.ini file works fine for the TWIG program installation. You can copy the default php.ini file from the PHP installation directory to the /usr/lib directory:

```
cp /usr/local/src/php-4.0.6/php.ini-dist /usr/lib
```

The Apache configuration file must be modified to support PHP documents. This file, called httpd.conf, is located in the /usr/local/apache/conf directory.

You need to modify five lines in the default httpd.conf file installed with Apache. First, you must tell Apache which TCP ports to listen on for incoming connections. Similar to SSL IMAP, SSL HTTP uses a different TCP port than the standard HTTP does. By default, the Apache software uses port 8080 for HTTP and port 8443 for HTTPS. These are not the standard values used by Web browsers, which use ports 80 and 443 respectively. Apache uses these default ports to avoid the possibility of a novice administrator bringing an unsecure Web server up on the standard HTTP and HTTPS ports. You can modify these values if you want.

You define the HTTP ports used with the Port and Listen directives. The Port directive defines the port used in standalone mode, and the Listen directive defines the ports used when accepting connections from the network. The directives are already defined in the default httpd.conf file, and should be modified for your particular Web environment:

```
Port 80
<IFDefine SSL>
Listen 80
Listen 443
</IfDefine>
```

The Apache configuration uses a VirtualHost directive to define which port is used by the SSL Web server. For the second configuration line change, you change the port value defined in the SSL VirtualHost directive to match a port that is configuring in the Listen directive:

```
<VirtualHost _default_:443>
```

This line sets the SSL HTTP port to 443 and allows normal HTTP on port 80. If only port 443 was defined, this Web server would support no regular HTTP sessions.

In the third configuration line change, you tell Apache to recognize the file index.php3 as a directory index file. This is done in the DirectoryIndex directive. A DirectoryIndex line already exists, containing an entry for index.html. This entry allows the default Web page for a directory to be called index.html. You can keep that value and add the index.php3 value, as shown here:

```
DirectoryIndex index.html index.php3
```

NOTE

TWIG uses PHP version 3 programs, so all the program files use the .php3 extension instead of the normal .php extension. If your Web server also supports PHP version 4 programs, you can include the index.php file in the DirectoryIndex.

The next two configuration line changes define the action Apache should take for Web pages that end with.php or .php3. You do that with the AddType directive. There are already two AddType directives for these values, but you might have to modify the entries to match your PHP environment:

```
AddType application/x-httpd-php .php3
AddType application/x-httpd-php .php
```

You will have to change the default .php3 application from x-httpd-php3 to x-httpd-php because you loaded PHP 4.0.6, which can also run PHP version 3 program files. When this is done, you are finally finished with installing and configuring the software.

Testing the Web Server

With everything installed and configured, you can create a sample PHP script file and test your installation. First locate the default Web page directory used for your Apache installation. The default location, and the location used in this example, is /usr/local/apache/htdocs. All HTTP documents are referenced in relation to this directory.

You can create a test PHP file by creating a file called /usr/local/apache/htdocs/test.php3 and placing the following text in the file:

```
<?phpinfo()?>
```

Again, the reason the file is named test.php3 instead of just test.php is that TWIG uses PHP version 3 program files, and you want to make sure your Web server can properly handle them.

After saving the test Web page, you can start the Apache Web server by using the apachectl command found in the /usr/local/apache/bin directory:

```
/usr/local/apache/bin/apachectl startssl
```

By specifying the startssl option, both the standard Web server and the SSL Web server will start. If you want to use only the standard Web server, you can use the start option instead.

After starting the server, you can connect from a standard Web browser on the network to see if the test PHP program works by using this URL:

```
https://server:port/test.php3
```

In this URL, server is your Web server address, and port is the SSL port you defined (if you used the default port 443, you do not need to include the port number in the URL). If things are installed properly, you should see a PHP information Web page describing your Web server environment.

Now all that's left is to install TWIG.

Installing the TWIG Webmail Server

With a database package and a secure Web server that supports PHP programs installed, you are finally ready to install and run TWIG. This section describes how to install and configure the TWIG package to provide Webmail services to your users.

Downloading TWIG

The TWIG software package can be downloaded from the TWIG Web site at http://twig.screwdriver.net/. At the time of this writing, the current version of TWIG is 2.7.3 and can be found at:

```
http://twig.screwdriver.net/download/twig-2.7.3.tar.gz
```

As with the other software packages, TWIG must be unpacked into a working directory:

```
tar -zxvf twig-2.7.3.tar.gz -C /usr/local/src
```

After unpacking TWIG, you can change to the working directory (/usr/local/src/twig-2.7.3 for this example) and perform the installation steps described in the next section.

Installing TWIG

TWIG has a simple installation process. It uses a single install script with a single option—the location of the final TWIG directory. You must install TWIG under the Apache documents directory so that it can be accessed from the Web server. This is the format of the TWIG install command:

```
./twig-install /usr/local/apache/htdocs/twig
```

This command places the TWIG program Web pages in the default Apache Web documents directory. This makes the TWIG program accessible by typing:

```
https://server:port/twig/
```

If your Web server is used only for TWIG, you can instead install the TWIG software directly in the htdocs directory so that it can be accessed as the default Web page on the server, without having to specify the twig directory.

After installing TWIG, you must create the MySQL database and set the TWIG configuration files for your environment.

Creating the MySQL Database for TWIG

TWIG uses a database system to maintain the calendar, schedules, meetings, to-do lists, and notes for each user. These features add functionality that makes the TWIG package competitive with many commercial office products.

You need to create the TWIG database environment, which includes a special username, a dedicated database, and several tables that contain the data. To start, connect to the default MySQL database using the root username and the password you configured when you installed MySQL:

```
$ mysql -u root -p mysql
Enter password:
Reading table information for completion of table and column names
You can turn off this feature to get a quicker startup with -A
```

```
Welcome to the MySQL monitor.  Commands end with ; or \g.
Your MySQL connection id is 27 to server version: 3.23.39

Type 'help;' or '\h' for help. Type '\c' to clear the buffer

mysql>
```

First, you create a new database using the CREATE command and a new MySQL user who has all access privileges to the new database:

```
mysql> CREATE DATABASE twig;
Query OK, 1 row affected (0.00 sec)

mysql> GRANT all privileges ON twig.* TO twiggy@localhost
➥ IDENTIFIED BY 'testpass';
Query OK, 0 rows affected (0.02 sec)

mysql> EXIT;
```

Next you must import the standard TWIG tables into the newly created database. The TWIG distribution includes script files for creating the necessary tables for different database types. These scripts are located in the setup subdirectory of the working directory (/usr/local/src/twig-2.7.3/setup for this example).

To import the new tables, you can redirect the script file to the database by using the mysql command at the Unix command line:

```
$ mysql -u root -p twig < /usr/local/src/twig-2.7.3/setup/twig.table.mysql
```

To verify that the tables were loaded properly, you can connect to the new database using the newly created username and list the tables, as demonstrated in Listing 17.2.

LISTING 17.2 Testing the MySQL TWIG Database Environment

```
$ mysql -u twiggy -p twig
Enter password:
Reading table information for completion of table and column names
You can turn off this feature to get a quicker startup with -A

Welcome to the MySQL monitor.  Commands end with ; or \g.
Your MySQL connection id is 30 to server version: 3.23.36

Type 'help;' or '\h' for help. Type '\c' to clear the buffer

mysql> show tables;
```

LISTING 17.2 Continued

```
+----------------------------+
| Tables_in_twig             |
+----------------------------+
| twig_accounts              |
| twig_acl_groups            |
| twig_acls                  |
| twig_announce              |
| twig_bookmarks             |
| twig_bookmarks_prefs       |
| twig_contacts              |
| twig_contacts_lists_entries |
| twig_contacts_prefs        |
| twig_context               |
| twig_folders               |
| twig_global_prefs          |
| twig_groups                |
| twig_lhsqltable            |
| twig_mail_prefs            |
| twig_main_prefs            |
| twig_meetings              |
| twig_meetings_invitations  |
| twig_meetings_prefs        |
| twig_meetings_registration |
| twig_members               |
| twig_news_prefs            |
| twig_notes                 |
| twig_notes_prefs           |
| twig_schedule              |
| twig_schedule_prefs        |
| twig_schedule_recurring    |
| twig_sclhsqltable          |
| twig_session               |
| twig_todo                  |
| twig_todo_lists_entries    |
| twig_todo_prefs            |
+----------------------------+
32 rows in set (0.00 sec)

mysql>
```

The SHOW TABLES command is used to list all the tables in the twig database. If you do not see any tables in the database, make sure you ran the proper script file for your database system and try again. Next, you need to set the TWIG configuration files to reflect your Webmail environment.

Configuring TWIG

There are lots of TWIG configuration files used to define how TWIG operates. All these files are located in the twig/config subdirectory under the default Apache data directory (/usr/local/apache/htdocs/twig/config in this example). Table 17.2 lists the different configuration files that TWIG uses.

TABLE 17.2 TWIG Configuration Files

File	Description
announcements.inc.php3	Contains announcements placed on the main page.
config.inc.php3	The main configuration file.
dbconfig.inc.php3	The database configuration file.
defaults.inc.php3	Contains default settings used for the server.
footer.inc.php3	Defines the footer used on all TWIG Web pages.
header.inc.php3	Defines the header used on all TWIG Web pages.
images.inc.php3	The list of images used by TWIG.
login.footer.inc.php3	The footer used on the forms-based login Web page.
login.form.inc.php3	The form used on the forms-based Web page.
login.header.inc.php3	The header used on the forms-based login Web page.
mailfooter.inc.php3	A footer message to include on all outbound messages.
mainmenu.inc.php3	The menu items to be displayed on the main menu Web page.
newusergroups.inc.php3	Allows you to list user groups for advanced security features.

The following sections describe the crucial configuration entries that must be changed for TWIG to work properly in your Webmail environment.

The Config.inc.php3 File

The config.inc.php3 file defines the main features of the TWIG software. For TWIG to work in your environment, you must change some of the default settings. This is the format for these settings:

```
$config["setting"] = "value"
```

Both the setting and value must be enclosed in quotes. There are lots of configuration settings you can modify. Fortunately, most settings have reasonable default values. Table 17.3 lists the settings that are most likely to be changed.

TABLE 17.3 Config.inc.php3 Settings to Change

Setting	Description
fromdomain	The host address used on all messages sent from the TWIG interface (default = "foo.com").
basedir	The base directory of the TWIG Web pages (default = "twig").
imap_server	The IMAP server to connect to (default = "localhost").
imap_path	The path of the IMAP folders in the users' directory (default = " ").
smtp_server	The SMTP server for outbound messages (default = "localhost").
news_server	The Network News server for newsgroups (default = "localhost").

If you are running a default TWIG installation on the mail server, the only value you should have to change is fromdomain, which should be set to the return address for your mail server.

NOTE

If you have decided to use SSL IMAP to retrieve messages for TWIG, you must change the `imap_port` value to `"993/imap/ssl/novalidate-cert"`. This odd-looking value reflects the SSL IMAP port, the IMAP SSL protocol, and the certificate method to use.

The Dbconfig.inc.php3 File

The dbconfig.inc.php3 configuration file must be modified to define your database environment. The format of the dbconfig.inc.php3 settings is as follows:

```
$dbconfig["setting"] = "value"
```

Similar to the config.inc.php3 file, both the setting and value must be enclosed in quotes.

If you created the database using the TWIG database scripts (as shown in the example earlier), you should not have to change many of the settings. Table 17.4 lists the database settings that most likely will need to be changed.

TABLE 17.4 Dbconfig.inc.php3 Settings to Change

Setting	Description
sqlserver	The hostname of the database server (default = "localhost").
sqlport	The TCP port of the database server (default = " ").
sqlusername	The username to log in to the database with (default = "nobody").
sqlpassword	The password to log in to the database with (default = " ").

TABLE 17.4 Continued

Setting	Description
defaultdb	The name of the TWIG database (default = "twig").
sqltype	The database package used (default = "mysql").

For the example in this chapter, the following values should be used:

```
$dbconfig["sqlserver"] = "localhost"
$dbconfig["sqlport"] = ""
$dbconfig["sqlusername"] = "twiggy"
$dbconfig["sqlpassword"] = "testpass"
$dbconfig["defaultdb"] = "twig"
$dbconfig["sqltype"] = "mysql"
```

With the new configuration values set, you are ready to test out the TWIG Webmail server.

Using TWIG

To test your TWIG installation, it is best to use a Web browser on a remote workstation. You can connect to your TWIG server with this URL:

```
https://server:port/twig/
```

Remember to include the "s" in the https, which indicates that the Web site is using the SSL protocol. If you forget it, you will not be able to connect to the Web server.

When the browser establishes a connection, you see a query box asking if you will accept the self-signed certificate that was created for the SSL Web server. You must answer yes to this query, or the HTTP session will be terminated. After answering yes, the TWIG login screen shown in Figure 17.3 appears.

You can create a customized login screen by modifying the HTML code in the footer.inc.php3 and header.inc.php3 files in the TWIG configuration directory. The customized footer and header files are then added to the TWIG Web pages.

After entering a valid IMAP username and password, the TWIG main menu page, shown in Figure 17.4, appears.

From the main menu page you can select to read your mail, check your calendar, schedule meetings, or enter items into your ToDo list or Notes area.

If you select the Mail menu, the INBOX folder is displayed, allowing you to select messages in the inbox for reading. Figure 17.5 shows the Web page layout for the mail area.

This test shows that indeed the TWIG software is working properly, and you can read messages from your inbox on the mail server.

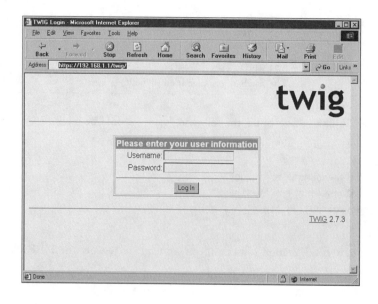

FIGURE 17.3

The TWIG login screen.

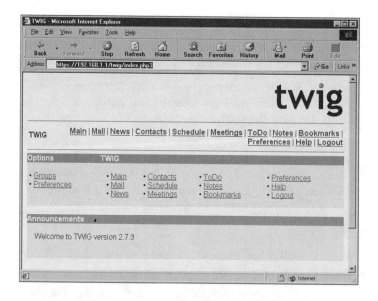

FIGURE 17.4

The TWIG main menu page.

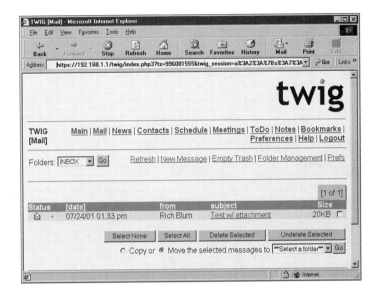

FIGURE 17.5

The TWIG mail page.

Summary

This chapter described how to install a secure Webmail server using the Apache Web server and TWIG Webmail software. Many components are required for this setup, all of which are available as open source packages.

The MySQL database provides SQL database support for storing user information, calendars, schedules, notes, and contact lists. The TWIG software is written using the PHP programming language, which must be installed with the Apache server software. For secure communication, you must also use the OpenSSL package to provide encrypted communications across the network between the Web browser on the workstation and the Web server. Finally, the UW IMAP software was used to allow TWIG to read messages in the users' mailboxes and display them on the Web pages.

Many different topics have been discussed over the past 17 chapters, but there's always more to learn about security. The only way to provide a secure e-mail environment is to keep abreast of the latest attacks and provide a method to avoid them on your mail server. You should constantly monitor the various MTA package mailing lists and security bulletins, always watching for security-related updates and patches to open source software used on your mail server.

Index

C

D

R

Hey, you've got enough worries.

Don't let IT training be one of them.

Get on the fast track to IT training at InformIT,
your total Information Technology training network.

 | **www.informit.com** | **SAMS**

■ Hundreds of timely articles on dozens of topics ■ Discounts on IT books
from all our publishing partners, including Sams Publishing ■ Free, unabridged
books from the InformIT Free Library ■ "Expert Q&A"—our live, online chat
with IT experts ■ Faster, easier certification and training from our Web- or
classroom-based training programs ■ Current IT news ■ Software downloads
■ Career-enhancing resources

Visit our Web site at
www.samspublishing.com

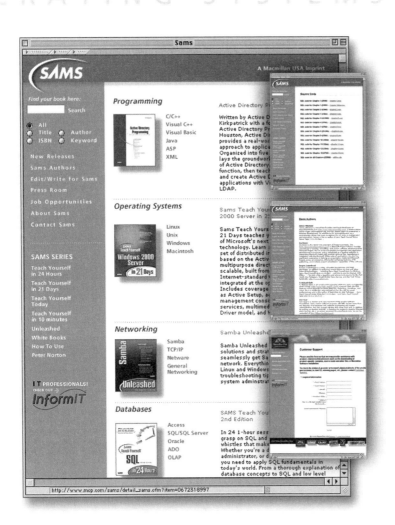

- New releases

- Links to deep discounts

- Full catalog of hot computer books

- Source code

- Author links and web sites

- Customer support